UNLOCKING
COMPANY REPORTS
AND ACCOUNTS

UNLOCKING COMPANY REPORTS AND ACCOUNTS

Wendy McKenzie

FINANCIAL TIMES
PITMAN PUBLISHING

FINANCIAL TIMES

MANAGEMENT

LONDON · SAN FRANCISCO
KUALA LUMPUR · JOHANNESBURG

*Financial Times Management delivers the knowledge,
skills and understanding that enable students,
managers and organisations to achieve their ambitions,
whatever their needs, wherever they are.*

London Office:
128 Long Acre, London WC2E 9AN
Tel: +44 (0)171 447 2000
Fax: +44 (0)171 240 5771
Website: www.ftmanagement.com

A Division of Financial Times Professional Limited

First published in Great Britain 1998

© Financial Times Professional Limited 1998

The right of Wendy McKenzie to be identified as author
of this work has been asserted by her in accordance
with the Copyright, Designs, and Patents Act 1988.

ISBN 0 273 63250 7

British Library Cataloguing in Publication Data
A CIP catalogue record for this book can be obtained from the British Library.

10 9 8 7 6 5 4 3 2 1

Typeset by Northern Phototypesetting Co Ltd, Bolton
Printed and bound in Great Britain by Clays Ltd, St Ives plc

The Publishers' policy is to use paper manufactured from sustainable forests.

ABOUT THE AUTHOR

Wendy McKenzie has been a financial training consultant and freelance lecturer for eighteen years, working closely with a number of major multinational companies and banks. She runs a wide range of finance courses for senior managers, directors and city analysts, and a key element of these courses is understanding and interpreting company accounts.

Her training experience has given her a unique insight into how to develop skills in this analysis, and how to unlock the hidden secrets from both UK and international company accounts.

She has also written the *Financial Times Guide to Using and Interpreting Company Accounts*.

To Bob, who made this possible

Contents

How to use this book

WHO SHOULD READ THIS BOOK

You should! This book is designed for anyone who wants to be able to read and understand a set of company accounts. It contains all the technical information that an accounting student would need, but has summaries for every section, so if you don't need to know all the detail you can read the key points on every subject. Summaries are clearly identifiable by grey shading behind the text.

The book starts from first principles and each point is illustrated by worked examples. Extracts are shown from published accounts, including those of overseas companies, to show you how the information is presented in real companies' accounts.

Accounting jargon is clearly explained twice, once in the chapter and then in the Jargon sections at the end of each chapter.

The book is not just concerned with UK accounting; international differences are discussed in every part of the book and can be easily recognised by the international symbol.

Legal aspects of accounting are covered and can be recognised by the law symbol.

Whilst the book shows you how to calculate the ratios that quantify a company's performance, it also shows you how to understand the information, and decide which ratios you need to calculate. This approach makes it easier for you to spot creative accounting. Opportunities for companies to engage in creative accounting are marked throughout the book by the creative accounting symbol.

THE STRUCTURE OF THE BOOK

The book is divided into five parts:

Part 1: Introduction to companies and their accounts – there are four chapters in this section:

- An introductory chapter that should be read by anyone that has not looked at accounts before. It follows a company through its first four months of trading, introducing the different accounting documents and illustrating what each document tells us about the business. These documents are introduced through a worked example that assumes no prior knowledge of accounts.
- The second chapter looks at accounting principles and the regulatory framework.
- The third chapter is largely concerned with companies, although there is some discussion of the option of being self-employed or forming a partnership. It looks at dif-

ferent types of companies and the impact that a stock exchange listing has on a company.

● The final chapter in this section introduces the accounts and the wealth of information that can be found in a set of company accounts.

Part 2: The accounts – there are 13 chapters in this section, covering all aspects of the accounts and the relevant accounting standards. They cover:

● the balance sheet;
● the profit and loss account, including an introduction to UK taxation;
● the cash flow statement;
● the statement of total recognised gains and losses.

Part 3: Other accounting issues – there are three chapters in this section which give the reader of accounts more information, or cover accounting issues that affect more than one accounting statement. They cover:

● other information disclosed in the accounts;
● accounting for groups, acquisitions and mergers;
● accounting for foreign currencies.

Part 4: Analysing company accounts – this section shows you how to analyse a company's financial performance. There are three chapters covering:

● ratio analysis and shareholder value; this shows you how to amend conventional ratios so that they become a better performance measure;
● a spreadsheet for financial analysis;
● an analysis of Boots' 1997 accounts and the group's performance over the past four years.

Part 5: Appendices – there are two covering:

● an introduction to discounted cash flow;
● international accounting formats.

Part 1

INTRODUCTION TO COMPANIES AND THEIR ACCOUNTS

① Introduction

This chapter covers:

● **What are the accounts?**

● **The published accounts**

● WHAT ARE THE ACCOUNTS?

This introductory chapter is designed for people who are unfamiliar with the accounts. It starts from first principles and identifies what you will find in a profit and loss account, balance sheet and cash flow statement. This chapter works through an example to show you how these documents are prepared and how they tell you very different things about the business.

So skip this chapter if you feel that you already know what the different accounting documents tell you, and how they are constructed. Otherwise, read on …

Everyone prepares accounts. We try to keep track of our own money, and this is exactly what the accounts do for a business. To illustrate this, we will follow the first four months of trading in a painting and decorating business.

JANUARY

We decide to start the company in January. We invested £14 000 in share capital, and borrowed £6000 from the bank. The bank loan has to be repaid in five years' time, and interest at 1 per cent each month is paid on the loan. We have £20 000 as cash on the first day, but this will not last long as we will find out!

In this chapter, we are going to follow the first four months of trading and prepare the company's accounts as we go. On the first day our business is worth £20 000 and this can be illustrated as follows:

Where the money came from		What the money was spent on	
Share capital	£14 000	Cash	£20 000
Bank loan	£6 000		£20 000
	£20 000		

This is a simple balance sheet. *A balance sheet is simply a snapshot of the business, showing us where the company's money came from, and where the company spent this money.*

In the first month we employed an assistant, paying him £250 a week and decide to take £350 a week ourselves. This means that the salaries will cost £2400 each month. We have

3

rented some premises at £800 a month, but had to pay a month's rent in advance. We also bought the following items for cash:

Painting and decorating tools	£1000	
Decorating materials	£2000	(£1300 remains in stock at
Van	£15000	the end of the month)
Petrol	£40	

We also have paid £60 interest on our loan.

In the first month we received £3000 in cash for decorating. Although we had £20 000 when we started the business, we are already starting to exhaust the cash:

January	**£**
Cash coming in:	
Share capital	14 000
Loans	6 000
Sales – cash	3 000
Total cash available	23 000
Cash going out:	
Van	(15 000)
Painting and decorating tools	(1 000)
Decorating materials	(2 000)
Salaries	(2 400)
Petrol	(40)
Rent	(1 600)
Interest on loan	(60)
Total cash spent	(22 100)
Surplus in the month	900

We started off with £20 000, but only have £900 left at the end of January. Whilst we still have some cash left, our first month will not be profitable. We only received £3000 for our decorating, and our wages alone were £2400, so it is not hard to predict that we will probably make a loss.

The profit and loss account

We will now move on to prepare a profit and loss account. The profit and loss account identifies whether we have received more for the decorating than it cost us to do. It is concerned with the costs that relate to the sales we have made in the first month, and we will see that this is *not* the same as the cash that has been paid. Only the cost of items *used* in sales will be charged to the profit and loss account.

To calculate the costs that have been used in sales we have to make a number of adjustments to the cash costs. We need to:

● exclude any stock and any payments we have made in advance;
● include a charge to cover the depreciation on our van and equipment;
● include any costs that we have incurred, but have yet to be invoiced for.

Exclude stock

We have purchased £2000 of decorating materials during the first month, but we have £1300 left in stock, so we have only used £700 during January. This £700 is the cost of paint that will be charged to the profit and loss account. The balance of £1300 will show on our balance sheet as *stock*, the Americans call this *inventory*.

Exclude stock

We have had to pay a month's rent in advance, so the cash outflow for rent was for two months of payments. However, the profit and loss account will just be concerned with the one month's rent that relates to January's sales. The remaining £800 will be shown on the balance sheet as a *prepayment*.

Include depreciation

We have spent £15 000 on a van, and the van is called a *fixed asset*. A fixed asset is something we mean to keep for more than a year, and will be used to help us make our sales. The tools will also be fixed assets. We cannot charge the whole £15 000 that we spent on the van to the profit and loss account, as the van should last longer than a month! However, we obviously must charge something to reflect the fact that we are using the van during the month. This charge is called *depreciation*. Depreciation is a charge that we make to reflect the shrinking in value of our assets. The basis for calculating depreciation varies from one country to another. In most countries it is determined by tax tables, but in others it simply reflects the management's view.

The principle of depreciation is easily illustrated. We have bought the van for £15 000, we expect it to last for three years and be worth £4200 at the end of that time. (We will see that this is a number deliberately picked to keep our arithmetic simple!) When preparing the profit and loss account, accountants are not concerned with the cash outlay, only with trying to match costs to revenues. The profit and loss account looks at the capital expenditure of £15 000 deducts the scrap value £4200 (this is called the *net residual value*). The balance of £10 800 will be spread over three years, as this is the intended period of use. There is £10 800 to be depreciated over three years, £3600 per year. This divides nicely by 12, to give a depreciation charge of £300 each month for the van. However, the van is not our only depreciating asset, the decorating tools also fall into the same category. We will have to make a similar depreciation charge for the tools, this will be £40 a month. Therefore, the total depreciation charge for our fixed assets will be £340 per month.

Include the costs that have been used in sales, but not yet invoiced

There will be some other hidden costs that we will need to consider. For example, we will have used electricity in our office. Electricity bills are paid in arrears. We must try to work out how much electricity we have used in the first month. This will be referred to as an *accrual*, or an *accrued expense*. This will be built into the profit and loss account, even though it may be another three months before we have to pay the bill. The amount we owe the electricity company will have to be shown on our balance sheet. It will be shown as part of our *creditors*. Creditors are people that the business owes money to. In America they are more usefully called *payables*.

To illustrate the principle of accruals, we will assume that we have used £40 electricity in our first month.

We can now prepare our profit and loss account:

	£
Decorating sales	3000
Decorating materials used in sales	(700)
Salaries	(2400)
Petrol	(40)
Electricity	(40)
Rent	(800)
Depreciation	(340)
Interest	(60)
LOSS	(1380)

The brackets are a give-away – in the first month we made a loss!

The balance sheet

We have made a loss. Unfortunately this means that our stake in the business will be worth less than it was when we started. We invested £14 000 in share capital, but in the first month we lost £1380, so now our investment in the business will only be worth £12 620 (14 000 – 1380). This is called the *shareholders' funds* or the *equity*. The loss, or any profits, are taken into the balance sheet, and reflected as part of the shareholder's stake in the business. The balance sheet tells us what the business is worth on a certain day. We know that, having made a loss during the first month, the investor's stake will not be worth as much as it was when we started. This will not be the only thing that has fallen in value during the month – we also have to recognise the fact that our fixed assets will not be worth what we paid for them.

The company's balance sheet, at the end of January, will be as shown in Table 1.1.

Table 1.1 **The balance sheet at the end of Janaury**

Where the money came from		What the money was spent on	
	£		£
Share capital	14 000	Fixed assets	
Loss in the month	(1 380)	Van and tools at cost	16 000
Shareholders' funds	12 620	Less depreciation	(340)
		Value of the fixed assets at the end	
		of January	15 660
Bank loan	6 000		
		Stock	1 300
Creditors – accrued electricity			
costs	40	Prepayment – rent	800
		Cash	900
Total liabilities	**18 660**	**Total assets**	**18 660**

In our balance sheet we are recognising that our money came from three sources:

(1) *the investors* (unfortunately we have lost some of their money – you may see this referred to in reports as 'the share capital is not intact');
(2) *the bank*;
(3) *the electricity company* (it has provided us with electricity that we have not paid for).

These three are called the business's *liabilities*, as the company will have to pay them back at some stage. (The shareholders will probably only be paid back if the company goes into liquidation.)

We have some cash and spent the rest of this money on:

● fixed assets, (these are not worth what we paid for them, as they have depreciated);
● stock;
● the deposit for our rent.

These are called the business's *assets*.

The balance sheet always balances, because all we are doing is matching where we got our money from, and what we spent it on!

SUMMARY

JANUARY

The profit and loss account

When preparing a profit and loss account, we are trying to see if we are selling our products and services for more or less than they cost us to deliver to our customers. Therefore, the profit and loss account does not reflect the company's cash position. The profit and loss account includes the costs that have been used in sales, not the cost that we have paid. So far, we have identified that we need to make four accounting adjustments.
We need to include charges to cover:

(1) depreciation of the fixed assets;
(2) accrued expenses; and exclude
(3) prepayments;
(4) stock.

The balance sheet

This is a snapshot of a business on one day, and shows where the business's money came from, and where the business spent that money.

The things that the business has are called the assets, and the money that the business owes is referred to as the liabilities. Fixed assets are things that the business means to keep for more than a year. This could be buildings, machinery, or vehicles. The accounts bring in this period's use through the depreciation charge. This measures the reduction in the value of the assets during the period.

FEBRUARY

We now move on to February. The company's sales improve; we invoice a local builder for £3600 (and he agrees to pay in four weeks) and do decorating work for £1000 cash. We buy decorating materials for £500, pay rent of £800, salaries of £2400, petrol of £60 and interest of £60. We continue to accrue £40 a month for electricity.

At the end of February we have £1000 decorating materials in stock, having used £800 during the month. Unfortunately this means that we have overspent and now have a bank overdraft:

February	£
Cash coming in:	
Cash sales	1000
Total cash available	1000
Cash going out:	
Decorating materials	(500)
Salaries	(2400)
Petrol	(60)
Rent	(800)
Interest on loan	(60)
Total cash spent	(3820)
Deficit in the month	(2820)
Opening cash	900
Closing overdraft	(1920)

Because the builder has not paid the company for the decorating, we spent £2820 more than the cash we had coming in during February. The opening cash of £900 was insufficient to cover the shortfall and we now have an overdraft of £1920.

The profit and loss account

But is the company profitable? The answer is – just, we've made £100! The profit and loss account uses the total sales in the period, regardless of whether we have been paid. This works on the same principle as the electricity costs. The amount that the builder owes the company will be shown on the balance sheet as a *debtor*, what the Americans refer to as a *receivable*.

Therefore, the profit and loss account is concerned with the sales that we have made in the period less the costs that have been used in making those sales. The profit and loss account for February will be as Table 1.2.

Table 1.2 **The profit and loss account for February**

	£
Sales	
Cash sales	1000
Credit sales	3600
	4600
Decorating materials used in sales	(800)
Salaries	(2400)
Petrol	(60)
Electricity	(40)
Rent	(800)
Depreciation	(340)
Interest	(60)
PROFIT	100

The profit and loss account will normally be presented in a slightly different way. First, our sales would normally be referred to as the *turnover* in the UK, Americans would call this *sales, or revenue*. Second, the costs need to be grouped into various categories. Interest is slightly different to the other costs, as it does not relate to sales – it is a cost of financing the business. The costs that relate to our sales are called the *operating* , or the *trading, costs*. Any profit after these costs is referred to as the *operating*, or the *trading, profit*.

The profit and loss account is presented in a more conventional format below.

Table 1.3 | **A more conventional format for the profit and loss account**

Profit and loss account for February	
	£
Turnover	4600
Decorating materials used in sales	(800)
Salaries	(2400)
Petrol	(60)
Electricity	(40)
Rent	(800)
Depreciation	(340)
OPERATING PROFIT	160
Interest	(60)
PROFIT AFTER INTEREST	100

We have made a small operating profit of £160, which is 3.5 per cent of sales (this is called the *operating/trading-profit margin*).

The balance sheet

We know the business is skint, but we are profitable, the difference between the two can be found on the balance sheet where we can see that we are owed £3600 by the builder (Table 1.4).

There are three things that need to be explained in this balance sheet:

(1) The accumulated loss of £1280 shown in the shareholders' funds is January's loss of £1380 plus February's profit of £100. As the balance sheet is a snapshot of the business on a certain day we need to show the total profit, or in this case loss, that the business has made since it started. This is called the *reserve*, or the *retained earnings*. (Retained earnings is a much better description than reserves. When we think of reserves, we think of cash. Unfortunately in accounting it does not mean that.)
(2) The bank overdraft of £1920 is shown as a liability. The bank is now giving the business additional funds in the form of an overdraft.
(3) The depreciation also accumulates and represents two months' depreciation of the fixed assets.

We have looked at the assets and liabilities as a total, but we could categorise them into short term and longer term. Stock will be sold in the short term, whereas the van will be kept for three years. The electricity bill will arrive and we will have to pay it, whereas the shareholders will probably only get their money back if we go into liquidation! We can see that all our assets and liabilities can be classified in this way (Table 1.5).

Table 1.4 **The balance sheet**

Where the money came from	£	What the money was spent on	£
Share capital	14 000	Fixed assets	
Accumulated loss for the two months	(1 280)	Van and tools at cost	16 000
		Less depreciation to date	(680)
Shareholders' funds	12 720	Value of the fixed assets at the end of February	15 320
Bank loan	6 000		
		Stock	1000
Creditors – accrued electricity costs	80	Debtors	3 600
		Prepayment – rent	800
Bank overdraft	1 920	Cash	0
Total liabilities	**20 720**	**Total assets**	**20 720**

Table 1.5 **Classification of assets and liabilities**

	Short term	Longer term
Assets	Cash Debtors Stock	Fixed assets
Liabilities	Bank overdraft Creditors Accrued expenses	Loans Shareholders' funds

In each box of Table 1.5 the assets and liabilities have been presented in the order that they could be realised. A bank overdraft is repayable on demand; the creditors will normally give us a month or more of credit; the accrued expenses will give us a month's credit when they send the invoice. This is referred to as *presenting assets and liabilities in decreasing order of liquidity* (liquidity simply means turning into cash). In other words, cash is shown first! Some countries such as the USA, present assets and liabilities in this way, but others, such as the UK, present them in *increasing order of liquidity* (cash is shown last).

This classification is used in published balance sheets. Short-term assets are called *current assets* and short-term liabilities are either called *current liabilities* or *creditors – amounts falling due within a year*. Longer-term assets are called *fixed assets*. Longer-term liabilities are divided into the shareholders' funds, which are hopefully permanent, and any other liabilities. The other longer-term liabilities are either called *long-term liabilities* or *creditors – amounts falling due in more than a year*.

We know that the balance sheet is a snapshot of the business on a certain day. This balance sheet is a snapshot of the business on 28 February. We have presented the balance sheet by looking at the business's assets and liabilities. However, there are different views of the business that you could take, in just the same way that there are different views that you could take of a person. The format we have been using for the balance sheet is the most popular view in the world. The layout could be slightly different, as some countries start with short-term assets and liabilities, and then show the long-term assets and liabilities.

However, most of the accounts that you will see in the UK would present the snapshot from a very different point of view. Most UK balance sheets try to identify what the business is worth to its shareholders. They start with the business's assets, and then deduct the money owed to outsiders to identify what the business is worth to its shareholders. This then balances with the shareholders' stake in the company. The February balance sheet is represented in this format as shown in Table 1.6.

Table 1.6 **Balance sheet as at 28 February 199–**

	£
Fixed assets	
Cost	16 000
Depreciation	(680)
Book value	15 320
Current assets	
Stock	1 000
Trade debtors	3 600
Prepayments	800
	5 400
Creditors: amounts falling due within a year	
Accrued expenses	80)
Bank overdraft	(1 920)
	(2 000)
Net current assets	3 400
Total assets less current liabilities	18 720
Creditors: amounts falling due in more than a year	
Loans	(6 000)
	12 720
Capital and reserves	
Share capital	14 000
Profit and loss account	(1 280)
	12 720

You will notice that all the numbers are the same, the difference lies solely in the presentation. This format:

- deducts the short-term liabilities from the short-term assets to arrive at the net current assets;
- adds the net current assets to the fixed assets to arrive at total assets less current liabilities;
- calls the accumulated profits and losses (the reserve), the profit and loss account. Consequently, there is a document called the profit and loss account which shows this period's profits, and a reserve called the profit and loss account that shows the accumulated profits and losses, since the business started.

SUMMARY

FEBRUARY

There are different layouts of both the profit and loss account and the balance sheet.

The profit and loss account

This takes the sales made in the period (the turnover) and deducts the costs that relate to these sales. It does not matter in the profit and loss account whether the cash has been received for the sales, or paid for the costs. Any outstanding amounts will be shown on the balance sheet as debtors or creditors.

The costs of materials, labour and overheads used in sales are called the operating costs and are deducted from turnover to arrive at the operating profit. Interest is shown afterwards.

The balance sheet

The balance sheet is a snapshot of what the business has, its assets, and what it owes (its liabilities) on a certain day. These assets and liabilities can be classified into short term and long term. Short-term assets are called current assets, and long-term assets are called fixed assets. The amounts owed by customers (the debtors), are shown as a current asset. In the UK, liabilities are divided into creditors falling due within a year, and more than a year. Similar analysis is done overseas, but the short-term liabilities are often called current liabilities.

There are several ways that a company can present its balance sheet. A UK balance sheet usually shows the business from the shareholders' point of view.

MARCH

In March we manage to get 30 days' credit for our decorating materials with a local builders' merchant. So, although we buy £800 materials, we do not have to pay for these until April. We pay cash for the following expenses:

Salaries	£2400	
Petrol	£70	
Electricity	£110	
Interest	£100	(we were charged £40 on our overdraft)

Although we have paid an electricity bill of £100, we decide to continue charging £40 a month to the profit and loss account, as the bill does not cover the full period. We receive £3600 from the builder for February's sales, and have £700 decorating materials in stock, having used £1100 during March.

By getting the money from the builder, and not paying for our materials, we have managed to turn around our cash and now have £200 surplus, rather than an overdraft.

March

	£
Cash coming in:	
Sales – cash	2000
Sales – credit	3600
Total cash available	5600
Cash going out:	
Decorating materials	
Salaries	(2400)
Petrol	(70)
Electricity	(110)
Rent	(800)
Interest on loan and overdraft	(100)
Total cash spent	(3480)
Surplus in the month	2120
Opening cash	(1920)
Closing cash	200

Profit and loss account

We have a cash surplus and we are also profitable, with an operating-profit margin of nearly 15 per cent (Table 1.7).

Table 1.7 **Profit and loss account for March**

	£
Turnover	5700
Decorating materials	(1100)
Salaries	(2400)
Petrol	(70)
Electricity	(40)
Rent	(800)
Depreciation	(340)
OPERATING PROFIT	950
Interest	(100)
PROFIT AFTER INTEREST	850

The decorating materials that have been used in the sales are still charged to the profit and loss account, even though they may not have been paid for.

The balance sheet

We now have another creditor on the balance sheet, the amount we owe to the builders' merchant for our decorating materials. This is a different type of creditor from the accrued expenses, as we have already received the invoice, and it is shown on the balance sheet as a *trade creditor* (Table 1.8).

Table 1.8 **BALANCE SHEET AS AT 31 MARCH 199–**

	£
Fixed assets	
Cost	16 000
Depreciation	(1 020)
Book value	14 980
Current assets	
Stock	700
Trade debtors	3 700
Prepayments	800
Cash	200
	5 400
Creditors falling due in a year	
Trade creditors	(800)
Accrued expenses	(10)
	(810)
Net current assets	4 590
Total assets less current liabilities	19 570
Creditors falling due in more than a year	
Loans	(6 000)
	13 570
Capital and reserves	
Share capital	14 000
Profit and loss account	(430)
	13 570

SUMMARY

MARCH

The profit and loss account
The materials used are charged to the profit and loss account, regardless of whether they have been paid for.

The balance sheet
Any amounts owed are shown on the balance sheet; the amounts owed to suppliers are shown as trade creditors – part of the creditors falling due in a year.

APRIL

During April we have some bad news, one of this month's customers is in receivership, and it looks probable that we will not receive £500 that he owes us. So, although we have invoiced him for the decorating, we decide that we ought to make a provision for bad debts to cover the amount, and not include the amount in debtors.

In April we did £1500 decorating for cash and £4400 on credit (including our probable bad debt), using £1200 decorating materials. We purchased £1000 decorating materials on credit and paid for last month's purchases of £800. We accrued £40 for electricity and paid cash for the following:

Salaries	£2400
Petrol	£80
Interest	£60

We have managed to improve our cash position:

April	**£**
Cash coming in:	
Sales – cash	1500
Sales – credit	3700
Total cash available	5200
Cash going out:	
Decorating materials	(800)
Salaries	(2400)
Petrol	(80)
Electricity	
Rent	(800)
Interest on loan	(60)
Total cash spent	(4140)
Balance	1060
Opening cash	200
Closing cash	1260

The profit and loss account

We have to charge our provision for bad debts against our profit and loss account (Table 1.9). The bad debt has almost halved our operating profit, without it we would have had operating profit of £1040 and an improved operating margin of 17.6 per cent.

The balance sheet

The debtors shown on the balance sheet represent the money we expect to collect from our customers, not necessarily the total outstanding invoices. Not all provisions reduce the value of an asset, some represent future expenditure (for example, rationalisation provisions). These would show as a liability on the balance sheet under a separate heading – *Provisions for liabilities and charges*. Provisions are different from other liabilities, as we do not precisely know what the cost will be or when we will have to pay that cost. It is possible that we may receive some money from the receivers, but we do not know how much and when we will receive the settlement (Table 1.10).

15

Table 1.9	**Profit and loss account for April**

	£
Turnover	5900
Decorating materials	(1200)
Salaries	(2400)
Petrol	(80)
Electricity	(40)
Rent	(800)
Depreciation	(340)
Provision for bad debts	(500)
OPERATING PROFIT	540
Interest	(60)
PROFIT AFTER INTEREST	480

Table 1.10	**Balance sheet as at 30 April 199–**

	£
Fixed assets	
Cost	16 000
Depreciation	(1 360)
Book value	14 640
Current assets	
Stock	500
Trade debtors	3 900
Prepayments	800
Cash	1 260
	6 460
Creditors falling due in a year	
Trade creditors	(1 000)
Accrued expenses	(50)
	(1 050)
Net current assets	5 410
Total assets less current liabilities	20 050
Creditors falling due in more than a year	
Loans	(6 000)
	14 050
Capital and reserves	
Share capital	14 000
Profit and loss account	50
	14 050

APRIL

The profit and loss account
Companies have to make provisions for likely costs that they will probably incur in the future, but which relate to the period's sales. These provisions are charged to the profit and loss account.

The balance sheet
The current assets shown on the balance sheet are those that we expect to realise. We would reduce the value of stocks and debtors by any provisions that we made during the period. Not all provisions represent a writedown of the value of assets. Some, like rationalisation provisions, reflect probable future cash outflows for the business. These would be shown as a liability, under the heading of 'provisions for liabilities and charges'.

● THE PUBLISHED ACCOUNTS

Companies publish accounts annually, with UK listed companies also providing interim statements covering a six-month period. In our example we were following the fortunes of a company monthly, like most companies would in their management accounts – those prepared for internal consumption. In the published accounts we would see:

- a profit and loss account for the period;
- a cash flow statement for the period;
- a balance sheet as at a certain day.

This means that profits and cash flows are totalled for the period, and we get very little indication of the monthly fluctuations. To illustrate this we will prepare a profit and loss account and a cash flow statement for the four-month period. The profit and loss account is simply prepared by totalling the four months' profit and loss accounts (Table 1.11).

● The profit and loss account

Table 1.11 **Profit and loss account for the four months ending 30 April 199–**

	£
Turnover	19 200
Decorating materials	(3 800)
Salaries	(9 600)
Petrol	(250)
Electricity	(160)
Rent	(3 200)
Depreciation	(1 360)
Provision for bad debts	(500)
OPERATING PROFIT	330
Interest	280
PROFIT AFTER INTEREST	50

We can see that the company has made a very small profit, 2.6 per cent of sales, barely enough to cover our interest payments. But what we cannot see is how this has been steadily falling over the last month, even though turnover was rising (Figure 1.1).

Figure 1.1 **TURNOVER AND OPERATING PROFIT**

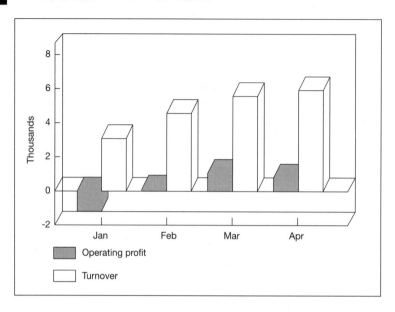

This is why it is important not to look at financial information in isolation. We should always have a number of periods' results before we can really comment on the businesses performance – we need to know if it is getting better or worse. A set of published accounts will always have last year's results alongside for comparison, and listed companies publish five-year summaries of their results.

● The cash flow statement

The cash flow statement uses the total cash flows in the business and groups the company's cash flows into eight categories:

(1) Cash flows arising from trading. These are called cash flows from *operating activities*.
(2) Cash flows arising from the payment and receipt of interest and the receipt of dividends are called cash flows from *returns on investment and servicing of finance*.
(3) Cash flows from taxation.
(4) Cash flows from buying and selling fixed assets and long-term investments. These are called *capital expenditure and financial investment*.
(5) Cash flows from buying and selling companies. These are called *acquisitions and disposals*.
(6) Dividend payments to ordinary shareholders. These are called *equity dividends paid*.
(7) Cash flows from buying and selling short-term investments. These are called *management of liquid resources*.
(8) Cash flows from borrowings and shareholders. These are called *financing*.

Totalling these cash flows will give the increase or decrease in cash.

Our example was too simple to have entries for all of these headings, but we can construct a cash flow statement once we have totalled our cash flows for the four months.

Cash flows January – April

	£
Cash coming in	
Share capital	14 000
Loans	6 000
Sales – cash	7 500
Sales – credit	7 300
Total cash available	34 800
Cash going out	
Van	(15 000)
Painting and decorating tools	(1 000)
Decorating materials	(3 300)
Salaries	(9 600)
Petrol	(250)
Electricity	(110)
Rent	(4 000)
Interest on loan	(280)
Total cash spent	33 540
Closing cash	1 260

Operating activities

First we need to identify the operating cash flows.

Sales – cash	7 500
Sales – credit	7300
Total sales	14 800
Less:	
Decorating materials	(3 300)
Salaries	(9 600)
Petrol	(250)
Electricity	(110)
Rent	(4 000)
Total	17 260
Operating cash flow	2 460

We have a cash outflow from operating activities of 2460.

Returns on investment and servicing of finance

This is simply the £280 interest paid.

Capital expenditure and financial investment

This is the purchase of the van and the decorating tools:

Van	(15 000)
Painting and decorating tools	(1 000)
Capital expenditure	16 000

Financing

This would be the proceeds of the share and the loan:

Share capital	14000
Loans	6000
Financing cash flow	20000

● Constructing the cash flow statement

We can now construct our reported cash flow statement for the four months (Table 1.12).

Table 1.12 **Cash flow statement**

OPERATING ACTIVITIES	
Net cash outflow from operating activities	(2 460)
RETURNS ON INVESTMENT AND SERVICING OF FINANCE	
Net cash outflow from returns on investment and servicing of finance	(280)
CAPITAL EXPENDITURE AND FINANCIAL INVESTMENT	
Net cash flow from capital expenditure and financial investment	(16 000)
FINANCING	
Net cash flow from financing	20 000
Changes in cash	**1 260**

What does this tell us? On its own, not a lot! We have managed to grow cash by £1260 in four months. The operations of the business were not managing to generate sufficient cash in the period, so, if we are profitable, we have a problem in either our *stock, debtors or creditors*. These three are what companies refer to as their *working capital*.

At the end of April we have £3400 tied up in the working capital:

Stock	500
Trade debtors	3900
Trade creditors	(1000)
Working capital	*3400*

The reason for the shortfall is the investment that a new business has to have in the working capital. We are owed £3900 by our customers, have to carry some stock, and we only owe suppliers £1000.

Plus we had to give a month's deposit on the rent, which is much greater than the £50 we owe the electricity company. The £20 000 capital that we raised from our shareholders and the bank was needed to fund the capital expenditure, working capital and interest.

The cash flow statement does not give us the monthly cash movement, as all it is doing is reconciling the opening position (we raised £20 000 in shares and loans) with the closing position (we spent £18 740) to show the movement in cash of £1260. We know that the monthly cash flows show a slightly different picture (Figure 1.2).

Figure 1.2   CASH FLOW

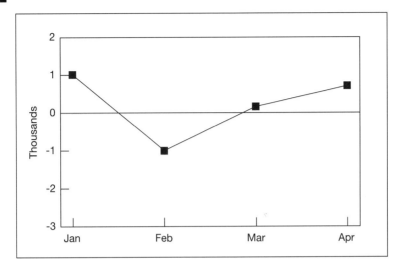

● The balance sheet

The balance sheet that will be shown in the published accounts will be the one that we pre-pared for the end of the period, in our example the balance sheet as at 30 April.

SUMMARY

The published accounts will show the profit and loss account and cash flow statement for the accounting period. The balance sheet will show the assets and liabilities of the company at the end of that period.

The cash flow statement shows the movement of cash during the period, and looks at cash flows functionally. There are eight categories of cash flow shown on a UK cash flow statement:

- *operating activities* – these are the cash flows from trading;
- *returns on investment and servicing of finance* – these are the cash flows from interest. Any dividends received would also be included.
- *taxation;*
- *capital expenditure and financial investment* – these are the cash flows from buying and selling fixed assets;
- *acquisitions and disposals* – these are the cash flows from buying and selling companies;
- *equity dividends paid* – this is the dividend that has been paid to ordinary shareholders;
- *management of liquid resources* – these are the cash flows from the purchase and sale of short-term investments;
- *financing* – these are the cash flows from shares and loans.

Accruals / accrued expenses   Charges made to the profit and loss account to reflect any outstanding invoices relating to items that have been used in sales.

Asset   Something of value that the business has. It is not necessarily owned by the company.

Balance sheet   A snapshot of the business on a certain day showing where the company's money has come from, and where the company has spent this money. It identifies the things that the company has (the assets) and the money that the company owes (the liabilities).

Cash flow statement   A document showing the movement of cash in the financial period.

Creditors   Money that the company owes, mainly to suppliers. These may also be called accounts payable.

Current assets   Assets that can be realised in the short term. In the UK, they are assets that are not fixed assets, so may include assets that cannot be realised within a year.

Current liabilities   Liabilities that have to be paid within 12 months. In the UK they are usually shown as creditors: amounts falling due within a year.

Debtors   Money that is owed to the company, mainly by customers. These may also be called accounts receivable.

Depreciation   A charge made to spread the cost of fixed assets over their useful life. The charge reduces both the profits and the asset value.

Equity   The share capital plus any reserves. This may also be called the shareholders' funds.

Equity dividends   Dividends paid to ordinary shareholders.

Fixed asset   Something that the business intends to keep, and, therefore, does not intend to resell.

Liability   A financial obligation – something that the business owes.

Operating profit   The sales in the period less the costs of materials, wages and overheads used in sales. This may also be called the trading profit.

Operating profit margin   Operating profit expressed as a percentage of the turnover. It may also be called the trading profit margin.

Prepayment   A payment that the company has made in advance, and does not relate to the sales that have been made in the period.

Profit and loss account   A document that identifies whether the company is selling its goods or services for more or less than it costs to deliver them to the customer. It takes the sales that the company has made in the period and deducts the costs that relate to those sales.

Provision   A charge made to reflect a likely future cost, that relates to the sales that have been made during the period. it could relate to the reduction of an asset (like a bad-debt provision) or a future cost (like a rationalisation provision).

Shareholders' funds   The share capital plus any reserves. This may also be called the equity.

Turnover   The sales that the company has made in the period. It may also be called sales or revenue.

② Accounting practice

This chapter covers:

- **The legal and regulatory framework**
- **The bases used in preparing accounts**
- **The accounting principles**

● INTRODUCTION

All accounts contain broadly the same information, the only real difference lies in the amount of detail that would be disclosed. The information increases with company size and public ownership. Small private companies show less detail than public companies that are listed on a stock exchange.

The amount of information disclosed in company accounts is influenced by four factors:

(1) the Companies Act
(2) the accounting rules
(3) the company's size and ownership
(4) the listing rules of the Stock Exchange.

These four factors combine to determine the amount of detail required in the accounts, and are discussed in detail below.

● THE LEGAL AND REGULATORY FRAMEWORK

● The Companies Act

Since the Companies Act 1947, British companies have been required by law to publish annual audited accounts containing a large number of disclosures. However, before the 1981 Act most of the detailed rules were to be found in the accounting standards rather than law. The implementation of the EC Directives (specifically the second, fourth, seventh and eighth directives) in 1981 and 1989 meant that detailed rules on accounting layout or measurement are now included in British law. The Companies Act 1985 now details the minimum information that must be both disclosed in the accounts, and subsequently filed at Companies House. All companies have a legal requirement to prepare accounts that are 'true and fair' and, with the exception of very small companies, that have been audited by an independent accountant. The Act also requires that the accounts include a Director's Report, a Profit and

Loss Account, a Balance Sheet, an Auditor's Report and specified notes to the accounts. Specific requirements of the Companies Act will be discussed throughout this book.

● The accounting rules

The accounting rules are called the Accounting Standards and are set, in the UK, by the Accounting Standards Board. The accounting rules that were issued before August 1990 are called Statements of Standard Accounting Practice (SSAPs), subsequently they have been called Financial Reporting Standards (FRSs). The UK rules cover things that would be set in law in many other countries. They clarify the way that profit should be measured, assets and liabilities should be valued, and require more information to be disclosed in the notes to the accounts. In addition to those financial statements required by the Companies Act, accounting standards require the publication of a number of other statements:

- a cash flow statement;
- a note on historical cost profits and losses;
- a statement of total recognised gains and losses.

Historical perspective

The accounting standard-setting regime started in January 1970 with the establishment of the Accounting Standards Committee (the ASC) by the Institute of Chartered Accountants in England and Wales. It was joined by other accounting bodies and was reconstituted in 1976 as a joint committee of the six member bodies. During the 1980s, despite the accounting standards, creative accounting boomed and many accounts plainly did not show a true and fair view. The problem was that the rules only told you what you could not do, not what you could. The standard-setting process was too slow, and, with six accounting bodies represented on the committee, was too often a compromise that satisfied no one. To make matters worse, the ASC had no powers of enforcement, and if companies did not comply, all the auditors could do was to say, 'The company has not complied with SSAP'. There was no legal sanction.

A committee was appointed in 1987, under the chairmanship of Sir Ron Dearing to review and make recommendations on the standard-setting process. The review resulted in two important changes:

Amendments to the Companies Act

The Companies Act 1989 introduced into the 1985 Act the following changes designed to strengthen the accounting standards:

- A definition of accounting standards was included in the Act.
- Directors, other than those of small and medium-sized private companies, must disclose whether the accounts have been prepared in accordance with applicable accounting standards. Any material departures must be both disclosed and explained.
- Section 245B of the Companies Act requires that when a company does not comply with the Act, the court has the power to order the preparation of revised accounts, with the costs of preparing these accounts being borne by the directors involved in the preparation of the defective ones!

New structure

The recommendations of the commission established a new structure for the setting, and enforcement of accounting standards. This was designed to coincide with the legislative changes.

The current structure

The current structure for the setting and enforcement of accounting standards is shown in Figure 2.1.

Figure 2.1 **THE BODIES RESPONSIBLE FOR ACCOUNTING STANDARDS**

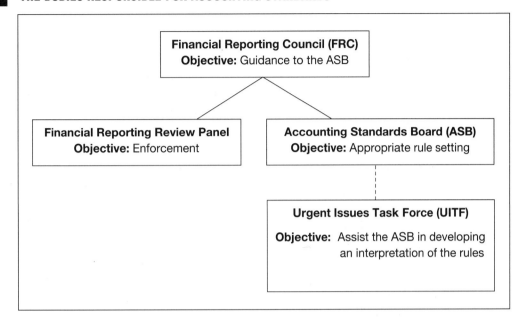

The Financial Reporting Council (FRC) has been established to determine the general policy for the standard-setting regime. It guides the ASB on work programmes and issues of public concern. Its chairman and three deputy chairmen are jointly appointed by the Bank of England and the Secretary of State for Trade and Industry. The balance of the council represent a broad cross-section of senior people who have an interest in the preparation of accounts, or in their use.

There are two bodies that report to the FRC:

The Financial Reporting Review panel

This investigates accounts that have been bought to its attention, where it is felt that the provisions of the Companies Act may have been breached. It is empowered under the law to take directors to court for issuing accounts which fail to comply with the law, for example where the accounts fail to give a true and fair view. Various penalties are laid down and the publicity combined with the threat of legal action usually persuades companies to comply with the panel's recommendations. Probably its most widely publicised success story occurred shortly after its establishment. In its 1991 accounts, Trafalgar House, now part of the Norwegian conglomerate, Kvaerner, had attempted to flatter its profits. It had wrongly classified some of its properties, to avoid a £102.7 million property writedown hitting the profit and loss account, and its policy on accounting for advance corporation tax had led to a £20 million understatement of the tax charge. Following discussions with the Financial Reporting Review Panel, the company agreed to change its accounts.

The Accounting Standards Board

The ASB replaced the ASC on 1 August 1990 and develops, updates and issues accounting standards. The ASB's accounting standards are called *Financial Reporting Standards* (FRSs) and the draft standards are called *Financial Reporting Exposure Drafts* (FREDs).

Companies now have to conform to accounting standards and so they have become much more important. The ASB has recognised this and tries to involve all interested parties in their development. Before a standard is issued, the ASB will probably issue a discussion paper (these are issued for all important or controversial topics) followed by a FRED to elicit the views of the interested parties.

The Urgent Issues Task Force is a committee of the ASB, whose role is to assist the ASB in maintaining and developing both good standards and accounting practice in financial reporting. It tries to achieve a consensus on the interpretation of existing rules in controversial areas and publishes this in an Abstract.

Legal opinion suggests that the status of accounting standards has been strengthened, and that accounting standards and UITF abstracts have to be followed in order to give a true and fair view.

● Statements of recommended practice

Statements of recommended practice (SORPs) are developed by bodies that are recognised by the ASB to provide guidance for the application of accounting standards to specific industries. For example, the Oil Industry Accounting Committee has issued a number of SORPs relating to the oil industry. These are not mandatory, but companies are encouraged to comply with them.

● International accounting standards

The international accounting standards are set by the International Accounting Standards Committee (IASC). This is an independent body, whose objective is to standardise the accounting principles that are used in financial reporting throughout the world. They were formed in 1973 through an agreement made by the professional accountancy bodies from Australia, Canada, France, Germany, the Netherlands, Japan, Mexico, the United Kingdom, Ireland, and the United States. Since then, the membership has widened and there are now 119 members and six associate members in 88 countries. These members try to persuade national standard setters to publish statements that are in accordance with international standards, and to work for international acceptance and recognition of the international standards. The standard-setting procedure is similar to the UK procedure, with the IASC inviting comment from interested parties at every stage.

Some of the early accounting standards offered a number of options and were felt to be too open to interpretation, and in the late 1980s the IASC embarked on its improvements project. It was hoped that this would encourage securities regulators to accept financial statements drawn up in accordance with international accounting standards (IASs) to be acceptable for multinational listings. A new feature of the revised standards is that any allowable options are classified; their preferred treatment is described as the 'benchmark' treatment, with the other option being the allowed alternative.

The process of improvement continues and the IASC now has a close relationship with the International Organisation of Securities Commissions. It has suggested a number of changes to IAS to enable them to be acceptable as 'core standards' for companies with cross-border listings. International accounting standards often form the basis for accounts prepared in countries that do not have an established accounting tradition (e.g. eastern Europe), and are becoming increasingly important in developing countries. Many companies overseas, with international markets (for example Anglo American of South Africa), prepare accounts conforming to international standards. The battle is on to decide whether US or international accounting standards will be those used by companies with cross-border listings.

Up to the end of 1993, any company complying with UK accounting standards would have complied with international accounting standards in all material respects. However, this does not always apply to revised standards of 1993 onwards, and further inconsistencies are likely to emerge over the next few years as the IAS develops its core standards. Most UK standards are broadly in line with the international view, and any points of difference will be discussed throughout this book. Every chapter in Part 2 (the accounts) will discuss any major differences between UK practice and international accounting standards.

● Company size and ownership

Until recently the accounts prepared by small and large companies were broadly similar, although smaller private companies were exempt from some of the accounting standards. (For example, they do not have to prepare a cash flow statement.)

In 1992 an amendment to the Companies Act introduced substantial disclosure exemptions for small companies. We are currently seeing the evolution of two different sets of generally accepted accounting practices, larger companies being required to comply with all statutory provisions and accounting-standard requirements, whereas smaller private companies comply with a shorter, more restricted set of rules that reduce the amount of disclosure in the accounts.

Definition of company size

The size of the company is determined by its turnover, total assets and average number of employees. (A small private company is currently a private company where two out of the three following conditions are met: the turnover must be less than £2.8 million, the total assets less than £1.4 million, and the average number of employees must be below 50. If these conditions are satisfied the company will qualify for the small-company disclosure exemptions under the Companies Act.)

Auditing of small company accounts

The November 1993 budget continued the divergence between small and larger companies' accounting practices by modifying the audit requirement for smaller companies. Companies with a turnover below £90 000 do not need to have their accounts audited. Those with a turnover between £90 000 and £350 000 only require an independent accountant to verify that the accounts accurately reflect the books.

Financial reporting for smaller entities

In 1997 the ASB issued an accounting standard, *Financial Reporting for Smaller Entities* (FRSSE). This standard tries to balance the need for small companies to provide accounting information that is sufficient to assess their financial performance, but is still simple enough for small companies to prepare. Therefore, it has been designed to ensure that all small companies will be required to prepare accounts that comply with the relevant company legislation and a simplified version of the accounting standards.

Consequently, most of the accounting standards have been modified, and a number are excluded from the proposed standard. However, most exclusions and simplifications would not normally be relevant for smaller companies anyway. The only major exception is FRS 1, as small companies will still remain exempt from FRS 1, although they have the option to disclose their cash flow.

● A stock exchange listing

Companies listed on a stock exchange must disclose additional information concerned with the company's status, affairs and activities, directors, shares and shareholders, and loans and interest. This is discussed in more detail in Chapter 3.

SUMMARY

UK accounting rules exist within a legal framework. The accounting standards have the backing of the law and since 1989 there are sanctions for non-compliance. The accounting standards are currently set by the Accounting Standards Board. The older accounting standards are called Statements of Standard Accounting Practice (SSAPs); whereas the newer ones are called Financial Reporting Standards (FRSs). Accounting standards evolve through a period of discussion, and the draft accounting standards are called Financial Reporting Exposure Drafts (FREDs). Sometimes there can be different interpretations of an accounting standard, or point of law. These are resolved by the Urgent Issue Task Force.

Guidance to the application of accounting standards within specific industries may be found in Statements of Recommended Practice (SORPs). These are not issued by the ASB, but by another relevant body that the ASB recognises. Compliance with SORPs is encouraged, but is not mandatory.

Other countries have their own accounting rules, which may either be incorporated into the law or be in the form of accounting standards. The International Accounting Standards Committee is trying to develop international accounting standards that can be used in any country, and will be acceptable on any stock exchange. This would be particularly useful for companies with multinational listings. Some of the later international standards differ significantly from UK standards. These differences will be discussed in this book.

The amount of detail that you will find in the accounts varies from one type of company to another, depending on size, ownership and whether the company is listed on a stock exchange. Small companies are now exempted from some accounting standards and from some of the more onerous terms and the disclosure requirements of many others.

THE BASES USED IN PREPARING ACCOUNTS

Companies can choose to prepare their accounts from two different perspectives, by asking:

● What are the profits that the business has made, and how much is the business worth on paper?
● What are the real profits and the real value of the business?

The difference between the two questions is inflation; the first ignores it and looks at historical cost, whereas the second adjusts the numbers to take account of inflation.

● Inflation and accounts

One of the things we all have to decide is, 'is inflation important?' Some of us are old enough to remember the 1970s when inflation was high, but at current levels does it really matter? We tend to think that it does matter when it comes to pay rises. If inflation is running at 3 per cent, and we are offered a 4 per cent pay rise, we would consider that we are only 1 per cent better off and we may be unhappy with only a 1 per cent real increase in our income. Shareholders will have the same concerns, and inflation will have an impact on their real earnings. This can be illustrated by considering a company whose earnings per share have remained constant at 20p. Twenty pence today will not have the same value as 20p at the end of the year (Table 2.1).

Table 2.1 **The impact of inflation on earnings per share**

	Inflation rate		
Received at the end of:	3%	5%	7%
Year 1	19.42	19.05	18.69
Year 2	18.85	18.14	17.47
Year 3	18.30	17.28	16.33
Year 4	17.77	16.45	15.26
Year 5	17.25	15.67	14.26
Year 6	16.75	14.92	13.33
Year 7	16.26	14.21	12.45
Year 8	15.79	13.54	11.64
Year 9	15.33	12.89	10.88
Year 10	14.88	12.28	10.17

Even when inflation is only running at 3 per cent, the value of the earnings has fallen by almost 26 per cent over ten years and at 7 per cent it has almost halved! Inflation does not just affect the earnings; imagine the effect that it can have on a company's asset replacements. We know that inflation affects the price of our own assets, because we see new car prices rising each year in a combination of inflation and technological improvements. The same is true for most of a company's tangible assets, but the problem may be exacerbated by the length of time that a company keeps its assets. (The only thing this does not seem to hold true for is computers, where costs have been falling in real terms over the last ten years.) A company with stable earnings would have to retain an increasing proportion of its earnings just to replace its assets. The conclusion has to be that inflation is important, but do we account for it?

We could ignore it, after all most companies do. Most companies base their accounts on *historical-cost accounting* using the costs the company has incurred during the year. The profit and loss account is based on the revenues and the costs that relate to the sales made in the period. The assets are shown on the balance sheet at the lower of cost or net realisable value.

If we wanted to adjust for inflation we could take a simple approach, and adjust the numbers for changes in RPI. This method of accounting for inflation is referred to as *current purchasing power*. However, this would not necessarily reflect a true and fair view. General inflation could be high, but an individual company could have deflation in some of its costs because of commodity price movements. Therefore, it may be more appropriate to consider the inflation in prices that the company has actually experienced during the year. This is called *current-cost accounting*.

The Dutch, with modest inflation, are the only people, to have developed a system of *replacement accounting* that is used by a number of major companies. Internally generated indices are used to calculate the replacement costs of fixed assets and stock.

In the UK accounts can be compiled using:

- **historical cost:** the costs that the business incurred. Most companies prepare their accounts on this basis;
- **current cost:** this is based on year-end costs, and adjusts for the inflation that is being experienced in the business. The charges to the profit and loss account are adjusted to take account of year-end costs and the balance sheet shows values based on year-end prices. Unfortunately, current costs are not allowed for tax purposes.

Historical cost is the most commonly used basis for preparing accounts, with some companies revaluing only their non-specialised properties. Utilities are the only large group of companies to use current-cost accounting, and then usually only in their regulatory accounts. Current-cost accounting is an attempt to cope with inflation, using the rate of inflation that is specific to their business.

● Current-cost accounting

Current-cost accounts adjust the historical-cost accounts to show the real profit, assets and liabilities for the year. It looks at the areas that are affected by inflation in the business:

- **Fixed assets** – these are bound to increase in cost because of inflation. It adjusts the reported profit prepared using historical cost by deducting the additional depreciation that would have been charged had depreciation been based on the year-end costs. This adjustment is referred to as the *depreciation adjustment*.
- **Stocks** – if we are paying more for our materials, labour and overheads it will be reflected in higher stock values when they are based on a current cost. The reported profit is reduced by the additional costs that would have been incurred if costs had been based on the year-end costs. This is called the *cost of sales adjustment*.
- **Trade credit** – if the difference between our debtors and our creditors was £100, and inflation was running at 3 per cent, we would not be surprised to see the difference increase to £103. The reported profit is reduced by the additional investment in trade credit that would have been required if the values of the debtors and creditors had been

based on the year-end costs. This is called the *monetary working capital adjustment*.

- **Gearing** – as the company does not raise all its capital from shareholders, they do not have to bear all the cost of inflation. An adjustment is made to the current-cost charges detailed above to reflect the benefit arising from partially funding the business by borrowings. This is called the *gearing adjustment*.

Profit is reduced by these additional costs and balance sheet values are increased to reflect the assets and liabilities at year end values. This can have a considerable effect on both the profit and loss account and the balance sheet. In its 1995 accounts, Eastern Group (now part of Energy group) reported £203.5 million profit before tax. Its current cost profit before tax was £152.2 million, with the largest current cost adjustment being the £53.7 million additional depreciation charge. The gearing adjustment reduced the other current-cost adjustments by £3.4 million. Their reported net assets were £831.1 million, compared to current-cost net assets of £1808.4 million.

SUMMARY

Most accounts are prepared using historical cost, with the profit and loss account based on the value of the revenues and the costs that relate to the sales that have been made in the period, and the assets shown on the balance sheet at the lower of cost or net realisable value. Many UK companies do not use strict historical cost, as they revalue properties. As most accounts are not adjusted for inflation, an analyst should adjust historical-cost profits to get some idea of the real underlying profit growth in the company.

Current-cost accounting is an alternative approach that uses year-end costs, and attempts to take account of the inflation that the business has experienced during the year. The reported profits are reduced by the effect of inflation, and asset values are increased. This approach tends only to be used in the regulatory accounts of utilities, and is not allowed for tax purposes.

● THE ACCOUNTING PRINCIPLES

There are six main accounting principles or concepts that determine the way that the accounts are prepared. The first four are incorporated into SSAP 2 (which looks at accounting policies) and the last two are reflected in many other accounting standards:

- matching/accruals
- prudence
- consistency
- going concern
- substance over form
- materiality.

It is important to understand these principles if you want to understand the accounts.

● The matching/accruals principle

This matches costs to revenues and brings them into the profit and loss account in the period to which they relate. This means that the profit and loss account does not necessarily reflect the cash that has come in and gone out of the business. The sales are the sales that have been legally made in the period and the costs are those that relate to these sales.

The fact that we have to consider the costs that relate to the sales in the period means that we make judgements about what those costs are. We shall consider these judgements later in Chapter 13. They are important as they give companies the opportunity to engage in creative accounting.

● The prudence principle

This is the most important principle. All others are subordinate to it. Prudence means you must take into the profit and loss account any probable losses, but you cannot take potential gains. Revenues and profit cannot be anticipated, but companies must make provisions for items such as possible bad debts. Companies also cannot include any increases in their asset values in the profit and loss account, as they have yet to be realised.

● The consistency principle

Items should be accounted for in a consistent manner within a period and from one period to the next. This ensures the comparability of accounts.

● The going-concern principle

This assumes that the business will continue in existence for the foreseeable future. Therefore, the accounts are based on the assumption that there is neither the intention, nor the need, to reduce the scale of the company's operations or go into liquidation.

● Substance over form

This tries to ensure that accounts reflect the commercial reality rather than the strict letter of the law. If a company has all the risks and reward associated with owning something, it should be included in the accounts, regardless of the legal position. The way that long-term leases (finance leases) are treated in the accounts is a good example of this. Finance leasing is just another form of borrowing, which can be particularly attractive to companies with tax losses. The company leasing the assets has all the benefits and risks that are associated with owning the assets. So although the leasing company legally owns the assets, they are shown in the company's accounts as fixed assets and depreciated in the usual way. The amount owed to the leasing company, over the life of the lease, is included in creditors.

FRS 5 (*Reporting the Substance of Transactions*) is based on the principle of substance over form as it requires that the accounts should reflect commercial reality rather than the strict legal form.

● Materiality

Accounts do not include items that are considered to be immaterial, but it is not possible to give a precise definition of what is and what is not material. In some situations an error of less than 5 per cent would be considered satisfactory, but in another situation any error would be unacceptable. For example, in a business with a multimillion pound turnover, a £10 000 error in the materials cost is unlikely to be considered material, but a £10 000 error in the chairman's salary, which is subject to specific disclosure requirements, would be regarded as material.

Accountants regard an item as material if there is a statutory requirement to disclose it accurately, or knowing about that item would influence your view about the company.

● Recent developments

In November 1995 the ASB published *The Statement of Principles for Financial Reporting*. This suggested that other principles should be included in the accounts. Two controversial additions have been suggested:

Financial adaptability

The company should be able to respond to changed circumstances and have both the flexibility and ability to manage change.

Comparability

Users of financial statements should be able to compare companies; both over time, and within a sector. This could have important implications for company accounts, as to make accounts truly comparable it would be necessary to:

● adjust for inflation to make the numbers comparable over time;
● have the same accounting policies, both over time and within a sector;
● finance the assets in the same way, or adjust the numbers to reflect the differences in financing.

SUMMARY   The accounting principles ensure that the accounts reflect an accountants' view of reality:

● Profitable businesses can go into liquidation – cash transactions are not necessarily reflected in the current period's profit and loss account.
● Companies are required to make judgements in arriving at the costs that relate to the sales.
● The book value of a company is unlikely to be realised if there is a liquidation.
● The accounts are not totally accurate; they are subject to approximations and may not reflect the legal position.

INTERNATIONAL DIFFERENCES

Whilst all countries have the same set of broad accounting principles there are many differences both in emphasis and interpretation. Accounting formats and practices vary widely across the world. These differences are inevitable and are likely to continue for the foreseeable future as the accounting practices and formats are shaped by a number of factors which include:

The legal system

Legal systems can be broadly categorised into two major groups: the Roman legal system and a system of common law. The two systems have generated different levels of government intervention. Roman law usually involves extensive governmental prescription, whereas common law survives on limited government intervention. It is inevitable that these different legal frameworks will lead to the development of different accounting systems.

Countries adopting Roman law have a strong legal framework, with accounting rules enshrined in law, accounting plans, or commercial codes. Whereas countries adopting case law have the principles and an overview in law, but the details are found in a separate set of accounting rules. Highly litigious societies, like the USA, have highly detailed rules that strive to be clear and unambiguous.

Corporate ownership

In some countries the ownership of most companies is still in the hands of the board of directors, whereas in others ownership is separated from the management of the company. Where the ownership is separated, there is an increased demand for financial reports and external audit.

Thus, both the quality and the quantity of accounting information will inevitably vary from one country to another with disclosure increasing as the ownership of the company becomes separated from its management.

The taxation system

The taxation rules will influence many day to day financial decisions such as provisioning and the valuation of assets. Some tax systems require the figures in the financial accounts to be the same as those shown in the tax accounts. This means that the accounting numbers will be largely determined by the tax rules. Whereas other countries are bedevilled with the problems of accounting for deferred tax, as the tax rules are substantially different from the accounting rules. In these countries, two sets of accounts will be prepared. The ones reporting performance to the shareholders, and those complying with the tax rules.

Political and historical factors

These have played a large part in a country's accounting practices. For example:

- Commonwealth countries have a legacy of UK accounting practices, prior to the 1981 Companies Act.
- French accounting has been strongly influenced by the German Occupation, with the *Plan Comptable* largely reflecting the ideas proposed by Professor Eugen Schmalenbach and adapted by the Vichy government in 1942. This has been subsequently modified but still clearly reflects the original proposals.
- Japanese accounting is a hybrid that has been influenced by both German and American practices.
- Entry into the European Union (EU) has affected the accounting practices of all the member countries, and will continue to do so for the foreseeable future.

These factors interact to provide us with a wide variety of accounting practices. Despite the attempts at standardisation embodied in the Fourth Directive, the formats of accounts within the EU are still different. The accounting practices are even more varied. This presents analysts with difficulties when making international comparisons – it becomes essential to know the detail of each country's accounting regulations. This book will discuss the main differences in accounting practices in Canada, France, Germany, the Netherlands, Japan and USA. This will help you to understand the accounts that are prepared in any country.

SUMMARY

Despite the pressures for the standardisation of accounting practices and presentation, there are still numerous differences. Although the differences will diminish over time, they are unlikely to disappear in the foreseeable future, as they arise from differences in the legal and taxation systems and from political and historical factors.

JARGON   **Accounting principles**   These are the underlying principles that affect the way that the accounts are prepared. There are six main principles: matching, prudence, consistency, going concern, substance over form, and materiality.

Accounting Standards Board (ASB)   The UK accounting standard-setting body.

Accounting Standards Committee (ASC)   The old UK accounting standard-setting body, replaced in 1990 by the ASB.

Cost of sales adjustment   An adjustment made in current-cost accounts to reflect the additional costs that would have been incurred had costs been based on year-end costs.

Current-cost accounting   A basis for accounting when values are based on year-end costs.

Depreciation adjustment   An adjustment made in current-cost accounts to reflect the additional depreciation charge that would have been made if depreciation had been based on the cost of buying fixed assets at the year end.

Financial Reporting Council (FRC)   This is the body that has determined the general policies for the UK accounting standard-setting regime since 1990.

Financial Reporting Exposure Draft (FRED)   A draft UK accounting rule.

Financial Reporting Review Panel   The enforcement arm of the UK standard-setting regime.

Financial Reporting Standard (FRS)   A UK accounting rule issued after 1990.

Gearing adjustment   The reduction made to the other current-cost adjustments to reflect the benefit of partially financing the business with borrowings.

Historical-cost accounting   A basis for accounting where values are based on the historical costs paid. This is the commonest basis for preparing accounts.

International Accounting Standard (IAS)   An international accounting rule.

International Accounting Standards Committee (IASC)   The international accounting standards-setting body.

Monetary working-capital adjustment   An adjustment made in current-cost accounts to reflect the additional investment in trade credit.

Statement of Recommended Practice (SORP)   A non-mandatory UK guideline for accounting practice in specific industries.

Urgent Issues Task Force (UITF)   Part of the ASB that develops a consensus interpretation of controversial areas of the existing UK accounting rules.

3 Companies

INTRODUCTION

The company in question could be a private company, an unlisted public company, or a public company that is listed on a stock exchange. We will look at each of these options in this chapter, concentrating on the more usual option of starting a company. As this chapter is largely concerned with the legal status of companies, the symbol denoting points of law will not be used.

ALTERNATIVES TO STARTING A COMPANY

Businesses do not always have to be companies. There are several different options open to us when we start a business.

Self-employment

Anyone who is self-employed takes all the business risks upon himself or herself. Being self-employed means that the individual and the business are the same. If the business gets into difficulties, the assets of the self-employed person are at risk. Whilst the risks belong to the individual, so do the rewards. Self-employed people only have to answer to the tax authorities; they are not subject to any corporate legislation and do not have to disclose any information.

Unincorporated associations

An unincorporated association is simply a collection of people who have come together to share a common interest; good examples of these are sports and social clubs. There are few

36

legal rules governing these associations. The management of the club's affairs is usually entrusted to a committee, that manages the club on behalf of its members.

● Partnerships

Partnerships are effectively unincorporated associations. The 1890 Partnership Act defines a partnership as 'the relation which subsists between persons carrying on business for profit'. Usually, all the partners in a business agree to put capital into the partnership and work on its behalf. In exchange for this, they will receive a share of the profits. The organisations of professionals, such as solicitors, are structured in the form of partnerships. Usually all partners are liable for the actions of the others. If the partnership gets into financial difficulties, each of the partners will usually be personally liable for the debts of the business. However, the Limited Partners Act (1907) does allow some partner's liability to be limited to the amount of capital that a partner has invested. In partnerships the risks and rewards are shared between the partners.

● COMPANIES

This chapter is primarily concerned with companies. A company is a corporation that has an existence, rights and duties that are completely separate from its shareholders (called the *members* in law). This means that the liability of the shareholders is usually limited in some way. Although it is possible, but very unusual, to have companies where the shareholders have unlimited liability. This would mean that the existence of a company gives no legal protection to the shareholders, who will still be personally liable for all the company's liabilities.

● Limitation of liability

Most companies limit the liability of their shareholders. The shareholder's liability can be limited by:

- **guarantee:** this is often use by charities, where no shares are issued. Each member personally guarantees to provide a specified maximum amount, in the event of the company going into liquidation. After 1980, a company's liability cannot be limited by guarantee if any shares are issued;
- **shares:** this is the most common form of limiting shareholder liability. The shareholders' liability is limited to any amount of any unpaid share capital. Consequently, if the shares are fully paid, the shareholder will lose his or her investment in the company, but will not be liable for anything else.

● Formation of companies

Companies can be formed in one of three ways:

(1) **By the grant of a Royal Charter:** this method was used before the Companies Acts, and some old companies were started in this way. Perhaps the best example is the Peninsular and Oriental Steam Navigation Company (known as P&O) which was started by Royal Charter in 1840. Another example would be the Institute of Chartered Accountants.

(2) **By a special act of parliament:** the various nationalising statutes of the 1940s established statutory corporations to own and operate the old nationalised industries. The Post Office is an example of a company created by statute.

(3) **By registration under the Companies Act 1985:** this is the most common method of company formation and is the one that we will consider in the rest of this chapter.

● Registration of companies under the Companies Act

To register a company the promoters, or their advisers, must draw up the company's constitutional documents – the *Memorandum of Association* and the *Articles of Association*.

The Memorandum

This is the more important of the two documents and is essentially the company's constitution, governing its relations with the outside world. It should disclose:

● the company's *name*;
● whether the company's *registered office* will be located in England and Wales, Wales, or Scotland;
● the *objects* of the company – this tells us what the company can do;
● how the *liability* of the company is limited, or that the company is unlimited;
● the *authorised share capital* and the *nominal value* of the shares.
● a *witnessed list of the initial shareholders* – there must be at least two shareholders for public companies, having at least one share each. Since 1992 it has been possible for private companies to have only one shareholder, following the Companies (Single Member Private Companies) Regulations.

The Articles of Association

This contains all the rules and regulations which relate to the company's internal management. The Articles are subsidiary to the Memorandum, and would usually include provisions relating to the following:

● *Share capital:*
  – the rights attached to each class of share, and how those rights may be varied;
  – the issue of shares and any restrictions on the transfer of shares;
  – the procedure for altering the authorised share capital of the company.

● *Annual general meetings:*
  – the notice and procedure for the annual general meeting.

● *Directors:*
  – directors' duties and powers (including borrowing powers);
  – the election, retirement and disqualification of directors.

● *Dividend declaration.*
● *Winding-up procedures.*

To obtain registration, these and other documents are submitted to the Registrar of Companies, who will then register the company on payment of certain fees and stamp duties and issue a *certificate of incorporation*. Unfortunately, this may take some time. As a result, it is possible to buy companies 'off the shelf'. These companies have already been registered, and a change of name is quickly effected.

SUMMARY

Companies are legally regarded as separate from their members, therefore, starting a company limits the liability of the company's members. The commonest way that companies limit members' liability is through the issue of shares. Each shareholder's liability is then limited to the amount of any unpaid share capital. Liability can also be limited by guarantee, each member guarantees a specified amount if the company is liquidated.

Most companies are started by registering them under the Companies Act. However, it is possible to form a company by a special Act of Parliament or by a Royal Charter. To register under the Act, companies must submit certain documents to the Registrar of Companies. The most important of these are the Memorandum and the Articles of Association. The Memorandum governs the company's relationships with the outside world and gives important details about the company. It tells us its name, where it is incorporated, what it can do, the shares the company can issue and nominal values of the shares, and who owns them. The Articles are concerned with the internal management of the company. They detail the procedures that should be followed in a range of situations, including the issuing and transferring of shares, the holding of annual general meetings, the appointment of directors, and liquidating the company.

● DIFFERENT TYPES OF COMPANY

Companies may be either public companies or private companies.

● Public companies

A public company is defined as one that has:

- allotted share capital of at least £50 000, of which at least 25 per cent has been fully paid;
- a minimum of two directors (unless it was registered before 1 November 1929), who must retire at 70;
- a qualified company secretary.

Its Memorandum must state that it is a public company, and it must be properly registered as a public company. It cannot start trading until it has been granted a Section 117 Certificate by the Registrar.

The name of the company must end with the words 'Public Limited Company' (which may be abbreviated to plc), unless it is incorporated in Wales, for which the Welsh equivalents should be used.

Contrary to popular belief, a public company is not necessarily listed on the Stock Exchange, although only public companies can achieve a listing. To be listed on the Stock Exchange the company must also satisfy the Exchange's listings requirements.

● Private companies

A private company is any company that is not a public company. It may trade from the date of its incorporation, and its name should be followed with the word Limited (Ltd), or its Welsh equivalent. Whilst all companies are required to prepare full statutory accounts for their shareholders, those for smaller companies may show less detailed information. Private companies are allowed to file limited financial information if they are classified as small, or medium sized.

A private company is defined as small or medium sized if it does not exceed more than one of the following criteria shown in Table 3.1.

Table 3.1 Criteria defining small and medium-sized companies

Criteria	Small	Medium sized
Turnover	£2.8 m	£11.2 m
Total assets	£1.4 m	£5.6 m
Average number of employees on a monthly basis	50	250

Accounting and filing criteria for small private companies

A small company is only required to file a modified balance sheet. This only shows the totals for each balance sheet category. It is a less detailed balance sheet than the one that is included in the statutory accounts prepared for the shareholders, and offers more limited notes.

In addition to the filing exemptions, small companies prepare for less detailed accounts. Until recently, the accounts prepared by small and large companies were broadly similar, although smaller private companies were exempt from some accounting standards. (For example, they do not have to prepare a cash flow statement.)

In 1992, an amendment to the Companies Act introduced substantial disclosure exemptions for small companies. We are currently in the process of evolving two different sets of generally accepted accounting practice. Larger companies being required to comply with all statutory provisions and accounting standard requirements. Whereas smaller private companies comply with a shorter set of rules that require less disclosure in the accounts.

Accounting and filing criteria for medium-sized private companies

Medium-sized companies must prepare full statutory accounts for their shareholders and there are fewer filing exemptions. Their filed accounts will comprise:

● a Director's Report
● a balance sheet
● a modified profit and loss account (this starts at gross profit and, therefore, does not disclose turnover or cost of sales).

Advantages of a private company

The only real disadvantage of private companies is that, since the Financial Services Act of 1986 (s 170) they are effectively denied access to the capital markets. As long as you do not want this access to the capital markets, private companies offer more flexibility than public companies. Private companies have a number of advantages over public companies, which include:

Share capital

● Subsequent share issues do not have to be in the form of a rights issue, unless the company's Articles require it (Companies Act, s 89).
● There is no requirement for any valuations to be made if shares are issued for assets, rather than cash.

- There is no minimum share capital.
- Private companies may provide financial assistance for the purchase of their own shares by following the statutory procedure (Companies Act, ss 155–158).
- Private companies may purchase or redeem their own shares out of capital (Companies Act, ss 170–177).
- There is no obligation to show the true ownership of a private company's shares, no matter how substantial the shareholding (Companies Act, ss 198–211).

Loss of capital

- There is no requirement to hold an extraordinary general meeting in the event of the company having lost half, or more, of its called up share capital (i.e. the net assets are at half or less of the of the called up share capital. This is referred to as a *serious loss of capital*).

Provision for unrealised capital losses

- A private company need not make a provision for an unrealised capital loss before making a dividend distribution (Companies Act, s 264).

SUMMARY The main differences between public and private companies are summarised in Table 3.2.

Table 3.2 **Differences between public and private companies**

	Public companies	Private companies
Minimum share capital	£50 000, at least a quarter of which must be fully paid	None
Minimum number of shareholders	Two	One
Minimum number of directors	Two	One
Qualified company secretary	Yes	No
Able to offer shares to the general public	No	Yes
Directors retire at 70	Yes	No, unless the company is a subsidiary of a public company
Extraordinary general meeting if the net assets fall to half the share capital	Yes	No

● Close companies

You will also see reference in accounts to a different type of company, *a close company*. This is not a term from the Companies Act, but from s 414 of the Income and Corporation Taxes Act (1988). The close company provisions were established to stop individuals avoiding personal tax liabilities. A close company is one that is either an:

- **unlisted company** – under the control of five, or fewer, people or its directors. Most private companies will be close companies; or a
- **listed company** – here less than 35 per cent of the shares are held by the public. The Stock Exchange rules require listed companies to disclose whether or not they are close companies.

● GETTING A LISTING ON THE STOCK EXCHANGE

From the company's point of view, the main advantage of having your shares listed on the Stock Exchange is the fact that their free marketability increases their value to a prospective investor. Until 1984, Stock Exchange listings were not legally regulated. However, in 1984 three European Directives bought about significant changes. These were:

- **the Admissions Directive:** this covers the conditions for admission to a stock exchange;
- **the Listing Particulars Directive:** this establishes the requirements for drawing up, scrutinising and the distributing the listing particulars that must be published before admission;
- **the Interim Reports Directive:** this requires information to be published on a regular basis.

In addition, the Mutual Recognition Directive deals with the UK listing of companies already listed on other EU markets. These four Directives have been implemented in part four of the Financial Services Act 1986; s 142 of the Financial Services Act (1986) provides that no securities can be quoted, unless part four is complied with. These, together with the Stock Exchange's additional rules, are covered in the Stock Exchange's listing rules, also known as the 'Yellow Book'.

The first thing that companies have to decide is the stock market where their shares will be listed. This may well be determined for them by the circumstances of their business. There are two different markets within the Stock Exchange:

- the main market designed for larger, established companies;
- the Alternative Investment Market (AIM), which is designed for smaller, younger companies.

Any company that wishes to have their shares or other securities listed on the Stock Exchange must also comply with the Stock Exchange rules. There are fewer rules for entrants to the AIM, but all companies offering their shares to the general public must provide a prospectus. The rules governing AIM listed companies are dealt with separately, towards the end of this chapter.

● Marketability – minimum criteria for listing

Before listing a company, the Stock Exchange has to satisfy itself that there will be sufficient trading in the company's securities to ensure a realistic market. Hence, the Yellow Book has two minimum criteria:

(1) The expected total market value for the listed security. Share issues must have a minimum market capitalisation of £700 000, whereas debt issue need only have a market capitalisation of £200 000.
(2) At least 25 per cent of the shares should be in the hands of the general public.

The prospectus

The information required in a company's prospectus is detailed in the listing particulars (Chapter 6 in the Yellow Book). The prospectus has been designed to ensure that the public has sufficient information about the company before buying the shares. The information that is contained in a company's prospectus is also very useful for the analysts, as it contains information about the company's history, its current position and its future prospects.

A prospectus must include the following information:

- Details of the offer, the company's share capital and its indebtedness.
- Details of the company's directors, secretary, auditors, financial advisers, solicitors, bankers and stockbrokers.
- A general description of the company including:
  - an introduction and brief history of the company;
  - a comprehensive description of its business;
  - information on both the management and the staff of the company;
  - details of the company's premises;
  - what the proceeds of the share issue will be used for;
  - a record of the earnings together with forecasted profit and dividends;
  - the company's future plans and prospects.

- The accountant's report containing the last three years' profit and loss accounts and balance sheets.
- Additional statutory and general information:
  - share capital and options;
  - the Articles of Association;
  - subsidiary and associated companies;
  - directors' interests and service agreements;
  - material contracts;
  - any pending litigation.

The Public Offers of Securities Regulations 1995 impose three prospectus requirements on companies offering their securities:

(1) when the securities are offered to the public for the first time, the published prospectus should be freely available to any member of the public, at a UK address during the period of the offer;
(2) before publishing this prospectus, it should be registered with the Registrar;
(3) any document, other than the prospectus, should state that a prospectus, if required, is, or will be, published.

Continuing obligations

Once the shares have been listed, the company must ensure that the shareholders' interests are protected and that they are kept informed of the company's activities and progress. Consequently, listed companies have to comply with the *Continuing Obligations*. (These are detailed in Chapters 9–16 in the Yellow Book.)

Companies are required to submit, for approval, to the Stock Exchange:

- all circulars to holders of securities
- notices of meetings

- forms of proxy
- advertisement notices to holders of bearer securities.

Companies are also required to notify the Exchange if any of the following occur:

- changes in directors
- dividend declarations
- material acquisitions
- profit announcements
- proposed changes in the nature of the business.

Companies are also required to disclose any information that is necessary to enable people to judge the position of the company and to avoid a false market in its listed securities. If there is any information that would lead to substantial price movements, and it is likely that secrecy cannot be maintained, the company must warn the Company Announcements Office and disclose this information.

● Additional accounting requirements for listed companies

As the shares are now in the hands of the general public, companies need to disclose more information about their financial position. Listed companies are expected to issue their accounts within six months of their year end, although they may apply for an extension if they have significant overseas interests. However, most listed companies will report within three months of their year end.

Listed companies are required to disclose the following additional information in their accounts:

- **borrowings:** details of bank loans, overdrafts and other borrowings;
- **Cadbury Committee Code of Best Practice:** (this applies only to companies incorporated in the UK) statement of whether the company complies with the requirements of the Cadbury Committee's Code of Best Practice, together with a review by the auditors and any reasons for non-compliance;
- **capitalised interest:** the amount of any interest capitalised;
- **close company:** a statement of whether or not the company is a close company;
- **contracts:**
  - details of any significant contract in which any director had, or has, a material interest;
  - details of any contract with, or for the provision of services by, any shareholder with 30 per cent, or more of the voting power (a substantial shareholder);
- **directors:**
  - details of the waiving of any emoluments by a director;
  - the identity of each independent non-executive director, together with their brief biographical details;
  - details of each director's beneficial and non-beneficial interests in the company's shares and options;
- **inaccurate profit forecasts:** if the period's results differ by 10 per cent or more from any published forecast and the reason for the difference;
- **investments:**
  - the principal country in which each subsidiary operates;
  - details of each associated undertaking;
- **non-compliance with relevant accounting standards:** any departures from UK Accounting Standards, US Accounting Standards, or International Accounting Standards,

as applicable to the company. This must be accompanied by a statement by the directors about the reasons for non-compliance;

● **shares and shareholders:**
 – details of the waiving of any dividends by a shareholder;
 – information on shareholdings of 3 per cent or more of any class of voting shares, that are not owned by the directors;
 – details of any authority for the purchase by the company of its own shares, and details of any purchases that were not made through the market;
 – details of shares that were issued for cash, unless this issue was in the form of a rights issue;
 – if the company has listed shares in issue and is the subsidiary of another company, it must disclose the parent's participation in any placing of its shares.

● How companies can get a listing

There are three ways that a company can get a listing on a stock exchange:

(1) an offer for sale or subscription
(2) a placing
(3) an introduction.

We will look at each in turn.

The offer for sale

This is the most common way of getting a listing. The shares are offered to the public, usually through a newspaper advertisement, containing both the prospectus and an application form for the shares. Either existing shares or new shares are offered for sale. We are obviously interested in who will be receiving the cash from the share issue: the existing shareholders or the company itself.

The shares must be sponsored; either by a merchant bank and a broker, or just by a broker. The sale could be effected either through a direct invitation to the public (*an offer for subscription*) or via an intermediary. The issuing house, or sponsoring broker, buys the shares and offers them to the public at a slightly higher price. The offer for sale will be either a fixed-price offer or a tender offer.

A fixed price offer

The sponsors will look at the historical financial performance and the profit forecasts and compare these to other companies in the sector. They will be able to consider the superior, or otherwise, growth prospects and indicated dividend policy of the company and use these to determine the price for the offer. It is always worth remembering two things:

(1) The company almost invariably is cautious in its profit forecast for the year. The last thing that it wants to have to do is to explain to shareholders, in its first year as a quoted company, why the company did not achieve the forecasts. Over-achievement, on the other hand, can always be put down to good management!
(2) The sponsors will want to make sure that the issue is successful, and preferably the share price following flotation (in the *aftermarket*) should be above the flotation price.

Consequently, all things being equal, with good management, sponsors and no market crash there should be money to be made on a flotation!

A tender offer

An offer by tender would be used when the company is very difficult to value. Investors are invited to subscribe for the shares and asked to state what price they are prepared to pay. (This will be a price above a stated minimum.) Assuming that all the shares can be sold (the issue is *fully subscribed*) the sponsors then work out at what price all the shares can be sold. This price is then referred to as the *striking price*, and anyone who has tendered at this price, or above it, has a chance of getting some shares. The striking price may not necessarily be the highest price, as the sponsors will want an aftermarket in the shares. Any one bidding below the striking price will not get any shares.

Even if your bid was at the striking price, you may not get all of the shares that you asked for, as the issue can be *over-subscribed*. In a tender offer this may be done to create an aftermarket.

Any issue can be oversubscribed be it via a fixed-price offer or a tender. The sponsors have then to decide who will get the shares, and how many each bidder will get. This process is referred to as *allotment*. This happened in 1997 with the Norwich Union flotation, when a lot of small investors were disappointed. The allotment can either be achieved through a ballot, where if you are lucky you get what you asked for, or the applications can be scaled down, according to a formula. Sometimes companies want to favour small investors, and they get a larger percentage of their applications.

A placement

In this case the company gets an initial spread of shares by arranging privately to sell shares to a range of investors. The placing is usually arranged by the company's broker and most of the shares will probably be placed with his clients. Therefore, there is no offer to the public, or general offer to the existing shareholders. After the placing, permission is given for the shares to be traded on the stock market, and anyone can buy the shares in the normal way. A variant on a placing is an *intermediaries offer*. The shares are offered to intermediaries, who then allocate them to their own clients. Many AIM issues, which tend to be smaller, are made via a placing.

An introduction

This is the rarest way of obtaining a listing, as the company does not raise any additional capital. It tends to happen where a company already has a large spread of shareholders, and is simply looking for permission for its shares to be traded in the stockmarket.

Introductions are common in two situations:

(1) the company is already listed on an overseas stock exchange;
(2) where a UK company has been financed by institutional investors in a management buy out.

It is the cheapest way of getting a listing.

● Subsequent share issues

Small quantities of shares can be directly placed in the market. The rules of the Stock Exchange require, in a rights issue, that the company offer its existing shareholders the opportunity to buy new shares at a discounted price. The shareholders then have three alternatives:

(1) they can exercise their right to buy the share;

(2) they can sell their rights to buy the share (in practice this option is only available to large shareholders, the smaller shareholders' profit will be wiped out by dealing fees);

(3) they can do nothing.

● Underwriting

Most share issues are 'underwritten'. This is a form of insurance, provided by banks and institutions, where the underwriters agree to buy the shares if no one else wants to buy them. This ensures that the company will receive some cash from the rights issue. The underwriters were forced to buy the shares in the BP privatisation in 1987. The stock market crash put the offer price above the market price, so that most of the shares were left with the underwriters.

SUMMARY

Marketability criteria

To qualify for a listing on the Stock Exchange, companies must meet the Exchange's marketability criteria. The minimum market capitalisation for share issues is £700 000 (£200 000 for debt issues) and at least 25 per cent of the shares should be in the hands of the general public.

The prospectus

To obtain a listing companies must issue a prospectus giving detailed information about the company, its advisers, its history, its current position and its prospects. Profit and loss accounts and balance sheets should be provided for the last three years. The prospectus enables the investing public to make an informed investment decision.

Obtaining a listing

There are several different ways that companies can obtain a listing. The commonest one is where the shares are offered for sale by an intermediary. The issuing house, or sponsoring broker, buys the shares and offers them to the public at a slightly higher price. This is called an offer for sale. Alternatively, the shares could be offered directly to the public. The price of the shares may be fixed (a fixed-price offer), or applicants could be invited to bid for the shares (a tender offer). In an offer for sale by tender, the price is determined by the market, rather than by the company's advisers.

A listing can also be obtained through a placing. Shares are privately sold to investors, usually by the company's broker placing the shares directly with his clients.

Most share issues are underwritten, where institutions have promised to buy the shares if no one else wants them.

If the company does not want to issue any additional shares as it already has a large spread of shareholders, it could have an introduction to the stock market. Introductions are used where the company is simply looking for permission for its shares to be traded in the stock market.

Continuing obligations

Once a company has obtained a listing, it must meet the stock market's continuing obligations. It must disclose additional financial information in its accounts and disclose whether or not it complies with the Cadbury Committee's requirements on corporate governance, and explain any non-compliance. Circulars and notices to shareholders should be approved by the Exchange prior to their issue. The company should also notify

▶

the Exchange of any changes in directors, changes in business, material acquisitions and dividend and profit announcements.

Subsequent share issues

Most subsequent share issues have to be in the form of a rights issue, although small amounts of shares can be directly placed in the market.

● THE ALTERNATIVE INVESTMENT MARKET (AIM)

The AIM has been designed for companies that are smaller and younger than those found in the main market. There are no marketability criteria and there are fewer rules:

- entrants need to have a nominated adviser and a nominated broker, who could come from the same company;
- their accounts must comply with UK, US, or International Accounting Standards;
- their directors, and certain employees, must conform to the model code (this covers the trading of shares whilst in possession of price-sensitive information);
- if the company has been generating revenues for less than two years, directors and employees must agree not to sell their shares for one year from the date of listing.

To obtain a listing on the AIM, companies must provide a prospectus, or a similar document, that meets EU Directives, and audited accounts conforming to company law. However, there is no minimum trading record. Subsequently, companies are required to publish unaudited interim figures and give details of all directors' dealings.

JARGON **Admissions directive**   An EU Directive covering the rules for admission to a stock exchange.

Alternative Investment Market (AIM)   A stock market for smaller and younger companies than those found on the main stockmarket. There are no marketability criteria and fewer rules.

Articles of Association   The rules governing the internal management of companies.

Continuing obligations   The stock market's ongoing requirements for listed companies.

Interim Reports Directive   An EU Directive requiring information to be published regularly.

Introduction   The cheapest way of getting a listing, as the company gets permission for its shares to be traded on a stock market. This usually happens when the shares are already traded on another stock market.

Listed company   A company listed on a stock exchange.

Listing Particulars Directive   An EU Directive detailing the requirements for drawing up, scrutinising and distributing the listing particulars.

Medium-sized private company   A private company which does not exceed two of the following:
- £11.2 million turnover
- £5.6 million total assets
- 250 employees, averaged on a monthly basis.

Memorandum   The company's constitution governing its relations with the outside world.

Offer for sale   Shares are offered to the general public. The company sells its shares to an issuing house, or sponsoring broker, who then offers the shares to the general public at a higher price.

Offer for subscription   The general public is invited to subscribe for shares.

Placement   Shares are sold privately to a range of investors.

Private company   Any company that is not a public company.

Prospectus   Effectively a marketing brochure containing all the details of an offer for the sale of securities. It would give information about the company and the securities that are being offered.

Public company   A company that has a minimum share capital of £50 000 (of which at least 25 per cent has been fully paid), a minimum of two shareholders and directors (unless registered before 1 November 1929) and a qualified company secretary. Only a public company can offer its shares to the general public.

Rights issue   Shares are offered to the company's existing shareholders in proportion to their current shareholding.

Small private company   A private company which does not exceed two of the following:
- £2.8 million turnover
- £1.4 million total assets
- 50 employees, averaged on a monthly basis.

Tender offer   Investors are invited to subscribe for shares and to state the price they would be prepared to pay (above a stated minimum). The price (the striking price) will be the one that ensures that all the shares have been sold. Anyone bidding below the striking price will not get any shares.

Underwriting   A mechanism to enable companies to receive a minimum amount of cash from a share issue. The underwriters agree to buy the shares for an agreed price if no one else wants them.

Unincorporated association   A group of people who come together to share a common interest, like a sports and social club.

4 Introduction to the accounts

This chapter covers:

- The chairman's statement
- The directors' report
- The operating and financial review
- The financial statements
- The auditors' report
- The Cadbury Committee's Code of Best Practice
- Greenbury
- The notes to the accounts

● INTRODUCTION

Company accounts contain a wealth of information. By law the accounts are required to contain:

- a directors' report
- a profit and loss account
- a balance sheet
- an auditors' report
- notes to the accounts.

The accounting standards also require a statement of total recognised gains and losses, and most companies have to prepare a cash flow statement. Listed companies' accounts will usually contain a chairman's statement.

● THE CHAIRMAN'S STATEMENT

The chairman's statement is a marketing document that larger companies use to satisfy the statutory requirement for a business review. It tries to present the company's performance in the best light and usually contains information on:

- the company's strategy and business plans;

- the general trading performance of the company in the context of the economic and competitive climate;
- the prospects for the next year;
- the performance of specific businesses within the company;
- any items of special interest during the year (for example, the acquisition and disposal of subsidiaries).

THE DIRECTORS' REPORT

This contains statutory information that may be found elsewhere in the accounts. In the directors' report you should find information on:

- the principal activities of the company and the business review, if this is not disclosed elsewhere in the accounts;
- the proposed dividend and the amount of profit that will be transferred to the reserves if the proposed dividend is paid;
- any major changes in fixed assets, and any significant difference between the market value and the book value of the assets;
- the directors, their interests and shareholdings, and any changes in directors during the year;
- employees, employee involvement in the running of the company, the company's policies relating to equal opportunities and the employment of disabled persons;
- any shares that have been purchased by the company during the year;
- any important events that have occurred after the company's year end;
- any political or charitable donations made during the year, that are over £200;
- insurance taken out for directors or auditors against liabilities in relation to the company;
- the company's status. Companies are required to disclose whether they are a 'close company'. The Income and Corporation Taxes Act (1988) defines a close company as one that is in the control of five, or fewer, persons or is under the control of the directors. A listed company is classed as a close company if less than 35 per cent of the voting power is held by the public;
- the appointment of the auditors.

THE OPERATING AND FINANCIAL REVIEW

The Accounting Standards Board published a document in July 1993 called *The Operating and Financial Review*. This is a 'statement of voluntary best practice' and is intended to cover public companies and any other large company 'where there is a legitimate public interest in their financial statements'. It is not mandatory, but is increasingly found in large companies' accounts.

The operating review

The operating review identifies the main factors that underlie the business, the way that these have varied in the past, and are expected to vary in the future. It gives a full discussion on the operating results and the dynamics of the businesses, including the main risks and uncertainties it faces.

● The financial review

This is of particular interest, as it should explain:

- The capital structure of the business:
  - the maturity profile of debt;
  - the types of capital instruments that are used in the company;
  - currencies;
  - the interest-rate structure.
- The company's treasury policy:
  - the control of treasury activities;
  - the currencies in which borrowings are made and cash and deposits are held;
  - the extent of fixed-rate borrowings;
  - the use of financial instruments for hedging;
  - the extent to which foreign currency net investments are hedged by currency borrowings, and other hedging instruments.
- The components of the tax charge, if the overall tax charge is 'significantly different from a standard tax charge'.
- Cash flows from operating activities:
  - a discussion of the cash flows, and any special factors that have influenced those flows;
  - segmental cash flows if these are significantly out of line with the segmental profits.
- The current liquidity:
  - the level of borrowings at the year end;
  - the seasonality of the borrowings;
  - the peak level of the borrowings;
  - the maturity profile of both the borrowings and the committed borrowing facilities;
  - the funding requirements for authorised capital expenditure;
  - any restrictions on the company's ability to transfer funds within the group, and any attendant restraints on the group;
  - negotiations with bankers on covenants that restrict the credit facilities;
  - the measures taken, or proposed, to remedy any breach, or probable breach, of banking covenants.
- Company resources and strengths that are not reflected in the balance sheet.

Unfortunately we rarely get all of this information, as the review tends to be a balance between discretion and disclosure.

● THE FINANCIAL STATEMENTS

There are four primary financial statements in the UK:

(1) the profit and loss account
(2) the balance sheet
(3) the cash flow statement
(4) the statement of total recognised gains and losses.

Only the first three would be found in accounts overseas.

● The profit and loss account

The profit and loss account shows whether the company has been selling its goods and services for more or less than it costs it to make and deliver them to the customer. It takes the income from sales made in the period and then deducts the costs that relate to those sales.

When looking at a profit and loss account it is important to remember three things:

(1) **It is historical.** All profit and loss accounts will tell you what has happened, not what is happening now. It usually takes a UK company three months, after the year end, to publish its profit and loss account. To reinforce the fact that they are historical, profit and loss accounts always say something like 'for the year ending ... for the six months ending ... for the period ending'.

(2) **It does not include capital expenditure.** The only impact that capital expenditure has on the profit and loss account is the depreciation charge. Consequently, a business can be profitable but run out of cash because of a capital expenditure programme.

(3) **It is not concerned about whether the cash has been received from customers or paid to suppliers, just that the sale has been made.** If I buy an apple for 5p and sell it for 8p, the profit and loss account records a profit of 3p. But I may have paid cash to buy the apple, and sold it on credit. The profit remains the same even though my cash is now at -5p. Thus, a business can be profitable, but run out of cash if the customers have not paid for the sales in the period. So, what looks like a 'profitable' business in the accounts may be making a loss today, and can easily go into liquidation because it runs out of cash!

The layout of the profit and loss account

The way a profit and loss account is laid out varies from one company to another. There are several different formats, and costs can be looked at in different ways. However, profit and loss accounts have a standard structure that is illustrated in Table 4.1.

Table 4.1 **Standard structure for profit and loss accounts**

```
Turnover
-    Operating costs
+    Other operating income
=    OPERATING PROFIT  (This is a profit that companies show, but it is not required by the
                        Companies Act)
+/-  Share of associates and joint venture profits/losses
+/-  Profits and losses on sale of fixed assets or subsidiaries[1]
-    Major restructuring costs[1]
+/-  Interest[1]
=    PROFIT BEFORE TAX
+/-  Tax[2]
=    PROFIT AFTER TAX
-    Dividends
=    RETAINED PROFIT

Notes:
[1]  The company's share of associates and joint venture will be shown on the profit and loss account.
[2]  This includes associate's and joint venture's tax, which will be separately disclosed.
```

The costs of materials, labour and overheads used in sales (the operating costs) can be calculated in two ways:

We can look at why we have incurred the costs – costs are analysed functionally:

● *cost of sales*

● *administration expenses*
● *selling and distribution expenses*.

Alternatively we can look at what the company has spent the money on, such as:

● *materials*
● *wages*
● *overheads*.

Within the EU there are four different ways of presenting the profit and loss account, and these are reflected in the Companies Act. Only two formats are used in the UK; the others being more popular in continental Europe. Formats 3 and 4 are essentially horizontal presentations of Formats 1 and 2.

A 'Format 1' profit and loss account

This is the most commonly used format in the UK, and classifies costs into:

● cost of sales
● administrative expenses
● distribution costs.

Unfortunately these terms are not defined in the Companies Act. Some companies include their sales and marketing costs in distribution costs, whereas others include these costs in administrative expenses. Some retailers define cost of sales as simply the cost of merchandise, others will also include distribution costs and store operating costs. Thus, it is not possible to compare these costs between companies; only within a company over time.

An example of a Format 1 profit and loss account is given in Table 4.2.

| Table 4.2 | Profit and loss account – 'Format 1' |

	£m	£m
Turnover		1000
Cost of sales		(600)
Gross profit		400
Distribution costs		(140)
Administrative expenses		(70)
Other operating income		10
Operating profit		200
Share of associate's operating profits		20
Profit on sale of fixed assets		10
Interest receivable – group		10
Interest payable:		
Group	(50)	
Associate	(10)	60
Profit on ordinary activities before taxation		180
Taxation on profit on ordinary activities*		(40)
Profit on ordinary activities after taxation		140
Minority interests		(10)
Dividend		(40)
Retained profit for the financial year		90
*Tax relates to the following: Group (38)		
Associate (2)		

A 'Format 2' profit and loss account

This classifies operating costs as materials, staff costs (which include social security and pension costs), other external costs and depreciation. As these are often the purchases that have been made in the period, rather than the costs that have been used in sales, two adjustments will have to be made to exclude:

● costs that relate to stock – *'changes in stock and work in progress'*;
● staff costs that have been spent on installing or improving capital items – *'own work capitalised'*.

Table 4.3 shows the same profit and loss account, but in a Format 2 presentation.

Table 4.3   **Profit and loss account – 'Format 2'**

	£m	£m
Turnover		1000
Raw materials and consumables		(470)
Staff costs		(195)
Other external charges		(100)
Depreciation		(90)
Changes in stock and work in progress		20
Own work capitalised		25
Other operating income		10
Operating profit		200
Share of associate's operating profits		20
Profit on sale of fixed assets		10
Interest receivable – group		10
Interest payable:		
Group	(50)	
Associate	(10)	
		(60)
Profit on ordinary activities before taxation		180
Taxation on profit on ordinary activities*		(40)
Profit on ordinary activities after taxation		140
Minority interests		(10)
Dividend		(40)
Retained profit for the financial year		90

*Tax relates to the following: Group   (38)
                                         Associate   (2)

Most listed companies would take a profit after minority interests, and before dividends. This is called the profit for the financial year.

If the company has sold assets that have previously been revalued, the profit and loss account will be followed by a note of historical-cost profits and losses. This shows what the profit would have been had there been no revaluations and is discussed in Chapter 14.

The profit and loss account is discussed in detail in Chapters 12–14.

● The balance sheet

This shows what the business is worth at the end of the year, given a set of assumptions that are detailed in the notes. The balance sheet represents a picture of the business on a certain day, identifying the assets and the liabilities. Like any photograph, it can be taken from different vantage points. A UK balance sheet identifies how much the business is worth to the shareholders; we will see that other countries look at the business from a different perspective.

The directors of the company know how important the balance sheet is. It will be used to determine things such as:

- how much credit the company will get
- how much money can be lent to the company
- the rate of interest that will be charged on borrowings
- whether someone is going to invest their life's savings in this company.

As a snapshot of the business on a certain day, it can be 'managed'. Companies will pick the best day in their year to take the snapshot, and always remember they have 364 days' notice of that day arriving! It may well be as like the business for the rest of the year as our passport photographs represent true and fair views of us! Balance sheets should be read very carefully, and we should always remember to look for trends. Every year the company tries to show the best picture of itself. Is the best picture getting better or worse?

It is possible to prepare the balance sheet from different perspectives. The balance sheet's content is broadly the same, no matter how it is presented. The degree of detail and the basis for valuations may vary from one country to another, but the information presented in the balance sheet will vary little. In Chapter 1 we discussed the two balance-sheet formats stipulated by the Companies Act. The layout of the two balance sheets is different, but the content of each balance sheet is identical. Most UK companies prepare the balance sheet from the shareholders' point of view, others from total assets and liabilities, looking at the business from the point of view of anyone who has put money into the business. Overseas, most companies use the asset and liabilities layout.

Examples of the two formats are shown in Tables 4.4 and 4.5.

Table 4.4 **Balance sheet – 'Format 1'**

	£m
FIXED ASSETS	
Intangible assets	50
Tangible assets	200
Investments	75
	325
CURRENT ASSETS	
Stocks	80
Debtors	270
Investments	40
Cash	10
	400
CREDITORS: AMOUNTS FALLING DUE WITHIN ONE YEAR	(300)
Net current assets	100
Total assets less current liabilities	425
CREDITORS: AMOUNTS FALLING DUE AFTER MORE THAN ONE YEAR	(100)
PROVISIONS FOR LIABILITIES AND CHARGES	(15)
MINORITY INTERESTS	(25)
	285

▶

	£m
CAPITAL AND RESERVES	
Share capital	50
Profit and loss account	175
Revaluation reserve	40
Share premium account	20
	285

Table 4.5 Balance sheet – 'Format 2'

	£m
FIXED ASSETS	
Intangible assets	50
Tangible assets	200
Investments	75
	325
CURRENT ASSETS	
Stocks	80
Debtors	270
Investments	40
Cash	10
	400
TOTAL ASSETS	725
CAPITAL AND RESERVES	
Share capital	50
Profit and loss account	175
Revaluation reserve	40
Share premium account	20
	285
MINORITY INTERESTS	25
PROVISIONS FOR LIABILITIES AND CHARGES	15
CREDITORS *	400
TOTAL LIABILITIES	725

* A Format 2 balance sheet shows creditors as a single item. In the notes each component of the creditors must be analysed between those falling due within a year and in more than a year. The totals should also be shown.

The balance sheet is discussed in detail in Chapters 5–12.

• The cash flow statement

The cash flow statement shows the movement of cash in the business in the past year. It identifies where the money has come from and where the business has spent the money. Cash flows are classified as arising from:

- **trading:** these cash flows are shown under the heading of *'operating activities'*;
- **dividends received from joint ventures and associates.** These will be shown under this heading following the implementation of FRS 9 in June 1998;
- **interest, dividends received and any dividends paid to 'non-equity' shares and minority interests**: these cash flows are shown under the heading of *'returns on investment and servicing of finance'*;
- **tax:** these cash flows are shown under the heading of *'taxation'*;
- **buying and selling fixed assets:** these cash flows are shown under the heading *'capital expenditure and financial investment'*;
- **buying and selling businesses and trades:** these cash flows are shown under the heading *'acquisitions and disposals'*;
- **dividends paid to ordinary shareholders:** these cash flows are shown under the heading of *'equity dividends paid'*;
- **short-term investments that are shown as current asset investments:** these cash flows are shown under the heading *'management of liquid resources'*;
- **shares and loans:** these cash flows are shown under the heading of *'financing'*.

Looking at the cash flow statement helps us see where the company has been spending and raising its money and whether the company is living within its means. This is probably the most important document of all; profit can be created, but you either have cash or you do not. You can always spot a business that is engaging in creative accounting – the cash runs out!

The cash flow statement is discussed in detail in Chapter 16.

● The statement of total recognised gains and losses

This is a relatively new document, much burdened by its title. It forms a bridge between the profit and loss account and the balance sheet bringing together profit, asset valuations and currency adjustments. It shows any gain or loss that the company has shown in its accounts, regardless of whether it has been realised and taken through the profit and loss account. The information found in the statement of total recognised gains and losses is not new; it has always been in the accounts, but buried far away in the notes.

The statement of total recognised gains and losses is concerned with movements on reserves and profitability, acknowledging that a non-professional reader of the accounts may not read all the notes and, therefore, may not know of all the gains and losses taken by the business in the year. By looking at this statement the reader can see instantly:

- whether the company has made a profit, before paying dividends
- whether the fixed assets have been revalued during the year
- the impact of any currency movements on the overall worth of the company.

The statement of total recognised gains and losses is discussed in more detail in Chapter 17.

● THE AUDITORS' REPORT

With the exception of very small companies, the accounts will include a report from the auditors. The auditors are required to report to the shareholders whether, in their opinion, the financial statements:

- have been properly prepared in accordance with the Companies Act and the relevant accounting standards;
- give a true and fair view of the company's financial position and profit or loss.

To do this the auditor will check that proper accounting records have been kept and that the accounts reflect those accounting records (Extract 4.1).

Extract 4.1 ## Auditors' report to the members of The Boots Company plc

> We have audited the financial statements on pages 50 to 75. We have also examined the amounts disclosed relating to emoluments, share options and long-term incentive scheme interests of the directors which form part of the board remuneration committee's reports on pages 40 to 45.
>
> **Respective responsibilities of directors and auditors** As described on page 46, the company's directors are responsible for the preparation of the financial statements. It is our responsibility to form an independent opinon, based on our audit, on those financial statements and to report our opinion to you.
>
> **Basis of opinion** We conducted our audit in accordance with Auditing Standards issued by the Auditing Practices Board. An audit examination, on a test basis, of evidence relevant to the amounts and disclosures in the financial statements. It also includes an assessment of the significant estimates and judgements made by the directors in the preparation of the financial statements, and of whether the accounting policies are appropriate to the group's circumstances, consistently applied and adequately disclosed.
>
> We planned and performed our audit so as to obtain all the information and explanations which we consider necessary in order to provide us with sufficient evidence to give reasonable assurance that the financial statements are free from material misstatement, whether caused by fraud or other irregularity or error. In forming our opinion we also evaluated the overall adequacy of the presentation of information in the financial statements.
>
> **Opinion** In our opinion the financial statements give a true and fair view of the state of affairs of the company and the group as at 31 March 1997 and of the profit of the group for the year then ended and have been properly prepared in accordance with the Companies Act 1985.
>
> **KPMG Audit Plc** Chartered Accountants
> Registered Auditor
> Birmingham
> 4 June 1997

The auditors' report is very important. Anyone looking at a set of accounts needs to be confident that those accounts are a true reflection of the company's performance. The growth of creative accounting in the 1980s generated increasing concerns about the reliability of the accounting information and the quality of the audit. The accounting rules were seen as too lax, and the auditors were accused of being the lapdogs rather than the watchdogs of the accounting profession. Some of the concerns were probably justified, but there was much confusion about the role of auditors. The general public seemed to have a higher expectation than was legally required. The auditors were not required to comment on the directors' stewardship or the future prospects for the company. The Cadbury Report (discussed later in this chapter) sought to clarify the position. It recommends that the directors should explain their responsibility for preparing the accounts and the auditors' reports should contain a clear statement of the auditors' responsibilities. The auditing profession has attempted to redress some of the other problems by revising the guidelines for conducting audits and expanding the audit report.

Auditing guidelines are issued by the Auditing Practices Board (APB). This was started in 1991 by the six principal accountancy bodies (the Consultative Committee of Accountancy Bodies). The APB issues Statements of Auditing Standards (SASs), and any auditors not following these are liable to disciplinary proceedings. It also issues practice notes and bulletins, reflecting good practice.

In May 1993 the APB issued SAS 600 *(Auditors' Reports on Financial Statements),* and this has changed the length and content of auditors' reports. Auditors' reports must now contain:

- a title specifying to whom the report is addressed;
- an introductory paragraph identifying the financial statements that have been audited;
- appropriately headed, separate sections discussing:
  - the respective responsibilities of the directors and the auditors;
  - the basis of the auditors' opinion;
  - the auditors' opinion on the financial statements.

The auditors' report should also be signed and dated.

SAS 600 requires that the report 'should contain a clear expression of opinion on the financial statements'. The auditors may offer an unequivocal opinion that the accounts are true and fair, or that they are not. However, the situation may not be that black and white, in some situations they may need to qualify their opinion in some way.

● Fundamental uncertainty

Auditors must now draw attention to any inherent uncertainties that they believe to be fundamental to the understanding of the accounts. For example, the auditors could be concerned about the continued support of the company's bankers or the outcome of a major litigation. The fundamental uncertainty may, or may not, lead to the accounts being qualified. If the uncertainty has been properly disclosed and accounted for in the accounts, there will be no reason for the accounts to be qualified.

● Qualification of the accounts

There are some situations where the auditors may be unable to arrive at unequivocal view on the accounts. Then they will qualify the accounts, by identifying the source of the problem. This will occur where:

- There is inadequate or insufficient information available to the auditors to enable them to determine whether proper accounting records have been kept. This is referred to as a limitation of scope. This often happens in small companies, where there is insufficient information to support some of the items shown in the accounts.
- There is a disagreement about the accounting treatment or disclosure of information contained in the accounts. The auditors may disagree with the amounts or the facts disclosed in the accounts. (For example, the auditors could be concerned about the level of provisioning.) Alternatively, they could disagree with the way things have or have not been disclosed in the accounts.

● Disclaimer of opinion

If an uncertainty or lack of adequate information could have a major impact on the accounts, the auditors will give a 'disclaimer of opinion'. This is given when the auditors have been unable to obtain sufficient evidence to support an opinion on the financial statements. The audit report will clearly state that they are unable to form an opinion that the accounts are true and fair.

● Adverse opinion

This is the report we do not want to see in the accounts! This is given when the auditors believe that the information in the accounts is seriously misleading. They will then state that in their opinion the accounts do not give a true and fair view.

● THE CADBURY COMMITTEE'S CODE OF BEST PRACTICE

The Cadbury Report was published in 1992 following public concern about the perceived lack of accountability of the directors of some large public companies. It is really a statement of best practice, and is an attempt to focus directors' attention on their own performance and working practices. It has been endorsed by the Stock Exchange, such that all listed companies must now disclose their compliance with the code. It is concerned with corporate governance, and specifically deals with four issues:

(1) the board of directors
(2) non-executive directors
(3) executive directors
(4) reporting and controls.

The Cadbury Report has increased the information found in the directors' report. Directors should report on their systems of internal control and their effectiveness. They also have to state in their report if the business is a going concern, giving the assumptions that they have used to determine this judgement. (The going-concern principle was discussed in Chapter 2.) In practice, this may not be included in the report as some companies report separately on corporate governance, whereas others disclose the required information in the financial review.

The role of the auditor in listed companies has been strengthened by the Cadbury Report. It proposed that:

● interim announcements should be subject to a review by the company's auditors;
● the auditors should review the company's compliance to the code;
● the accountancy profession should draw up guidelines for the rotation of audit partners.

It also requires that all listed companies should have audit committees. The objective of the audit committee is to strengthen the independence of the external auditor, and to reinforce the position of the internal auditor.

Other committees are also required to be set up under the code:

● **a board-nominations committee:** this is concerned with the selection and appointment of directors;

● **remuneration committee:** this is concerned with the remuneration of the directors.

● GREENBURY

During the 1990s the tabloid press was full of 'fat cat' stories. These were not about overweight moggies, but overpaid directors – particularly those in some of the recently privatised, former nationalised industries. The public pressure resulted in the Greenbury Committee (more correctly called the Study Group on Directors' Remuneration) being set up to look at directors' pay. It specified the best practice for remuneration committees, remuneration policy, and directors' service contracts and compensation. This has been adopted by the Stock Exchange in its listing rules, and companies now give very detailed information about their directors' remuneration in the remuneration committee's report. For all accounting periods ending after 31 December 1995, companies have had to disclose details of benefits, compensation for loss of office, and any other payments for each director, by name.

The information contained in the report is always interesting, but often has little relevance for financial analysis. However, it is always worth looking to see the basis for directors' bonuses, and to reflect if this could be an influence on some of the company's policies.

● THE NOTES TO THE ACCOUNTS

This will probably be the largest part of the accounts, and they should probably be read first of all. They tell you the accounting policies used in the preparation of the accounts and how all the numbers in the accounts have been calculated. Careful reading of the notes is essential if you want to be able to spot creative accounting.

JARGON **Auditor's report** A report from the company's auditors disclosing whether in their opinion, the accounts have been properly prepared, and are a true and fair view of the company's financial position and profit or loss.

The Cadbury Committee's Code of Best Practice A best-practice code for corporate governance that is specifically concerned with: the board of directors, non-executive directors, executive directors, and reporting and controls. Listed companies must disclose their compliance with the Code.

Chairman's statement A statement found in most listed companies' accounts that forms part of the business review.

Directors' report This document contains information that is often disclosed elsewhere. Information is given about the company's activities, profits and dividends, fixed assets, share capital, directors, employee involvement and employment policies, post balance sheet events, political and charitable donations, and the appointment of auditors.

Equity dividends Dividends paid to ordinary shareholders.

Financial review A review of the company's: capital structure, treasury policy, tax charge, cash flows from operating activities, current liquidity, and any resources that are not reflected in the balance sheet.

Operating review A review of the main factors affecting the company's performance and the company's operating results.

Statement of total recognised gains and losses A document showing all the gains and losses that have been recognised by the company during the year. Consequently it will disclose profits, revaluations, currency adjustments and prior-year adjustments.

5 The balance sheet: share capital and reserves

This chapter covers:

- **Share capital and share issues**
- **Reserves**
- **Debt–equity hybrids**

INTRODUCTION

The capital and reserves represent the owners' stake in the business. The share capital represents the shares in issue at the year end, and the reserves can come from a variety of sources. The main ones are:

- the accumulated retained profits, less any losses, since the business started – this reserve is called t*he profit and loss account* and is the only distributable reserve (there is a document called the profit and loss account showing this year's profit, and a reserve called the profit and loss account showing the accumulated profits since the business started;
- the extra premium that has been paid, over the nominal value, for the shares that have been issued – this is called *the share premium account*;
- the revaluation of the businesses' assets – this is called *the revaluation reserve*.

It is possible to find other reserves on the balance sheet, and these will be discussed later in this chapter.

SHARE CAPITAL AND SHARE ISSUES

In this section we will consider:

- the difference between the authorised and the issued share capital;
- the different types of shares found in company accounts;
- share issues;
- capital reconstructions through bonus issues, share splits and consolidations and reductions in share capital;
- share buy-backs;
- information that is disclosed in the accounts.

● Authorised and issued share capital

There will be two share capital numbers in the notes to the accounts: the *authorised share capital* and the *issued share capital*. The authorised share capital is simply the amount that the company can issue, not what it has issued. If the directors of the company wish to issue more shares than have been authorised they will have to seek shareholder approval, normally this just requires the passing of a resolution by a majority of the shareholders. The procedure for increasing the authorised share capital is contained in the Articles of Association.

The issued share capital shown on the balance sheet is the total number of shares currently in issue at their original value (this is called the *nominal* or the *par value*). All UK shares must have a par value, which is determined when the company is started. Legally shares cannot be issued at a discount to this value (s 100, Companies Act). (This is not always true overseas, for example in the USA it is possible to have shares with no par value and to be able to issue shares at any price.) The nominal value and the authorised share capital is included in the company's Memorandum of Association.

The notes to the accounts usually describe the issued shares as *allotted* (the company has decided who is going to hold the shares), *called up* (they have asked for the money) and *fully paid*. (Not all shares are fully paid, many of the privatisations required shareholders to pay in instalments. Had the companies gone into liquidation the shareholders would have had to pay the outstanding amounts on their shares!)

● Different types of share

Different kinds of shares can be found in company accounts:

● ordinary shares
● deferred shares
● preference shares.

Companies may also issue warrants to allow people to subscribe for shares at some future date.

FRS 4 (*Capital Instruments*) categorises shares as *equity shares* and *non-equity shares*. Non-equity shares are shares that have any of the following characteristics:

● **fixed dividend:** the dividend is fixed and, therefore, its payment does not depend on the financial performance of the company, or on the dividends paid to other shareholders;
● **limited rights in a liquidation:** there are limited rights to share any 'winding-up surplus' if the company is liquidated;
● **redeemable.**

If a share has none of these characteristics, it would be regarded as an equity share. Most ordinary shares would be regarded as equity shares and most preference shares would be regarded as non-equity shares.

Ordinary shares

These are the commonest form of shares, and comprise most of a company's share capital. (They are referred to as common stock in America and shown as common stock in translations of overseas accounts.) Ordinary shareholders are usually entitled to all of the profits after tax, minority interests and preference dividends – although usually not all of the available profits are distributed as dividends.

However, it is possible (but unusual) to have different types of ordinary share; with differences in:

- voting rights
- entitlement to dividend
- entitlements and ranking in the event of liquidation.

The commonest variation is in voting rights; where some shares may have restricted voting rights or no voting rights at all (these are often called A shares). Whilst this practice used to be fairly common in recent years, most companies have now enfranchised the non-voting shares.

 Another variation on the ordinary share is the redeemable ordinary share. Companies may issue these (Companies Act, s 159) if they have unredeemable ordinary shares and are allowed to do so in their Articles.

Deferred shares

These are often the founders' shares and are now rarely seen in company accounts. They either:

- do not receive a dividend until some future date, usually several years after issue; or
- they only receive a dividend after ordinary shareholders' dividends have reached a predetermined level.

Preference shares

Preference shares have a fixed dividend that must be paid *before* other dividends can be paid. (They are referred to as preferred stock in America and shown as preferred stock in translations of overseas accounts.) There are various types of preference shares; they can include one or more of the features outlined below:

- **cumulative preference shares:** if the company does not pay a preference dividend on a cumulative preference share, it is only postponing the payment, which accumulates. The preference dividend is known as 'in arrears' (which must be noted in the accounts) and no other dividend can be paid until all the preference dividend arrears have been paid;
- **redeemable preference shares:** these have to be redeemed (repaid) at a fixed date. This makes them fundamentally the same as debt, but with the dividend being paid out of after-tax profits. They are common in two situations: management buy-outs and bank rescues (the bank undertakes a debt–equity conversion, turning loans into redeemable preference shares);
- **participating preference shares:** shareholders may receive two dividends: the fixed dividend, and a variable dividend (usually a proportion of the ordinary dividend);
- **convertible preference shares:** these are becoming increasingly common. Preference shareholders have the right to convert into ordinary shares at a predetermined rate, at some future date.

Warrants

A warrant is a type of option that gives the holder the right to buy a specified number of shares in the company at a predetermined price on or before an expiry date. They are often attached to bonds to make the issue more attractive (these are called *covered warrants*), although they can be traded separately. Warrants can also be issued and traded in their own right (*naked warrants*).

Trading in warrants, like any form of option trading, is high risk with a potential high return. If a warrant gives an option to buy a share for £1.75 and the share is trading at £2.00, the warrant would be worth at least 25p. If the share price moves up by 30p (17 per cent), the warrant price would also move by 30p (120 per cent). However, if the share price falls by 30p the warrant would be worthless.

Accounting for warrants

Warrants used to be disclosed in the notes to the accounts rather than the balance sheet itself. However, FRS 4 (*Capital Instruments*) now requires warrants to be disclosed as part of shareholders' funds.

If a company has issued warrants, the notes to the accounts have to disclose the exercise price and the expiry date. When the warrants are issued, the proceeds are included in the reconciliation of movements in shareholders' funds. If the warrant is subsequently exercised, the proceeds will include both the value that was previously recognised and any additional consideration. If the warrant lapses and is unexercised, a gain to the existing shareholders is reported in the statement of total recognised gains and losses.

ADRs

You will find reference in some accounts to American Depository Receipts (ADRs). These are not another type of share. It is a mechanism used in the USA to simplify the procedures for holding shares in foreign companies. The shares are bought, on behalf of the American investor, and deposited in a bank outside of the USA. An American bank then issues ADR certificates to the American shareholder. The custodian bank then processes the payment of dividends, rights issues etc. ADRs may be traded on American stock exchanges (they are then called sponsored ADRs) if the company is registered with the Securities Exchange Commission and complies with their requirements.

● Share issues

The company's ability to issue further shares is determined by two things:

(1) the authorised share capital;
(2) the Stock Exchange rules. The continuing obligations for listed companies limit the amount of shares that can be placed with new investors, requiring any issues of shares, convertibles or warrants to have been approved by the shareholders in a general meeting, or by the Stock Exchange. Placings are restricted unless the market conditions or the company's circumstances can justify them. This essentially forces listed companies to have major new issues in the form of a *rights issue* (new shares are offered to existing shareholders in proportion to their existing shareholdings).

Whilst most major share issues are in the form of a rights issue, shares can also be placed directly in the market, issued to employees or issued instead of a cash dividend.

Rights issues

In a rights issue, the company offers its existing shareholders the opportunity to buy new shares at a discounted price.

EXAMPLE For example, a shareholder could be invited to buy one share at £1.00, for every five shares he already owns. If the current market price is £1.60, the shareholder is being offered the shares at a discount to encourage him to buy the shares. This does not mean that he will necessarily make more money. It is possible to calculate a theoretical ex-rights price. If the shareholder exercises his right to buy, the shares the value of his shareholding will be:

5 existing shares at the current market price of £1.60	£8.00
1 new share issued for cash	£1.00
Total for 6 shares	£9.00
Theoretical ex-rights value of each share (9.00 ÷ 6)	£1.50

This should be the price that the shares will be trading in the market following the rights issue. The price will fall from £1.60 to £1.50, reflecting the fact that the new shares were issued below the market price.

Shareholders have three options in a rights issue:

(1) they can exercise their right to buy the share;
(2) they can sell their rights to buy the share (in practice this option is only available to large shareholders, the smaller shareholders' profit will be wiped out by dealing fees). The value of the rights will depend on the difference between the issue price and the current share price;
(3) they can do nothing. In practice, when the shareholder does nothing, the company will usually sell the shares on the shareholder's behalf and send the proceeds to the shareholder.

Most share issues are 'underwritten'. This is a form of insurance, provided by banks and institutions, where the underwriters agree to buy the shares if no one else wants to buy them. This ensures that the company will receive some cash from the rights issue. The underwriters were forced to buy the shares in the BP privatisation in 1987. The stock-market crash put the offer price above the market price, so that most of the shares were left with the underwriters.

Other ways of issuing shares

As long as the company has its shareholders' or the Exchange's permission, there are other ways that a company can issue shares. These issues are normally at a lower discount than a rights issue, and so have the advantage of generating more cash for the company. The other options available to the company are:

● **a placing:** the company creates new shares and its financial adviser places them with a range of investors. Companies often use this in overseas markets, placing shares overseas without offering them to investors in London;
● **a vendor placing:** these are usually used when the company is making an acquisition. The company is acquired through a share exchange, but the acquired company's shareholders may not want the acquirer's shares. Therefore, the acquirer arranges, in advance, for the shares to be sold to other investors, usually institutions;
● **a bought deal:** in a bought deal, the company invites bids from investment banks and other securities houses for the shares. The shares are then sold to the highest bidder, who subsequently sells them to investors;
● **a placing and an open offer:** the company's existing shareholders lose in the three methods outlined above. The company offers shares at a discount to the market price to new shareholders, thus transferring value from existing shareholders to new shareholders.

A placing and an open offer, also called a *clawback*, eliminates this objection. The company sells the shares to its financial adviser, and has, therefore, guaranteed a cash inflow. The financial adviser then offers the shares to the existing shareholders, in proportion to their existing holdings. The existing shareholders then have the opportunity to buy the shares, but they have no rights to sell for cash.

Employee share schemes

Many companies offer employees and directors the opportunity to buy shares in the company at a discounted price. The Companies Act, s 153 allows companies to make loans to employees (but not directors) to buy shares. These loans should be disclosed in the company's balance sheet. However, these tend to be rare, as other schemes offer more tax advantages.

The government has given tax concessions to three types of employee share scheme, which will not be subject to income tax, although profits are subject to capital gains tax:

(1) **save-as-you-earn (SAYE) schemes:** this is a savings-related scheme where an employee enters into a savings contract to save a maximum of £250 per month for a minimum period of five years. The company grants an option for the employee to buy shares at a maximum discount of 20 per cent of the share's market price on the date when the option is granted. At the end of the savings period, the employee has the option to convert his option into shares or to take the cash;

(2) **profit-sharing schemes:** under the current legislation companies are allowed to allocate £3000 a year (or 10 per cent of salary to a maximum of £8000) for each employee to be used to buy shares for employees. These shares are bought by employee share-ownership trusts, and are held in trust for at least two years. As long as the shares are held for five years they are not subject to income tax, but profit made on the sale of shares is subject to capital gains tax in the usual way. If the shares are sold within five years, they are subject to income tax on a sliding scale, determined by the time they have been held;

(3) **company share-option plans:** these plans grant employees the option to buy shares in the company at the current market price. The options are limited to a maximum market value (at the time when the option is granted) of £30 000 per employee. If the plan is approved by the Inland Revenue it will not be subject to income tax. Some share-option plans are used as performance incentives for senior managers and directors and are conditional on certain performance criteria being met.

Accounting for employee share ownership plan trusts (ESOP trusts)

The accounting for ESOPs is covered by UITF 13 (*Accounting for ESOP Trusts*). It states that where a company has effective control of an ESOP trust, the company should recognise the shares as an asset and charge any associated costs to operating profit on an accruals basis. For this reason, companies should:

● recognise the shares as assets until they are passed to the employees. These should be appropriately shown as fixed or current assets. Any permanent diminution in the value of shares shown as fixed assets should be recognised immediately;

● any difference between the book value and the option value (or the conditional gift value) should be charged as an operating cost over the employees' service period when they are granted;

● the company should record its liabilities for any borrowings of the ESOP trust that it has guaranteed;

● finance and administration costs should be charged on an accruals basis.

The benefits arising under some schemes, usually for directors and senior management, are determined by the achievement of performance criteria. UITF 17 (*Employee Share Schemes*) is concerned with performance related schemes and is obligatory for accounting periods on or after 22 June 1997. It covers the accounting treatment of share schemes other than SAYE schemes, and any other scheme which is offered to all or substantially all employees. Consequently, it is concerned with share schemes for directors and senior employees, where shares are often given as part of a bonus payment.

The cost of the scheme should be based on the fair value of the shares when the award is made, and will represent the difference between the fair value and the consideration that has been paid, unless the shares are held in an ESOP trust accounted for in accordance with UITF 13. Then the cost will be the difference between the book value of the shares and the consideration paid. This cost should then be recognised over the period to which the employee's performance relates. If the scheme is long term, and the award is dependent upon performance, it should be assumed that the performance criteria will be met.

Scrip dividends

A scrip dividend is paid in shares, rather than cash, and so involves a share issue. The shareholder usually has the option to take the dividend in either cash or shares. Scrip dividends have two advantages to the company: there is no cash outflow, and they are not subject to ACT. (This is advance corporation tax, which is paid to the Inland Revenue shortly after the dividend payments. It may then be reclaimed later by the company. This tax is discussed in detail in Chapter 14.)

Smaller investors will often take the scrip dividend, as it allows them to increase their holding without incurring dealing fees. If the company wants to make the scrip alternative attractive to institutional investors, it will be *enhanced* (the value of the shares will be considerably greater than the cash). This was particularly important when pension funds were able to reclaim the ACT.

Accounting for scrip dividends

When the company declares a scrip dividend alternative, it usually does not know how many shareholders will elect to take the scrip alternative. Consequently, FRS 4 (*Capital Instruments*) requires that the dividend should be accounted for as if all shareholders will take the cash dividend. When shares are issued as a scrip dividend the value of the shares will be deemed to be equal to the cash-dividend alternative.

• Capital reconstructions

Bonus issues

There are other forms of share issues that do not involve any cash coming into the business. Companies can have scrip, bonus, or capitalisation issues (they all mean the same thing!). In these issues the company converts some of the reserves into share capital. Distributable reserves (the profit and loss account) and the undistributable revaluation reserves, capital redemption reserve, and the share premium account can be used to create bonus shares, as long as it is allowed by the company's Articles. Companies will usually capitalise undistributable reserves rather than distributable ones.

EXAMPLE

A company has the following capital and reserves:

	£000
Share capital	1000
Share premium account	450
Profit and loss account	6200
	7650

It decides to have a 1 for 4 bonus issue, capitalising the share premium account. Following the bonus issue the capital and reserves will be:

	£000
Share capital	1250
Share premium account	200
Profit and loss account	6200
	7650

The share price will fall after the bonus issue, reflecting that the market value of the company has not changed and there are more shares in issue. Companies often have a bonus issue when they want the individual share price to fall, if they believe that the market price for their shares is too high.

Share splits

Another way of reducing the share price, without capitalising reserves, is to have a share split. This reduces the nominal value of each share in issue, and must be approved by the shareholders. For example, if the share has a nominal value of £1.00, the company could split each share into four 25p shares. A share split, like a bonus issue, does not generate any cash for the company.

Both bonus issues and share splits reduce the market value of the shares, as they increase the number of shares in issue. However, the procedure for bonus issues and share splits is slightly different. In a bonus issue the shareholder receives additional shares. In a share split the shareholder receives new shares in place of the old share.

Share consolidations

This is the opposite of a share split. Several shares are consolidated into one with a higher nominal value. For example four 25p shares could be consolidated into a £1.00 share. The company's shareholders must approve the consolidation of shares.

● Share buy-backs

Share buy-backs have become very popular following the government's decision to abolish the repayment of ACT tax credits to pension funds and companies. Since 1996 buy-backs have been treated as though they are a *Foreign Income Dividend*. (A foreign income dividend is one that is paid from overseas earnings that have borne tax overseas. They are still liable to ACT, but the ACT can be reclaimed by the company, rather than the shareholder. These are usually known as *FIDs*.)

A buy-back incurs ACT, which can then be offset against corporation tax. Any surplus ACT can be reclaimed by the company. The government announced in July 1997 that it would be abolishing FIDs from 6 April 1999. Abolishing FIDs looks likely to abolish the tax efficiency of share buy-backs. This will probably mean that we will see a rush of buy-backs until April 1999, as companies try to maximise the tax efficiency of buy-back offers.

The Companies Act (s 162–169) allows companies to buy back their own shares if they are also allowed to do so by their Articles as long as a company:

● does not buy itself out completely; and
● the buy-back leaves some unredeemable shares.

Public companies may buy back their shares using the procedures laid down in s 166. The company needs the prior approval of its shareholders in an ordinary resolution at an annual general meting. This resolution will authorise the purchase of the shares in a specified price band, and within a specified time period that should not be greater than 18 months. In practice, most companies pass a resolution at each AGM authorising the directors to purchase shares. Usually directors seek authority to purchase up to 10 per cent of the issued share capital at a maximum premium of 5 per cent to the middle-market price. This is illustrated in the following extract from Community Hospitals Group's 1996 accounts.

Extract 5.1   **SHARE CAPITAL (COMMUNITY HOSPITALS GROUP)**

> **SHARE CAPITAL**
> Details of the changes in the issued share capital of the Company are set out in Note 20 to the Financial Statements on page 44.
>   As in 1995, a Special Resolution will be proposed at this year's Annual General Meeting seeking authority for the Directors to allot shares for cash up to a maximum nominal amount of £1,693,000 which represents approximately 5% of the Company's issued share capital, without first offering them to existing ordinary shareholders within certain constraints as set out in the Notice of the Annual General Meeting.

The Stock Exchange has additional rules covering a company's purchase of its own shares, designed to increase investor protection. For example, companies are not allowed to buy back their own shares for two months before the announcement of company results (both half yearly and final results), as they would be in possession of sensitive information that would not be publicly known.

Accounting for share buy-backs

Generally shares can only be bought out of distributable profits or from the proceeds of a new share issue. Any shares that are bought by the company are cancelled, but this does not mean that the authorised share capital is reduced.

The accounting for share buy-backs and the redemption of shares is as follows:

● **share capital:** this is reduced by the nominal value of the shares purchased or redeemed. This amount is then transferred to a *capital redemption reserve*. (This is a non-distributable reserve of the company, which is separately disclosed on the balance sheet.) This is required by the Companies Act, s 170 to prevent a reduction in capital. The principle is that the total of the share capital and the undistributable reserves should remain unchanged following the repayment of share capital;
● **profit and loss account:** as shares are usually purchased using distributable profits, the profit and loss account reserve will be charged with the cost of the purchase.

EXAMPLE A company purchases 1 000 000 shares, with a nominal value of £250 000, for £750 000. Its summarised balance sheets before and after the buy-back are as follows:

	Before buy-back	Buy-back adjustments	After buy-back
	£000	£000	£000
Cash	2 500	(750)	1 750
Other net assets	74 500	—	74 500
	77 000	(750)	76 250
Share capital	10 000	(250)	9750
Profit and loss account	67 000	(750)	66 250
Capital redemption reserve		250	250
	77 000	(750)	76 250

● Disclosure requirements

Both the Companies Act and the accounting standards have detailed disclosure requirements for share capital.

The Companies Act (Sch 4, s 38–41) requires the disclosure of the following information in the notes to the accounts:

● The authorised share capital and the nominal value of each class of shares that have been allotted.
● If the company has allotted redeemable shares, it must disclose:
  – the earliest and latest dates for redemption;
  – whether the company is obliged to redeem the shares, or just has the option to do so;
  – whether a premium is payable on redemption, and if so the company must disclose the size of the premium.
● If shares have been issued during the year, the company must disclose:
  – the reason for the issue;
  – the number and class of share that has been issued;
  – the total nominal value and the consideration that has been received for each class of share.
● If the company has outstanding share options and warrants, it must disclose:
  – the number, description and amount of the shares involved;
  – the period during which the right is exercisable;
  – the price payable for the option.

Additionally FRS 4 requires companies to disclose:

● Equity and non-equity interests in shareholders' funds and minority interests.
● A summary of the rights of each class of share, other than non-redeemable voting ordinary shares with unlimited rights in the event of a liquidation. This information on other shares should include:
  – the right to dividends;
  – their priority and the amounts receivable in a winding up;
  – their voting rights;
  – the dates of redemption and the amount of the redemption.
● The total dividend for each class of share.

Extract 5.2 is from the 1996 accounts of the building and home improvements products group, Caradon plc. It illustrates the disclosures that companies are required to make about their share capital.

Extract 5.2   EXTRACT FROM THE ACCOUNTS OF CARADON PLC

Notes to the accounts continued

17 SHARE CAPITAL

	1996 Authorised £	1996 Allotted, called up and fully paid £	1995 Authorised £	1995 Allotted, called up and fully paid £
(a) NOMINAL VALUE OF SHARES				
Equity shares – Ordinary shares of 25p each	**217 000 000**	**150 284 128**	217 000 000	149 901 751
Non-equity shares – 7.25p Convertible Cumulative Redeemable Preference shares of 150 each	**27 000 000**	**24 310 985**	27 000 000	24 311 239
		174 595 113		174 212 990

Each holder of 7.25p Convertible Cumulative Redeemable shares of 15p nominal value is entitled to convert into Caradon plc Ordinary shares of 25p each at the rate of 42.533 Ordinary shares for every 100 Convertible Preference shares (and a conversion price of 235p per Ordinary share) in June in any year from 1996 to 2005, or otherwise to redeem the Convertible Preference shares in 2005 at the price of £l per share.

No voting rights attach to the 7.25p Convertible Cumulative Redeemable Preference Shares of 15p each unless at the date of a general meeting the dividend thereon is six months or more in arrears, or the business of that meeting includes a resolution for the winding up of the Company, the appointment of an administrator; approval of a voluntary arrangement, capital reduction or the purchase of any Ordinary shares or any resolution directly or indirectly adversely affecting the rights or privileges attached to those shares. The Preference shareholders have the right to be paid a fixed cumulative preference dividend at the rate of 7.25p net per share per annum on a half-yearly basis in equal amounts.

The Preference shareholders have no further rights to participate in the profits of the Company except that in the case of a winding up the Company's surplus assets, after payment of its liabilities, shall be applied, firstly to pay Preference shareholders any arrears of dividend; secondly, to repay to the Preference shareholders the capital and a premium amounting to a total of £1 per share; thirdly, to repay the capital paid up on Ordinary shares; and fourthly, to distribute rateably amongst Preference and Ordinary shareholders (each Preference share being treated as if converted into fully paid Ordinary shares for this purpose). The Company shall, subject to the requirements of the Companies Act, redeem on 31 August 2005 all outstanding Preference shares and the amount payable shall be £1 per share, together with any arrears of dividend. The above is a summary of the Preference shareholders' rights, but full details are contained in the Company's Articles of Association.

	Ordinary shares of 25p each Number	7.25p Convertible Cumulative Redeemable shares 15p each Number
(b) SECURITIES ISSUED DURING THE YEAR		
At 1 January 1996	599 607 004	162 074 927
Exercise of executive share options	402 719	–
Exercise of savings-related share options	265 903	–
Conversion of 7.25p Convertible Cumulative Redeemable Preference shares of 15p each	719	(1 692)
Allotment for Personal Equity Plans	26 741	–
Scrip dividend issues	833 425	–
At 31 December 1996	601 136 511	162 073 235

Ordinary shares with a nominal value of £0.4m were issued during the year for a total consideration of £3.3m.

SUMMARY

Types of share

There are many different types of shares found in company accounts. The commonest shares are ordinary shares. Ordinary shareholders are usually entitled to all of the profits after tax, minority interests and preference dividends. It is possible to have different types of ordinary share with differences in voting rights, entitlement to dividend, and entitlements and ranking in the event of liquidation. However, this would be unusual as most ordinary shares have one vote, their dividends are determined by the directors, and they have the same rights in the event of a liquidation.

Preference shares usually have a fixed dividend, but participating preference shares may receive an additional dividend reflecting the company's financial performance. Preference shares can also:

- be redeemed – *redeemable preference shares;*
- carry forward any dividend arrears – *cumulative preference shares;*
- have the option of being converted into ordinary shares – *convertible preference shares.*

Ordinary shareholders may only receive a dividend after the preference dividend, and any arrears of cumulative preference dividends.

Another class of share that is rarely seen is deferred shares. These are the founders' shares, and only receive a dividend when certain conditions have been met.

FRS 4 (*Capital Instruments*) requires shares to be classified as non-equity and equity shares. Non-equity shares are those that have any of the following characteristics:

- a fixed dividend
- limited rights in the event of a liquidation
- redeemable.

Consequently, most preference shares would be classed as non-equity shares. All other shares are classed as equity shares.

Share issues

Companies may issue up to the amount of their authorised share capital, but major new issues should be in the form of a rights issue. A rights issue offers existing shareholders the right to buy new shares in the company in proportion to their existing holding. To encourage shareholders to buy the shares, the shares are offered at a discount to the current market price. The size of the discount is largely irrelevant to the shareholders as the price will fall to reflect the increased number of shares in issue and the discount offered.

As long as the company has the permission of its shareholders, or the Stock Exchange, shares can be placed in the market. They can be placed with institutions or securities houses, which may then offer the shares to the existing shareholders. This is called a *clawback.* If the company is trying to acquire another company via a share exchange, it may have a *vendor placing.* If the acquired company's shareholders do not want the acquiring company's shares, the acquirer arranges in advance for the shares to be sold to other investors, usually institutions.

Shares may also be issued to employees and directors, or offered as an alternative to a cash dividend.

Capital reconstructions

A company can change its capital structure by having:

- *a bonus issue* (also called a scrip or capitalisation issue): the company converts some of the reserves into share capital, thus there is no cash inflow for the company. This tends to be done when the company decides that the current share price is too high;
- *a share split:* this reduces the share price without capitalising the reserves. A share split reduces the nominal value of each share in issue, by offering a number of shares, with a lower nominal value, for every share held;

▶

● *a share consolidation:* this is the opposite of a share split. Several shares are consolidated into one that has a higher nominal value;

● *a share buy-back:* a company may buy back its own shares, with its shareholders' permission, as long as it has sufficient distributable reserves or uses the proceeds of a share issue. When a company buys-back its own shares, the shares are cancelled; the nominal value of the shares is transferred to a capital redemption reserve and the profit and loss account is charged with the cost of the buy-back.

● RESERVES

The reserves on a company's balance sheet arise from a number of sources, the commonest being:

● the accumulated retained profits and losses of the business – this reserve is called *the profit and loss account.*
● the revaluation of fixed assets – this reserve is called *the revaluation reserve.*
● the premium paid, above the nominal value, on the issue of shares – this reserve is called *the share premium account.*
● the reserve arising from the cancellation or redemption of shares – this reserve is called *the capital redemption reserve.*

Other reserves may be established by the company's Articles or at the company's choice. For example, some companies show exchange rate movements in a separate reserve, often called the foreign-currency equalisation reserve.

 Overseas statutory reserves are commonly found in company accounts. These are undistributable reserves and are made for the protection of creditors. They are established by transferring a percentage of the dividends or profit each year to the reserve until it equals a predetermined percentage of the share capital.

In France and Germany 5 per cent of the annual profit is charged to the legal reserve until it equals 10 per cent of the issued share capital. In Japan the legal earned reserve is established by allocating a minimum of 10 per cent of appropriations until the reserve equals 25 per cent of the issued share capital. The legal reserve can be clearly seen in Extract 5.3 from Hitachi's 1997 accounts.

Extract 5.3   **EXTRACT FROM THE ACCOUNTS OF HITACHI**

	Millions of Yen		Thousands of US dollars
	¥ 1997	1996	**$ 1997**
Stockholders' equity:			
Common stock, ¥50 ($0.40) par value. Authorised 10 000 000 000 shares; issued 3 337 796 005 shares in 1997 and 3 329 138 508 in 1996 (notes 9 and 12)	**281 684**	278 178	**2 271 645**
Capital surplus (note 12)	**486 695**	480,718	**3 924 960**
Legal reserve (note 13)	**101 146**	95 377	**815 694**
Retained earnings (notes 9 and 13)	**2 447 391**	2 404 388	**19 737 024**
Foreign currency translation adjustments	**(33 026)**	(58 589)	**(266 339)**
Total stockholders' equity	**3 283 890**	3 200 072	**26 482 984**

The capital surplus arises as the Japanese commercial code requires that half of the price arising from the conversion of debt issued after October 1982 be credited to the capital surplus account, with the balance credited to the common stock account.

The Companies Act classifies reserves as *distributable* (called *revenue reserves* in some countries), and *non-distributable* (called *capital reserves* in some countries). Distributable reserves are the only reserves that can be used to pay dividends. Both distributable and undistributable reserves can be used in bonus issues, unless the company's Articles specifically prohibit this. Undistributable reserves are allowed to be used as they are regarded as part of the company's capital base, and the transfer is from a reserve to the share capital.

Undistributable reserves are:

- the share premium account
- the revaluation reserve, as it arises from unrealised profits
- the capital redemption reserve
- any other reserve that the company is prohibited from distributing by its Memorandum or Articles.

● Profit and loss account

This is the accumulated profits and losses made since the company started, adjusted by two factors – currency adjustments and any goodwill that was written off through reserves before 23 December 1998. It is the only reserve that is distributable and that can be used to pay dividends. In some countries this called a revenue reserve.

● Revaluation reserve

This represents the accumulated revaluations of fixed assets. When previously revalued assets are sold, and the revaluation is realised, the revaluation is transferred between reserves. It will be transferred from the revaluation reserve to the profit and loss account. The revaluation reserve is not a distributable reserve, but can be used for a bonus issue.

● Share premium account

When shares are issued at a premium to their nominal value, the premium should be shown in the share premium account. The only exception to this is where shares are issued for an acquisition. The company may then qualify for statutory share premium relief under s 131 of the Companies Act. This allows companies to write off any goodwill arising on consolidation through the share premium account, via a merger reserve. (This is discussed in Chapter 19.)

Once a share premium has been created, it is legally treated as part of the share capital of the company, and is not a distributable reserve. It may however be used for:

- writing off any expenses, commissions, or discounts relating to share or debenture issues;
- writing off the company's preliminary expenses;
- providing for any premium repayable on the redemption of debentures;
- a bonus issue.

It may only be paid out to the shareholders when the company is liquidated, or in a capital reduction scheme that is approved by a court of law.

SUMMARY Reserves can be classified into *distributable reserves*, which can be used to pay dividends and *undistributable reserves*. The only distributable reserve is *the profit and loss account*. This is the accumulated retained profits and exchange adjustments. It may also be reduced by goodwill arising on business acquired before December 1998.

Undistributable reserves usually arise from:

● unrealised profits – *the revaluation reserve*;
● a premium paid, above the nominal value, to acquire the company's shares – *the share premium account*;
● the cancellation or redemption of shares – *the capital redemption reserve*.

● DEBT–EQUITY HYBRIDS

There are increasingly more instruments which are bridging the debt and equity. The three discussed below are typical examples.

● Convertible bonds

Convertible bonds give the holders the option to convert into ordinary shares, rather than have a cash repayment of the bond. They have two advantages:

(1) the interest rate is lower because of the conversion option
(2) the company may not have to repay the loan, just issue additional shares (subject to shareholder approval in the UK).

These bonds will now show as part of the company's debt, as FRS 4 requires that the debt conversion should not be anticipated. They are discussed in detail in Chapter 6.

● Redeemable preference shares

Redeemable preference shares are a form of equity that is repaid at a fixed date, normally at the nominal value. FRS 4 requires that these should be included in the shareholders' funds and classified as non-equity shares. As the dividend is usually fixed and the payment is not dependent upon the company's performance, they can be regarded as a quasi-debt instrument.

● Mezzanine finance

Mezzanine finance is another example of a debt–equity hybrid. It tends to be used in young companies or management buy-outs and buy-ins. In these situations, there is a limited amount of debt that can be raised and/or a limited amount of cash available for a share issue.

Mezzanine finance is a loan that ranks behind the company's other loans, with a higher rate of interest than the other debt, to reflect the increased risk. It is convertible into shares and is discussed in detail in Chapter 6.

SUMMARY There are several instruments that have some of the characteristics of both debt and equity. Only redeemable preference shares will be shown as part of the shareholders' funds. The others are classified as debt instruments, and are separately disclosed as part of convertible debt.

JARGON   **American Depository Receipts (ADRS)**   A mechanism used in the USA to simplify the procedures for holding shares in foreign companies.

Authorised share capital   The shares that the directors are currently authorised to issue.

Bonus issue/scrip issue/capitalisation issue   Some of the company's reserves are converted into share capital.

Convertible preference shares   Preference shares that have the right to be converted into ordinary shares at a predetermined rate at a future date.

Cumulative preference shares   A share where the entitlement to dividend is carried forward. Consequently, a company not paying a dividend to these shareholders is postponing the payment.

Deferred shares   Shares where the dividend is deferred until a future date, or when ordinary shareholders' dividends have reached a certain level.

Employee share ownership plan (ESOP)   A plan that offers employees the opportunity to buy shares in the company at a discounted price.

Equity shares   Shares that are not classified as non-equity shares. Most ordinary shares would be classed as equity shares as long as they are not redeemable and do not have limited rights in a liquidation.

Issued share capital   The shares that have been issued on the date of the balance sheet.

Mezzanine finance   A loan that ranks behind other loans and is convertible into ordinary shares at a predetermined rate.

Nominal/par value   A notional value for a share. Share issues should be at this or a higher amount. Any premium paid above the nominal value will be shown in the share premium account.

Non-equity shares   Shares that have any of the following characteristics: entitlement to a fixed dividend, limited rights in a liquidation, or that they are redeemable. Most preference shares are non-equity shares.

Ordinary share   The commonest form of share. However, it is possible to have different types of ordinary shares with differences in: voting rights, entitlement to dividends, redemption, and entitlement and ranking in the event of a liquidation.

Participating preference shares   Shareholders may receive two dividends: a fixed dividend and a variable dividend that is dependent upon the company's performance.

Placing   New shares are placed directly with investors.

Placing and open offer clawback   A company sells shares to its financial adviser, who then offers the shares to existing shareholders in proportion to their existing holdings.

Preference shares   Shares that have a fixed dividend that must be paid *before* other dividends can be paid.

Redeemable preference shares   These have to be repaid by a fixed date. These are often regarded as debt, and dividends can even be linked to interest rates.

Revenue reserve   Another name for the profit and loss account. It is the company's distributable reserve.

Rights issue   The existing shareholders are offered the opportunity to buy new shares in proportion to their existing holding.

Scrip dividend   A dividend that is paid in shares, rather than cash.

Share buy-back   The company buys shares in the open market and then cancels them, thus reducing the number of shares in issue.

Share consolidation   Several shares are consolidated into one, increasing the nominal value of each resulting share.

Share premium account   A non-distributable reserve reflecting the premium that has been paid, above the nominal value, in share issues.

Share split   The nominal value of the share is reduced and extra shares are created. A share split does not involve the capitalisation of the company's reserves.

Vendor placing   This is often used in acquisitions where the company wishes to acquire a company through a share exchange. The acquirer arranges, in advance, for the shares to be sold to other investors.

Warrant   A type of option, often attached to bonds, that gives the holder the right to buy a specified number of shares in the company at a predetermined price on or before an expiry date. Warrants issued on their own are called naked warrants, whereas those attached to bonds are called covered warrants.

6 The balance sheet: borrowings

This chapter covers:

- How much should a company borrow?
- How much can a company borrow?
- What sort of borrowings does a company have?
- The lender's perspective
- Managing interest rate exposure
- Accounting treatment
- FRED 13
- The borrowing ratios

• INTRODUCTION

We all borrow money. How much money we are prepared to borrow is normally determined by three things:

(1) our attitude to debt – some individuals do not like having loans, whereas others feel quite comfortable with high levels of debt;
(2) how much we can afford borrow – considering both interest and loan repayments;
(3) interest rates – we are likely to borrow more when interest rates are low and likely to borrow less when they are high.

The same factors affect companies, although it becomes a little complicated by tax, as interest is tax deductible and can, therefore, appear cheaper than dividends. We borrow because we cannot raise the money any other way, but most companies have two alternatives: borrowings or share issues. Some companies choose to borrow, as they believe that it is a cheaper form of finance. This form of finance is referred to in a statement made in Eastern Group's 1995 accounts, in its operating and financial review:

| Extract 6.1 | OPERATING AND FINANCIAL REVIEW (EASTERN GROUP) |

BALANCE SHEET AND FINANCIAL RESOURCES
During the latter part of 1993/94 and into 1994/95, we took significant steps towards improving the financial efficiency of the Group's balance sheet, through a share repurchase programme. The aim of the programme is to allow us to maintain a better balance of debt and equity (i.e., share capital) financing for our operations, given that debt up to reasonable levels is a cheaper form of financing than equity.

This may or may not be true, and certainly there has to be a balance. If a company increases its borrowings, it may increase the risk to the shareholders, who would then want a higher return from the company to compensate them for the higher risk.

HOW MUCH SHOULD A COMPANY BORROW?

Whilst it is not possible definitively to determine an ideal level of borrowings, it is possible to make the generalisation that stable businesses can borrow more than cyclical businesses. Two things can be used to help determine if the company's borrowings may have a damaging effect on earnings:

- calculating earnings at different returns on capital;
- considering the company's cost structure.

Borrowings and returns on capital

Borrowing money can be good for shareholders if the company is expanding, or where the returns are stable, but it can completely destroy shareholder returns if the company is contracting. This is illustrated in the following example.

EXAMPLE Two companies have total capital of £10 million which is structured slightly differently; Cautious plc has no loans, whereas Optimistic plc has borrowed 50 per cent of its capital. Table 6.1 shows a summarised profit and loss account and earnings per share for both companies at different returns on capital.

In this example, we can see that the earnings per share are better in Cautious plc in a bad year, but worse in every other year. In fact both companies have the same earnings per share when the return on capital reaches 10 per cent; below that, Cautious plc gives a better return for its shareholders, above it Optimistic plc wins. This is illustrated in the Figure 6.1.

Table 6.1 The impact of borrowing on capital returns

Cautious plc				Optimistic plc		
Share capital – £1 shares	10 000 000			Share capital – £1 shares		5 000 000
Loan capital				Loan capital @ 10%		5 000 000
Total capital	10 000 000			Total capital		10 000 000
	Poor year	**Average year**	**Good year**	**Poor year**	**Average year**	**Good year**
Return on capital	5%	12%	20%	5%	12%	20%
	£000	£000	£000	£000	£000	£000
Operating profit	500	1200	2000	500	1200	2000
Interest				(500)	(500)	(500)
Profit before tax	500	1200	2000	0	700	1500
Tax @ 31%	(155)	(372)	(620)	0	(217)	(465)
Profit after tax	345	828	1380	0	483	1035
Earnings per share (pence)	3.45	8.28	13.80	0	9.66	20.70

Figure 6.1 **BORROWINGS AND EARNINGS PER SHARE**

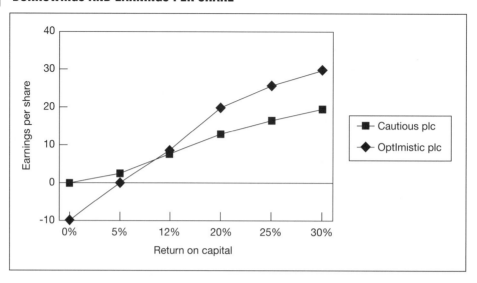

The critical thing, then, to think about is what range of returns this business is likely to get. If you think it unlikely that the returns will fall below 10 per cent, it would pay the company to borrow the £5 million. Increasing the borrowings would not necessarily increase the earnings, as unfortunately an increase in borrowings would lead to an increase in interest charges. Interest rates can also rise and fall, the situation would be very different if interest rates rose to 15 per cent. However, it is possible to work out at what level of borrowings and interest rates the shareholders' real risk would increase, leading to an increase in the required rate of return.

Cyclical businesses can have problems with high levels of borrowing, as their returns on capital can easily range from 5 per cent to 30 per cent at different points in the cycle. We would then need to look at the impact of borrowings on shareholder return over the life of the cycle to be able to calculate optimum borrowing levels.

● Borrowings and the cost structure

Another thing that influences the amount that a company should borrow is its cost structure. Costs behave in different ways – some costs increase with our sales (e.g. materials), whereas other costs remain fairly constant regardless of the level of sales (e.g. rent). Costs can be classified into those that are variable and those that are fixed. *Variable costs* are those that move with volume. *Fixed costs* tend not to move in the same way; within a certain level of sales they remain constant. However, sometimes getting an extra order can lead to an increase in the fixed costs – it may, for example, require putting on an extra shift, or even having another factory. This is illustrated in Figure 6.2.

Figure 6.2 COSTS

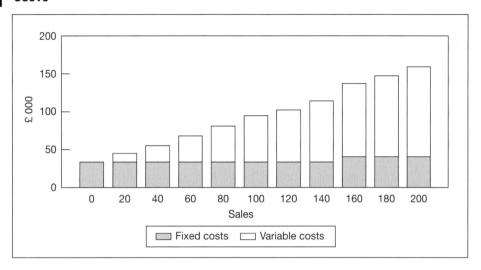

When sales reach 160, the fixed costs increase from £30 000 to £40 000. Fixed costs do increase with volume, but they do not increase proportionately – they move in steps. In some industries, where the company is operating at maximum capacity, small changes in volumes can lead to large changes in fixed costs. We can also see that when the sales fall, the variable costs will also fall, whereas the fixed costs will only fall when we move down to another 'step'. However, we must not confuse fixed costs with uncontrollable costs. Fixed costs can be reduced. Even seemingly fixed costs like insurance premiums can be reduced simply by changing insurance companies. A significant proportion of a company's fixed costs are controllable and reducible by management actions.

One thing that we would want to know about any company is the level of income it would need to achieve to cover all of its costs – to be able to break even. Unfortunately, we cannot find this out from the published accounts, but it is important to understand some basic principles. To illustrate these principles, and how we could calculate break even if we had the right information we will consider the following example.

EXAMPLE A company has sales of £100, variable costs of £60 and fixed costs of £30. So, it has made a profit of £10. We know that if sales increase, the variable costs will increase; if they fall, the variable costs will fall. In reality, any movement may not be directly proportional, because of the impact of other factors like quantity discounts. However, for the purposes of simplicity in our example, we will assume that variable costs move in direct proportion to the sales. Consequently, if sales move to £110, variable costs will rise to £66; if they fall to £90, variable costs will fall to £54. Variable costs are, therefore, 60 per cent of sales. If 60 per cent of our sales go to pay for the variable costs, we have 40 per cent as a contribution towards our fixed costs. Once we have reached our break-even point and the fixed costs have been paid, any sales above this point will generate 40 per cent profit. This is illustrated in Figure 6.3.

Figure 6.3 **BREAK-EVEN CHART**

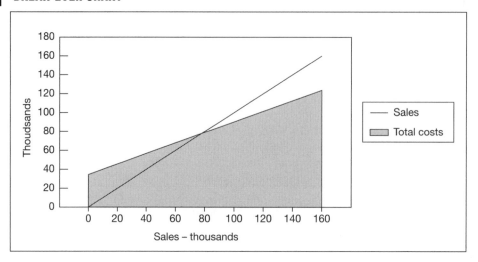

Once the sales and costs lines meet, the company has covered all its costs, if sales are above the break-even point it makes a profit, below this it makes a loss. Looking at the chart, it would appear that the company breaks even when sales reach £75. We can check this arithmetically. To do this we will use the profit and loss account below:

Sales	100	
Variable costs	(60)	*60% of sales*
Contribution	40	*40% of sales*
Fixed costs	(30)	
Operating profit	10	

The variable costs have been deducted from the sales to arrive at *the contribution*. (This is also called the gross profit, but we will use the term contribution to avoid confusion with the gross profit that is shown in the published accounts. The gross profit shown in the published accounts has not been calculated by deducting variable costs, and should *not* be used to calculate the break-even point.)

The company breaks even when the contribution reaches £30, the level of the fixed costs. We know that contribution is 40 per cent of our sales. Therefore, calculating the break-even point is a matter of simple arithmetic:

$$\frac{\text{Fixed costs}}{\text{Contribution \%}} \quad = \quad \frac{30}{40\%} \quad = \quad 75$$

Unsurprisingly this agrees with the answer we worked out from Figure 6.3.

The company covers all its costs when the sales reach £75. If it sold £100, sales could fall by £25 before they reach the break-even point. Expressing this as a percentage, the company could afford to lose 25 per cent of its sales. This is referred to as *the margin of safety*.

EXAMPLE Let us now consider a company that has the same total costs of £90 on sales of £100, but with a different cost structure.

Sales	100	
Variable costs	(30)	30% of sales
Contribution	70	70% of sales
Fixed costs	(60)	
Operating profit	10	

The break-even point is calculated using our formula:

$$\frac{\text{Fixed costs}}{\text{Contribution \%}} = \frac{60}{70\%} = 85.7$$

This business has a much higher break-even point and lower margin of safety (14.3 per cent). Its profits will be much more sensitive to changes in volume. This is illustrated in Table 6.2.

Table 6.2 **The break-even point and the margin of safety**

	COMPANY A Lower contribution and fixed costs		COMPANY B Higher contribution and fixed costs	
	Sales fall by 10%	Sales rise by 10%	Sales fall by 10%	Sales rise by 10%
Sales	90	110	90.00	110
Variable costs	(54)	(66)	(27)	(33)
Contribution	36	44	63	77
Fixed costs	(30)	(30)	(60)	(60)
Operating profit	6	14	3	17

The profits of the company with the higher contribution and fixed costs are much more susceptible to changes in sales. If sales halve, Company B's losses are two-and-a-half times greater than those of Company A (Company A will report a loss of £10, compared to Company B's reported loss of £25). If sales double, without any increases in fixed costs, Company B's profits are 60 per cent higher than Company A's (Company A reports a profit of £50, compared to Company B's profits of £80).

The differences between the two companies can be quantified by looking at their *operational gearing*. This is usually expressed as the change in operating profits for each percentage point change in the company's sales. (To confuse the situation some analysts would also take borrowings into account. This is discussed towards the end of this chapter.)

Operational gearing is calculated by dividing the contribution by the operating profit. The operational gearing for our two companies, using the contribution based on sales of £100, would be:

COMPANY A

$$\text{Contribution} = \frac{40}{10} = 4$$
$$\text{Operating profit}$$

COMPANY B

$$= \frac{70}{10} = 7$$

87

This reflects our conclusions above. Company A's sales rise by 10 per cent; their profit rises by 40 per cent (from 10 to 14). When the sales rose by 100 per cent, its profits rose by 400 per cent (from 10 to 50). On the other hand, Company B's reported profits move by 70 per cent when sales moved by 10 per cent. Therefore, its profits move by 7 per cent for every percentage increase in its sales. Company B has higher operational gearing than Company A.

SUMMARY

The amount of money that a company should borrow is influenced by a combination of two factors: its return on capital and its cost structure.

It is possible to calculate the minimum return on capital that the company needs to achieve to support a given level of borrowing. If the return falls below this level, the borrowings will reduce the earnings per share; above it earnings per share will improve. As long as the return on capital is unlikely to fall below this minimum, companies should usually have some level of borrowing to optimise the shareholders' return.

A company's cost structure also influences the level of borrowing that a company can support. Companies with high fixed costs have high break-even points. Small changes in their sales will have a disproportionate impact on their reported profits. This is measured by *operational gearing*. Operational gearing measures how much profits will change following a change of 1 per cent of sales.

There are three important learning points from looking at break even and operational gearing. If a company wants to improve its profitability it can:

(1) Improve its contribution percentage (usually called the gross margin); or reduce its fixed costs. We know that share prices move in line with company profit announcements. Share prices rise if a company announces a rationalisation programme, as fixed costs will fall. Any reduction in the company's fixed costs moves straight to operating profit. Equally, they will fall if the company announces that its gross margins have fallen. If Company A's sales are 100 and the gross margin falls to 30 per cent, the contribution will only cover the fixed costs and it will be at break even.

(2) A company with high fixed costs has a high break-even point. This means that it will make bigger losses if sales fall, or better profits if sales rise, than a company with the same total costs but higher variable costs. Therefore, in times of falling sales, one way to improve reported profits is to switch from fixed to variable costs. This is part of the accounting logic behind outsourcing, which has recently become very popular in the UK. Outsourcing has the effect of exchanging fixed costs for variable costs. In the short run it can improve profitability, although in the long run the company is at the mercy of its contractors.

(3) If a company has high operational gearing and is operating in cyclical markets, it should not borrow too much money. The interest charge will have the effect of increasing its fixed costs. If we continue our previous example, Company B can support less borrowing than Company A. This is clearly illustrated in Table 6.3, which assumes that both companies incur interest charges of £5 and sales move by 20 per cent.

Table 6.3 **Operational gearing and cyclical markets**

	COMPANY A Lower contribution and fixed costs			COMPANY B Higher contribution and fixed costs		
	Sales @ 80	Sales @ 100	Sales @ 120	Sales @ 80	Sales @ 100	Sales @ 120
Operating profit	2	10	18	(4)	10	24
Interest	(5)	(5)	(5)	(5)	(5)	(5)
Profit before tax	(3)	5	13	(9)	5	21

HOW MUCH CAN A COMPANY BORROW?

You and I can borrow as much as someone is prepared to lend us. Not all companies are in this position, as some company's borrowing powers are restricted. The borrowing powers of directors are often limited by the company's Articles of Association, and can only be altered with the approval of the shareholders at the annual general meeting. The company's borrowing powers are usually defined as a multiple of the shareholders' funds (this may or may not include goodwill).

In addition to the restrictions that arise from the Articles, there may be covenants attached to the company's existing loans that restrict future borrowing. It is quite common for loans to have a clause that prevents the company from issuing any further loans that would rank above the existing debt in the event of a liquidation. Therefore, although the company could have more debt, it would have to be *subordinated* to (in other words, rank behind) the existing loans.

WHAT SORT OF BORROWINGS DOES A COMPANY HAVE?

When we think of loans we think of bank loans, but to companies borrowings are more complex than that. If you look at the notes of any listed company's accounts you will find a large variety of different types of debt. Company treasurers have become increasingly sophisticated, and will raise funds from the cheapest market that matches their needs. They are innovative in their use of both short- and long-term debt instruments, often tailoring them to attract a specific investor. Consequently, we need to expand our definition of borrowings to encompass all interest-bearing debt.

Company borrowings fall into two broad categories:

(1) loans and overdrafts from banks and other financial institutions;
(2) issues of debentures, and other forms of loan stock which are offered to investors, and, therefore, can be held by the general public. They are bought and sold in the same way as shares, and could be long-term borrowings, like bonds, or short-term borrowings, like promissory notes. These are referred to as *financial instruments*. This term covers most forms of short- and long-term investments traded in the money markets or the stock market. A financial instrument gives rise to an asset in one organisation (the investment) and a liability (the borrowing) in another. These financial instruments are also negotiable instruments. This means that they can be bought and sold, and the ownership will often change during their life.

In this chapter we will discuss company borrowings in more detail, analysing them as long-term and short-term borrowings.

● Security given to the lender

Any borrowings can be secured in one of two ways:

A fixed charge

When we take out a mortgage on our house, the building society or bank has a fixed charge on our property. They have a legal right to our house if we do not pay our mortgage, and we cannot sell our house without the lender's permission. Fixed charges on company's assets work in exactly the same way. The lender has the legal right to specified assets and the company cannot dispose of these assets without the lender's permission. The asset normally then has to be replaced by another asset. Fixed charges tend to be given on long-term fixed assets such as land, properties and ships. There may also be a provision for securing other assets, if the value of the secured assets falls below an agreed figure.

If the company falls into arrears or defaults on the agreement the lender can either:

- repossess and sell the assets, giving any surplus to the company. This is also known as foreclosure;
- appoint a receiver to receive any income from the asset (e.g. property rents).

A floating charge

This is a general charge on the company's assets. Floating charges usually relate to short-term fixed assets (plant and machinery, and vehicles) and current assets. Whilst the lender has the legal right to a group of assets, the company may continue to manage those assets in the normal course of business. After all, the company has to be able to sell its stock, otherwise it will be unable to trade!

It is also common for a lending bank to require a company to seek the bank's permission before giving security to anyone else – this is called a *negative pledge*.

Some loans may be secured, but they rank after all the other borrowings in the event of a liquidation. These are called 'subordinated loans'.

● Long-term borrowings

A long-term loan

The simplest form of long-term borrowing is a long-term bank loan. A traditional long-term loan is rather like an endowment mortgage, but without the endowment policy. All the company has to do on a day-to-day basis is pay interest, the loan is repaid either in full at the end of the term, or in stages. It is also possible to take the loan in stages; if the company does not want all the money at once, it can draw it down in specified tranches. The loan could either be with one bank or syndicated amongst a number of banks.

Debentures and unsecured loan stock

A debenture is simply a document that acknowledges or creates company debt – effectively it is an IOU. It is a negotiable instrument for a specified amount that must always be transferred in its entirety. It is usually, but not always, secured and is covered by either a debenture deed or a trust deed:

- **a debenture deed** – details the security offered for the debenture;
- **a trust deed** – contains all the details of the debenture, including the interest payable and the security available to debenture holders. It will also include any clauses that restrict the operations of the company.

When the debenture is issued to a number of holders, or listed on the stock market and, therefore, available to the general public, a trustee will be appointed. The trustee, usually either an insurance company or a specialist debenture company, represents the debenture holders. The trust deed contains all the details of the issue, other than the issue price and will include clauses covering the following:

Borrowing details

There will be a covenant, by the company, covering payment of interest and repayment of the debenture. The repayment details will include the redemption price, repayment date (or period), and any other redemption arrangements.

Security

The security of the debenture issue, if any, will be detailed (further information on the type of security that may be offered to debenture holders is given earlier in the chapter). Most debentures are secured, even though they may not be reported as such in the company's accounts. They become secured on breach of covenant, when debenture holders often have a legal mortgage on all the company's properties. Consequently, there will be a clause specifying the events that trigger the enforceability of the security (for example, non-payment of interest or the appointment of a receiver).

Subsequent borrowings

Any additional borrowing usually would have to rank equally (*pari passu*) with the debenture, or be subordinate to it in the event of a liquidation. There may even be restrictions placed on prior borrowings and the company's overall borrowing limit.

Trustee powers

There will be clauses giving the trustees power to repossess the properties, or appoint a receiver, when the security becomes enforceable. The trustee may also have the power to approve modifications to the debenture terms and conditions.

Bonds

There is no real difference between a debenture and a bond, both are sold to the general public and they may be secured or unsecured. Bonds are actually defined as debentures in the Companies Act (s 744 defines a debenture as including debenture stock, bonds and any other security of a company, whether secured or unsecured).

Bonds are also negotiable instruments that are offered to the general public and may, or may not, be secured on the company's assets. The bondholder's rights, and the company's duties, are covered by a trust deed. A bondholder is entitled to receive a stream of interest payments, and the repayment of the principal at maturity. Before a company has a bond issue it will have the debt credit rated. There are two types of rating agencies looking at companies:

(1) agencies that look at the company from a supplier's point of view (e.g. Dun and Bradstreet) and help to answer the question, '*Will I get paid if I supply goods to this company?*'
(2) agencies that look at the company from the investor's point of view (e.g. Standard and

Poor, Moody) to help to answer the question, '*Will I lose all my money if I invest in this company?*'

It is the latter group of agencies that rates corporate debt, and the best quality corporate debt is rated triple A. The rating is very important as it affects both the ability to sell the bonds and the rate of interest that the company will have to pay. The higher the rating, the lower the risk; the lower the risk, the lower the interest! Bond interest is called the 'coupon' and is expressed as a percentage of the face value of the bond. The face value of the bond may not be the same as the current bond price. Bond prices are influenced by two things:

(1) relative interest rates, if current interest rates are 6 per cent and the bond is paying 10 per cent the investors will be prepared to pay a premium to buy the bond;
(2) the current credit rating of the company, if the credit rating has fallen the interest rate will not reflect the current level of risk and the bond price will fall.

There are many different types of bonds found in company accounts. Banks and companies have been very innovative, custom designing bonds to attract specific investors. They have been an ideal vehicle for financial innovation, as there are four variables which can be modified:

(1) The security given for the bond

For example, banks issue bonds that have our mortgages and credit card balances as collateral.

(2) The coupon paid

For example, some bonds are issued that do not pay interest, these are called *Zeroes*. They are issued at a discount. For example, a £10 million five-year bond may be issued for £6.209 million. This has an implied interest rate of 10 per cent and the value of the bond would increase by 10 per cent a year. All other things being equal, at the end of the first year the bond would be worth £6.83 million, at the end of the second £7.513 million, and so on, until the end of the fifth year when the investors would receive the £10 million. Some bonds increase the interest over the life of the bond (these are called *step-up bonds*), others reduce it (*step-down bonds*).

(3) The repayment of the principal amount borrowed

For example, the repayment of the principal in some bond issues is index linked. In others, the bond may be issued in one currency and repaid in another (these are called *dual currency bonds*).

(4) The bond maturity

For example, a bond may have two options on maturity – it might have a maturity of 30 years, with an option to reduce this to ten years (*a retractable bond*). Alternatively it could have a maturity of ten years with an option to extend it to 30 years (*an extendible bond*).

Eurobonds

Large companies often issue Eurobonds. If we are to understand a Eurobond we must understand what the term 'Euro' is. A currency goes 'Euro' when it is traded outside of the country of origin, and its banking regulations. Japanese yen on deposit in London are Euroyen; American dollars deposited in Tokyo are Eurodollars. *Euro does not mean European.* A

Eurobond is simply a bond that is issued outside the country of its currency and has few restrictions on its issue and trading.

Companies do not keep a register of Eurobond holders (they may for a domestic or foreign bond). The bond is sold in *bearer* form (whoever holds the bond claims the interest and repayment of the principal). As Eurobond interest has no tax deducted at source, they are very attractive to investors who wish to keep their affairs secret from the tax authorities! Eurobonds are available to large, internationally known, high-quality borrowers.

Convertibles

Bonds and other loan stocks, for example debentures, may have rights that enable the holders to convert their loans into ordinary shares, rather than cash. From a company's point of view, this enables it to get cheaper borrowing, as the coupon on a convertible bond will normally be lower than on a normal bond. This arises from the fact that the value of a convertible bond consists of two parts – the value of the bond and its potential value as shares. Therefore, the price of a convertible is influenced by two factors:

(1) the normal basis for bond valuation, i.e. corporate ratings and relative interest rates;
(2) the market value of the company's shares.

If the company's share price is rising the bond value will rise, as the value of the conversion option increases. Consequently, the markets regard convertible bonds as a form of deferred equity. Pricing convertibles is much more complicated than a conventional bond as the pricing formula has to take account of both the share option and the bond.

The holder of the convertible has the option of converting his bond into ordinary shares at a predetermined rate during a specified period. Usually the holder cannot convert into shares during the first two or three years, or for a number of years at the end of the bond's life. (The period between the issue of the bond and the conversion period is called the *rest period*, and the period after the conversion period is called *the stub*.) Companies like to have this rest period at the end. It is a breathing space, because if the holders have decided not to take the conversion option, the company's performance is probably poor.

The fact that the convertibles are effectively deferred equity gives the company both problems and opportunities. Issuing convertibles requires the permission of the shareholders unless:

- they are part of a rights issue; or
- they are part, or the whole, of the consideration given for an acquisition.

In acquisitions they can be used to steer the victim's shareholders away from accepting the cash alternative. If the victim's shareholders have been holding their shares for the yield, and the predator's shares have a low yield, a straightforward share exchange would be unattractive. Convertibles could be the solution, as it is possible to structure the convertible issue to give a higher initial income. Convertibles tend to attract investors who are looking for income, but who wish to have the benefit from any improvement in the market's performance.

Convertibles can, therefore, have advantages to both the issuer and the holder. The issuer benefits from cheaper interest rates and the holder has flexibility. The holder has the opportunity to benefit from improvements in the company's share price, but if the price falls, the holder can take repayment in cash. Holders pay for this flexibility by taking a small loss in their income.

We know that the holders of convertibles are hoping to benefit from market movements in the company's share price. There is a risk, however, that the holder may not benefit from market improvements if the company is taken over, outside of the conversion period. Consequently, to make the convertibles more attractive, most companies have some form of bid protection clause in their convertibles. This protection could be structured in different ways. The holder could be compensated by structuring a redemption premium linked to the premiums that would have been paid in the previous years. Alternatively, the protection could be simply an enhancement of the conversion terms.

Warrants

A company may issue warrants that give holders the opportunity to subscribe for shares in the company at a future date. As the price is usually fixed above the current share price, the warrant has no initial value. If the share price rises above the fixed price, the warrant will start to have an *intrinsic value* equal to the difference between the current share price and the fixed price. The warrant-exercise period generally starts soon after the issue date and, when they are issued with debt, they are usually traded separately from the bond and become exercisable when the bond is fully paid.

Warrants are sometimes issued to improve the attractiveness of a bond issue. For example, it may be difficult to have a fixed-rate bond issue if inflation is high, but it could be made more attractive to investors if warrants were attached. Or, in the same way as a convertible, a company could issue warrants to reduce the coupon that it would have to pay on the bond.

The equity entitlement of the warrants, in relation to the issue price, varies from company to company. The greater the equity entitlement, the greater the saving in coupon. It is this flexibility of warrants that makes them a useful addition to debt when a company is involved in a takeover. They can significantly reduce the coupon that has to be paid on the bond. However, they are less attractive if the company is hoping to get a cash inflow from the warrant. Warrants are rarely exercised until close to the exercise date.

Mezzanine finance

Mezzanine finance is a term used by venture capitalists to cover debt–equity hybrids. They can be in the form of:

- redeemable preference shares (usually with a conversion option)
- convertible debt
- debt with warrants attached.

This finance is commonly associated with management buy-outs where the amount of equity that can be issued is limited, as is the amount of debt that can be raised. If the finance is in the form of loans, they are usually subordinated, and therefore have a higher interest rate to compensate for the increased risk.

Sinking funds

Some debentures make provisions for part, or all, of the borrowing to be repaid by a *sinking fund*. Money is transferred to a sinking fund to enable loans to be repaid. The original concept is very like our endowment policies, but without the life cover. The company invests a sum of money each year, usually in safe investments, such as government securities. The sums, together with the interest, accumulate and are shown on the balance sheet. When the debentures have to be repaid (redeemed) there should, with luck, be sufficient money to repay the borrowings. This sounds very familiar to anyone with an endowment policy, the only difference is that there is no intermediary investing the money. This method is so simple that it is rarely used. Two other forms of sinking funds have emerged to allow earlier repayment of the debt: non-cumulative sinking funds and cumulative sinking funds.

Non-cumulative sinking funds

In this case the company puts aside sufficient money each year to redeem a fixed amount of the borrowings. This is often expressed as a fixed percentage. The sinking fund is non-cumulative as the interest does not accumulate. The early repayment means that the average life of the debenture may not be what it seems. This is illustrated in the following example.

EXAMPLE A company issues a twenty-year debenture. A sinking fund is established to redeem the debentures at the rate of 3 per cent a year at the end of years five to 19, leaving 55 per cent of the debentures to be redeemed at the redemption date. Redemption is at par. The average life of the debenture is calculated by working out the average life of the debentures that are redeemed by the sinking fund and weighting this by the percentage of the total that will be redeemed by the sinking fund. In our example the average life of the debentures redeemed through the sinking fund is 12 years and 45 per cent are redeemed by the fund. Calculating the average life is now a matter of simple arithmetic:

$$(12 \times 0.45) + (20 \times 0.55) \quad = \quad 16.4 \text{ years}$$

This average return is important as it will affect the lender's return that is discussed later in the chapter.

Cumulative sinking funds

In a cumulative sinking fund the amount that the company uses to redeem the debentures is variable, as it is a fixed amount of cash coupled with the interest that has been saved by the prior redemption of the debentures. This is illustrated in the example below.

EXAMPLE Continuing our previous worked example, the issue was as above, but comprised £10 million debentures, paying 10 per cent interest. The first ten years' calculations are shown in Table 6.4.

Table 6.4 **Redemption of a twenty-year bond issue (ten years)**

End of year	Fixed cash @ 3% redemption	Interest saved on debentures redeemed	Debentures redeemed in the year	Total redemptions to date	Remaining debentures
1			0	0	10 000
2			0	0	10 000
3			0	0	10 000
4			0	0	10 000
5	300	0	300	300	9 700
6	300	30	330	630	9 370
7	300	63	363	993	9 007
8	300	99	399	1 392	8 608
9	300	139	439	1 832	8 168
10	300	183	483	2 315	7 685

Most of the debentures are redeemed through the sinking fund; only £468 000 are redeemed in year 20. As different amounts are redeemed each year, the average life of the issue is calculated using a time-weighted average [(300 000 x 5) + (330 000 x 6) + (363 000 x 7) ... ÷ 10 000 000]. This gives an average issue life of 14.02 years.

In our example some debenture holders get their money back in five years, whereas others have to wait for 20 years. The company determines which holders will benefit from the sinking fund by:

- drawing out debenture certificate numbers, like the lottery
- purchasing them in the market
- inviting holders to tender for redemption.

● Short-term borrowings

We are all familiar with bank overdrafts, but may be less familiar with the short-term debt instruments that companies use. Some of the more common ones found in company accounts are:

- bills of exchange
- notes
- commercial paper.

These are discussed in detail below.

Bills of exchange

We have probably all written a post-dated cheque at some time or another. Companies' post-dated cheques are called bills of exchange. Bills of exchange differ from our post-dated cheques in two respects:

(1) they are written by the supplier, and signed by the customer in an acknowledgement of the debt;
(2) they can be sold. Bills of exchange are what lawyers call 'negotiable instruments', this simply means that you can sell them!

Bills of exchange normally have a maturity of three months. If the supplier wants the cash today, rather than in three months' time, he or she sells the bill. They are bought by discount houses. Discount houses are specialist banks which borrow short-term money from commercial banks, and use the cash to buy various forms of short-term IOUs, like bills of exchange. If the buyer of the bill is going to have to wait three months for his money, he will not pay £100 today for a bill that will yield £100 in three months' time. The buyer will be losing three months of interest. Bills of exchange are 'discounted', effectively interest is paid in advance – the discount reflecting the three months of interest lost. This type of bill is called a *trade bill*; there is another kind called a *bank acceptance*.

An acceptance is basically the same as a post-dated cheque, with a cheque-card number on the back – the bank has guaranteed payment. The real difference is that, unlike our cheques, the acceptance can be sold. A bank puts its name on the bill, in so doing the bank is guaranteeing payment, even if the company issuing the bill defaults. The top tier of merchant banks historically comprised the banks which 'accepted' the bills and that were known as the accepting houses. An acceptance sells at the lowest interest rates because the payment of the bill is certain.

Bills of exchange have been around for centuries, and have always been part of the normal trade practice in import and export businesses. Treasurers however, often use acceptances as

Extract 6.2 **DISCLOSURE OF DEBT (ANGLIAN WATER)**

Loans and Other Borrowings Falling Due After More Than One Year	Group		Company	
	1997 £m	1996 £m	1997 £m	1996 £m
Repayable wholly after five years				
51/8% Index Linked Loan Stock 2008 (a)	128.6	125.8	128.6	125.8
12% Fixed Rate Bonds 2014	100.0	100.0	100.0	100.0
European Investment Bank 2002 (Interest at 8.0%)	60.0	60.0	–	–
European Investment Bank 2003 (Interest at 6.6%)	10.0	10.0	–	–
European Investment Bank 2005 (Interest at 8.2%)	60.0	60.0	–	–
US$122m Private Placements 2006 (b)	79.1	79.1	74.6	79.1
81/4% Fixed Rate Bonds 2006	149.0	–	149.0	–
Repayable by instalments,				
any of which is due for repayment after five years				
European Investment Bank 2004 (Interest at 11.5%)	13.2	14.1	–	–
European Investment Bank 2005 (Interest at 85%)	45.0	50.0	–	–
European Investment Bank 2007 (Interest at 10.25%)	9.1	10.0	–	–
European Investment Bank 2007 (Interest at 9.9%)	30.0	30.0	–	–
US$10m Private Placement (Interest at 6.71%)	5.8	6.5	5.8	6.5
Finance leases (c)	121.9	122.3	–	–
Other borrowings (d)	22.8	23.1	–	–
Repayable wholly within five years				
European Investment Bank 1999 (Interest at LIBOR minus 0.2%)	25.0	25.0	–	–
European Investment Bank 2001 (Interest at LIBOR minus 0.15%)	50.0	50.0	–	–
61/4% Fixed Rate Bonds 1998	64.1	63.4	64.1	63.4
£20m Private Placement 1997 (Interest at 9.07%)	20.0	20.0	20.0	20.0
Other loans (d)	3.5	2.7	0.4	0.4
Total loans and other borrowings	997.1	852.0	542.5	395.2
Less amounts included in creditors falling due within one year	(33.0)	(8.0)	(20.9)	(0.1)
	964.1	844.0	521.6	395.1
Due for repayment as follows:				
Between one and two years	77.6	32.0	64.9	20.0
Between two and five years	127.5	134.5	1.9	63.7
After five years	759.0	677.5	454.8	311.4
	964.1	844.0	521.6	395.1

part of their short-term financing programmes, and a marked increase in acceptances may indicate a cash shortage.

Notes

Notes are unsecured IOUs. They are negotiable instruments and can have a maturity of up to ten years and, therefore, could be part of a company's long-term borrowings. However, most have a much shorter maturity and a number of note issues are repayable at the option of the holders.

Commercial paper

Commercial paper has been widely used internationally since it started in America in the nineteenth century. The commercial paper market started in the UK in 1986 and represents another form of short-term unsecured borrowing in the form of a negotiable instrument. It is only available to high-quality borrowers and in some markets (for example, the USA) companies must have their commercial paper credit rated.

Commercial paper is only an option for large companies, as, in order to have an issue, the company should have net assets of over £25 million. Whilst commercial paper can have a maturity as long as five years, most issues tend to be very short dated. It is not unusual for commercial paper to have a maturity of three weeks. In the sterling commercial paper market the maturity ranges from a week to a year. Large companies use commercial paper as an alternative to bank overdrafts, as they are very cheap to establish. (It can cost as little as £15 000 to set up £50 million commercial paper programme!).

Commercial paper is issued at a discount to the face value, and is often 'rolled over' – with one tranche being repaid by the issue of another.

The wide variety of debt that companies can have and the required disclosures is clearly shown in Extract 6.2 from Anglian Water's 1997 accounts.

SUMMARY

Loans are not necessarily from banks and financial institutions as many large companies' borrowings are in the form of *financial instruments*. A financial debt instrument is one that is traded in the stock market or money markets, meaning that these may be held by any investor.

Company borrowings may be secured or unsecured. Loans may be secured in one of two ways:

A fixed charge

Here the lender has the legal right to specified assets and the company cannot dispose of these assets without the lender's permission. Fixed charges are usually given on long-term assets such as properties. If the company defaults on the agreement, or falls into arrears, the lender can either:

- repossess (foreclose) and sell the assets; or
- appoint a receiver to receive any income from the asset (e.g. property rents).

A floating charge

This is a general charge on the company's assets that usually relates to short-term fixed assets (plant and machinery, and vehicles) and current assets. Whilst the lender has the legal right to a group of assets, the company may continue to manage those assets in the normal course of business.

Loans may, or may not, be secured, but security is not the only thing that banks are interested in. Not all loans have the same priority in the event of a liquidation, some loans

▶

rank behind other loans (*subordinated loans*). Companies may also give an undertaking not to have any other loans without the bank's permission (*a negative pledge*).

Company borrowings have different maturities. These have been simply described as long term and short term. Long-term borrowings can be in the form of:

Long-term loans

These are conventional loans from banks, and other financial institutions where interest is paid throughout the loan and the loan is repaid according to an agreed schedule. Most long-term loans are repaid at the end of the loan period.

Debentures

A debenture is a document that acknowledges, or creates company debt. It is a negotiable instrument and so can be bought and sold. Debentures are usually secured by a debenture deed or a trust deed. Some debentures make provisions for part, or the entirety, of the borrowing to be repaid by a sinking fund. Money is transferred to a sinking fund to enable loans to be repaid. There are three different types of sinking fund:

(1) *the original concept:* this is similar to endowment policies that repay mortgages. Money is invested to repay the debenture at the end of the period. The other types of sinking fund are designed to repay some of the loan early;

(2) *the non-cumulative sinking fund:* the company puts aside sufficient money each year to redeem a fixed amount of the borrowings;

(3) *the cumulative sinking fund:* the amount that the company uses to redeem the debentures is variable, as it is a fixed amount of cash coupled with the interest that has been saved by the prior redemption of the debentures.

Bonds

These are also negotiable instruments that are offered to the general public and may or may not be secured on the company's assets. The bondholder's rights and the company's duties are covered by a trust deed. Companies are innovative in the design of their bonds, as they can vary:

- the security offered for the bond;
- the bond coupon;
- the repayment of the amount that is borrowed;
- the maturity of the bond.

Eurobonds

These are bonds that are usually issued outside of the country of their currency. Eurobond issues are available to internationally known, high-quality borrowers and have few restrictions on their issue and trading.

Convertible bonds

These are bonds that give the holders rights to convert their loans into ordinary shares, rather than cash. An attractive conversion option allows the company to pay a lower rate of interest than that paid on a conventional bond.

Bonds with warrants

A warrant is an option to buy shares at an agreed price that is usually fixed above the current share price, at a future date. The warrants are usually traded separately from the bond and become exercisable when the bond is fully paid.

▶

Short-term debt does not have to be in the form of conventional bank loans and over-drafts. Companies may also use:

Notes

These are unsecured negotiable instruments that span long- and short-term borrowings, as it is possible to have notes with maturities of ten years.

Bills of exchange

These are negotiable instruments that are written by the supplier and signed by the customer in an acknowledgement of a debt. They can be sold at a discount and usually have a maturity of three months.

Acceptances

These are bills of exchange whose payment has been guaranteed by a bank.

Commercial paper

Commercial paper is a short-term negotiable instrument, usually issued to investors at a discount to the face value. Commercial paper has become very popular with large companies in the UK because it is a cheap form of borrowing.

● THE LENDER'S PERSPECTIVE

People lend money to make a return on their investment. The size of the return largely depends on the risk, the bigger the risk the bigger the return. This return is measured by the *yield*. This simply relates the interest to the price of the instrument.

When we are looking at the return on shares we are interested in the dividend yield, yields are also important when we are looking at debt. The calculation can be as simple as the dividend yield calculation on shares; the interest divided by the price. Consequently, if a bond is issued for £100 and the coupon is 8 per cent, the yield will be 8 per cent, if it was issued for £95 with a coupon of 8 per cent, the yield would be 8.42 per cent (8 ÷ 95). This is called the *running yield*.

This may be appropriate for simple issues, but would be totally inappropriate for deep discount bonds and zeroes. There has to be a way of measuring the total return. If a bond was issued at £80.04 per cent, had an coupon of 3 per cent paid annually, and was redeemed for £100 per cent in five years' time – the coupon would only be part of the return. We have to find a way of combining the interest with the capital gain that will be made in five years' time. To do this we need to use present-value techniques (a detailed discussion of these techniques can be found in Appendix 1). We need to find the discount rate that would give a present value of £80.04 from the following cash flow:

Year 1	£3
Year 2	£3
Year 3	£3
Year 4	£3
Year 5	£103

This gives a yield of 8 per cent, and this is referred to as the *gross redemption yield*. This identifies the real return that the holder will get if he or she keeps the bond until redemption. However, the redemption date may not be as clear-cut as it sounds. Some bonds will give a period for the redemption, e.g. 2001–2006. In this case it is assumed, when calculating the yield, that the company will choose the earliest redemption date. We know that some debentures and bonds are covered by sinking funds, and so there may be early redemptions. If the company has a 'lottery' to determine redemption, the average life of the fund will be used. However, if it purchases in the market or invites tenders, the holder cannot be certain that early redemptions will occur and the average life will be inappropriate.

The gross redemption yield on corporate borrowing will be higher than the benchmark government borrowing to reflect the increased risk. The premium will vary according to:

● the security offered on the borrowing
● the credit rating of the company involved.

More complex yield calculations can be made, taking account of specific issues:

● interest that can be earned on interest (*realised compound yield*)
● tax (*net redemption yield*).

SUMMARY

The yield measures the return on the investment. A number of different yields can be calculated:

● *running yield:* this compares the interest to the current price;
● *gross redemption yield:* this combines the interest with the capital gain on maturity to give a measure of the total return;
● *net redemption yield:* this is an after-tax measure of the total return;
● *realised compound yield:* this compounds the return by reflecting the fact that interest can be earned on interest.

● MANAGING INTEREST RATE EXPOSURE

Large companies try to manage their exposure to changes in interest rates. Treasurers in large companies regularly use forward markets, swaps and options to hedge against risk. Whilst these are vehicles that are used to try to avoid risk, they can be risks in themselves.

● The forward markets

Using the forward markets can help a company to limit its exposure to interest rates. It is possible to both borrow and lend money forward – agreeing a rate of interest for a loan that will start in the future. This type of agreement has become less common and has now largely been replaced by *forward rate agreements* (FRAs). FRAs are simply contracts between two parties to exchange cash amounts that compensate for any interest rate movements between specified dates. They can provide considerable flexibility for managing interest rates, usually for a maximum of two years.

The forward market offers a company certainty.

● Options

An option is just what it says, if the company buys an option it has the opportunity to buy something at an agreed price. Options can be bought and sold on shares, bonds, currencies, interest rates and futures contracts (a futures contract is a contract to buy or sell something at some agreed date in the future). Companies can buy, or sell, a *cap* (the maximum interest rate) or a *floor* (the minimum interest rate) over one or more periods. A cap suits borrowers, whereas a floor has an obvious appeal to lenders. These can be combined in a *collar*, which locks the company in a range of interest rates. When a company takes out an interest rate option it pays the market rate and is compensated when the rates are outside of the agreed level.

● Swaps

Both currency and interest rates can be 'swapped'. Again, this means what it says. Interest-rate swaps exploit the credit quality standards between the fixed-rate bond market and the floating-rate, short-term credit market. These markets have different interest rates for different quality borrowers.

EXAMPLE To illustrate this, a company rated BBB might be able to borrow short-term at LIBOR (London inter-bank offered rate) +3/4 per cent. Whereas a company rated AAA might borrow at LIBOR + ¼ per cent, a difference in the short-term markets of 1/2 per cent.

In the bond market, the interest rate differential widens considerably, the size of the difference is determined by market conditions prevailing at the time, but it can be between 1 per cent and 2 per cent. We will assume that the AAA-rated company could issue a ten-year bond at 10 per cent, whereas the BBB-rated company would have to pay 111/4 per cent. With a bank as an intermediary they enter into a swap arrangement. The BBB-rated company raises short-term, variable-rate money and the AAA-fixed-rate money. They swap their interest, as is shown in Figure 6.4.

Figure 6.4 **AN INTEREST RATE SWAP**

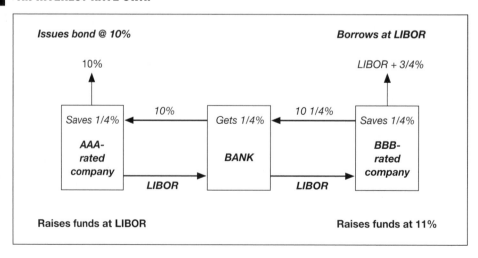

The AAA-rated company issues a fixed-rate bond at 10 per cent, and the BBB-rated company borrows at LIBOR + 3/4 per cent. Unfortunately this is not what they want; the AAA-rated company wants variable rates (maybe it thinks that interest rates are going to fall) and the BBB-rated company wants fixed rates. The swap should work to both parties' benefit.

The AAA-rated company gives the intermediary bank LIBOR; the bank then passes this on to the BBB-rated company. So, the BBB-rated company has received LIBOR from the AAA-rated company. The BBB-rated company then pays LIBOR +3/4 per cent on its loan, so it has to pay 3/4 per cent. It then gives the bank 10 1/4 per cent, the bank keeps 1/4 per cent for itself, and passes the 10 per cent to the AAA-rated company. The AAA-rated company can then pay its bondholders. The BBB-rated company's borrowings end up costing 11 per cent, and it has locked itself into these rates for the long term. It has managed to get fixed-rate money via the swap, 1/4 per cent cheaper than it could get direct. It has what it wants. The AAA-rated company has switched out of fixed rates into variable rates and effectively borrowed at LIBOR (a quarter of a per cent cheaper than it can normally get). The bank has made a profit.

Although everybody seems to win there are two risks in an interest-rate swap:

(1) counterparty failure
(2) adverse interest rate movements.

Whilst it is possible to 'unwind', (cancel) a swap, this is usually expensive. A number of companies discovered this when Britain left the ERM and interest rates fell. They had locked themselves into high-fixed rates of interest, and had to pay to get themselves out of the swap.

Interest rate swaps are useful tools for company treasurers as they:

- allow companies to obtain long-term, fixed-rate money, which might not otherwise have access to the bond markets;
- reduce the cost of borrowing;
- allow companies to respond to changing economic conditions – moving from fixed to floating rates, without changing the underlying debt instrument.

SUMMARY

There are three main ways that companies manage their exposure to interest rates:

(1) *forward rate agreements:* the company locks itself into an agreed interest rate – whatever happens to interest rates, this is the rate that the company will get. Forward rate agreements offer certainty;

(2) *options:* the company buys an option for an interest rate over one or more periods. The option may be for a *cap* (the maximum interest rate), a *floor* (the minimum interest rate), or a *collar*, which locks the company in a range of interest rates. Options offer flexibility because, if the market offers a better rate; the company does not have to take the option;

(3) *swaps:* these allow companies to move from fixed interest rates, or vice versa, by swapping their interest payments with another company. They exploit the credit quality standards between the fixed-rate bond market and the floating rate, short-term credit market. The spread between different quality borrowers is larger in the long-term, fixed-rate market than in the short-term market.

● ACCOUNTING TREATMENT

Until FRS 4 (*Capital Instruments*) became effective on 22 June 1994, there was no accounting standard offering guidance on the accounting for capital instruments. Historically, the Companies Act probably gave sufficient guidance until the late 1980s, which saw both increasing innovation in the development of capital instruments, combined with a lack of uniformity in their accounting. (Listed companies were always required to give more information than the minimum that was prescribed by the Act.) The Companies Act requires that companies disclose:

- Whether any debentures, bonds, and any other securities have been issued during the year, in which case the company must disclose:
  - the reason for the issue;
  - the instruments that have been issued;
  - the amount issued and the proceeds of the issue.
- An analysis of borrowings between those repayable by instalments and those not repayable by instalments, disclosing separately for each:
  - the amounts falling due after five years;
  - the repayment terms and interest rates.
- The amount of secured borrowings and the security offered on the loans.

FRS 4 has additional disclosure and accounting requirements:

● All borrowings

Accounting treatment

The direct issue cost should be deducted from the proceeds of the issue. Any other costs should be charged as expenses when they are incurred. The finance costs should be allocated to periods at a constant rate based on the amount shown on the balance sheet. This means that, in line with the accruals principle, the charges to the profit and loss account may not be the same as the cash paid. Any accrued finance cost will be added to or subtracted from the value of the debt that is shown on the balance sheet. This sounds more complicated that it is and we will illustrate this by looking at how we would account for a zero-type coupon bond.

EXAMPLE

A company issues a zero coupon bond for £100 million, repaying £161.051 million at the end of the fifth year. The difference between the bond proceeds and the redemption value equates to the finance cost, which would not usually be referred to as interest. Present-value techniques are used to find the implied financing rate of the bond – it is 10 per cent. (See Table 6.5.)

Table 6.5 Accounting treatment of a zero coupon bond

		Profit and loss account	Balance sheet	
	Bond value at the start of the year	Finance cost	Bond value at the end of the year	Less cash payment
	£m	£m	£m	£m
Year 1	100.000	10.000	110.000	
Year 2	110.000	11.000	121.000	
Year 3	121.000	12.100	133.100	
Year 4	133.100	13.310	146.410	
Year 5	146.410	14.64	161.051	(161.051)
Total		61.051		

Disclosure

Borrowings should be analysed between those due for repayment:

- on demand, or within one year;
- between one and two years;
- between two and five years;
- in more than five years.

Using the specified repayment date can sometimes be misleading. A company may have debt that falls due within a year, but has already agreed with the bank that it will provide the same level of finance for longer (*committed facilities*, i.e. the bank has committed itself to providing the company with the debt on those terms). As long as the company meets the criteria laid down in FRS 4, it can use instead a repayment schedule based on the maturity of the committed facility. If the company chooses to base the schedule on the committed facilities, it should also disclose:

- the amount of debt that has been treated in this way;
- the earliest date the lender may demand repayment if the facility was not available.

Companies have to disclose any unusual legal differences that are associated with the debt (for example, conditional repayment).

Convertible borrowings

These should be separately disclosed as part of the debt, and their conversion should not be anticipated. The notes should disclose:

- the dates of possible redemption, and the amounts payable on redemption;
- the number and class of shares that the debt can be converted into, together with the conversion period;
- whether the conversion is at the option of the holder or the issuer.

Bonds with warrants

FRS 4 requires that if a bond is issued with warrants attached, the proceeds of the issue should be split between the debt and the warrants. This means that the proceeds that are recognised as debt will be less than the par value of the bond. This discount should be treated as finance costs and apportioned to accounting periods giving a constant rate on the outstanding debt. The warrants are shown as part of the shareholders' funds.

● Repurchase of debt

A company can buy back its own debt, or pay it off early. FRS 4 requires that any difference arising from re-purchase or early settlement of debt should be taken to the profit and loss account in the period it is done.

● FRED 13

FRED 13 (*Derivatives and Other Financial Instruments: Disclosures*) was issued by the UK Accounting Standards Board in July 1997, and is solely concerned with the disclosure of financial information about *derivatives* and similar instruments. It is not concerned with how we account for them.

So what is a derivative? A *derivative* is a financial instrument that is a spin-off from either the basic product or the markets. The FRED defines it as 'a financial instrument that derives its value from the price or rate of some underlying item'. All of the hedging instruments we talked about above would be regarded as derivatives. What is a *financial instrument*? A financial instrument is a term that covers most forms of investments that are traded in the money market or the stock market. The FRED defines it as 'any asset that gives rise to both a financial asset of one entity and a financial liability, or equity instrument, of another entity'.

The accounting for and disclosure of financial instruments are the subject considerable international concern. In July 1993 the Group of Thirty, an international association of bankers and former government officials, published a study entitled *Derivatives: Practices and Principles*. This stressed the need for better disclosures about derivatives in financial statements.

The International Accounting Standards Board published IAS 32 (*Financial Instruments: Disclosure and Presentation*) in 1995. The USA will be the first country to have a standard concerned with the accounting for derivatives, which is due to become effective in 1998.

The objective of the FRED is disclosure in the accounts that will enable users of the financial statements to understand the major aspects of the risks affecting the company's performance and financial condition, and how the company is managing these risks.

FRED 13 proposes additional disclosures to be given in listed company's accounts:

● Discursive disclosures

This is a discussion of the main financial risks it faces, and the way it manages its exposure to these risks. The discussion could be given in the financial review or the directors' report.

● Numerical disclosures

The company must give those following, usually after taking account of the effects of financial instruments (such as swaps) that alter the interest base or the currency involved:

- an analysis of borrowings showing the interest rate, currency and maturity profiles;
- an analysis of the company's interest-bearing assets, showing their interest rate and currency profile;
- a summary of the company's undrawn committed borrowing facilities;
- the total fair value of each category of financial asset and financial liability;
- a summary of the fair value of financial instruments that are held for trading purposes, together with an analysis of the trading profits and losses arising from trading these instruments;
- where a company has accounted for a financial instrument as a hedge associated with future transactions, information should be given to show the effect of this treatment on the profit and loss account, balance sheet and the statement of total recognised gains and losses.

INTERNATIONAL DIFFERENCES

There is a fundamental difference between IAS 32 (*Financial Instruments: Disclosure and Presentation*) and FRS 4. IAS 32 classifies financial instruments by their substance, whereas FRS 4 usually classifies them on the basis of their legal status. This means that, under IAS 32, redeemable preference shares that are obliged to be redeemed would be shown as debt (rather than equity). The treatment of debt–equity hybrids, like convertibles, is also different as they have to be split into their component parts. This means that they have to be treated in a similar way to bonds with warrants, with the fair value of the option being shown as part of the equity.

● THE BORROWING RATIOS

In this chapter we introduce the borrowing ratios; further illustrations of these, showing some technical adjustments, are given in Chapter 21.

● Interest cover

When we are looking at a company's borrowings we are concerned about its ability to pay the interest and repay the loans when they fall due. To see if the company is having any difficulties in paying the interest, we need to look at both the profit and loss account and the cash flow statement.

Interest cover identifies how many times the company can pay the interest out of the available profit or cash. It is simply calculated:

$$\frac{\text{Profit before interest}}{\text{Interest payable}}$$

The higher the number the better. Ideally, we would want to see an interest cover falling between four and six times, depending on the risk profile of the company. The riskier the company the more cover we would want to see, as the profits would be more volatile.

Most interest cover ratios are prepared from the profit and loss account, but interest is paid from cash. it is useful to look at the cash interest cover. To do this we need to look at the cash flow statement:

$$\frac{\text{Operational cash flow}}{\text{Interest paid}}$$

High levels of borrowing and poor interest cover is an indication of possible *future* solvency problems. Looking at companies is just the same as looking at people in real life. In the 1980s banks and building societies were prepared to lend up to four times a couple's joint salary to buy a house, and people took out enormous mortgages. They were highly geared. Had they borrowed less, their gearing would have been irrelevant. Their mortgages would have been a smaller percentage of their 'take-home' salaries. But many people borrowed the maximum amount that they could, believing that 'there's nowt as safe as houses'. For them, being highly geared became *the* problem. They had a poor interest cover. Real people experienced exactly the same problems as companies. People's 'profits' fell: they lost bonuses (and some lost jobs), just at the time when interest rates doubled. And there was a limit to the number of lodgers that could fit into a house! For a lot of people it was even worse! people in southern England had the same problems that the property companies had. Their mortgage payments were larger than their salaries, but they could not sell their house because they would not get enough money back from the sale to repay the loan! Negative equity is not just a domestic problem; it is a corporate problem.

Interest cover is crucial, if you look at the large companies that went into liquidation in the last recession, they were highly geared companies with low interest covers. In fact, you probably do not even need to be highly geared, your borrowings could be relatively low, but you could still have poor interest cover. The important question is, can the company afford to service its debt?

● Sensitivity to interest rates

If we knew the variable interest rates a company was paying (unfortunately we usually do not, and so have to approximate) we could work out the effect that a 1 per cent change in interest rates would have on both earnings and interest cover.

● Gearing

Accountants and analysts use the gearing ratios to quantify the proportion of borrowed capital. Financial gearing is a measure of the amount of debt a company has, and the debt can be expressed as a percentage of either the debt (the old UK accountant's approach) or the shareholders' funds (the City of London and banking approach). Alternatively, we could use the net debt as a percentage of shareholders' funds; this is becoming increasingly popular and is probably the most common definition of gearing.

The different ways of calculating gearing will quantify variants of the same thing.

Accounting gearing

The traditional way of calculating gearing measured long-term loans as a percentage of the long-term capital available to the business. This shows us what percentage of the total long-term capital has been borrowed:

$$\frac{\text{Long-term loans}}{\text{Capital employed}} \quad \text{x} \quad 100$$

Gearing calculated in this way will always generate a percentage below one hundred, the City of London's methods of calculating gearing (see below) can generate percentages way in excess of 100 per cent.

City gearing

This looks at the relationship between long-term debt and the equity (the shareholders' stake in the business), in the USA it is referred to as *leverage*. There are three different ways that this can be calculated, using:

- long-term debt
- all debt
- net debt.

These are discussed below.

Long-term debt

This is calculated as follows:

$$\frac{\text{Long-term loans}}{\text{Capital and reserves}} \quad \times \quad 100$$

All debt

This is a measure that is often used by banks and credit rating agencies. it may also be a more appropriate measure when looking at smaller private companies, which have limited access to long-term loans.

$$\frac{\text{All debt}}{\text{Capital and reserves}} \quad \times \quad 100$$

Net debt

This is the commonest way of calculating gearing in the City of London. It deducts any cash and short-term deposits from the debt. the total debt is usually the figure used. This tends to be a better measure when looking at multinational companies which may have both cash balances and bank overdrafts. These are often in different countries; with the cash balances in one country and bank overdrafts in another. There are two reasons why this may occur:

- it is very difficult to take cash out of some countries. For this reason, companies may have an overall cash surplus, but are reluctant to use it in a country with these remittance restrictions, so they will borrow money in these countries instead of transferring the cash;
- some companies take advantage of interest rate differentials, borrowing money in countries with low interest rates and depositing in countries with high interest rates. This is discussed in detail in Chapter 13. Whilst this may flatter profits in the short term, it can create problems in the long term. Countries paying higher interest rates are not doing so because they feel generous towards investors! Their economy is viewed as being a less attractive one to invest in, so they have to pay higher rates to attract investors. Companies doing this always run the risk of incurring future exchange losses. If the economy does not perform well, the relative value of the currency will fall.

Or it could simply be that the loans have early redemption penalties, and its cheaper to keep the loans rather than pay them off!

To return to the gearing calculation, gearing on this basis would be:

$$\frac{\text{All interest-bearing debt} - \text{cash and short term deposits}}{\text{Capital and reserves}} \quad \times \quad 100$$

Net debt is probably the most common way of calculating gearing today, but we should select the definition of gearing that seems most appropriate for the company that we are analysing. The way we choose to calculate gearing is largely irrelevant, as long as we are consistent in the way that we calculate it – we should still see the same trends. It is important to calculate our own gearing figures, and not to rely on the ones chosen in the company accounts. Finance directors will always pick the most flattering definition, which may change from one set of accounts to the next!

● The leverage effect

It is possible to calculate how sensitive a company's earnings are to small changes in operating profits. This can be done by calculating the *leverage effect*. We know that gearing affects earnings. One thing that might be useful to know is the effect that a 1 per cent increase in profit before interest would have on earnings. (This is a similar principle to operational gearing, which looked at the change in operating profits from a 1 per cent change in sales.) It is calculated by using the following formula:

$$\frac{\text{Increase in earnings from a 1\% increase in profit before interest}}{\text{Current total earnings}} \quad x \quad 100$$

● Operational gearing

Operational gearing can rarely be calculated from published financial statements, as it requires an analysis of the fixed and variable costs. However, you will find reference to it in brokers' reports as many analysts try to estimate the fixed and variable cost split. If the information is available operational gearing may be calculated using the following formula:

$$\frac{\text{Contribution}}{\text{Operating profit}}$$

● Combined gearing effect

If we are able to identify the company's variable costs, it is possible to calculate the impact that changes in sales have on earnings (assuming constant interest and tax rates and no exceptional items) by combining operational gearing and interest cover:

Operational gearing   x   interest cover

This shows percentage change in earnings arising from a percentage change in sales and is referred to as *the combined gearing effect*. However, its use probably lies more in the realm of exam questions than practical financial analysis.

Acceptance   A bill of exchange whose payment has been guaranteed by a bank.

Bill of exchange   A negotiable instrument that is written by the supplier and signed by the customer in an acknowledgement of the debt.

Bond   A negotiable instrument offered for sale to the general public.

Commercial paper   A short-term negotiable instrument, often used by large companies as a cheaper alternative to bank overdrafts.

Convertible bond   A bond that gives the holder the right to convert their bonds into ordinary shares at a predetermined price.

Debenture   A document creating or acknowledging company debt. It is a negotiable instrument and can, therefore, be bought or sold.

Eurobond   A bond that is usually issued outside of the country of the currency and has few restrictions on either its issue or its trading.

Fixed charge   This gives the lender a legal right to specified assets that the company cannot sell without the lender's permission.

Fixed cost   A cost that does not increase with the number of units sold. Within certain levels of volume, these costs will not change.

Floating charge   A general charge on the company's assets, usually relating to short-term fixed assets and current assets.

Forward-rate agreement (FRA)   An agreement to buy something, at an agreed price, in the future. They lock companies into a price, and are commonly used to reduce currency and interest rate risks.

Negative pledge   A promise, given by a company to its bankers, to get the bank's permission before taking out any more loans.

Note   An unsecured negotiable instrument that can be a source of long- and short-term borrowings.

Operational gearing   A measure of the percentage change in profit for a 1 per cent change in sales.

Option   An opportunity to buy something at an agreed price. Options are available on shares, bonds, currencies, interest rates and futures.

Sinking fund   A fund established to repay loans. there are different types of sinking fund:

- traditional fund – this repays the debt at the end of the period and is similar to an endowment policy;
- non-cumulative fund – this repays a fixed amount of the borrowings each year;
- cumulative fund – the amount that is redeemed is a fixed amount of cash plus the interest that has been saved by the early redemptions.

Subordinated loan   A loan that ranks behind other loans in a liquidation.

Swap   An exchange of cash flows, usually interest rates or currencies.

Variable cost   A cost that moves in proportion to the number of units sold.

Warrant   A type of option that allows the holders to buy shares at an agreed price at a future date.

Yield   A measure of the return on the investment.

7 The balance sheet: intangible fixed assets

This chapter covers:

- **Capitalised research and development costs**
- **Patents and trade marks**
- **Brand names**
- **Goodwill**

● INTRODUCTION

The Companies Act gives some limited guidance about the accounting treatment of intangible assets, and identifies the following categories of intangible fixed assets:

- development costs;
- concessions, patents, licences, trade marks and similar rights and assets
- goodwill
- payments on account.

Although most companies do not currently show any intangible assets on the balance sheet, there are many that could be included. For example:

- capitalised research and development costs
- concessions
- patents and trade marks
- brand names
- goodwill.

Where an intangible asset has a finite life, it must be written down in the same manner as tangible assets. (Companies talk about *amortising*, rather that depreciating, intangible assets. The process is essentially the same.)

FRS 10 *(Goodwill and Intangible Assets)* covers the accounting treatment for intangible assets. It defines an intangible asset as a non-financial fixed asset that does not have physical substance, but is identifiable and controlled by the company through custody or legal rights. For the intangible asset to be identifiable, the company should be able to dispose of it separately from the rest of business. If it can only be disposed of by the disposal of the business it is regarded as goodwill and accounted for as such.

It covers the accounting treatment for goodwill and intangible assets and becomes effective on 23 December 1998. The difference between the purchase price of a company and its net asset value is referred to as 'purchased goodwill'. The accounting standard requires that purchased goodwill and purchased intangible assets should be recognised as assets on the balance sheet. This will mean that intangible assets will be found more frequently on UK accounts.

The intangible assets should subsequently be amortised over their useful economic life, usually a maximum of twenty years, but companies can extend this period beyond twenty years, or even indefinitely, if they can prove in an annual impairment review that their value has not been eroded. Intangible assets that are believed to have an indefinite life should be reviewed annually to identify any impairment, which should then be charged to the profit and loss account. This means that companies need not amortise intangible assets and goodwill, but only if they can clearly establish that their values have not fallen. All companies will be reqired to have an impairment review at the end of the first full financial year following the acquisition of the intangible asset and also when events indicate the value of the asset may have fallen.

The Companies Act requires that all fixed assets should be depreciated if they have a limited life. Consequently those companies not amortising intangible assets with indefinite lives must disclose that they are not amortising these assets, give detailed reasons for their decision, and show the effect of not amortising these assets.

Internally generated goodwill should not be shown on the balance sheet. Internally generated intangible assets should usually be expensed to the profit and loss account, ensuring consistency with the accounting treatmet for goodwill. The only allowed exception is where the internally generated asset satisfies both of the following criteria:

- it is clearly distinguishable from goodwill;
- it has a readily ascertainable market value that is readily measurable.

SUMMARY

FRS 10 covers the accounting treatment for goodwill and intangible assets and becomes effective from 23 December 1998. Following its implementation, purchased goodwill and intangible assets should be shown as assets on the balance sheet. Other internally generated intangible assets can only be shown if they have a readily ascertainable market value that is easily measurable. The other requirements of FRS 10 are:

- **goodwill:** purchased goodwill should be shown as an intangible asset and amortised over its useful life.
- **other intangible assets:** these should only be recognised if the company can establish a market value. They should be amortised over their useful economic life.
- **amortisation period:** the asset life would usually not exceed twenty years, but it can be indefinite. If the asset life exceeds twenty years the intangible assets should be reviewed annually to ensure that their value has not eroded.

CAPITALISED RESEARCH AND DEVELOPMENT COSTS

Research and development challenges traditional accounting principles. On the one hand, there is considerable uncertainty that it will be successful, therefore, prudence would seem to indicate that it should be charged to the profit and loss account. Whereas on the other hand, it is a socially desirable activity that promotes economic growth and employment. Charging it immediately to the profit and loss account could discourage companies spending money on research and development. A distinction is usually drawn between research (which is original and strives to gain new scientific knowledge and understanding) and development (which is the translation of this knowledge into a new product or process). Research is rarely capitalised, whereas development costs may be capitalised in most countries.

SSAP 13 (*Research and Development*) requires that the fixed assets used for research and development are always included within the fixed assets, and most research and development expenditure should be charged to the profit and loss account as it is incurred. Both pure and applied research should always be charged to the profit and loss account. However, the accounting standard does identify some specific criteria which, if met, would allow the company to show development expenditure as an intangible fixed asset:

- there is a clearly defined project;
- the related expenditure is separately identifiable;
- it is reasonably certain that the project is both technically feasible and commercially viable;
- it is expected to be profitable, having considered all current and future costs;
- the company has the resources to complete the project.

Research and development costs are specifically excluded from FRS 10, consequently capitalised development costs do not have to meet the additional requirements for the recognition of internally generated intangible assets. If the company capitalises development costs, they should be amortised over the periods that are expected to benefit from their use. Companies must disclose their accounting policy for research and development in the notes to the accounts.

SUMMARY

- *Research costs:* all research costs should be charged to the profit and loss account.
- *Development costs:* development costs relating to specific projects may be capitalised if the project is technically feasible, likely to be profitable, and the company has the resources for project completion and launch. Any capitalised development costs should be amortised over the period expected to benefit from the development.
- *Tangible fixed assets:* there is no distinction between fixed assets used for research and development and other fixed assets.

INTERNATIONAL DIFFERENCES

Whilst it is rare for a UK company to capitalise development costs, it is not unusual on the continent. For example, Volvo shows the development costs of aircraft engines as an intangible asset on its balance sheet.

International accounting standards

IAS 9 (*Research and Development Costs*) separately defines research and development; with development being the application of research to production. All research costs should be charged to the profit and loss account, but development costs *must* be capitalised if they meet the following criteria:

- it is a clearly defined product or process;
- the costs can be separately identified and reliably measured;
- the technical feasibility is demonstrable;
- a market exists for the product, or if it is to be used within the group, its usefulness is demonstrable;

- the company intends to go ahead with the product or process;
- the company can demonstrate that it has adequate resources.

The capitalised costs cannot exceed the probable net recoverable proceeds and they should be amortised in a systematic way to reflect the related benefits. If the circumstances change, with the net recovery becoming improbable or the project no longer meeting the criteria, any capitalised costs should be written down. This treatment can be reversed if the circumstances change again.

Europe
In France research and development costs are generally written off as they are incurred. However, it is possible to capitalise clearly defined projects which have a reasonable chance of success. Once the development costs have been capitalised, they should be written off over five years – although in exceptional circumstances this period could be extended. Until these costs have been fully amortised, dividends can only be paid where there are sufficient reserves to cover the capitalised development costs.

In Germany development expenses are not capitalised.

In the Netherlands clearly defined projects may be capitalised as long as they meet certain criteria (these criteria are similar to those found in IAS 9). Capitalised development costs should be amortised over five years and the total research and development cost for each year should be disclosed.

Japan
In Japan specific research and development projects may be capitalised, and the criteria for capitalisation are less stringent and rely on the identification of a specific project. The research costs may also be capitalised. Any capitalised research and development costs must be amortised within five years.

North America
In the USA all research and development expenditure should be charged to the profit and loss account and disclosed separately. Any fixed assets which do not have a future alternative use should also be charged to the profit and loss account.

In Canada development costs can be capitalised if they meet certain criteria, which are broadly the same as those of IAS 9.

● PATENTS AND TRADE MARKS

A *patent* is a government grant to an inventor for the sole right to use and sell the invention for a limited period, and this obviously has a value during that period. A *trade mark* is a name or other symbol that differentiates a company's products from those of its competitors. The trade mark can be officially registered, giving the company legal protection.

As both patents and trade marks can have an identifiable value they can be capitalised as intangible assets and amortised over their useful life. Schedule 4 of the Companies Act (Note 2) allows capitalisation of these, and similar rights, if they have been acquired for 'valuable consideration' or 'were created by the company itself'. If these assets have been purchased they will normally be shown at cost, but they may be stated at valuation (usually depreciated replacement cost). The choice of the useful life is usually fairly straightforward as it is usually linked to the legal life, although the principle of prudence may shorten it. FRS 10 allows the extension of the life beyond the legal rights only when the legal rights are renewable and the renewal of rights is certain.

The household-products group, Jeyes, shows trade marks and other rights as intangible assets on its balance sheet. Patents and trade marks are one of the many rights that companies can choose to capitalise. Similar rights would be:

Copyrights and similar publishing rights

A copyright provides the holder with the exclusive rights to control and produce copies of an original literary, musical, or artistic work. Within the EU there is now standard copyright protection, this was enacted in the UK in 1996 by the statutory instrument, the Duration of Copyright and Rights in Performance Regulations (1995). Copyrights obviously have a value and some companies choose to show these as intangible assets in their accounts. Sony includes 'artists contracts and music catalogs' as part of its intangible assets. EMI shows all music publishing copyrights acquired after 1 April 1989 on its balance sheet.

Licences

A licence is an agreement entered into with a third party or the government to carry out certain actions. Two licences that most of us are familiar with are pub and betting licences. We are probably also familiar with software licences, which license us to use the software that we have purchased. SmithKline Beecham shows licences and patents as part of its intangible assets (it also shows goodwill and brands as intangible assets).

SUMMARY Any patents, trade marks and similar rights may be shown as an intangible asset on the balance sheet. They will be initially recorded at cost, or valuation, and are normally amortised over the shorter of the legal period attached to the right and the period expected to benefit from the asset.

● BRAND NAMES

The inclusion of brand names on company balance sheets is a recent phenomenon, and has become common practice in the food and drinks industry where brand names are a large hidden asset. At 30 September 1996, Grand Metropolitan, now part of the drinks group Diageo, had brands on its balance sheet of £3884 million compared to net assets of £3647 million and borrowings of £4439 million. These brands clearly do have a value (we are talking about names such as Burger King, Green Giant, Pillsbury and Smirnoff), the problem is – what should that value be?

Most companies have their brands valued independently by companies such as the Interbrand Group. The valuation is derived from applying a multiple (based on the brand's strength in certain areas) to the brand's earnings. Both components of the formula (the multiple and the future earnings) are subjective. The other alternative valuation method is to discount the present value of the future cash flows arising from the brand, using the company's after-tax-weighted average cost of capital as the discount rate. The problems with this method lie in predicting the future cash flows. Hence, whatever method the company uses to value its brands, the assumptions used will make the valuation subjective and open to debate.

Brands are undoubtedly important in some industries, and this is reflected in the amount of goodwill paid for the acquisition. But the valuation of brands is very subjective and the inclusion of brands in the balance sheet reduces the comparability of accounts and affects the ratio calculations. This is compounded by the fact that most companies showing brands on their balance sheets do not amortise them, arguing that they have an indefinite life. However, FRS 10 (*Goodwill and Intangible Assets*) would require those companies using indefinite lives to conduct an annual impairment review. This is already the accounting policy in Grand Metropolitan, as seen in the following extract from its accounts.

Extract 7.1   **INTANGIBLE ASSETS (GRAND METROPOLITAN)**

INTANGIBLE ASSETS

Significant owned brands, acquired since 1st January 1985, the value of which is not expected to diminish in the foreseeable future, are recorded at cost, less appropriate provisions, as intangible fixed assets. No annual amortisation is provided on these assets but their value is reviewed annually by the directors and the cost written down as an exceptional item where permanent diminution in value has occurred.

SUMMARY   Brands may be shown as intangible assets on the balance sheet, and where they are shown, they are often a significant proportion of the net assets. They are initially shown at cost or valuation. Valuing brands is not an exact science. Brands are not normally amortised, as they are believed to have an indefinite life. This will have to be proven in an annual impairment review from 23 December 1998, with the implementation of FRS 10.

● GOODWILL

What would you pay for a company that has a net worth of £5 million, but is generating £1 million profit a year? The answer would undoubtedly be more than £5 million, as you would not just be buying the assets, you would also be gaining access to £1 million profit every year. The difference between the purchase price and the value of the business shown in the accounts is called goodwill. Goodwill is simply the difference between the purchase price of a company and the value of the net assets acquired – the premium paid to acquire the company.

We will illustrate goodwill by using a simple example, but it is discussed in more detail in Chapter 19 – Groups.

EXAMPLE Imagine that the net assets of my business are currently £20 million, and I agree to buy the company we discussed above for £7 million in cash. I have to consolidate my newly acquired subsidiary in my accounts. My summarised balance sheet, before the acquisition, was as follows:

	£ million
Fixed assets	22
Cash	8
Other current assets	15
Current liabilities	(15)
Long-term loans	(10)
	20
Capital and reserves	
Share capital	5
Profit and loss account	15
	20

Following the acquisition, my cash was reduced by the £7 million that I have paid to acquire the business. In exchange, I will receive £5 million net assets. This will give me a major problem when I come to consolidate the two balance sheets:

	My business	Acquisition cost	Acquisition	Consolidated balance sheet
	£ million		£ million	£ million
Fixed assets	22		3	25
Cash	8	(7)	0	1
Other current assets	15		5	20
Current liabilities	(15)		(2)	(17)
Long-term loans	(10)		(1)	(11)
	20		5	18
Capital and reserves				
Share capital	5			
Profit and loss account	15			
	20			

    The consolidated balance sheet's net assets does not balance with my capital and reserves of 20! Balance sheets are supposed to balance! However, it does not balance in this case because I have paid more for the business than it was worth on its balance sheet. The difference is the £2 million goodwill. I can make it balance in one of two ways:

● I can reduce the capital and reserves, by reducing the profit and loss account; or
● I can increase the net assets, by creating an intangible asset.

The first option writes goodwill off against *past* profits, the second option increases the assets and opens the debate about whether the goodwill should be amortised. Both the international accounting standards and FRS 10 suggest that goodwill should be amortised. (From 23 December 1998 it must be amortised unless the company can prove that the value has not fallen.) This has the effect of charging goodwill against *future* profits.

Historically companies in the UK wrote off goodwill through reserves (the first option). Most companies overseas use the second option. However, FRS 10 requires them to follow the second option and show goodwill as an intangible asset. This will bring the UK in line with international accounting practice.

In the past the accounting treatment, shown in Option 1, overstated the returns on the investment and made it harder to spot those companies who had overpaid for their acquisitions. It actually reduces the capital and reserves, which may make some of the accounting ratios improve – as the denominator reduces the percentage increases! The new accounting treatment will ensure that the management will be held accountable for all aspects of the acquisition, and should identify whether the acquisition had added value for the shareholders. However, the transitional requirements allow companies to leave the goodwill written off against reserves before the implementation of FRS 10 to remain eliminated against reserves. This will mean that there will still be differences between companies in the value of the reserves that are shown in the accounts.

Goodwill must be reviewed at the end of the first full financial year to ensure that the premium that has been paid to acquire the company will be covered by the acquisition's future cash flows. The review is carried out in two stages. Initially, the company compares the first year performance of the acquired company with the pre-acquisition forecasts for the first year. A full impairment review is then undertaken if there is evidence that the post-acquisition performance does not meet the pre-acquisition expectations. The impairment review compares the value of the acquisition with the present value of its future cash flows. This impairment review ensures that if there has been an overpayment the loss is recognised immediately.

INTERNATIONAL DIFFERENCES

International differences in accounting for goodwill are discussed in Chapter 19.

Extract 7.2 is from the French retailing and distribution company, Pinault Printemps-Redoute illustrates the information that is disclosed about intangible assets in the notes to the accounts. (French companies analyse goodwill in detail.)

Extract 7.2 **GOODWILL AND OTHER INTANGIBLE ASSETS (PINAULT PRINTEMPS-REDOUTE)**

9 – GOODWILL

(in FF millions)	1996 Gross	1996 Amorti-zation	1996 Net	1995 Net
Retail Division				
Printemps	245	(33)	**212**	219
Prisunic	147	(16)	**131**	115
Conforama	1,099	(130)	**960**	988
La Redoute	1,023	(160)	**863**	897
Fnac	2,736	(127)	**2,609**	2,340
Financial Services Division	162	(22)	**140**	144
Wholesale Division				
Rexel	1,781	(152)	**1,629**	846
Pinault Distribution	282	(72)	**210**	216
International Trade	608	(104)	**504**	282
Total	**8,083**	**(825)**	**7,258**	**6,047**

The main changes in goodwill during the year were (in FF millions):

Net book value at December 31, 1995	**6,047**
Add:	
Rexel: acquisitions	833
PPR: IENA	218
Fnac: acquisition of Sodal	121
CFAO: acquisitions	192
Other	23
Less:	
Other	
Exchange differences and changes in Group structure	52
Amortization charge	(228)
(excluding write-backs of negative goodwill)	
Net book value as at December 31, 1996	**7,258**

10 – OTHER INTANGIBLE ASSETS

(in FF millions)	1996 Gross	1996 Amorti-zation, provisions	1996 Net	1995 Net
Trading names and market share	10,158	(117)	**10,041**	9,795
Goodwill and leasehold interests	1,302	(65)	**1,237**	1,264
Other	413	(247)	**166**	98
Total	**11,873**	**(429)**	**11,444**	**11,157**

The heading Trading names and market share breaks down as follows:

(in FF millions)	1996 Gross	1996 Amorti-zation, provisions	1996 Net	1995 Net
Retail Division: Trading names				
Printemps	1,100	(55)	**1,045**	1,045
Prisunic	400	–	**400**	400
Conforama	2,363	(1)	**2,362**	2,362
La Redoute	3,600	–	**3,600**	3,600
Other (less than FF 100 million)	4		**4**	6
Wholesale Division: Market share				
Rexel	810	–	**810**	810
Rexel Inc. (Formerly Willcox & Gibbs)	604	–	**604**	480
Grouplec	292	–	**292**	292
S.E.W.	223	–	**223**	188
C.E.I.M.	110	–	**110**	109
Other (less than FF 100 million)	625	(35)	**590**	499
Other (less than FF 100 million)	27	(26)	**1**	4
Total	**10,158**	**(117)**	**10,041**	**9,795**

SUMMARY Goodwill is the premium paid to acquire a company, and represents the difference between the purchase price and the net assets acquired. Most UK companies have historically written goodwill off through reserves, and do not show it as an intangible asset. However, from December 1998 goodwill will be capitalised and amortised over its useful life.

JARGON   **Amortisation**   A charge made to reflect the reduction in value of intangible fixed assets.

Development costs   The costs associated with developing a new product, or process. Development costs may be shown as intangible fixed assets under certain circumstances.

Goodwill   The difference between the cost of an acquisition and its net asset value.

Licence   An agreement with a third party to carry out certain actions.

Patent   A government grant to an investor giving him the sole right to use and sell his invention for a limited period.

Research costs   The costs associated with gaining new scientific or technical knowledge. It may or may not be directed towards a specific objective. Only the costs of fixed assets used for research may be capitalised (and shown as fixed assets in the normal way). All other costs should always be charged to the profit and loss account.

Trade mark   A name or other symbol that differentiates one company's products from those of its competitors.

8 The balance sheet: tangible fixed assets

This chapter covers:

- Identifying the cost of an asset
- Government grants
- Depreciation of assets
- Changing the basis of depreciation
- Ownership of assets
- Revaluation of assets
- Disposal of tangible assets
- Information disclosed in the notes
- The fixed asset ratios

INTRODUCTION

An asset is regarded as a fixed asset if a company intends to use it on a continuing basis in its activities. There are three types of fixed assets shown on UK accounts:

(1) **tangible assets:** these are called fixed assets outside the EU, and are the assets that are held by a business for use in generating sales, and are not held for resale. This term would cover land and buildings, plant and machinery, and vehicles;

(2) **intangible assets:** these are currently only found in the accounts of some UK companies, and are more common in overseas accounts, where acquisition premiums are shown as an intangible fixed asset. There are numerous items that could be included as intangible assets, ranging from brand names to drug patents;

(3) **investments:** this covers any investment shown as a fixed asset that is being held for the long term.

This chapter is concerned with tangible fixed assets – intangible fixed assets and fixed-asset investments are covered in other chapters.

There is no definition of tangible fixed assets in company law. FRED 17 *(Measurement of Tangible Fixed Assets)*, issued in October 1997, contains the only definition of tangible fixed assets. It defines them as 'Assets that have physical substance and are held for use in the production or supply of goods and services, for rental to others, or for administrative purposes on a continuing basis in the reporting entity's activities.'

When we are doing our personal balance sheets and look at our friends' fixed assets, we have a fair idea of what they are worth. Unfortunately, the book value of a company's assets rarely reflects the market value.

When looking at the tangible assets on a company's balance sheet we must always bear in mind three things:

(1) the cost may not be the purchase price of the asset;

(2) they are not shown at their market value and their values are affected by the company's depreciation and revaluation policies;

(3) they may not be owned by the company.

● IDENTIFYING THE COST OF AN ASSET

Most people think that working out the cost of an asset should be easy. If we buy some furniture, we know precisely how much it cost, so why should companies find it more difficult to determine the costs than we do? Most of the time they do not; usually, it is fairly easy to determine the cost of a tangible asset. It will be easy to determine the cost if the asset has been purchased and is used immediately. However, it can be difficult to identify the cost precisely if:

● the company has constructed the asset, rather than bought it from an outside organisation;
● the asset is bought to replace or improve an existing asset;
● the asset is paid for in foreign currency (this is discussed in detail in Chapter 20).

The Companies Act (Sch 4) gives some assistance, as it states that the cost of an asset will be the purchase price plus any incidental expenses. These are the incidental expenses that the company incurs to make the asset operational. Consequently, the cost of machinery would include freight and commissioning costs.

Paragraph 26 of Schedule 4 of the Act states that if a company constructs an asset the following costs may be included:

● the direct costs of raw materials and consumables;
● a reasonable proportion of the indirect costs that relate to the construction period;
● interest on any borrowings used to finance the construction, for the period of construction only, if the company's accounting policy requires the capitalisation of interest.

There is no accounting standard that addresses the problem of how we calculate the cost of constructed assets. However, it is discussed in FRED 17 (*Measurement of Tangible Fixed Assets*). It covers commissioning costs, subsequent expenditure and the capitalisation of interest:

Commissioning costs

The FRED suggests that only costs that are directly attributable to bringing the asset into use should be included. Commissioning costs should only be included where the asset is incapable of operating normally without a commissioning period.

Subsequent expenditure

Additional expenditure is often incurred on existing assets, and there are always difficulties in deciding whether the expenditure is an enhancement, or a repair which should be charged to the profit and loss account. This can only be capitalised if:

- a component, that has been treated as a separate asset and depreciated separately, is replaced or restored;
- the subsequent expenditure improves the asset and its performance.

Capitalisation of interest

The FRED allows the capitalisation of attributable borrowing costs, if the company's accounting policy is to capitalise borrowing costs. However, it is proposed that the capitalisation is only allowed during the period of construction and must not exceed the total borrowing costs in the period. (On a major construction contract, capitalised interest can be a major element of the total cost.)

 INTERNATIONAL DIFFERENCES

Internationally there is no agreement about whether interest should be capitalised. Generally it is allowed, but not required, although in the USA, FAS 34 (*Capitalisation of Interest Costs*) requires interest relating to constructed assets to be capitalised if certain conditions are met. The international accounting standard (IAS 23, *Borrowing Costs*) prefers non-capitalisation, but capitalisation is the allowed alternative. In Canada it is allowed, but not mandatory. It is allowed, but unusual outside of the construction industry, in France, the Netherlands, and Germany. In Germany there must be a close and identifiable relationship between the borrowings and the asset before interest can be capitalised.

SUMMARY   The cost of tangible assets is not necessarily the same as the purchase price of the asset. The cost can include commissioning costs and capitalised interest and it may well increase if the company later improves the asset.

● GOVERNMENT GRANTS

Government assistance can take many forms and will change over time to reflect the social and economic priorities of the day. The accounting for government grants is covered by SSAP 4 (*Accounting for Government Grants*) which is concerned with financial government assistance in the form of cash or transfers of assets. Other assistance (for example, advice) should be disclosed, where possible, but not necessarily recorded in the financial statements. Grants do not need to come from central government to be regarded as a 'government grant'; they can be from local government or the EU. If the company receives a grant to buy a fixed asset, it is possible that the grant could affect the cost of the asset shown in the balance sheet.

The accounting standard identifies:

- two types of grant – revenue grants and capital grants. However, it does recognise that there are grants that are hybrids, in which case the grant will need to be apportioned between the capital element and the revenue element, treating each part appropriately;
- the appropriate accounting treatment for each type of grant – this is essentially determined by the principles of accruals and prudence.

● Revenue grants

These are grants that relate either to the company's activities, or to a specific period. Prudence states that they should not be shown in the profit and loss account until the company has complied with all of the conditions applying to the grant. If a grant has to be subsequently repaid it will normally be treated as an expense in the period that it becomes clear that the grant has to be repaid.

The accruals principle requires companies to match costs to revenues. Therefore, if the grant is to reimburse the company for specific expenditure, it should be credited to the profit and loss account when the expenditure is incurred. Where grants are made to cover the general costs of a period, rather than specific costs, they should be credited to the profit and loss account when they are paid.

● Capital grants

These are grants that are received to enable the company to purchase an asset. In theory, these grants could be deducted from the cost of the asset and the balance depreciated over the life of the asset. This had used to be the most common way of accounting for government grants and, therefore, the availability of grants did affect the cost of the asset. However, this treatment now appears to be forbidden by the Companies Act (Sch 4, para 17). This means that UK companies now treat the grant as deferred income that will be reduced over the life of the asset. This is illustrated in the example below:

EXAMPLE

A company purchases a machine for £50 000 and receives a grant of £10 000 towards the cost. The machine is expected to last for five years having no residual value. The company uses the straight-line method of depreciation, as set out in Table 8.1.

Table 8.1 **Straight-line depreciation**

	Balance sheet		Profit and loss account		
	Tangible asset value	Creditor – deferred income	Depreciation charge in the year	Grant income in the year	Net charge to the profit and loss account
On acquisition At the end of:	50 000	10 000			
Year 1	40 000	8 000	(10 000)	2 000	8 000
Year 2	30 000	6 000	(10 000)	2 000	8 000
Year 3	20 000	4 000	(10 000)	2 000	8 000
Year 4	10 000	2 000	(10 000)	2 000	8 000
Year 5	0	0	(10 000)	2 000	8 000

INTERNATIONAL DIFFERENCES

The accounting treatment required by IAS 20 (*Accounting for Government Grants and Disclosure of Government Assistance*) is broadly the same as the UK standard. There are small differences in the accounting treatment for probable repayments of grants (the cumulative additional depreciation should be recognised immediately) and the disclosure requirements. Within Europe, grants are often deducted from the cost of the asset. In Germany the treatment is determined by the tax situation; if they are tax free they are included as income, if they are subject to income tax they are deducted from the cost of the asset. In the Netherlands grants are either deducted from the cost or a provision is amortised over the period of benefit. Whereas in France grants are either treated as income when received, or shown as a separate component of equity and amortised to the profit and loss account over the depreciable period of the asset.

SUMMARY

Government grants should only be recognised when it is likely that the company will comply with the conditions relating to the grant and will therefore receive the grant. In the UK, government grants are regarded as deferred income and include its creditors on the balance sheet. They are then credited to the profit and loss account over the life of the asset. This accounting treatment may not be followed overseas, but the different practices will have little impact on the reported profitability.

● DEPRECIATION OF ASSETS

● Introduction

Depreciation is something we all know about. We buy something today, and it is not worth the same tomorrow. Some things depreciate faster than others. Cars and computers generally depreciate much faster than our other assets. The Companies Act requires companies to make a charge for depreciation in their accounts to reflect the shrinking in value of their assets. The original cost of the asset is spread over its useful life to match the costs of the asset to the benefits that it has generated. This depreciation charge is not a cash cost to the business. (We do not pay depreciation in the same way that we pay rent; we physically pay depreciation when we trade our car in. That is when we find that it is not worth what we paid for it.)

The company's definition of costs (how much should be capitalised and charged to fixed assets), and their depreciation policy affects both the profitability of the company and the value of the assets shown on the balance sheet. Capitalising costs and extending asset lives can flatter both profits and net worth, and should always be spotted by the analyst.

● What should we depreciate?

In the UK most fixed assets must be depreciated, the only exceptions are:

(1) Investment properties

These are stated at market value and not depreciated under UK accounting standards (SSAP 19, *Accounting for Investment Properties*). An investment property is one that is:

- held for its investment potential;
- having rental income determined on an
- not occupied by the company or any ot

They are not depreciated as it is felt that d
generate income would be illogical! Only
erties would be charged to the profit and l
ment of SSAP 19, Accounting for Investmen
from the Companies Act requirement
economic life. Consequently, compar
is necessary for a 'true and fair view'.

(2) Land

This should only be depreciated if there is a
value.

All other assets must be depreciated, although some re
(They will be unable to continue with this policy if the proposals in
dard.) This and the note for investment properties is illustrated by Extrac
accounting policies in Marks & Spencer's 1997 accounts:

Extract 8.1 **FIXED ASSETS (MARKS & SPENCER)**

FIXED ASSETS
b Depreciation

…

(ii) Given that the lives of the Group's freehold and long leasehold properties are so long and that they are maintained to such a high standard, it is the opinion of the directors that in most instances the residual values would be sufficiently high to make any depreciation charge immaterial. The directors have based their estimates of residual values on prices prevailing at the time of acquisition or revaluation. Where residual values are lower than cost or valuation, depreciation is charged to the profit and loss account. Any permanent diminution in value is also charged to the revaluation reserve or the profit and loss account as appropriate.

c Investment properties
Investment properties are revalued annually and are included in the balance sheet at their open market value. In accordance with SSAP 19, no depreciation is provided in respect of investment properties. This represents a departure from the Companies Act 1985 requirements concerning the depreciation of fixed assets. These properties are held for investment and the directors consider that the adoption of this policy is necessary to give a true and fair view.

The UK accounting practice of not depreciating investment properties runs contrary to the Fourth Directive's instructions, and is not found anywhere else in the EU. Similar treatment is allowed under international accounting standards. Investment properties may be treated as ordinary properties or classified as investments and covered under IAS 25 (*Accounting for Investments*), which permits periodic revaluation (although not necessarily annual) and, therefore, no depreciation. In the USA depreciation should be provided on all assets except land, whereas in Canada all fixed assets should be depreciated. Japan has no special treatment for investment properties.

ciate?

ion charge should take account of the asset's:

residual value (the scrap value, at the end of its life).

an asset's value has fallen permanently, the Companies Act requires that it should be shown at its new value. This is called a *permanent diminution*. SSAP 12 requires that the assets should be written down immediately to the estimated recoverable amount, and any associated depreciation charged to the profit and loss account. The recoverable amount can then be written off over the remaining life of the asset, in the normal way.

FRED 17 (*Measurement of Tangible Fixed Assets*) states that 'the fundamental objective of depreciation is to reflect in operating profit the cost of using the assets (i.e. amount consumed) that generate the revenue in the period'. There are several ways that companies can do this and the different depreciation methods are illustrated in the example below.

EXAMPLE A company buys a machine for £10 490, which it believes will last for five years and have a scrap value of £490 in five years' time.

The straight-line method

The company has £10 000 to depreciate over five years, and would make an annual charge to the profit and loss account of £2000 (10 000 ÷ 5). This is the most popular method of depreciating assets in the UK.

The depreciation charge is constant at £2000 per year and the value of the asset is decreasing in a straight line:

	Depreciation	Asset value
	£	£
1st year	2000	8490
2nd year	2000	6490
3rd year	2000	4490
4th year	2000	2490
5th year	2000	490

Whilst this is the most common method, it is not the only method of depreciating assets. There are many other methods that companies can use, and the main ones are illustrated below.

Reducing balance

This is also called the declining-balance method. It uses a fixed percentage each year and applies this to the diminishing value of the asset. The percentage is calculated by using the following formula, which will give the chosen residual value at the end of the chosen life.

$$1 - \sqrt[n]{\frac{\text{residual value}}{\text{cost}}}$$

(*n* is the anticipated life).

Using the example above, the percentage that would be used is 45.8 per cent, and this would give the following depreciation charges and asset value:

		Depreciation	Asset value
		£	£
1st year	(10 490 x 45.8%)	4805	5685
2nd year	(5 685 x 45.8%)	2604	3081
3rd year	(3 081 x 45.8%)	1411	1670
4th year	(1 670 x 45.8%)	765	905
5th year	(905 x 45.8%)	414	491
			(rounding error of 1)

Do not let the formula fool you. Although there is a root sign in it, it is no more accurate than any other way of calculating depreciation. All it does is calculate the percentage that would allow us to arrive at what, for UK companies, is a purely arbitrary residual value. Some companies prefer the reducing-balance method, as they believe it gives a closer approximation to 'real' depreciation. However, as many UK companies write assets down to zero, the reducing-balance method becomes almost impossible to use. (Try calculating the percentage when the residual value is zero!) Plus, there are problems with this method if there are small residual values. The method gives unrealistically high charges in the early years.

Sum of the digits

In the UK this method is usually used by leasing companies, but it is more widely used overseas, particularly in the USA. It gives a depreciation charge that falls between the straight-line method and the reducing-balance method. The sum of the digits is simply the total of the number of years the asset is expected to last (1 + 2 + 3 + 4 + 5 = 15) and can be found quickly by using the formula:

$$\frac{n(n + 1)}{2}$$

(n is the anticipated life).

Having found the sum of the digits, the next step would be to find the depreciation factor for each year. In the first year depreciation is calculated at 5/15 x £10 000, in the second 4/15 x £10 000 and so on:

		Depreciation	Asset value
		£	£
1st year	(5/15 x 10 000)	3333	7157
2nd year	(4/15 x 10 000)	2667	4490
3rd year	(3/15 x 10 000)	2000	2490
4th year	(2/15 x 10 000)	1333	1157
5th year	(1/15 x 10 000)	667	490

Some companies prefer this method as it reflects 'real' depreciation, but is not as extreme as the reducing-balance method.

Usage-based method

All of the depreciation methods discussed above are fairly arbitrary. Some companies use a depreciation method that is based on the use of the asset, as this more directly relates the cost of the asset to the sales and production in an accounting period. This method expresses the life of the asset as production units, or hours, rather than years. It is often used for machinery and planes.

Continuing our example, if the company believed that the machine would last for 20 000 hours, the annual depreciation charge would be based on the usage, at 50p an hour.

	Usage (hours)	Depreciation charge £	Asset value £
1st year	3 600	1 800	8 690
2nd year	4 800	2 400	6 290
3rd year	3 600	1 800	4 490
4th year	2 800	1 400	3 090
5th year	5 200	2 600	490
	20 000	10 000	

The annuity method

This method takes account of the cost of capital tied up in the asset. The objective is that both the interest and the cost of capital should be constant. Consequently, when the asset is new, the debt and interest will be high and the depreciation will be low. It may be appropriate for large fixed assets that are funded externally, and is occasionally used to write off the premium on leasehold properties over the period of the lease.

The annual depreciation charge is calculated by using present-value techniques and annuity tables. (If you are unfamiliar with the principles of present value, they are explained in detail in the introduction to discounted cash flow chapter in Appendix I.) This method can be criticised on two grounds:

(1) it is hard to understand why the depreciation should be linked to the way that the asset has been financed;
(2) it would appear to be imprudent, as it assumes future profitability.

UK companies give limited information on their depreciation policies, as the extract below from the accounting policies of speciality chemicals and materials group Laporte's 1996 accounts shows (Extract 8.2).

Extract 8.2 **DEPRECIATION (LAPORTE)**

DEPRECIATION
Fixed assets, less estimated residual values, are depreciated on a straight-line basis over their estimated useful lives, which are reviewed periodically. The criteria for future lives are:

- plant, plant-specific buildings and equipment – maximum of 15 years
- freehold buildings (excluding plant-specific buildings) – maximum 50 years
- leasehold properties – term of lease
- freehold land – not depreciated

As depreciation is somewhat subjective, it is possible that the market value of fixed assets could be different from the value shown in the accounts. The proposals in FRED 15 (*Impairment of Fixed Assets and Goodwill*) would ensure that they are not shown at a value that is higher than their market value. FRED 15 proposes that all fixed assets should be subject to an 'impairment review' when circumstances indicate that their value may have fallen. The proposed standard offers a wide range of situations when an impairment review would be appropriate, including rationalisation programmes, operating losses, cash outflows from operating activities, as well as the decline in the market value. Most losses would be charged to the profit and loss account in the year that the loss is recognised, impairment of fixed assets that have previously been revalued are shown in the statement of total recognised gains and losss to the extent of the previous revaluation. Any further impairment should be shown in the profit and loss account.

SUMMARY

In the UK companies can choose the method of depreciation, and the straight-line method is usually used. The reducing-balance method and the sum-of-the-digits method give higher charges in the earlier years than the straight-line method. This probably more closely reflects the reduction in the market value of the asset. Whereas usage-based methods bring in depreciation charges that reflect the use of the asset, rather than its market value. The straight-line method is the simplest of all, and allocates the costs equally over the life of the asset. The annuity method is very rarely used.

The different methods of depreciation will give different depreciation charges, and these are illustrated in Figure 8.1.

FRED 15 proposes that any impairment in the value of assets should be charged to the appropriate financial statement in the year that the impairment is recognised. Most impairments would be shown in the profit and loss account. The only exception is assets that have previously been revalued, where the impairment will be shown on the statement of total recognised gains and losses to the extent of the previous revaluation. Further impairments should be charged to the profit and loss account in the normal way.

Figure 8.1 **FOUR DEPRECIATION METHODS AND THEIR DIFFERING CHARGES**

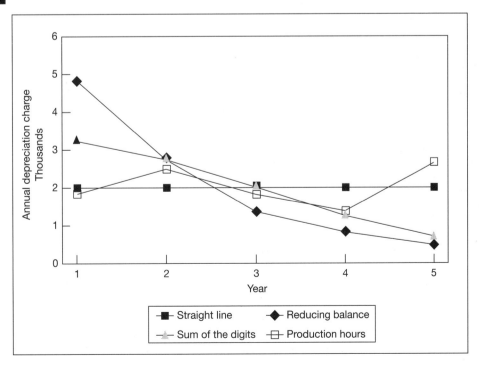

INTERNATIONAL DIFFERENCES

Companies outside of the UK have less flexibility in calculating their depreciation charge, as depreciation is often linked to tax allowances.

International accounting standards

There are two international accounting standards covering depreciation; IAS 4 (*Depreciation Accounting*) and IAS 16 (*Property, Plant and Equipment*). Neither standard currently gives any guidance about the method that should be used for calculating depreciation.

Europe

The depreciation charge is linked to tax allowances in the accounts of individual companies in France and Germany, but in the consolidated accounts it is more common to show a true and fair view. In Germany asset lives and depreciation are commonly based on the tax tables, however there will be disclosures about this in the notes to the accounts. Since 1994, it has become common practice for large German groups to adopt options that comply with international accounting standards but would not be tax efficient under the principle of *Massgeblichkeitsprinzip*. In 1995 the Justice Ministry announced that it would tolerate the use of international accounting standards in listed group company accounts. In France individual companies' accounts would follow the tax tables, but the numbers are usually corrected to reflect the true and fair view when consolidated. In the Netherlands accounting depreciation usually follows tax depreciation, although it can be different.

Japan

Depreciation in Japan follows the tax tables, with the reducing-balance method being the most popular, as it gives a higher charge (and, therefore, tax allowance) in the earlier years.

North America

In the USA the asset lives should be reviewed annually and the annuity method is not acceptable. If a company changes the method they must show an adjustment for the cumulative effect of the change in the income statement.

In Canada depreciation should be recognised in a systematic manner that is appropriate to the asset and its use.

● CHANGING THE BASIS OF DEPRECIATION

In calculating the charge for depreciation companies have four variables to consider:

(1) cost
(2) asset life
(3) net residual value
(4) depreciation method.

UK companies can change the way they depreciate assets if they believe it gives a truer and fairer view, and any changes in any of these will affect profitability, asset values and the financial ratios. For example we could:

● use the straight-line method, instead of the reducing-balance method;
● depreciate over ten years, instead of five years;
● have a net residual value of £2490, instead of £490.

This would improve the reported profitability for the first three years and increase the value of the asset shown on the balance sheet. The effect of this change is illustrated in Table 8.2.

In practice, the difference is unlikely to be as pronounced as suggested in Table 8.2. The net book value should be written off over the remaining life, starting with the year that the new method is adopted. So if we were using the straight-line method, but shortened the asset life from ten years to five during the third year, the revised depreciation would be calculated as follows:

Previous annual depreciation charge	800	((10 490 – 490)/10)
Asset value at the end of the second year	8890	(10 490 – (800 x 2) = 8890)
Annual depreciation based on three more years	2800	((8890 – 490)/3 = 2800)
Net book value at the end of the third year	6090	(8890 – 2800 = 6090)

If the amounts were material, the company would have to disclose that profits and fixed assets had been reduced by £2000 (the additional depreciation charge), following the change in asset lives. The same procedures would apply to a change in the depreciation method.

SUMMARY

In the UK all assets, apart from investment properties, are depreciated. The depreciation is charged to the profit and loss account over the life of the asset, using an appropriate method. Companies may choose the life and the method, as in the UK the depreciation charged in the published accounts does not affect the tax charge. Any change in the method, asset life, or scrap value will have an impact on a company's reported profitability and asset value. The impact of any material changes in asset lives and methods will have to be disclosed in the notes to the accounts.

Table 8.2   **Changing the basis of depreciation**

Profit and loss account				Balance sheet		
Depreciation charge			Increase in profit	Asset value		Increase in asset value
	Reducing balance over 5 years	*Straight line over 10 years*		Reducing balance over 5 years	*Straight line over 10 years*	
Residual value	490	*2490*		490	*2490*	
1st year	4805	*800*	4005	5685	*9690*	4005
2nd year	2604	*800*	1804	3081	*8890*	5809
3rd year	1411	*800*	611	1670	*8090*	6420
4th year	765	*800*	(35)	905	*7290*	6385
5th year	415	*800*	(385)	490	*6490*	6000
6th year	0	*800*	(800)	490	*5690*	5200
7th year	0	*800*	(800)	490	*4890*	4400
8th year	0	*800*	(800)	490	*4090*	3600
9th year	0	*800*	(800)	490	*3290*	2800
10th year	0	*800*	(800)	490	*2490*	2000

● OWNERSHIP OF ASSETS

In Chapter 2 we discussed the accounting principle of substance over form. This says that if the company has the benefits and risks associated with owning an asset, the asset should be incorporated into the accounts, regardless of the legal position. This is now embodied in the accounting standards (SSAP 21, *Accounting for Leases and Hire-Purchase Contracts* and FRS 5, *Accounting for the Substance of Transactions*), and has a large impact on the tangible fixed assets that are shown on the balance sheet.

The assets will be shown, regardless of the legal ownership, if the company has access to the benefits and the risks of owning the asset. Assets purchased under hire-purchase agreements will be included as fixed assets, even though the company does not own the asset until it has met certain conditions (normally when it has paid the final instalment). Assets leased on long-term leases where the company has all the benefits of ownership (*finance leases*) will also appear as part of the tangible assets. Whereas those leased on a short-term basis giving none of the benefits of ownership (*operating leases*) will not, and their lease rentals will be charged to the profit and loss account.

The accounting standard (SSAP 21, *Accounting for Leases and Hire-Purchase Contracts*) defines these two types of leases and the appropriate accounting treatment for them.

● Finance leases

SSAP 21, in its introductory notes, recognises that it may be difficult to define precisely the difference between a finance lease and an operating lease. It states that a finance lease is one that 'transfers substantially all the risks and rewards of ownership to the lessee'. The difference between the two types of leases is largely one of degree, not of any fundamental difference.

However, the accounting standard does give a primary test for a finance lease, which is:

● the present value of the lease payments is at least 90 per cent of the fair value of the leased asset;
● the present value will be calculated using the interest rate implicit in the lease and is the discount rate where the present value equals the fair value of the asset. (If any of these terms are unfamiliar, they are explained in detail in Appendix I on discounted cash flow.)

Accounting treatment

There are two types of companies that are involved in leasing – the *lessees* (who lease and use the asset, but do not legally own it) and the *lessors* (who own the asset and lease it to another company).

Most companies are lessees, so we will consider the accounting treatment for lessees in more detail than that of lessors.

Lessee

The basic principle is that both the asset and the underlying liability should be shown on the balance sheet. Therefore, assets leased under finance leases are capitalised and depreciated over their life. (The life must be the shorter of the lease term and the anticipated useful life.) The lease rentals are then split between the interest element and the capital element. Interest will be charged to the profit and loss account in the normal way. The capital amount owed to the leasing company is included in creditors, and any capital repayments will reduce the amount owed to the leasing company.

The allocation between capital and interest payments is not as straightforward as it sounds, as the standard requires companies to use present-value techniques to determine the split. There are three accounting methods that can be used to calculate the charge to the profit and loss account and the remaining leasing liability shown on the balance sheet that are illustrated in SSAP 20. These are:

(1) the actuarial method, also known as the implicit interest-rate method;
(2) the sum-of-the-digits method, also known as the Rule of 78 (this name arose because if finance charges were allocated over a one-year period, the sum of months one to 12 add up to 78).
(3) the straight-line method.

The different methods are illustrated through the use of the example below.

EXAMPLE

A company buys a machine on a ten-year finance lease, with an option to extend the lease for a further five years. The first payment of £10 000 is made on the delivery of the machine, and the remaining payments of £10 000 per annum are made annually in advance. The machine cost the finance company £67 590 to buy and this gives an approximate implied interest rate of 10 per cent (the present value £10 000 per annum for ten years, at 10 per cent, is £67 590.24). The machine is expected to last for ten years, and have no residual value.

Payment date	Present value of £1 on the payment date	Present value of £10 000
On delivery in year 1	1.000	10 000
Year 2	0.909	9 090
Year 3	0.826	8 260
Year 4	0.751	7 510
Year 5	0.683	6 830
Year 6	0.621	6 210
Year 7	0.565	5 650
Year 8	0.513	5 130
Year 9	0.467	4 670
Year 10	0.424	4 240
		67 590

The machine will be shown as a fixed asset with a value of £67 590, which will be the same as the creditor. Therefore, the recognition of the fixed asset will have no initial impact on the company's net worth. The machine will be depreciated on a straight-line basis over ten years, as this is shorter than the lease term (a possible 15 years) and the anticipated useful life (ten years). Consequently, the depreciation charge will be £6759 a year.

The actuarial method

EXAMPLE

At the end of the first year the machine will be worth £60 831 (67 590 – 6759).

To find out the value of the creditor at the end of the first year, it is necessary to recalculate the present value of the outstanding payments. There are only nine years of payments remaining, so the present value can be simply calculated as £67 590 – £4240 = £63 350.

The lease rental must now be split between the capital repayment and the interest charge. £10 000 has been paid as a lease rental, £4240 is the capital repayment that has been deducted from the liability. The balance of £5760 is regarded as interest, and is charged to the profit and loss account. Consequently the impact on the profit and loss account and the balance sheet will be as shown in Table 8.3.

Table 8.3	Split between capital and interest: impact of lease rental

	Balance sheet		Profit and loss account	
End of:	Fixed-asset value	Total creditor – remaining lease payments	Interest charge	Depreciation charge
Year 1	60 831	63 350	5 760	6 759
Year 2	54 072	58 680	5 330	6 759
Year 3	47 313	53 550	4 870	6 759
Year 4	40 554	47 900	4 350	6 759
Year 5	33 795	41 690	3 790	6 759
Year 6	27 036	34 860	3 170	6 759
Year 7	20 277	27 350	2 490	6 759
Year 8	13 518	19 090	1 740	6 759
Year 9	6 759	10 000	910	6 759
Year 10	0	0	0	6 759
Total			32 410	67 590

If we add together our interest charge of £32 410 and the depreciation charge (asset value) of £67 590 we have the total lease payments of £100 000.

The same split between the capital and the interest can be identified by using a slightly different basis for the calculation as shown in Table 8.4.

Table 8.4	Identifying the capital/interest split

	Liability at the beginning of the year	Payment made at the beginning of the year	Remaining liability after the payment	Interest on the remaining liability @ 10%	Total creditor – liability carried forward at the end of the year
Year 1	67 590	10 000	57 590	5 759	63 349
Year 2	63 349	10 000	53 349	5 335	58 684
Year 3	58 684	10 000	48 684	4 868	53 552
Year 4	53 552	10 000	43 552	4 355	47 908
Year 5	47 908	10 000	37 908	3 791	41 698
Year 6	41 698	10 000	31 698	3 170	34 868
Year 7	34 868	10 000	24 868	2 487	27 355
Year 8	27 355	10 000	17 355	1 735	19 090
Year 9	19 090	10 000	9 090	909	9 999
Year 10	9 999	10 000	(1)	(0)	(1)
Total				32 409	

You will see that there are some small rounding differences, but whilst the logic is different the numbers remain essentially the same.

The sum-of-the-digits method

Another way of calculating the interest charge, and the corresponding leasing liability, is to use the sum of the digits, which is an approximation to the actuarial method. It is based on the depreciation formula that we discussed earlier in the chapter.

First, we need to calculate the number of lease payment periods (the number of periods between the beginning of the lease and the last payment). This is the number of periods over which interest accrues, and in our example it is nine. (This is because our payments are made in advance, if they had been in arrears it would have been ten.)

The formula for the sum of the digits is:

$$\frac{n(n + 1)}{2}$$

EXAMPLE

We have calculated that $n = 9$ and so we have a value of 45 (90/2 = 45). The total interest paid over the period of the lease is £32 410 and this now has to be charged to each period of the lease.

Table 8.5 The capital/interest split: sum of the digits

	Liability at the beginning of the year	Payment made at the beginning of the year	Sum-of-the-digits formula used for the interest	Profit and loss account	Balance sheet
				Interest charge for the year	Total creditor – liability carried forward at the end of the year
Year 1	67 590	10 000	9/45 x 32 410	6 482	64 072
Year 2	64 072	10 000	8/45 x 32 410	5 762	59 834
Year 3	59 834	10 000	7/45 x 32 410	5 042	54 875
Year 4	54 875	10 000	6/45 x 32 410	4 321	49 197
Year 5	49 197	10 000	5/45 x 32 410	3 601	42 798
Year 6	42 798	10 000	4/45 x 32 410	2 881	35 679
Year 7	35 679	10 000	3/45 x 32 410	2 161	27 839
Year 8	27 839	10 000	2/45 x 32 410	1 440	19 280
Year 9	19 280	10 000	1/45 x 32 410	720	10 000
Year 10	10 000	10 000		0	0
Total				32 410	

The straight-line method

EXAMPLE

This is the simplest method and works in the same way as that discussed in depreciation. The total interest charge of £32 410 is allocated equally to each year, giving an annual interest charge of £3241.

SUMMARY

The actuarial method and the sum-of-the-digits method give very similar results; whereas the straight-line method gives a comparatively lower charge in the earlier years and a higher charge in the later years. This is shown by Figure 8.2.

Figure 8.2 | **INTEREST CHARGED TO THE PROFIT AND LOSS ACCOUNT**

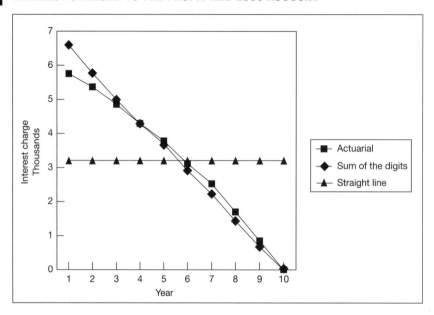

Lessors

So far we have assumed that the company we are analysing is the one that is leasing the asset from the finance company – the lessee. If the company we were analysing was the finance company (the lessor), the accounting treatment would be different.

The lessor legally owns the asset, but passes all the risks and rewards of ownership to the lessee in exchange for a stream of rentals. Thus, essentially the lessor is providing finance and expects a return on that finance. In consequence, the finance lease is accounted for as a loan, not as a fixed asset. The lessor records the amounts due from the lessee as a debtor. This debtor reflects the net investment in the lease, which will usually be the cost of the asset less:

- any government or similar grants that have been received; and
- provisions for any bad and doubtful debts.

If the asset has a residual value, this will be shown on the balance sheet at the end of the lease.

The standard requires that the lease rentals should be split between the interest earned (*the gross earnings*), and repayment of the capital. Whilst the debtor is based on the lessor's net investment in the leased asset, the income taken in the profit and loss account will be determined by a different figure. Income should be allocated to accounting periods based on the *net cash investment* of the lease. This is the amount of money that the lessor has tied up in the lease. It takes account of other factors (for example, taxation and interest on any borrowings used to finance the purchase of the asset, profit taken out of the lease). The gross earnings in each period are then allocated to accounting periods to give a constant return on the lessor's net cash investment in the asset.

● Disclosure requirements

Both lessors and lessees have to disclose information about their finance-leased assets, and the detailed disclosure requirements are discussed below.

Lessees

Companies should disclose the accounting policy adopted for finance leases, the value of the leased assets and the obligations to the leasing company. Any leases entered into before the balance sheet date, but which have not yet started, should also be disclosed.

The disclosure of assets held under finance leases may be given in one of two ways:

(1) **summarised disclosure:** the company can combine the owned and leased assets, disclosing the net book value of assets held under finance leases, together with the related depreciation. This is the most common form of disclosure;
(2) **detailed analysis:** the company may show the gross amounts of assets held under finance leases and the related total depreciation. This should be given for each major class of asset.

The capital obligations under any finance lease should be disclosed in the accounts, split between creditors due within a year, and more than a year.

Lessors

Lessors will need to disclose:

- the accounting policy adopted for finance leases;
- the net investment, in finance leases, split between that due within a year and more than a year;
- the total rents receivable from finance leases during the period;
- the cost of assets acquired for use in finance leases.

SUMMARY

The accounting treatment for finance leases follows the accounting principle of substance over form, therefore the party that has all the risks and rewards of ownership shows the asset in their accounts. The interest and the capital repayment should be accounted for separately, with interest being reflected in the profit and loss account, and the capital element shown on the balance sheet. Accounting policies and details of leased assets should be shown in the accounts.

Lessors

The legal owner of the asset, the lessor, will not show the asset on his balance sheet. Instead, the lessor will show a debtor, representing the net investment in the asset, which is analysed between amounts falling due within a year and in more than a year. The lessor must calculate two investment figures:

(1) the net investment in the asset. This is used for the valuation of the debtor shown on the balance sheet; and
(2) the net cash investment in the asset. This is the amount of money the lessor has tied up in the lease, and is used for the calculation of gross earnings.

The earnings in each period are calculated to give a constant return on the lessor's net cash investment in the asset.

Lessees

Both the asset and the underlying liability should be shown on the balance sheet. The asset should be depreciated over the shorter of the lease term and the anticipated useful life. The lease rentals are then split between interest and the capital repayment; this is ▶

determined by present-value techniques. The total interest must be allocated to the profit and loss account, usually by using one of three different methods:

- the actuarial method
- the sum-of-the-digits method
- the straight-line method.

Both the actuarial method and the sum-of-the-digits method give very similar results. The capital amount owed to the leasing company is included in creditors, which is split between amounts falling due within a year and in more than a year.

INTERNATIONAL DIFFERENCES

International accounting standards

IAS 17 (Leases), revised in 1997, has a looser definition of a finance lease than SSAP 21, defining it simply as one that transfers substantially all the risks and rewards of ownership. The asset is shown at the lower of the fair value and the present value of the minimum lease payments and is depreciated over the asset's useful life, if it is reasonably certain that the lessee will own the asset by the end of the lease term. Otherwise the asset is depreciated over the shorter of the lease term or the useful life.

Europe

Within Europe, finance leases may be capitalised, but this practice is less common than in the UK. In the Netherlands finance leases are capitalised, and in France finance leases may be capitalised in the group accounts. In Germany they are also capitalised, but the definition is related to tax rules and most leases are designed to avoid capitalisation.

Japan

Japanese practice is similar to the German, as both countries concentrate on the legal substance and the tax basis rather than commercial substance. The capitalisation of finance leases is allowed, but is unusual. When leases are not capitalised, the number and description of the assets would be given in the supporting schedules.

North America

There are four criteria for identifying finance leases (*capital leases*) in the USA:

(1) the lease transfers ownership to the lessee
(2) the lease contains a bargain purchase option
(3) the lease term covers 75 per cent of the remaining economic life of the asset
(4) the present value is 90 per cent or more of the asset's fair value.

Canadian practice has been influenced by the USA. Leases are capitalised if:

- there is reasonable certainty that ownership will be transferred
- the lease term covers 75 per cent of the remaining economic life of the asset
- the present value is 90 per cent or more of the asset's fair value.

These percentages are only guidelines, and leases can be capitalised even though the percentage criteria are not met.

● Operating leases

An operating lease is any 'lease other than a finance lease'.

Accounting treatment

Operating leases are treated in the same way as any other short-term hire agreement. The lease rental is charged to the profit and loss account as an operating cost. Neither the asset, nor the commitment to the leasing company is shown on the balance sheet. Consequently, operating leases can be regarded as 'off balance-sheet financing'. The lease rental is charged to the profit and loss account on a straight-line basis, unless another method is more appropriate. UITF 12 (*Lessee Accounting for Reverse Premiums and Similar Incentives*) states that incentives received should be spread over the lease term or, under some circumstances, a shorter period.

Disclosure

The notes to the profit and loss account will disclose the amount charged during the period, split between the hire of plant and machinery and other assets. As the leasing agreement represents a contingent liability, the notes on contingent liabilities will disclose the annual commitment for operating leases. These will be analysed between:

- leases expiring in one year
- leases expiring between two and five years
- leases expiring in more than five years.

SUMMARY Operating lease rentals are charged to the profit and loss account on a straight-line basis. The note on contingent liabilities will disclose the agreed annual rentals that have been taken off the balance sheet.

A thought on leases

Whether a lease is a finance lease or an operating lease is clearly important. The accounting standard tries to define the differences between the two, but stresses that it can only be a matter of degree. The standard recognises that it is often difficult to decide whether the lease is a finance or an operating lease. This grey area has allowed finance companies to try and develop finance leases that can be classified as operating leases under the standard. However since FRS 5, the opportunities for off balance-sheet funding through leases has been limited. If the company has the liability associated with ownership, it will be required to show both the asset and the associated liability on the balance sheet.

Hire-purchase agreements

SSAP 21 defines a hire-purchase contract as one which is for the hire of an asset, where the ownership of that asset transfers to the hirer when he has fulfilled certain conditions. (This is different from a credit-sale agreement where the ownership of the asset passes immediately and consequently ownership is not separated from the risks and rewards associated with the asset.)

Hire-purchase agreements are accounted for in a similar way to leases, the only real difference being that the hire-purchase company allocates income on the net investment in the contract (rather than the net cash investment).

● REVALUATION OF ASSETS

If we think for a moment about our own assets, not all of them depreciate. Some, such as properties, may increase in value. We have already discussed the fact that UK companies must show investment properties at market value to comply to the accounting standards. This means that they must conduct an annual revaluation of these properties.

However, most companies' properties are not held for investment purposes. Whilst they must disclose any significant differences between book values and market values, they currently have the option of whether to incorporate any surplus into the accounts. The Companies Act (Sch 7, para 1) requires most companies to disclose in the directors' report any material difference between the book value and the market value of properties.

Revaluation of assets is allowed by the alternative accounting rules in Sch 4 of the Companies Act. The alternative accounting rules allow companies to include fixed assets either at their market value, on the date that they were last revalued, or at their current cost. The European Fourth Directive states that where a company departs from historical cost, details must be given of the valuation methods used and what the historical cost figures would have been. If the company revalues its assets, it must also disclose in the notes to the balance sheet:

● the basis of the valuation
● the name and qualifications of the valuer.

To illustrate how a company would account for the revaluation of assets we will consider the following example.

EXAMPLE A company has tangible fixed assets of £100 000 and share capital of £100 000. The share capital has been used to buy the tangible assets, which include property that originally cost £60 000. Property prices have been rising steeply and the company has had the property valued at £80 000 and decides to incorporate this value into the balance sheet.

The new balance sheet will be:

	£
Tangible fixed assets	120 000
Share capital	100 000
Revaluation reserve	20 000
	120 000
Share capital	100 000
Revaluation reserve	20 000
	120 000

Four things should be noted:

(1) the revaluation of assets is shown on the balance sheet, not in the profit and loss account;

(2) the revaluation does not affect the profit and loss account directly as it is not a realised gain (the principle of prudence means that only realised gains are shown in the profit and loss account). It may affect the profit and loss account indirectly, as the depreciation charge will be based on £80 000, not on the original cost of £60 000. However, it would be recognised in the statement of total recognised gains and losses;

(3) the revaluation reserve is not a distributable reserve, and so cannot be used for the payment of dividends;

(4) the net worth of the company has increased by £20 000. This may improve the company's borrowing powers and will affect the ratios calculated on the company's accounts. Many ratios use the share capital and the reserves as part or all of the denominator. Simple arith-

metic says that if we increase the denominator, the percentage will automatically fall! (The impact of this will be discussed in detail in Chapter 21.)

If the property subsequently falls in value (as commercial property did in the UK during the late 1980s and early 1990s), it should be recognised in the accounts if the fall in value is believed to be permanent. Any revaluation deficits which are believed to be permanent can only be charged to the revaluation reserve to the extent of any revaluation surpluses that relate to those assets. This became a major problem for UK companies in the early 1990s.

In our example above, the company could absorb a fall of £20 000 on the balance sheet. If the value of the property fell to £65 000, the revaluation reserve would fall by £15 000 to £5000. But if the value of the property fell to £50 000 a charge of £10 000 would have to be made to the profit and loss account.

Trafalgar House was a good example of a company whose profits were hit by asset write-downs. Its hotels were revalued at open-market value on 30 September 1993. This resulted in a 'writedown of their carrying values of £51.5 million of which £11.7 million has been charged to the profit and loss account and £39.8 million to the revaluation reserve'. Only part of their writedown could be absorbed by the reserves; the balance had to be charged to the profit and loss account.

When we mentally revalue our own property we use an approximate market value for the valuation, for companies it is more difficult to calculate that value. The problems that Queens Moat Houses experienced in the valuation of its hotels illustrates the difficulties. Two firms of surveyors had put widely different values on the assets. Weatherall Green & Smith valued the hotels in May 1993 at £1.35 billion, following a draft valuation of £1.86 billion. Jones Lang Wootton valued the same assets at £861m. Both of these companies had used the same basis for the valuations.

But different bases do exist. Should the company use an open-market value based on existing use or an alternate use? Should it, as Trafalgar House did before 1993, underpin the valuations by indicative offers from potential purchasers?

Currently few companies revalue anything other than their non-specialised properties. Under current revaluation rules, there is no requirement for the valuation to be either professionally conducted or independent. Revaluations by directors should always be treated with suspicion.

• FRED 17

Fred 17 (*Measurement of Tangible Fixed Assets*) has been developed to ensure consistency in the accounting for tangible assets. Its proposals on the definition of a fixed asset's cost and its depreciation were discussed earlier in this chapter. It also has far-reaching proposals on the revaluation of assets, the reporting of revaluation gains and losses and profits on disposal of assets. These proposals are discussed below.

Revaluation of assets

The definitions of specialised and non-specialised properties and the proposed valuation methods are those used by the Royal Institution of Chartered Surveyors.

- Where tangible assets are revalued, all similar assets should also be revalued.
- Where non-specialised properties are revalued they should be shown at their current value at the balance sheet date, using an existing use valuation. The FRED proposes that there are two ways that current values can be determined:

- by a full valuation at least every five years, with an interim valuation in year three, with interim valuations in other years if there has been a material change in value; or
- by a full valuation on a rolling basis every five years, with interim valuations on the other assets if there has been a material change in value.

● The valuation of specialised properties should be based on depreciated replacement cost and updated at least every five years, with interim valuations if there has been a material change in value.

● Investment properties should be revalued annually based on their open-market value.

● Any properties that are surplus to requirements should be shown at open-market value.

● If non-property assets are revalued, and market comparisons or appropriate indices exist, annual valuations should be made using these indices. If no comparisons or indices are available, the company should update the valuations at least every five years, with interim valuations if there has been a material change in value.

Revaluation gains and losses

● Revaluation gains should usually be recognised in the statement of total recognised gains and losses, but should be shown in the profit and loss account when they reverse revaluation losses that were previously shown on the profit and loss account.

● Any revaluation losses that arise from an increase in the cost of using the asset, e.g. damage to the asset, (the FRED talks about 'losses that are clearly due to the consumption of economic benefits') should be charged to the profit and loss account. Other losses are shown on the statement of total recognised gains and losses if:
  - they reverse previous revaluation gains shown in the statement;
  - the value, in use, of the asset is greater than the replacement cost.
    Otherwise they are charged to the profit and loss account.

Profit on disposal of fixed assets

● The book value of the asset should be adjusted immediately before the sale to reflect the sale proceeds, with any resulting gain or loss recognised as discussed above. As these gains and losses represent an adjustment to depreciation, they should be charged to operating profit in the same way as depreciation. This means that they will no longer be shown below operating profit as an exceptional item.

SUMMARY

Companies in the UK can currently choose whether or not to revalue their assets. This can cause distortions in many of the financial ratios, and some adjustments would have to be made when comparing companies with different revaluation policies.

Revaluations made during the year will be reported in the statement of total recognised gains and losses and the cumulative revaluation is shown in the non-distributable revaluation reserve in the balance sheet.

If a company revalues its assets it is important to find out who did the revaluation, and what basis was used for the revaluation.

Any permanent falls in the value of assets should be recognised immediately. If the asset has previously been revalued, the fall in value can only be charged against the revaluation reserve to the extent of any revaluation surpluses relating to those assets. All other falls in value should be charged to the profit and loss account.

The proposals in FRED 17 will have a far-reaching impact on the revaluation of assets. If a company wishes to revalue, all assets in the same class will have to be revalued at least once every five years. Profits or losses on disposal of fixed assets will no longer be shown as an exceptional item.

INTERNATIONAL DIFFERENCES

Internationally revaluations of assets are unusual, unless the country is experiencing hyper-inflation, with most countries showing assets at historical cost.

International accounting standards

International accounting standards allow revaluation. In IAS 16 (*Property, Plant and Equipment*) historical cost is the preferred treatment, although revaluation based on fair value is the allowable alternative. IAS 16 differs from the UK Companies Act in that it does not make any distinctions between permanent and temporary diminutions in value – all should be charged to the profit and loss account unless covered by a revaluation reserve.

Europe

Within Europe, revaluations are often either not allowed or subject to taxation and, therefore, not done. Germany's accounting is based on strict historical cost and so assets are not revalued. In France assets had to be revalued in 1978 using government published indices that were based on December 1976 prices – this is referred to as 'fiscal revaluation'. Any other revaluations are subject to tax, except for property companies which may revalue tax free. Revaluations are legally allowed, and therefore may be found, in French group accounts, which are not subject to tax. In the Netherlands most companies do not revalue assets, although many large companies use net replacement cost or net realisable values for various types of tangible asset – not just properties.

Japan

In Japan both the rules of the Finance Ministry and the Commercial Code do not allow revaluation. Assets must be shown at historical cost adjusted for depreciation and any permanent diminution. The 'hidden reserves' that arise from showing properties at depreciated historical cost are disclosed by some companies in their accounts.

North America

The USA and Canada show assets at historical cost and so do not revalue.

● DISPOSAL OF TANGIBLE ASSETS

Fixed assets are by definition things the business means to keep. But all businesses try to sell their tangible assets when they reach the end of their useful life. If a company bought a machine for £60 000 and has depreciated it by £10 000 a year for five years, it would have a book value of £10 000. Assuming that the company manages to sell the asset for £12 000, it will report £2000 profit on sale of assets in the profit and loss account. If it was only sold for £8000, a loss of £2000 will be shown. Hence, when assets are sold they have a value in the books. If the company receives more than the book value it shows as a profit, any less would show as a loss.

FRS 3 (*Reporting Financial Performance*) requires this profit or loss to be shown on the face of the profit and loss account after operating profit, and before interest, and attributed to continuing or discontinued operations. (This may change if FRED 17 becomes a standard.)

It also states that if the assets have previously been revalued, the profits or losses should be the difference between the book value (the valuation less accumulated depreciation – this is also called *the carrying value*) and the cash received. Therefore, any profits or losses on sale of assets are determined by the value of these assets in the accounts in the books. These profits are sometimes excluded from earnings calculations (for further information on this subject, see Chapter 13).

● INFORMATION DISCLOSED IN THE NOTES

Companies will disclose the following information in the notes to the accounts:

- their depreciation policy;
- whether the assets have been revalued, the date of any revaluation, the basis of the revaluation, the identity of the valuer and the year of the revaluation;
- an analysis of the fixed assets by type.

The detailed analysis of fixed assets found in the notes is illustrated in Extract 8.3 from Whitbread's 1996 accounts.

● THE FIXED ASSET RATIOS

When we are looking at a company's tangible assets we have a number of concerns:

- *Is the company replacing them?* A company can make its ratios look very good in the short term by not replacing its assets, but in the longer term it will lose business as its machinery wears out and becomes unreliable.
- *Is it replacing them with the right fixed assets?* Additional fixed assets should lead to additional profits. Either the fixed assets are being bought to increase capacity, and the additional sales will lead to additional profits, or they are purchased as part of a cost reduction programme.

● Asset replacement

Companies will normally disclose their capital expenditure in the operating review, if not it will be found in the additions line in the note on fixed assets. On the same note, they will disclose the depreciation that has been charged in the year. One way of checking whether the company is replacing its machinery is to compare the capital expenditure and the depreciation charge. We would expect capital expenditure to be much greater than depreciation, as depreciation is based on historical costs and technologies. This can be measured by the following ratio:

$$\frac{\text{Capital expenditure}}{\text{Depreciation}} \times 100$$

Like all ratios, this is pretty meaningless in isolation; you would need to have a number of years to establish whether the company has a problem. It also needs to be considered in the light of the probable age of the assets. This can be roughly guessed by comparing the book value of the assets with the cost. For example, if a company's plant and machinery, originally costing £1 million, had depreciated by £800 000 to give a current book value of £200 000 they are 80 per cent through their life. If we know the asset life for plant and machinery we could work out an average age. Unfortunately, most companies disclose asset lives in bands, but even so we have some useful information. If the assets are 80 per cent through their life, the company should be replacing them at a much faster rate than one where the assets are only 20 per cent through their life.

Extract 8.3   **ANALYSIS OF FIXED ASSETS (WHITBREAD)**

12 Tangible fixed assets Whitbread Group	Industrial property £m	Retail property £m	Plant & machinery £m	Total £m
Cost or valuation 25 February 1995	100.6	2,053.3	773.2	2,927.1
Foreign exchange movements	–	3.1	1.1	4.2
Businesses acquired	0.4	269.8	43.4	313.6
Additions	2.1	224.3	128.5	354.9
Interest capitalised	–	3.4	0.3	3.7
Disposals	(2.5)	(68.5)	(53.6)	(124.6)
Provision for permanent diminution	–	(4.2)	–	(4.2)
Revaluation	(1.3)	14.7	–	13.4
Reclassifications	1.0	8.0	(9.0)	–
Cost or valuation 2 March 1996	100.3	2,503.9	883.9	3,488.1
Depreciation 25 February 1995	(5.8)	(30.7)	(426.0)	(462.5)
Foreign exchange movements	–	(0.7)	(0.8)	(1.5)
Businesses acquired	–	(8.2)	(16.6)	(24.8)
Depreciation for the year	(2.7)	(8.5)	(82.1)	(93.3)
Disposals	–	5.9	47.1	53.0
Revaluation	(0.1)	(0.6)	–	(0.7)
Reclassifications	–	(4.5)	4.5	–
Depreciation 2 March 1996	(8.6)	(47.3)	(473.9)	(529.8)
Net book amounts 2 March 1996	91.7	2,456.6	410.0	2,958.3
Net book amounts 25 February 1995	94.8	2,022.6	347.2	2,464.6

A provision of £4.2m has been made for a permanent diminution in the value of properties which have been identified for sale. This has been charged to the profit and loss account.

It is the group's policy to revalue approximately 20% of its UK properties in each year, so that each property will be revalued once every five years. Breweries are valued on a depreciated replacement cost basis and all other properties are valued at open market value for the purpose of their existing use. During 1995/96 the directors carried out a revaluation in accordance with this policy in conjunction with the group's own professionally qualified staff and external chartered surveyors, principally Gerald Eve. The revaluation in 1995/96 was £3.3m above book value. Incuded within the net surplus are individual diminutions relating to properties identified for sale. £0.5m of these diminutions, representing the deficit below historical cost, has been charged to the profit and loss account. The remaining net surplus of £3.8m has been added to the revaluation reserve. In addition, adjustments have been made to previous years' revaluations with the result that the net book amount has been increased by a further £9.4m. This has also been added to the revaluation reserve.

If this and previous revaluations had not taken place, the net book amounts of fixed assets would have been:

	Industrial property £m	Retail property £m	Plant & machinery £m	Total £m
Cost	79.4	1,901.6	883.9	2,864.9
Depreciation	(31.9)	(87.4)	(473.9)	(593.2)
Net book amounts 2 March 1996	47.5	1,814.2	410.0	2,271.7
Net book amounts 25 February 1995	51.2	1,387.2	347.2	1,785.6

Net book amounts of properties	Freehold £m	Long leasehold £m	Short leasehold £m	Total £m
2 March 1996	2,024.2	429.8	94.3	2,548.3
25 February 1995	1,827.7	215.1	74.6	2,117.4

Cost or valuation of properties	1996 £m	1995 £m
As valued 1995/96	363.2	–
As valued 1994/95	364.4	366.3
As valued 1993/94	369.1	377.0
As valued 1992/93	777.0	1,122.1
As valued 1988/89	6.4	8.7
As valued 1984/85	1.9	3.2
At cost	722.2	276.6
	2,604.2	2,153.9

Capital expenditure for which no provision has been made		
Commitments	49.1	33.4
Authorised, not committed	215.4	132.6
	264.5	166.0

• Asset utilisation

Increasing fixed assets should lead to increased profits, although there may be a time lag between the two. Profits can be increased by increasing sales or increasing margins.

Increasing sales

The sales can be simply measured:

$$\frac{\text{Turnover}}{\text{Tangible fixed assets}}$$

This can either be left as a number showing you how many pounds of sales the business generates for every pound invested in tangible assets, or expressed as a percentage. If it is left in pounds it is referred to as *the tangible asset turn*. If this is increasing, it may be that the company is becoming more efficient or had excess capacity in earlier years, but it may mean nothing. Beware of this ratio, as like many others, the results can be misleading.

To illustrate this we will consider a company with sales of £1000 and fixed assets of £500. Inflation is running at 3 per cent and sales increase in line with inflation. The fixed assets are depreciated at £50 a year, and the company buys no new fixed assets during the next five years. If we look at the tangible asset turn we get some interesting and totally misleading results:

	Year 1	Year 2	Year 3	Year 4	Year 5
Sales	1000	1030	1061	1093	1126
Tangible assets	500	450	400	350	300
Tangible asset turn	*2.00*	*2.29*	*2.65*	*3.12*	*3.75*

The business appears to have a significant increase in its operating efficiency, but the truth is that by not replacing its assets, it is storing up problems for the future! We could solve this problem by:

- making some adjustment for inflation over the five-year period;
- using the cost of fixed assets rather than the book value (I have yet to see an analyst do this, but you could be the first!)

Increasing profit margins

Many companies buy new fixed assets in an attempt to reduce their costs. If they are successful there should be an increase in their operating profit margins.

SUMMARY

> We need to see whether the company is replacing its fixed assets, and whether those fixed assets are improving the company's profitability. Companies' capital expenditure should be greater than the depreciation charge, as the depreciation charge reflects historical costs and historical technologies.
>
> The tangible asset turn tells us how many pounds of sales have been generated for each pound invested in tangible assets. However, we should be careful in interpreting this ratio as it is easily distorted by inflation and depreciation.
>
> Operating margins should improve if the company has justified its replacement of fixed assets through cost reduction.

JARGON

The annuity method   A method of depreciation that produces a depreciation charge that reflects a constant cost of capital.

Book value/carrying value   The net book value of an asset at the balance sheet date. It will be the cost/valuation less the accumulated depreciation to date.

Capital grant   A grant to enable the company to buy an asset.

Finance lease   A lease that transfers most of the risks and rewards of ownership to the lessee.

Operating lease   This is defined by default, as it is a lease other than a finance lease.

Reducing-balance method   The depreciation charge is based on a fixed percentage that is applied to the reducing value of the asset. Using this method gives higher depreciation charges in the early years and lower charges in later years.

Revenue grant   A grant relating to either the company's activities or to a specific period.

Straight-line method   The depreciation charge is calculated at a constant amount each year.

Sum of the digits   A method of depreciation, often used by leasing companies, that produces a depreciation charge similar to, but not as extreme as, the reducing-balance method.

9 The balance sheet: fixed asset investments

This chapter covers:

- Subsidiaries
- Participating interests
- Associated undertakings
- Other investments

INTRODUCTION

Investments can be found in two places on the balance sheet – fixed assets or current assets. Where they show on the accounts is determined by why the company is holding the investment, not what the investment is. An investment should be classed as a fixed asset when the company has an intention to keep it on a long-term basis, or where the company is forced to keep it on a long-term basis. (For example, the company may be unable to sell it.)

Therefore, an investment will be classed as a fixed asset if the company does not intend to, is not able to, or will not be required to, sell it within the next year. Otherwise, it will be classed as a current asset investment.

Like any other fixed asset, investments must be shown at cost less any necessary provisions. So, if the net realisable value falls below the cost or the valuation, a provision will have to be made to cover the 'diminution in value'. Investments are not normally regarded as depreciating assets, as they do not have a finite useful economic life.

Companies may have three different types of fixed asset investments:

(1) investments in subsidiaries
(2) investment in associated undertakings and other participating interests
(3) other investments.

SUBSIDIARIES

Subsidiaries are defined in detail in Chapter 19. A subsidiary is a company that is controlled by another company. Prior to 1989 we referred to subsidiaries as subsidiary companies. However, in 1989 the Companies Act was amended to comply with the European Communities Seventh Directive. This required the consolidation of all subsidiaries, not just those that were companies. Consequently, the Companies Act now refers to subsidiary 'undertakings'. This means that subsidiaries can now be companies, partnerships and associations carrying on a trade or a business. an undertaking does not have to have to be a company, or have a profit motive. subsidiaries can be companies, partnerships, or unincorporated associations where a holding company controls the board of directors of another undertaking.

The holding company is legally required to prepare consolidated accounts for the group, thus subsidiaries will not be shown in the group's fixed asset investments, as their assets and liabilities are included in the group's accounts. However, they will show as a fixed asset investment in the parent company's balance sheet (usually published alongside the group balance sheet).

SUMMARY

A subsidiary is not necessarily a company, because since 1989 the definition has included partnerships and unincorporated associations where the investing company controls the business. Hence, the term undertaking. Subsidiaries only appear as fixed assets in the parent company's balance sheet. In the group accounts the assets and liabilities are consolidated.

● PARTICIPATING INTERESTS

A participating interest is defined by the Companies Act (s 260) as: 'an interest held by an undertaking in the shares of another undertaking which it holds on a long-term basis for the purpose of securing a contribution to its activities by the exercise of control or influence arising from or related to that interest'.

The rules for determining participating interests are similar to those used for associates (see below). A shareholding of 20 per cent (including any options or convertible securities) or more is deemed to be a participating interest, unless evidence to the contrary can be shown. Most participating interests are also associates, as a participating interest becomes an associate when a significant influence is exercised over the operating and financial policy.

● ASSOCIATED UNDERTAKINGS

An associated undertaking is one where the company has a participating interest in a long-term investment and exercises significant influence over the operational and financial policies of the associate.

● Accounting for associates

Accounting for associates is covered by FRS 9 (*Associates and Joint Ventures*), which becomes effective on 23 June 1998. The investment in associated undertakings must be accounted for using some version of the 'equity method'.

● The equity method

The equity method is effectively consolidation on one line of the balance sheet. Rather than detailing all of the associate's assets and liabilities , the group determines its share of the associate's net assets. The value of the investment on the balance sheet will also include any unamortised goodwill arising on the acquisition of the associate. The investment is initially shown at cost, and the subsequent value is then adjusted for the investing company's share of any changes in the associate's net assets. Consequently, the balance sheet will show the investor's share of the associate's net assets plus the goodwill arising from the acquisition of the investment. Any goodwill will be disclosed in the accounts, but is shown as part of the value of the investment and is not included with the goodwill shown as an intangible asset.

The investing company incorporates into its consolidated profit and loss account its share of the associate's operating profit, and all subsequent profit and loss account items, other than dividends. The consolidated cash flow statement discloses the dividends received from associates as a separate heading, with other cash flows between the investor and its associates being shown under the appropriate heading. The consolidated statement of total recognised gains and losses will include the investor's share of gains and losses, which are separately disclosed either within the statement or in the notes to the statement.

The investor will also have to disclose:

- The name of each associate, showing for each the proportion of each class of shares owned by the group, disclosing any special rights or constraints.
- Material notes to the associate's accounts that are necessary for an understanding of the effect on the investor of its investments, noting the investor's share of any contingent liabilities and capital commitments.
- The extent of any restrictions on the distributions of reserves arising from exchange controls, statutes, or contracts.
- Disclosure of amounts owed and owing to associates, together with other disclosures required FRS 8 (*Related Party Transactions*).

The Stock Exchange's listing rules require listed companies to disclose the following information for all companies where the investing company's holding is 20 per cent or more:

- the principle country of operation
- the issued capital and debt securities
- the percentage interest in each class of security.

These apply regardless of whether the company is accounted for as an associate.

The accounting treatment for associates is illustrated in the following example.

EXAMPLE

We will assume that our predator buys 30 per cent of the victim for £20 000. The total net assets of the victim were £50 000. Therefore the goodwill will be £5000 as the predator's share of the net assets will be £15 000. (£20 000 – £50 000 x 30 per cent). On the date of acquisition the investment will be shown at the cost of £20 000 and the goodwill of £5000 will be disclosed in the accounts.

The balance sheet of the predator will be as follows:

	Pre-acquisition £000	Post-acquisition £000
Fixed assets:		
Tangible fixed assets	100	100
Investments		
Associate		20
		120

Business Library - Issue Receipt

Customer name: Lui, Sze Hoi

Title: Financial statement analysis and security
valuation / Stephen H. Penman.
ID: 1006921930
Due: 04/05/2015 23:59

Title: Unlocking company reports and
accounts / Wendy McKenzie.
ID: 1001692664
Due: 04/05/2015 23:59

Total items: 2
09/03/2015 15:51

All items must be returned before the due date
and time.
The Loan period may be shortened if the item is
requested.

WWW.nottingham.ac.uk/is

Current assets:		
Stock	30	30
Debtors	70	70
Cash	100	80 (100–20)
	200	180
Creditors: amounts falling due within a year:		
Creditors	(110)	(110)
Net current assets	90	70
Total assets less current liabilities	190	190
Creditors: amounts falling due in more than a year:		
Loans	(30)	(30)
	160	160
Capital and reserves:		
Share capital	50	50
Profit and loss account	110	110
	160	160

The predator and victim's profit and loss accounts for the year following the acquisition were:

	Predator £000	Victim £000
Turnover	1000	100.0
Operating costs	(750)	(80.0)
Operating profit	250	20.0
Interest payable	(50)	(10.0)
Profit before tax	200	10.0
Tax	(60)	(3.3)
Profit after tax	140	6.7
Dividend	(20)	–
Retained profit	120	6.7

The predator has to include its 30 per cent share of the victim's operating profits (£6000), interest (£3000) and tax charge (£1000) into its consolidated profit and loss account, which is shown below:

	£000	£000
Turnover		100.0
Operating costs		(750)
Operating profit		250
Share of associate's operating profits		6
Interest payable:		
Group	(50)	
Associate	(3)	(53)
Profit on ordinary activities before tax		203
Tax on profit on ordinary activities*		(61)
Profit after tax		142
Dividend		(20)
Retained profit for the group and its share		
of associates		122
The tax charge relates to the following:		
Parent and subsidiaries	(60)	
Associate	(1)	

The earnings have risen but there has been no additional cash input into the predator's business, as the associate did not pay a dividend! (Dividends would be the main source of cash to the predator, and the only form of permanent cash. There are occasions when the associate will lend the investing company money. These are disclosed, separately among the creditors, as amounts owed to associated undertakings.)

The value of the investment shown in the predators' balance sheet will rise to £22 000 – the £20 000 cost plus the £21 000 retained profit from the associate. The predator's proportion of the victim's profit, less any dividends paid from this profit, will be added to the value of the investment shown on the balance sheet. This ensures that the value of the investment reflects both the cost and the predator's proportion of the victim's retained profit or loss, since the date of acquisition.

If the victim had paid a dividend of £5000, its retained profits would be £1700 (£6700 – £5000 dividends paid). The predator would have received £1500 cash from the dividend that would not have shown on the consolidated profit and loss account, but will be reflected on the balance sheet in increased cash balances. Therefore the predator would increase the value of the investment on the balance sheet by £500 (£2000 shown in the profit and loss account, less the £1500 dividends received). This reflects the predator's share in the victim's net worth. Thus, the value of the investment shown on the balance sheet would be £20 500 – the cost plus the predator's share of the post-acquisition retained profits. (This also equals the predator's share of the net assets, 30 per cent of £50 000, £15 500, plus the goodwill of £5000.

Equity accounting is clearly illustrated in Extracts 9.1 and 9.2 from Taylor Woodrow's 1996 accounts. Taylor Woodrow's accounting policy for associates is shown in Extract 9.1.

Extract 9.1   ASSOCIATED UNDERTAKINGS (TAYLOR WOODROW)

An associated undertaking is defined as an undertaking other than a subsidiary undertaking or an unincorporated joint venture in which the group has a participating interest and over whose operating and financial policy it exercises significant influence.

The group's share of the post-acquisition results of associated undertakings is shown in the consolidated profit and loss account.

Investments in associated undertakings are included in the consolidated balance sheet at cost less premiums including loans plus the appropriate shares of post-acquisition results and reserves as disclosed in the latest balance sheets. Premiums are written off against retained profit and loss account.

Taylor Woodrow's unincorporated joint ventures are accounted for using proportional consolidation (this method of accounting is discussed later in the chapter).

Its operating profits were £73.3 million in 1996. Its share of associates' profits showed below operating profit and was £2.9 million.

The note on investments in associates is shown in Extract 9.2.

2 + 2 = 5   Borrowing from associates could be very important. In the creative accounting boom of the 1980s, companies would use associates as a way of getting loans off their balance sheets. The associate would have a loan that the investing company was liable for, and the associate would then lend the money to the investing company. Neither the loan nor the interest showed in the investing company's accounts as borrowings or interest. The associate was equity accounted, not consolidated. There were, however, two clues – loans from associates and a note in the contingent liabilities that the company had guaranteed the debt of an associate. The off-balance-sheet funding was usually very blatant, but was often ignored by analysts. The ASB has tried to close this loophole with FRS 2 (*Accounting for Subsidiary Undertakings*) and FRS 5 (*Reporting the Substance of Transactions*). The additional disclosure requirements of FRS 9 will make any off-balance-sheet funding transparent.

● Joint ventures

A joint venture is a long-term investment in a business that is trading in its own right and is jointly controlled by the reporting company and others under a contractual arrangement. Following the implementation of FRS 9, in June 1998, joint ventures are consolidated using the gross equity method, which expands the information shown in the balance sheet and profit and loss account using the equity method. The information in the cash flow statement and the statement of total recognised gains and losses is the same as that given for associates using the equity method.

The equity method is one-line consolidation on the balance sheet, the gross equity method is a three-line consolidation showing the gross assets and liabilities underlying the net investment in the joint venture. It also expands the information shown in the consolidated profit and loss account showing the joint venture's turnover, which should be clearly distinguished from the turnover of the group. The company's share of the operating profit and subsequent profit and loss account items will be shown in the normal way. Items from operating profit to profit before tax should be shown separately from group figures, whereas items following profit after tax may be included in group numbers on the face of the profit and loss account but should be separately disclosed.

Extract 9.2   INVESTMENTS IN ASSOCIATED UNDERTAKINGS (TAYLOR WOODROW)

Cost and share of reserves	Shares unlisted £m	Share of reserves £m	Loans £m	Total £m
31 December 1995	7.5	6.0	1.4	14.9
Changes in exchange rates	(0.1)	(0.9)	–	(1.0)
Additions	–	1.2	–	1.2
Reductions	(1.5)	(2.6)	(1.4)	(5.5)
31 December 1996	5.9	3.7	–	9.6
Amounts provided				
31 December 1995	2.6	–	–	2.6
Changes in exchange rates	(0.5)	–	–	(0.5)
Reductions	(0.2)	–	–	(0.2)
Charge for year	1.4	–	–	1.4
31 December 1996	3.3	–	–	3.3
Net values				
31 December 1996	2.6	3.7	–	6.3
31 December 1995	4.9	6.0	1.4	12.3
The directors' estimate of the value of unlisted investments was				
31 December 1996	6.3			
31 December 1995	10.9			
Dividends received				
31 December 1996	2.5			
31 December 1995	0.3			

If the associate shown in the example had been a joint venture where the group had a 30 per cent interest, the consolidated profit and loss acount would be as follows:

	£000	£000
Turnover: group and share of joint ventures	1030	
Less: share of joint venture's turnover	(30)	
Group turnover		1000
Operating costs		(750)
Operating profit		250
Share of joint venture's operating profits		6
Interest payable:		
Group	(50)	
Joint venture	(3)	(53)
Profit on ordinary activities before tax		203
Tax on profit on ordinary activities*		(61)
Profit after tax		142
Dividend		(120)
Retained profit for the group and its share of associates		122

*The tax charge relates to the following:	
Parent and subsidiaries	(60)
Joint venture	(1)

If the group's share of the joint venture's net assets was £24 000, comprising £40 000 gross assets and £16 000 gross liabilities, the consolidated balance sheet would show the investment as follows:

	£000	£000
Investments		
Investment in joint ventures:		
Share of gross assets	40	
Share of gross liabilities	(16)	
		24

● Significant associates and joint ventures

Additional disclosures have to be made where a significant part of a company's business is conducted through associates or joint ventures. These are required when the associates or joint ventures exceed 15 per cent of the investing group's:

● gross assets
● gross liabilities
● turnover
● operating result (on a three-year average).

If these thresholds are exceeded the investing company gives additional information about the gross assets and liabilities, disclosing:

- fixed assets
- current assets
- liabilities due within a year
- liabilities due in more than a year
- any other information that is necessary to understand the total amounts disclosed, for example the size of the debt and its maturity.

If an individual associate or joint venture exceeds 25 per cent of the thresholds shown above, the same information should be disclosed for the individual investment.

INTERNATIONAL DIFFERENCES

The UK practice is broadly representative of practice internationally in accounting for associates, but there are differences in accounting for joint ventures.

The accounting requirements for associates in FRS 9 and IAS 28 (*Accounting for Associates*) are broadly similar. There are some minor differences, but the most important between the two standards lies in the definition of an associate. The two standards have different definitions of 'significant influence'. IAS 28 defines significant influence as 'the power to participate in the financial and operating decisions in the investee', whereas FRS 9 requires the actual exercise of this influence. Consquently a company would not be regarded as an associate under UK rules if the investor had the power to influence financial and operating decisions, but did not do so. The additional disclosures for major associates are not required by the international standard.

There are a number of differences in both the definition and accounting for joint ventures. IAS 31 (*Financial Reporting of Interests in Joint Ventures*) defines a joint venture as a contractual arrangement whereas FRS 9 defines a joint venutre as an entity that is under joint control. Therefore, jointly controlled assets and operations would not be a joint venture under UK accounting rules, whereas they would be under the international standard. Proportional consolidation is the benchmark treatment in IAS 31 with the equity method as the allowed alternative. The international standard requires additional disclosures for all jointly controlled entities, whereas FRS 9 only requires certain additional disclosures for joint ventures exceeding the thresholds given earlier in the chapter.

The definition of an associate is broadly similar in all of our comparative countries, and they all use the equity method to account for associates. There are, however, some differences in accounting for joint ventures. The European Seventh Directive allows member states to permit or require proportional consolidation for joint ventures. In France it must be used, whereas in Germany and the Netherlands it may be used. In Canada, Japan and the USA the equity method is used.

• Other statutory disclosure requirements

The Companies Act requires that the following additional information about associates be disclosed in the investing company's accounts:

- its name;
- the country in which it is incorporated (together with the country of registration if the company is incorporated in Great Britain), or the principal place of business if it is unincorporated;
- the proportion and identity of each class of share held by the parent and the group as a whole.

This information has an obvious interest to the analyst, and is illustrated by the following extract from Taylor Woodrow's 1996 accounts.

Extract 9.3	PARTICULARS OF PRINCIPAL JOINT VENTURES (TAYLOR WOODROW)

Name of joint venture (*Interests held by subsidiary undertakings)	Address of principal place of business	Taylor Woodrow plc interest in joint venture capital
Construction		
Costain Building & Civil Engineering Limited/ Taylor Woodrow Civil Engineering Limited Jubilee Line Extension 104 Joint Venture *	345 Ruislip Road, Southall, Middlesex UB1 2QX	50%
Translink Joint Venture*	Terminal Sub Project, Beachborough, Newington, Folkestone, Kent CT18 8NP	20%
Housing		
Harrington Park Joint Venture*	Level 1, 96 Phillip Street, Parramatta, New South Wales 2150, Australia	50 %
Taylor Woodrow/Kenco Limited (a limited partnership)	7120 South Beneva Road, Sarasota, Florida 34238-2150, USA	39%

The above joint ventures are managed jointly through management boards on which subsidiary undertakings of the group and the other joint venturers are represented in accordance with the respective interests held in the joint ventures.

SUMMARY

An associate is an undertaking where the investor has a participating interest and exercises significant influence in a long-term investment. Associates are accounted for by using the equity method. This brings the investor's share of the associate's operating profit and subsequent profit and loss account items into the investor's profit and loss account. The investment in the associate is separately disclosed on the balance sheet at cost, plus the group's share of retained profits, since its acquisition. Additional information will have to be provided if the associate is material within the group.

A joint venture is a long-term investment in an entity trading in its own right that is jointly controlled with other parties under a contractual agreement. Joint ventures are accounted for using the gross equity method. This is a three-line consolidation on the balance sheet showing gross assets and liabilities, and shows more information on the profit and loss account. The joint venture's turnover is shown and the investing company brings its share of the joint venture's operating profit and subsequent profit and loss account items into its profit and loss account. Additional information will have to be provided if the joint venture is material to the group.

Investing companies have to disclose information that can be very useful for the analyst, namely:

● who their associates and joint ventures are;
● where they are based;
● the proportion of the associate that they, and the group, own;
● the goodwill relating to the purchase of associates;
● any loans to or from associates;

▶

● any material trading balances.

Listed companies also have to disclose:

● the principle country of operation (this can be different from where they are incorporated);
● the issued capital and debt securities;
● the percentage interest in each class of security.

Equity accounting was used during the 1980s to take debt off the balance sheet. A company could have loans that were hidden in an associate. The only references to the loan would be an innocuous sounding note in the contingent liabilities that the company had guaranteed the loans of an associate, and of amounts owed to associates in the creditors. The ASB has significantly reduced the scope for 'off balance-sheet' funding with FRS 2 (*Accounting for Subsidiary Undertakings*) and FRS 5 (*Reporting the Substance of Transactions*) and it should become transparent with the additional disclosure provisions of FRS 9.

● OTHER INVESTMENTS

Investments in companies listed on a stock exchange should be divided into those listed in the UK and those listed overseas. They will be shown at cost, and the aggregate market value will be disclosed if this differs from the cost. Unlisted investments should be shown at cost or valuation.

Usually other investments will be those where the company owns less than 20 per cent, as most holdings of 20 per cent or over are accounted for as associates. The disclosure requirements for company's other fixed asset investments decline with the size of the investment.

● Company owns 20 per cent

Under the Companies Act, if the company does not exercise significant influence, the investment would not be regarded as an associate. If the company has investments of 20 per cent or more and decides not to account for these as an associated company it must disclose:

● the reason for its decision in the notes to the accounts;
● the total capital and reserves and the profit or loss for the most recent year;
● the information required for significant investments shown below.

A holding of 20 per cent should give the investing company significant influence. It is often interesting to reflect on why a company which could exercise significant influence does not. It may be that it is seen as hostile and, therefore, not given a seat on the board.

● Significant investments

If an investment is deemed to be 'significant' under the Companies Act, the company must disclose additional information about it. A significant investment is where the company holds 10 per cent, or more, of the nominal value of any class of shares, or where the investment represents more than 10 per cent of the company's assets.

If the investment is significant, companies have to disclose:

- the name of the investment;
- the country of incorporation (together with the country of registration, if the company is incorporated in Great Britain), or the address if it is unincorporated;
- the size and nature of the investment.

There is a possibility that the DTI will exempt companies from the disclosure requirements if the directors believe that it will be prejudicial and the company trades overseas.

Investments do not necessarily have to be in companies to classify as a fixed asset investment. The Anglo-French paper group, Arjo Wiggins Appleton, showed £103.1 million security deposits on its 1996 balance sheet. These were held as fixed assets 'in order to secure lower finance costs'. The group 'provided these deposits as security for lease obligations in respect of certain sale and lease-back obligations'.

• Other disclosure requirements

 The Companies Act requires that where a company has material fixed-asset investments, the accounts should disclose in the parent's balance sheet:

- shares in group undertakings;
- loans to group undertakings;
- interests in associated undertakings;
- other participating interests;
- loans to associated undertakings and participating interests;
- other investments other than loans;
- other loans;
- own shares (these cannot be legally be held by the company as its own investment, but you may see companies including the shares in fixed asset investments when they are held for employee share option schemes).

SUMMARY Most other investments are in companies. The accounting requirements are different for listed and unlisted investments, and additional information is given for significant investments.

Listed investments
Investments in companies listed on a stock exchange should be divided into those listed in the UK, and those listed overseas. They will be shown at cost, and the market value should be disclosed if this is different from the cost.

Unlisted investments
Unlisted investments should be shown at cost or valuation.

Significant investments
An investment will be classified as a significant investment under the Companies Act if either of the following applies:

- the company holds 10 per cent or more of the nominal value of any class of shares;
- the investment represents more than 10 per cent of the company's assets.

Companies must disclose the following information for significant investments:

- who they are;

▶

- where they are based;
- the proportion of the company that they own.

If a company owns 20 per cent or more of an undertaking and decides not to account for it as an associated company, it must disclose:
- the reason for its decision in the notes to the accounts;
- the total capital and reserves and the profit, or loss, for the most recent year.

Listed companies also have to disclose the following information if they own 20 per cent or more of a company:

- the principle country of operation (this can be different from where they are incorporated);
- the issued capital and debt securities;
- the percentage interest in each class of security.

JARGON **Associated undertaking**   A company, partnership, or association where the company has a participating interest, and exercises significant influence.

Equity method of accounting   Equity accounting is consolidation on one line of the balance sheet. The group's share of the associates' total net assets is shown on the group balance sheet. Consequently, the individual assets and liabilities are not shown. The group's share of the associates' operating profit and subsequent items is shown on the consolidated profit and loss account.

Gross equity method of accounting   This is used in the UK for accounting for joint ventures and is an expansion of the information provided by the equity method on the balance sheet and profit and loss account. The net investment is expanded to show the underlying gross assets and liabilities. The joint venture's turnover is also shown on the consolidated profit and loss account.

Joint venture   A long-term investment in a business that trades in its own right and is jointly controlled contractually with other parties.

Participating interest   The investing company can influence the operational and financial decisions of another undertaking.

Proportional consolidation   A method of consolidation often used for joint ventures. The company reports its interests in the income, expenses, assets and liabilities of the joint venture. These are either combined with other group items or may be shown separately.

Significant investment   Defined by the Companies Act as one where the company holds 10 per cent or more of the nominal value of any class of share or where the investment is more than 10 per cent of the company's assets. Additional disclosures are required for significant investments.

Subsidiary   A company that is controlled by another company.

10 The balance sheet: stock

This chapter covers:

- **Valuing stock**
- **The stock ratios**

● INTRODUCTION

Stock is one of the most important items in many companies balance sheets, and the valuation of stock will have a direct impact on a company's reported profits. Stock shows on the balance sheet because of the matching principle. This says that we should match our costs to our revenues. Consequently, anything that is unsold or not consumed will show as stock at the balance sheet date. The prudence principle means that the stock should be shown on the balance sheet at the lower of cost and net realisable value. (Net realisable value is defined as the selling price less any further costs to completion, sales, marketing and distribution costs.) This limits the costs that can be charged to stock.

Surprisingly, given its importance, there is no clear definition of stock. The accounting standard (SSAP 9, *Stocks and Long-Term Contracts*) requires the sub-classification of stocks to be 'in a manner which is appropriate to the business and so as to indicate the amounts held in each of the main categories'. It does include a list of the sort of items that could be included in stock:

- goods or other assets purchased for resale;
- consumable stores;
- raw materials and components purchased for incorporation into products for sale;
- products and services in intermediate stages of completion;
- long-term contract balances;
- finished goods.

The Companies Act requires stocks to be disclosed under the following sub-headings:

- raw materials and consumables;
- work in progress;
- finished goods and goods for resale;
- payments on account (for items yet to be received).

Companies can adapt these statutory headings if they feel that it provides a better reflection of the stock that they hold. Therefore, additional classifications can be used, and we can see in Extract 10.1 from Taylor Woodrow's 1996 accounts that land and buildings can be included in stock.

Extract 10.1 **STOCKS (TAYLOR WOODROW)**

	1996	1995
	£m	£m
Raw materials and consumables	2.3	1.8
Finished goods and goods for resale	23.5	19.7
Residential developments		
Land	166.6	176.7
Development and construction costs	177.4	170.6
Commercial, industrial and mixed development properties	62.7	57.7
	432.5	426.5

This is acceptable as:

● costs have been incurred in their production or purchase;
● it is intended that they will be sold in the near future;
● the assets cannot be classified as fixed assets.

Companies will generally show the total stock on the balance sheet and will disclose the detail in the notes.

When looking at stock it should also be recognised that:

● Not all items included as stock are intended for resale. Consumable stores, which are things like oil for the machines, are included in stock, but will never be sold. They will be used within the business.
● Not all stock is tangible. For example work in progress will include work on long-term contracts.
● A company may hold stocks that are subject to reservation of title clauses. The accounting principle of substance over form means that it will still show on the company's accounts, unless they are part of consignment stock where they may, or may not, be shown.
● Consignment stock is treated slightly differently. It is essentially the same as stock covered by a reservation of title clause. It is held by one party, but legally owned by another. Consignment stock is covered by one of the accounting rules (FRS 5, *Accounting for the Substance of Transactions*). This says that consignment stock should show on the accounts of the party who has the risks and rewards of ownership. To help companies identify who has the risks and rewards four variables have been identified:
   (1) the manufacturer's right of return;
   (2) the customer's right of return;
   (3) the stock transfer price and deposits;
   (4) the customer's right to use the stock.

FRS 5 became effective for accounting periods ending on or after 22 September 1994. The accounting for consignment stock and sale and repurchase agreements (common in property companies and distilleries, where stock may be held for a number of years) has changed significantly. The stock now appears on the accounts of the party who benefits from the stock and who has all the risks associated with ownership.

● VALUING STOCK

To calculate the value of goods used in sales companies have to measure the volume of units that have been used in sales, and calculate their value.

Measuring the volume of goods used in sales is theoretically very simple, all companies use some form of stocktaking. This would follow the procedure shown below:

	Opening stock	
Plus	Purchases	
Equals	Goods available	
Less	Closing stock	*shown on the balance sheet*
Equals	Goods used in sales	*charged to the profit and loss account*

However, anyone who has been involved in stocktaking knows just how imprecise this measurement can be!

Once the company has measured how many units it has in stock, it then has to value them. Valuing stock accurately is important, small changes in the stock values can have a disproportionate impact on reported profits in businesses where the materials cost is a large proportion of the total costs.

Whilst it is important, in practice valuing stock can be difficult. Some guidance is given in SSAP 9. It defines the cost of stock as the 'cost of purchase ... such costs of conversion ... as are appropriate to that location and condition'. The accounting standard says that the costs of conversion comprise:

- costs which are specifically attributable to units of production (e.g. direct labour, direct expenses and sub-contracted work);
- production overheads;
- other overheads, if any, attributable in the particular circumstances of the business to bringing the product or the service to its present location and condition.

Production overheads are subsequently defined in SSAP 9 to be those 'overheads incurred in respect of materials, labour, or services for production, based on the normal level of activity, taking one year with another'.

Therefore, the cost of stock must include the direct costs, a proportion of production overheads relating to normal activities, and may include a proportion of other overheads as well. It may also include interest on any capital borrowed to finance the production of the stock. The accounting standard argues that the principle of prudence should be applied through the requirement to show stock at the lower of cost and net realisable value, not through the exclusion of relevant costs. This is a logical argument that relies on the auditor's ability to verify net realisable value, and to find his way through the minefield of cost apportionment.

Any manager who has worked in a manufacturing company understands the difficulties involved in allocating overheads. It is an area fraught with difficulties, involving many, often arbitrary, judgements. If you asked four accountants how a cost should be apportioned, you would probably have five different views! Thus, the allocation of overheads to stock involves judgement and so gives scope for creativity.

Any interest capitalised must be disclosed in the notes to the accounts. This is illustrated in Extract 10.2 below from Guinness's 1996 accounts, where the relatively high costs of financing maturing whisky are clearly disclosed.

Extract 10.2 **STOCKS (GUINNESS)**

	1996 £m	1995 £m
Raw materials and consumables	131	151
Work in progress	16	19
Stocks of maturing whisky and other spirits	1516	1498
Finished goods and goods for resale	204	231
	1867	1899

Stocks of maturing whisky and other spirits include financing costs amounting to £563m (1995 – £563m). The adjustment to stocks credited to the profit and loss account amounted to £Nil (1995 – £Nil) within net trading costs, comprising £112m (1995 – £111m) of interest incurred during the year less £112m (1995 – £111m) in respect of sales during the year.

To illustrate the difficulties of stock valuation we will consider three different types of company:

(1) a retailer who is holding goods for resale;
(2) a manufacturer which has raw materials stock, work in progress and finished goods stock;
(3) a construction company that has long-term contracts.

● The retailer

The retailer has fewer problems as there is only one type of stock, the goods that are held for resale. A number of retailers, for example Marks & Spencer, find it useful to show stock at resale value in their internal accounts. When they publish their accounts they adjust this figure to arrive at 'cost', by deducting the gross margin they would expect to make on the product. For instance if they had a dress that would retail at £70.00 and the estimated gross margin was 50 per cent, the stock value would be £35.00. The accounting standard requires companies using the estimated margin method of valuing stock to test that this is a 'reasonable approximation of the actual cost' before using it in their published accounts.

● The manufacturer

Manufacturing businesses have more problems when trying to determine the cost of goods sold and the value of stock. These problems can be classified as relating to:

- **differential prices:** most manufacturers carry their stock for much longer than retailers, and so are more likely to have goods in stock that have been bought at different prices;
- **complex valuation:** they have different types of stock. At the year end they are likely to have raw materials stock, work in progress and finished goods stock. Labour and overhead costs need to be added to the value of the materials as they move through the production process.

To cope with these difficulties accountants have developed a number of different approaches to valuing stock. The most common methods are valuing stock on:

- a first-in first-out basis (FIFO)
- an average cost
- a last-in first-out (LIFO).

Whatever method is chosen for valuing stocks, companies must disclose any material difference between the cost shown on the balance sheet and the replacement cost of stock.

EXAMPLE   We will use the following example to illustrate the impact of using the different methods.

		Units	Unit cost £	Total £
1 January	Opening stock	1 500	1.00	1 500
28 February	Purchases	2 000	1.05	2 100
1 April	Purchases	1 500	1.06	1 590
30 June	Purchases	2 000	1.08	2 160
31 August	Purchases	2 200	1.10	2 420
30 November	Purchases	1 500	1.13	1 695
		10 700		11 465
31 December	Closing stock	1 000		

To determine the cost of sales we must ascertain the value of the closing stock.

First in, first out

This applies the principle of stock rotation to stock valuation. The first goods into the warehouse are assumed to be the first despatched to the customer, therefore, it will be the latest deliveries that will be in stock.

The value of stock shown on the balance sheet will be £1130 (1000 units times the latest price of £1.13) and the cost of sales charged to the profit and loss account will be £10 335 (11 465 – 1130).

Average cost

A weighted average cost is used, as unfortunately a simple average will not give the degree of accuracy required. This is illustrated below.

A simple average cost per unit would be:

$$\frac{£1.00 + £1.05 + £1.06 + £1.08 + £1.10 + £1.13}{6} = £1.07 \text{ per unit}$$

This would mean that £10 379 (9700 x 1.07) would be charged to the profit and loss account and stocks would be £1070. Unfortunately, when we use a simple average the addition of the stock and the cost of sales does not equal the total cost of purchases, £11 465. The stock and the cost of sales total £11 449. To be exactly right a weighted average must be used.

A weighted cost per unit would be:

$$\frac{(1500 \times £1.00)+(2000 \times £1.05)+(1500 \times £1.06)+(2000 \times £1.08)+(2200 \times £1.10)+(1500 \times £1.13)}{10\ 700}$$

= £1.0714953

The extra decimal places ensure the accuracy! Using the weighted average gives cost of sales of £10 393.504 and closing stock of £1071.4953. These add up to the total cost of purchases, £11 465.

167

Last in, first out

Last in, first out charges the most recent deliveries into the profit and loss account. From our earlier example, the closing stock on the balance sheet will be shown at £1000 and the cost of sales in the profit and loss account will be £10 465. As this does not reflect the commercial reality, where the oldest will be used first, SSAP 9 only allows this if it is necessary to ensure the accounts show a true and fair view.

Continuing with our example, the cost of sales would be £10 465 and the stock £1000. However, our example is too simple, to operate LIFO properly companies would have to calculate the last in at the time of making the sale. This means that they would have to have a complicated accounting system to cope with the demands of operating LIFO. It also has the additional disadvantage that it is not allowed for tax purposes in the UK.

The three methods of valuing stock will give different profits and different stock values on the balance sheet:

	Cost of sales £	Stock values £
First in, first out	10 335.00	1130.00
Weighted average	10 393.50	1071.50
Last in, first out	10 465.00	1000.00

If we consider the effect on the profit and loss account:

	FIFO £	**Average** £	**LIFO** £
Turnover	18 000.00	18 000.00	18 000.00
Materials	(10 335.00)	(10 393.50)	(10 465.00)
Staff costs	(4 000.00)	(4 000.00)	(4 000.00)
Other costs	(2 000.00)	(2 000.00)	(2 000.00)
Operating profit	1 665.00	1 606.50	1 535.00

Last in, first out gives us the smallest profit, but is unlikely to be seen in a UK company, as LIFO should only be used if it is the only method that would show a true and fair view, and is not allowed for tax purposes.

Other costing methods

There are other methods of costing that may be used to value stock that will be found in accounts. Whilst they may not be widely used in the UK, they are more common overseas. The main alternative methods of costing are discussed below.

Base stock

The base stock level is the minimum amount of stock that a company would need to operate, and it is shown at a fixed price. Any amounts of stock above the base stock are valued differently. Effectively the base stock is treated as though it is a fixed asset as a fixed quantity of stock is shown at a fixed price. This is an allowable method under the Companies Act (s 4 para 25) for valuing raw materials and consumables if:

● the overall value of the stock is not material in assessing the company's state of affairs;
● the quantity, value and composition of the stock is not subject to material variation.

However SSAP 9 implies that using base stock is likely to make the presentation of current assets misleading. Base stock is not allowed for tax purposes in the UK.

Standard cost

This type of costing creates standard costs for the materials, labour and production overhead costs of products. It is part of a company's budgeting process, as it calculates what each product should cost, given some detailed assumptions. These standards are often subsequently revised in the light of the company's performance. The use of standard costing for stock valuation is acceptable under SSAP 9, as long as the standards are reviewed frequently to ensure that they are a reasonable approximation to the actual cost.

Replacement cost

This is where the stock is valued at what it would cost to replace at the balance sheet date. Replacement cost is not an acceptable method of stock valuation if the company is preparing its accounts using the historical-cost convention. However, it is one of the factors to be considered if the company is preparing its accounts under the current-cost convention.

Current cost

This is the lower of replacement cost and net realisable value, and should be used where the costs are being prepared under the current-cost convention. Any resulting profit or loss should be taken through the revaluation reserve.

Including overheads in stock values

These methods give us the basis for calculating the costs of goods used in sales, but do not cope with the problem of including labour and production overhead costs into the value of work in progress and finished goods stock. Our earlier example was very simple, as it showed stock valuation based purely on the materials cost. Direct labour costs, direct manufacturing expenses and manufacturing overheads also have to be included in the valuation of stocks. Most companies' accounting procedures allow them to build in the cost of labour and production overheads as the materials move through the production process. But problems can arise when production falls or rises dramatically, as the procedures assume 'normal' production levels.

We have to define 'the normal level of activity'. The accounting standard gives some guidance in its appendix. It says that companies should consider the plant capacity, the budgeted level of activity, and current and previous year's performance. The problems start when the company has a fall in sales. It then has to determine whether this is a short-term problem or a continuing one. This is illustrated in the following example.

EXAMPLE

A company has a production facility that has been designed to produce 100 000 units a year. In the first year it produced, and sold 94 000 units, in the second 95 000 units, and in the third 96 000 units. This year the company produced 90 000 units, 10 000 of which are still in stock. They have almost achieved their budgeted production of 95 000 units but achieving budget sales has proved more elusive, as they only managed to sell 80 000. The company was operating close to budget until the last quarter, when sales fell off dramatically. The production overheads for the period were £2 million.

The real problem here is trying to define the level of normal activity. The plant has never operated at maximum capacity, although in most businesses 100 per cent efficiency is probably an impossible dream! Average production over the first three years is 95 000 units, the same as the budgeted production and sales for this year. If the overheads were apportioned across 95 000 units, there would be a unit overhead cost of £21.053 (2 000 000 ÷ 95 000) and the overheads allocated to stock would be £210 530. This would be an appropriate allocation if it was believed that the fall in sales was only temporary (for example, customers could have been de-stocking towards the year end and the sales will return to normal levels next year). However, if the fall in sales is thought to be permanent, then the 80 000 units sold would be a more appropriate basis for apportioning the overheads. This would give a unit charge of £25, a total overhead charge to stock of £250 000, an increase of nearly 19 per cent. So, should the overheads be apportioned over 95,000 units or 80,000? This does not just have implications for stock values, it also has implications for the profit and loss account. The company has incurred the £2 million overhead cost, part of which will be charged to stock, and the balance to the profit and loss account (Table 10.1).

Table 10.1 **Overheads charged to profit and loss account and stock**

Overhead allocated to stock based on:	Amount charged to:	
	the profit and loss account	Stock
95 000 units	1 789 470	210 530
80 000 units	1 750 000	250 000

Reducing the level of normal activity flatters profits. The more overhead that is included in the stock value, the higher the profit for the year (but the lower the profit for the next year, unless the company can have a price increase to reflect the increased 'costs'). Whilst the auditors would want to see some consistency, the company could argue that it was taking a prudent view!

Net realisable value

We have been looking at what costs should be assigned to stock, but we must not forget that stock should be shown at the lower of cost or net realisable value. Charging all these costs to stock does not help if the 'cost' then exceeds the net realisable value! But what is net realisable value? The definition, in the accounting standard, has been given in the introduction to this chapter. However, trying to ascertain whether the stock has fallen below its market value, in its current state, is an area for discussion. Small companies, in particular, are loath to make provisions for obsolete stock. Provisioning reduces both profits and net worth.

2 + 2 = 5 There is considerable scope for creative accounting in stock valuation. Stock and profits can be flattered by:

- **changing the method** – in our previous example a move from average cost to FIFO increased profits by £58.50, a number not significant on its own, but it increased operating profits by nearly 4 per cent. The percentage improvement in profits would increase as the materials cost percentage increases. Companies would have to disclose a change in the valuation method in their accounting policies;
- **reducing the level of 'normal activity'** – in the example illustrated above, reducing the normal activity improved profits and stock values;
- **overstating the net realisable value** – companies are required to show stock at the lower of cost and net realisable value, with any writedown in values being charged to the profit and loss account, but net realisable value is a matter of judgement. These provisions are only disclosed separately if it is necessary in order to show a true and fair view.

Analysts in fact have limited information about stock valuations, as the note from the accounting policies of the engineering group IMI's 1996 accounts illustrates (Extract 10.3).

STOCKS (IMI)

STOCKS
Stocks are valued at the lower of cost and net realisable value. In respect of work in progress and finished goods, cost includes all direct costs of production and the appropriate proportion of production overheads.

Therefore, we are forced to rely on our common sense. Is the stock number believable when we look at the company's history of managing stock and the performance of other companies in the industry?

● The construction company

Construction companies have different problems in stock valuation, as large construction contracts often span a number of years. The normal accounting rules are fine when the sales and the purchases are close together, but may be inappropriate when the company is incurring costs over a number of years. If the company waited until the completion of the project before including the contract in the profit and loss account, the accounts would not reflect a true and fair view of their financial performance. They could have high stocks one year and nothing in the following year, as they complete nothing in one year and three contracts in the following year. Both stocks and profits would become very erratic. Treating companies which are involved in long-term contracts in the same way as other companies would render their accounts meaningless.

In view of this, SSAP 9 allows construction companies, and others with long-term contracts, to include both turnover and profit from uncompleted long-term contracts in their profit and loss account. As the contracts are valued on a percentage of completion basis, with profit being taken before completion, the asset is often recorded as a debtor (amounts recoverable on contracts) rather than stock. The amount shown as long-term contract balances as part of stock will have been determined by taking the costs that have been incurred and deducting:

● cost of sales
● foreseeable losses
● payments on account that are not matched by turnover.

The notes to the balance sheet should separately disclose:

● the net cost less any foreseeable losses
● the applicable payments on account.

As profit is taken on percentage of completion, and any unmatched payments on account are deducted for the contract work in progress, it may well mean that there is little or nothing included stock. This illustrated in the following example:

EXAMPLE   A company with a long-term contract has certified work completed of £590 000 during a year. This will be shown as the turnover of the project. It has received a total of £630 000 payments on account from its customer. The total costs incurred on the project during the year are £550 000, of which £500 000 has been transferred to cost of sales.

	£
Project costs incurred during the year	550 000
Transferred to cost of sales	(500 000)
	50 000
Excess of payments on account to be offset against long-term contract balances	(40 000)
Classified as long-term contract balances	**10 000**

The payments in advance were £40 000 greater than the turnover and, therefore, the reported stocks are reduced to £10 000. The balance sheet note on stock should separately disclose the net cost of £50 000 and the applicable payments on account of £40 000. Had the payments on account been £60 000 greater than the turnover, the stock would be eliminated and £10 000 would be payments on account and separately disclosed in creditors. If all of the project costs had been transferred to the profit and loss account the payments on account would be the whole £40 000.

A detailed discussion of accounting for turnover and the profits of long-term contracts can be found in Chapter 13.

SUMMARY

Stocks are an important asset on the balance sheet and their values affect the reported profits of the business. They should be shown at the lower of cost or net realisable value.

Cost
The cost of stock includes production and other overheads that have been incurred by the business to bring the stock into its current condition. Overheads are allocated to stock based on the normal levels of activity. This means there are two problems involved in the allocation of overheads to stock. Companies have to decide on the:

- method of apportionment
- normal activity levels.

Interest may also be charged to stock, and this must be disclosed in the notes to the accounts.

Companies often buy their materials (and other expenses) at different prices through the year, and it is possible to have the same products at different prices in stock. Cost can be calculated in a number of different ways. The main methods used are:

- first in, first out (FIFO) follows the principles of stock rotation and assumes that the most recent deliveries will be found in stock;
- a weighted average price;
- last in, first out (LIFO) is the opposite of FIFO and assumes the most recent deliveries have been charged to the profit and loss account. Whilst this is allowed by the Companies Act, SSAP 9 only allows it to be used when it is necessary for a true and fair view as it does not reflect commercial reality.

Net realisable value
Net realisable value is effectively a market price for the stock in its current condition. The accounting standard defines it as the selling price less any further costs to completion, and sales, marketing and distribution costs.

Long-term contracts
There are special rules that apply to long-term contracts:

- the turnover should be recorded as a contract progresses, rather than when it is completed;

▶

● profit is also recorded when it arises.

Consequently, it is unlikely that large long-term contract balances will be found. Any long-term contract balances are reported net of:

● any payments on account that are in excess of the turnover;
● any foreseeable losses.

INTERNATIONAL DIFFERENCES

International accounting standards

Stocks
Stocks are covered by IAS 2 *Inventories*. SSAP 9 and IAS 2 are broadly similar, with some minor differences on capitalisation of interest and presentation. When valuing stocks, FIFO and weighted average are the benchmark treatment, with LIFO as the allowed alternative. If LIFO is used, the notes should disclose the difference between LIFO and either FIFO or the current cost.

Long-term construction contracts
Long-term construction contracts are covered by IAS 11 *Construction Contracts* which is similar to SSAP 9. The main differences are:

● **Turnover recognition** – when the outcome of a project is uncertain IAS 21 requires that turnover only be recognised to the extent that the costs are probably recoverable.
● **Grouping of contracts** – IAS 11 has detailed definitions of when contracts should be shown separately or grouped. A group of contracts should be treated as a single contract when:
  – they are negotiated as a single package;
  – they are so interrelated that they are in effect a single contract with an overall profit margin;
  – they are performed concurrently, or in a continuous sequence.

Europe

Stocks
The Fourth Directive requires stock to be shown at the lower of cost and market value, with cost being calculated by FIFO, LIFO, a weighted average, or any other similar method. Any adjustments that have been made for tax purposes, should be disclosed in the accounts.

In France, stocks should be shown at the lower of cost or market value, where the market value can be either the net realisable value or the replacement cost. Weighted average is the most common way of determining cost, and LIFO is only permitted in the group accounts. Any related financial costs may be included in work in progress if the production cycle is greater than 12 months. In the individual company accounts you will see tax-deductible provisions for rises in stock prices (*hausse des prix*), however these provisions are not usually shown in the group accounts.

Dutch accounting allows stocks to either be shown on a historical cost or a current value basis. When replacement costs are used the stocks are shown at the lower of replacement value and net realisable value. FIFO and weighted average are the most common methods of valuing stocks, but LIFO is allowed and is fairly common. Base-stock accounting may also be used. If either LIFO or base-stock accounting is used, the current value of the stock must also be shown.

In Germany the tax rules have a large impact on the reported stock values. Stock should be stated at the lower of historical cost, replacement cost, or any other value that is permitted by the tax rules. Cost is usually determined by an average cost, FIFO being the next most common method used. LIFO is allowed where it reflects the stock usage, and may become more popular now that it is allowed for tax purposes. Both tax rules and accounting rules use absorption costing (also known as full costing) for determining the cost, and allow an appropriate proportion of administrative overheads to be included in the cost.

Long-term contracts

In the Netherlands long-term contracts are accounted for on a percentage of completion basis, and the asset would normally be shown as stocks. In France there is no consistency of accounting treatment for long-term contracts; they may be recognised on completion, percentage of completion, or a combination. In Germany contracts are usually recognised on completion, although in certain circumstances the percentage of completion method may be used. This means that German companies have considerable balances of long-term contract work in progress.

Japan

Stocks

Stocks are generally valued at historical cost, although they may be shown at the lower of cost and 'market' (this may be either replacement cost or selling cost). Where cost is used as the basis of valuing stock, there is no requirement under the Commercial Code for it to be written down. The accounting principles prefer that an actual cost should be used, but most companies use a weighted average for valuing their stocks. FIFO, LIFO, or the retail inventory method are also allowed.

Long-term contracts

Long-term contracts are normally recognised on a completed contract basis, but percentage of completion is also allowed.

North America

Stocks

In the USA stock is normally shown at the lower of stock or market value. Market value usually means the current replacement cost, but it cannot be:

- greater than net realisable value; or
- less than net realisable value less the normal profit margin.

LIFO, FIFO, or a weighted average may be used to calculate the cost.

In Canada stock is normally shown at the lower of stock or market value. The Handbook setting out the rules suggests that the term market value should be replaced with replacement cost, net realisable value or net realisable value less normal profit margin. The method chosen by the company should be the one that results in the fairest matching of costs against revenues, regardless of the actual flow of goods. FIFO, LIFO and average cost are common, but other methods can be used if they satisfy the criterion above.

Long-term contracts

Long-term contracts in the USA are divided into cost-plus contracts and other long-term contracts.

- **Cost-plus contracts** – these should be recognised by a method that reflects their realisation. Therefore, the method of accounting reflects the specific circumstances of the contract. So, it could be based on billings, partial deliveries, percentage of completion, or any other method the company felt was appropriate.

- **Other long-term contracts** – the method used should be determined by the circumstances of the project. The percentage-of-completion method would usually be used where the cost estimates and the progress valuation are reasonably reliable. Otherwise the completed contract method should be used.

In Canada long-term contracts can be recognised on a percentage-of-completion basis, as long as it relates appropriately to the work that has been done. The completed contract basis would only be appropriate if either of the following applied:

- the performance consists of the execution of a single act;
- the company cannot reasonably estimate the extent of the progress towards completion.

● THE STOCK RATIOS

As stock is so important to the reported results of a company, we have evolved a number of different ways of assessing a company's control of stock. Companies need to keep a certain level of stock to ensure that their business runs efficiently and so that they can satisfy demand for their products. Managing stock is a balancing act; the company wants to have sufficient stock, but also it wants to minimise its investment in stock. Tying up money in stock can be costly, not only in interest charges, but also in lost opportunities. The company may get a better return investing in fixed assets, or even just placing the money on deposit. All companies try to optimise their investment in stock, having just enough to satisfy demand. The amount of stock a company needs is determined largely by the nature of its business. Large grocers, with sophisticated information systems, can predict demand on a daily basis, whereas for other companies demand can only be predicted annually. Therefore, we need to understand a company's business if we are to understand its stock. However, we can find out useful information from the accounts. We can find out if the company we are analysing is carrying more or less stock than it used to; or more or less stock than other companies in its sector. If the stock is changing, We can discover what proportion of any change in stock has come from changes in the level of sales, and how much has come from changes in the company's practices.

Once the company has achieved their optimum level, stock should be related to the company's sales in a period. If the sales double, it is not unreasonable to assume that the value of stock will double. There are two ways of measuring the company's control of stocks. Either you can see how many times a year the company turns its stock over, or you can work out how many days' stock the company is carrying. There are slightly different ways of making both calculations.

● Stockturn

This shows you how many times a year a company converts its stock into sales. Whilst the principle is simple, the calculation is open to debate.

Stocks relate to the merchandise that has been sold in the period for a retailer, and to the materials, labour and overheads used in sales for a manufacturer. Therefore, we would want to compare stocks with the materials that have been used. We do not necessarily have these figures available to us in the published profit and loss account. In the UK, only a Format 2 profit and loss account (unfortunately the least popular presentation) will give us this information. Even if we did have the information, manufacturing businesses will also include direct labour and a proportion of overheads in their stock values. So, either way, we are unlikely to be able to get an accurate figure.

Some analysts would use cost of sales as an approximation to production costs, but this can mean different things to different companies. If you want to compare companies you need to look at stocks in relation to turnover. Although it is wrong, it is consistently wrong and enables you to compare one company with another! You must remember that you are only trying to identify whether the company has a problem, or a commercial advantage. You are always going to be unable to quantify anything accurately as the balance sheet has already been managed to give you the best view. We could use cost of sales if we were only analysing one company, as it probably more nearly reflects production costs. However, if we were comparing companies internationally, or within a sector, we would use turnover. Most people use turnover. Whichever way you choose to calculate stockturn, you should still get the same trend (unless profit margins have fluctuated wildly during the period), although not exactly the same answer as we shall see!

If we look at the stockturn calculation using both turnover and cost of sales as the numerator:

Turnover based

$$\frac{\text{Turnover}}{\text{Stock}}$$

Cost of sales based

$$\frac{\text{Cost of sales}}{\text{Stock}}$$

EXAMPLE To illustrate the stock ratios, we will calculate all the stock ratios using the following information:

	Year 1	Year 2	Year 3	Year 4
Turnover	1000	1050	1150	1300
Cost of sales	(400)	(420)	(450)	(510)
Other operating costs	(300)	(310)	(330)	(350)
Operating profit	(300)	320	370	440
Stock at the year end	100	110	125	150

We can see at a glance that the company is carrying its stock for longer. Sales in the period have risen by 30 per cent, and stocks by 50 per cent. Now we need to quantify the size of the problem. In our example the stockturn for the company would be:

	Year 1	Year 2	Year 3	Year 4
Stock turn:				
Turnover based	10 times	9.6 times	9.2 times	8.7 times
Cost of sales based	*4.0 times*	*3.8 times*	*3.6 times*	*3.4 times*

You can see how using turnover, rather than cost of sales, has the effect of understating stocks. As this number is not calculated in a way that ensures its accuracy, it is important that it is looked at in context. Is the control of stocks improving, does this company have lower stocks than other companies in the sector?

It is also important to recognise that the way we calculate the ratio can affect the answer that we get.

Cost of sales as a percentage of turnover

We can see that the company is converting its stock into sales at a slower rate each year. The trend we show is exactly the same whether we use turnover or cost of sales, as the company's cost of sales is at a fairly constant percentage of turnover:

	Year 1	Year 2	Year 3	Year 4
Cost of sales as a percentage of turnover	40.0%	40.0%	39.1%	39.2%

If it had not been fairly constant, we would have had a different trend for the turnover-based ratio compared to the cost-of-sales based ratio. But a changing cost of sales ratio could tell us something else about the company:

- there could be changes in the product mix, this may lead to changes in the required stock levels too;
- there could be changes in the costs that are not passed on to the customer;
- the company could be more, or less, efficient and is not passing on the effect of efficiency changes to its customers;
- if the cost of sales is falling, the company could be investing more in fixed assets to reduce costs and keeping the benefits for itself.

This list is far from exhaustive, but we should have information elsewhere in the accounts that may support one, or more, of the possibilities.

● Stock days

Another way of looking at stock is to calculate how many days stock the company has at the year end. This tells us how many days of sales are currently being held as stock and is calculated using one of the following formulas:

Turnover based

$$\frac{\text{Stock}}{\text{Turnover}} \times 365$$

Cost of sales based

$$\frac{\text{Stock}}{\text{Cost of sales}} \times 365$$

We are multiplying by 365 as we are looking at the sales for the year and the stock on a given day; 365 represents the number of days in the accounting period.

Using our earlier example, the stock days would be:

	Year 1	Year 2	Year 3	Year 4
Stock days:				
Turnover based	36.5	38.2	39.7	42.1
Cost of sales based	*91.3*	*95.6*	*101.4*	*107.4*

Over the four years the company's stock levels have moved from 36.5 days (based on sales) to 42.1 days. The company is carrying much more stock than it used to, but does this really matter?

Using either stockturn or stock days we can calculate what the company's investment in stock would have been, if the stock had been maintained at the previous years levels by using the formulas below:

Stockturn

$$\frac{\text{Turnover / cost of sales}}{\text{Previous year's stockturn}}$$

Stock days

$$\frac{\text{Turnover / cost of sales}}{365} \times \text{previous year's stock days}$$

Whether we use turnover or cost of sales, stockturn or stock days, we can calculate the extra investment that the company has had to have in stock. Different ways of calculating the investment will give slightly different answers, but the principle remains the same. The calculation of the additional investment is illustrated, using a turnover-based stockturn, in Table 10.2.

Table 10.2	**The investment in stock**

	Year 3	Year 4	Year 4 stock @ Year 3 stockturn	Additional investment in stock
Turnover	1150	1300		
Stock value	125	150	141.3	8.7
Stockturn	9.2	8.7		

We know that the company is now holding more stock than it used to, and this has meant that it has had to have another 8.7 tied up in stock during year four. This is almost 6 per cent of the stock value for year four. Had the company been able to maintain stocks at the levels of year one, it would only have required 130 (based on turnover) or 127.5 (based on cost of sales) invested in stock. (If we use the turnover number, we eliminate the difference that has come from the reduction in the cost of sales as a percentage of turnover from 40 per cent to 39.2 per cent.) Every extra day the company holds its stock costs 3.56 (total stock of 150 ÷ number of days stock held 42.1). If the stocks could have been maintained at the same levels as the first year, the company would have had another 20 to invest elsewhere in the business.

We know that stocks appear to have increased, we now need to think about why this might have happened. Analysis is not about measurement, it is about understanding! A few of the possible reasons could be:

● The company could be forced to carry more stocks because the nature of their business has changed. Possible changes could be:
  – a change in the mix of products that the company sells;
  – its customer base may have changed;
  – the market has become more volatile and it is more difficult to predict demand patterns.
● The volume of the stock may be unchanged, but the costs may have increased. This could be due to:
  – negotiations with suppliers occur towards the end of the year, so the increased costs are reflected in stocks, but have yet to work through to sales. If we had the opportunity to question the company, we would simply ask that question, but we could check our guess by looking at stock in relation to the following year's sales (we obviously cannot do this for the last year). This gives some interesting results with stock days (based on turnover) running at a fairly constant level of around 35 days;
  – a combination of material cost increases and a competitive market where the company is unable to pass on the price increases. However, this does not fit well in our example, as we would expect the cost of sales as a percentage of turnover to be increasing, rather than falling.
● The company could be buying in larger quantities to get better prices. This should be reflected in falling cost of sales.

SUMMARY

When analysing a company we need to know whether any changes in its stocks have arisen from changes in sales or from changes in management practice. We should be able to spot changes in stock at a glance; ratios will help us measure them. We have two ratios that help us to measure any changes in stocks levels: stockturn and stock days.

Stockturn

This tells us how many times in the period the company has converted its stock into sales. It is calculated by dividing either the turnover, or the cost of sales, by the stock. The higher the number, the shorter the conversion period.

Stock days

This tells us how many days sales (or cost of sales) are held in stock. The stock is divided by the turnover, or cost of sales, and then multiplied by the number of days in the accounting period.

Once we have identified a trend in the management of stocks, we should try to understand why the management practice may have changed. There will often be other information in the accounts that we can use to help us understand why the stock levels have changed.

JARGON

Base stock A method of stock valuation that values the minimum stock that a company must have in order to operate, at a fixed price. Any stock above this minimum would be valued differently.

Consignment stock Stock that is held by one party, but legally owned by another.

Current cost The lower of the net realisable value and the replacement cost.

First in, first out (FIFO) A method of stock valuation that charges the oldest deliveries to the profit and loss account, and shows the most recent deliveries as stock.

Last in, first out (LIFO) A method of stock valuation that charges the most recent deliveries to the profit and loss account, and shows the oldest deliveries as stock.

Net realisable value The selling price less any further costs to completion, sales, marketing and distribution costs.

Percentage of completion A method of accounting for long-term contracts where turnover is recorded as the contract progresses, and profit is recorded as it arises. This means that contract work in progress is rarely shown in a company using this method to account for long-term contracts.

Replacement cost The cost of replacing the stock at the balance sheet date. It is used to determine the current cost of stock.

Standard cost A budgeted cost, based on detailed assumptions. This can be used for stock valuation as long as it is frequently reviewed and approximates to the actual cost.

11 The balance sheet: other current assets

This chapter covers:

- **Debtors**
- **Businesses held for resale**
- **Investments**
- **Cash at bank and in hand**

● DEBTORS

Debtors represent amounts of money that are owed to the business. This is not exclusively the amounts that are owed for sales. Any money that the company is owed, together with any prepayments, will be shown as part of debtors. In the UK debtors will comprise the total amounts owed to the company, including money that is not realisable within a year.

 Schedule 4 of the Companies Act requires that debtors be sub-divided into:

- trade debtors – this is money owed for the company's sales;
- other debtors – this is money owed for sales of fixed assets and other non-trading items;
- prepayments and accrued income;
- unpaid, called-up share capital (discussed in Chapter 5);
- amounts owed by group undertakings – this will be shown on the parent company's balance sheet only (discussed in detail in Chapter 19);
- amounts owed by undertakings in which the company has a participating interest (discussed in Chapter 9).

The Act requires that amounts falling due within a year, and more than a year, should be disclosed for each heading. Long-term debtors are not required to be discounted to present values. In addition to the types of debtors identified in the Act, other items that can be included in debtors are:

- *tax-related* – these could include corporation and advance corporation tax recoverable, or deferred tax (see Chapter 14);
- *pension fund prepayments* (see Chapter 13);
- *finance-lease receivables* (see Chapter 8);
- *loan notes* (see Chapter 6).

The different debtors that can be found in company accounts is illustrated by the following extract from Unilever's 1996 accounts.

Extract 11.1 DEBTORS (UNILEVER)

	£ million	
Due within one year:		
Trade debtors	3107	3325
Prepayments and accrued income	289	313
Other debtors	744	762
	4140	4400
Due after more than one year:		
Prepayments to funded pension schemes	305	191
Other debtors	132	133
	437	324
Total debtors	4577	4724

From this we can see that the amounts owed to a company come from a variety of sources. Most companies would show total debtors on the face of the balance sheet, disclosing the detail in the notes.

One of the sad facts of life is that not everyone pays the money that they owe. In common with other current assets, debtors should be shown at the lower of cost or net realisable value. This means that companies are required to make provisions for doubtful debts, and the value of debtors shown on the balance sheet should be after making doubtful debt provision. These doubtful debt provisions are not usually disclosed, although some companies do disclose them, as the extract from British Steel's 1997 accounts shows.

Extract 11.2 DEBTORS (BRITISH STEEL)

	The Company		The Group	
	1997 **£m**	1996 £m	**1997** **£m**	1996 £m
Amounts falling due within one year:				
Trade debtors	**688**	733	**1287**	1565
Less allowances for doubtful debts	**(22)**	(26)	**(36)**	(38)
	666	707	**1251**	1527

If we are analysing a company we need to know the composition of the debtors, and the split between the debtors that are due within a year, and more than a year. If the company has a lot of money falling due in more than a year, we would ideally like to know precisely what it is and when it is likely to be paid. Unfortunately companies do not have to disclose this unless it is necessary for a true and fair view.

● Trade debtors

Trade debtors are one of the most important components of debtors, as they relate to the company's sales during the period. In some businesses they are more important than in others. In its 1997 accounts Tesco, on a turnover of £13 887 million, had no trade debtors – do you get an invoice at the checkout? Whereas, in its 1997 accounts British Steel had £666 million net trade debtors, on a turnover of £7224 million. In a manufacturing business such as British Steel, debtors will always feature in the accounts.

Debtor days

Debtors relate to the sales that have been made in the period and this is how we measure them. In the same way that we calculated stock days, we can calculate the number of days that it is taking the company to collect money from its customers. The formula for calculating debtor days, also called the *collection period*, is:

$$\frac{\text{Trade debtors} \times 365}{\text{Turnover}}$$

Unfortunately we are comparing slightly different numbers. The turnover excludes VAT, whereas the debtors includes it. Some businesses do show their VAT-inclusive sales, but unfortunately they tend to be companies like Tesco, which do not have any trade debtors. So, as usual, we are working with imperfect information.

This calculation of debtor days is illustrated by using the following example:

EXAMPLE

	Year 1	Year 2	Year 3	Year 4
Turnover	1000	1050	1150	1300
Trade debtors	170	190	220	260

We can see that the company is taking longer to collect its money than it used to, as sales have increased by 30 per cent but debtors have increased by over 50 per cent. This is quantified by using the debtor days ratio:

	Year 1	Year 2	Year 3	Year 4
Debtor days	62.1	66	69.8	73

The debtor days have increased by almost 11 days over the four years. This is important as every extra day's credit the company gives its customers in year four requires the company to find another 3.562 in cash (1300 ÷ 365). Over the past four years the debtors have increased partly through increased sales values and partly through extended credit terms.

There are different ways of showing the collection period. Whilst it is usually expressed in days, it could also be expressed in months, or debtors could be expressed as a percentage of turnover.

	Year 1	Year 2	Year 3	Year 4
Debtor months	2.0	2.2	2.3	2.4
Debtors as a percentage of turnover	17.0%	18.1%	19.1%	20.0%

However we choose to calculate it, the company is giving longer payment terms to its customers. The one thing that we can say for certain is that this will not have been through choice. All companies would like to be like Tesco and get cash for their sales, but unfortunately life is not like that. Companies have to give the same credit as everyone else in the industry, otherwise they do not get the sales! But it is a balance, extending credit is essentially the same as a price cut. However, some companies will give extended credit to get a large order.

Debtor days could increase for a number of reasons. The company could be giving more credit, or its customers may be experiencing cash flow problems themselves and are delaying payment, or are just unwilling to pay. (This could be a particular problem if the company has a few, very large, customers who may almost be able to dictate their own credit terms.) Whilst some companies are more efficient at credit control than others, large companies do put a lot of effort into controlling their debtors, and would monitor the *age profile* of their debtors. (A debtor age profile analyses the total debtor figure into amounts outstanding for less than 30 days, 30 to 60 days, 61 days to 90 days, and over 90 days. Unfortunately it is only prepared as an internal control document.)

One thing that we must recognise is that increasing debtor days is not necessarily a sign of inefficiency. The debtor figure represents the amount of money that the company is owed by its customers at the year end. Small changes in the pattern of trading can distort the ratio. This is illustrated in the example below, which is an extension of our previous example.

The sales in the last quarter of the financial year are a slightly greater percentage (+2 per cent) of the total sales in year four than in year three. As the trade debtors are the sales that have not been paid for, these should relate to the sales that were made in the last quarter. If you recalculate debtor days based on the sales for the last quarter (multiplying by 91 – the number of days in the period) debtor days have improved slightly, rather than deteriorated ([260 ÷ 500] x 91 days = 47.3 days, compared to 47.4 days based on the same period last year).

Table 11.1 **Analysis of sales by quarter**

	Quarter 1	Quarter 2	Quarter 3	Quarter 4	Total
Year 4					
Sales	200	300	300	500	1300
Percentage of annual sales	15.4%	23.1%	23.1%	38.5%	
Debtors at the year end				260	
Debtor days based on last quarter's sales				47.3	
Year 3					
Sales	190	270	270	420	1150
Percentage of annual sales	16.5%	23.5%	23.5%	36.5%	
Debtors at the year end				220	
Debtor days based on last quarter's sales				47.7	

Consequently, if the company says elsewhere in the accounts that sales increased in the last period, expect that the calculated debtor days will also have increased. A fall in sales may well lead to an apparent improvement in credit control. A similar distortion could occur if the company sells high-value items. A small increase in its sales towards the end of the year would be reflected in higher debtors.

● Factoring

An expanding manufacturing business can rapidly run into cash flow problems. Sales double, stocks and debtors will probably double, and they will be unable to fund this from the doubling of their creditors. We saw the trend during the early 1990s for large companies to delay paying smaller companies, recognising them as a source of interest-free borrowing. (a practice not too dissimilar to our payments to the electricity companies – how many of us paid on the blue bill before discounts were given for prompt payment?) As a result, companies have found ways of using their debtors to generate finance. Increasingly, companies have turned to factoring as a way of releasing cash from their debtors.

In *factoring* the company sells the invoices to a factoring house (which is usually part of a bank or an international factoring organisation), which will then give the company up to an agreed percentage (usually 80 per cent) of the invoice value as cash. The balance will be paid (less the factoring company's fees) on the payment of the invoice by the customer.

There are different types of factoring agreements, they can be:

- **disclosed:** the customer deals with the factor, rather than the company, that manages the sales ledgers);
- **undisclosed:** the customer deals with the company, which still manages the sales ledger in the normal way. This is also called invoice discounting;
- **with recourse:** if the customer does not pay, either in full or by a certain date, the company will repay any advances that have been received from the factor;
- **non-recourse:** the factor cannot force the company to repay in the event of non-payment by the customer;
- **with partial recourse:** some non-refundable proceeds are received by the company.

FRS 5 (*Accounting for the Substance of Transactions*) discusses the accounting treatment of the different types of factoring agreements and invoice discounting agreements in Application Note C. All companies whose agreements have any recourse back to the company will have to disclose in the notes to the accounts:

- that they are factoring
- the amount of factored debtors at the end of the year.

Accounting treatment

The underlying principle of FRS 5 is that the party who has the significant risks and benefits from the agreement should show the transaction in its accounts. Consequently, the specific accounting treatment will depend on the nature of the recourse involved in the agreement.

Non-recourse agreements

Neither the debtors nor the advance from the factor will show on the balance sheet. It will be *derecognised*. The cost of factoring will be charged to the profit and loss account.

Limited recourse agreements

The debtors will be reduced by the amount of any non-recourse advances, to show a net debtor position. This is called a *linked presentation* in the standard. This should only be used where the company selling the invoices cannot be forced to re-acquire them in the future. The non-recourse advances could take several forms. For example, they could be in the form of credit insurance, or a credit protection policy. The cost of factoring will be separately disclosed in the notes to the accounts. The factoring cost will be split between any administration costs and interest charges, which should show on the appropriate lines of the profit and loss account.

Full recourse agreements

The gross debtors will be shown on the balance sheet, less any provisions for bad debts and the advances from factors will show as a separate line within the notes to the creditors. This is called *separate presentation*. The factoring cost will be split between any administration costs and interest charges, which should show on the appropriate lines of the profit and loss account.

INTERNATIONAL DIFFERENCES

There are few international differences in accounting for debtors. The Fourth Directive requires separate disclosure of any debtors falling due in more than a year in member states. These would not be classified as current assets in either the USA or Canada.

Some countries' provisions are affected by the tax rules. In Germany a provision must be taken through the profit and loss account to be allowable for tax. Japanese companies tend to provide at the maximum level that is allowable for tax purposes, regardless of whether it is true and fair.

SUMMARY

Types of debtor

Not all debtors shown in a set of UK accounts are current, as some fall due after a year. The notes to the accounts will disclose the separate components to the debtors. The debtors are not necessarily related to sales, they could be:

- trade debtors – these debtors represent the money owed for sales during the year;
- other debtors – this is money owed for sales of fixed assets and other non-trading items;
- prepayments and accrued income;
- any unpaid called-up share capital;
- pension fund prepayments;
- finance-lease receivables in finance company's accounts;
- loans.

Additionally, a parent company's accounts must also legally disclose:

- any amounts owed by group undertakings – this will be shown on the parent company's balance sheet only;
- any amounts owed by undertakings in which the company has a participating interest.

TRADE DEBTORS

Trade debtors are one of the most important elements of the debtor figure in most companies' accounts. All companies should be trying to reduce their investment in debtors, to give as little credit as possible. However, a balance has to be struck between shortening the collection period and gaining sales. Extending the credit period is effectively the same as a price discount.

▶

It is possible to quantify how long it takes the company to collect money from its customers. The commonest way of calculating this is to calculate the debtor days. This is simply calculated by using the following formula:

$$\frac{\text{Trade debtors}}{\text{Turnover}} \times \text{ the number of days in the accounting period (365 if it is a year)}$$

The results can be misleading if the company's sales patterns change from one year to the next, or are erratic.

Factoring

Factoring and invoice discounting are ways of using debtors to obtain finance. The company assigns the legal ownership of the debtors to the factoring company in exchange for a cash payment. The factor may, or may not, provide a credit control service for the company. The cash payment may, or may not, be refundable. If the payment is refundable, the factoring agreement is said to be 'with recourse', if not it is a 'non-recourse' agreement.

FRS 5 applies to factoring agreements, therefore, if there is any recourse to the company, the debtors should be shown on the accounts to the extent of any recourse. The advances from factors would then be shown as a creditor. If the factor has no recourse back to the company, neither the debtor, nor the advance would be shown on the company's accounts.

● BUSINESSES HELD FOR RESALE

Whilst technically businesses held for resale could be included in current-asset investments they are usually shown separately in the current assets. FRS 2 (*Accounting for Subsidiary Undertakings*) requires these businesses to be shown at the lower of cost and net realisable value.

● INVESTMENTS

Investments shown as part of current assets are not intended to be held long term. They are held on a short-term basis, either as a way of generating income from its cash balance, or the company intends to sell the investments. The following may be disclosed as current asset investments in a company's accounts:

● money market and other deposits;
● listed and government securities;
● certificates of deposit. This is a way of getting higher interest on deposits whilst still retaining the flexibility of cash. The company deposits cash with the bank for an agreed period of time. In exchange the bank issues the certificate of deposit, which is a negotiable instrument. If the company needs the money sooner it can sell the certificate;
● certificates of tax deposit;
● commercial paper (discussed in Chapter 6);
● options (see Chapter 6 and Chapter 20);.
● short-term local authority bonds.

● Accounting for short-term investments

Investments are usually shown at the lower of cost (including any expenses associated with the purchase of the investment) and the net realisable value. However, the Companies Act also allows investments to be shown at:

- market value (this is called *marking to market*);
- any method that the directors feel is appropriate to the company circumstances.

The valuation method, and the reasons for selecting it, should be disclosed in the accounts. As companies have considerable flexibility in the valuation, and subsequently of the accounting, this note should be read carefully. It is also unclear in the Companies Act whether the gains, and losses, relating to investments shown at market value should be taken to the profit and loss account.

The notes to the accounts will categorise the investments, with listed investments shown on London and overseas markets shown separately. Additional information is required for significant investments (see Chapter 9).

The following extract from Boots' 1997 accounts illustrates the disclosures that are given in the note on current asset investments:

Extract 11.3   **CURRENT ASSET INVESTMENTS AND DEPOSITS (BOOTS)**

	Group 1997 **£m**	Group 1996 £m	**Parent** 1997 **£m**	Parent 1996 £m
Listed investments	**0.1**	199.8	–	199.7
Short-term deposits	**592.1**	683.1	**573.2**	657.9
Certificates of tax deposit	**10.8**	11.0	**10.8**	11.0
	603.0	893.9	**584.0**	868.6
Market value of investments	**0.1**	202.8	–	202.7

The income from current asset investments is not separately disclosed, it is combined with that of fixed asset investments.

INTERNATIONAL DIFFERENCES

International accounting standards

Current asset investments are covered by IAS 25 (*Accounting for Investments*). The definition of a current asset investment is different from the UK one of not being held for continuing use. IAS 25 defines it as readily realisable and intended to be held for up to a year. The investments must be shown at either market value, or the lower of cost and market value. If they are shown at market value, the gains or losses can either be shown in the profit and loss account, or the revaluation reserve.

In other countries there is less flexibility on the valuation of current assets investments and they are usually shown at the lower of cost and market value. The market value is often disclosed in the notes to the accounts.

SUMMARY There is considerable flexibility in the valuation of current asset investments, consequently the notes on the company's accounting policy should be read carefully. Most investments are shown at the lower of cost and net realisable value.

● CASH AT BANK AND IN HAND

The definition of cash is not covered by the Companies Act, it is defined only for the purposes of preparing the cash flow statement by FRS 1 (*Cash Flow Statements*). It is hard to believe that the large sums that are often shown in company's accounts are not placed on deposit, and probably not always repayable on demand.

Groups often have companies in the group with cash balances, and others with bank overdrafts. The group usually then comes to an agreement with the bank to offset the bank overdrafts against the cash balances. The amounts can only be offset in the accounts where a legal right of set-off exists, and where the company has the right to insist on net settlement (this has arisen following FRS 5). These offset agreements are often disclosed in the notes to the accounts.

JARGON   **Debtor days** The number of days of credit that a company is giving to its customers. This is based on year-end debtors and total turnover, and can be distorted by a number of factors.

Factoring A way of raising finance from debtors. Invoices are sold to a factoring company, which then advances an agreed percentage of the invoice value. The balance, less the factor's fee, is given to the company when the invoice has been paid.

Marking to market Showing investments at the current market value.

Offset agreement A legal agreement, with a bank, allowing bank overdrafts to be set off against cash balances.

Trade debtors The amount of money owed to a company for the sales that it has made during the period.

12 The balance sheet: creditors and other liabilities

This chapter covers:

- **Creditors**
- **Provisions for liabilities and charges**
- **Contingent liabilities**
- **Capital commitments**

CREDITORS

The Companies Act requires that companies disclose the following categories of material creditors in their balance sheets, analysed between those falling due within a year, and more than a year:

- payments received on account
- trade creditors
- amounts owed to group undertakings
- amounts owed to undertakings in which the company has a participating interest
- other creditors, including taxation and social security
- accruals and deferred income.

The disclosure is usually more detailed than that laid out in the balance-sheet format. Proposed dividends are usually shown separately from other creditors. Taxation and social security are normally shown separately; analysed between corporation tax, and other taxes and social security.

The different types of creditor

Payments received on account

These would be deposits that customers have made for goods that will be received in the future. They are shown as creditors as the company has a liability to either produce the goods, or return the deposit (although in some circumstances the deposit can be non-refundable).

Trade creditors

This is the amount of money that the company owes for goods and services that have been supplied during the period. In many businesses this is an important source of funds, with trade creditors funding the company's stock.

Other creditors

These are many other creditors that do not fall into another category. Proposed dividends are also classed as creditors and are usually shown separately.

Corporation tax

This will include both the corporation tax and the advance corporation tax.

Other taxation and social security

This includes VAT, National Insurance contributions, PAYE, and excise duties.

Accrued expenses and deferred income

Accrued expenses are the invoices that are outstanding for the goods and services that have been used during the year. They will have been charged to the profit and loss account.

Deferred income is money that has been received by the company (or is due to the company), and has yet to be earned. If we buy an annual season ticket we are paying for our travel a year in advance. The train operating company will then have deferred income – it has received the cash, but has yet to provide the travel. Companies that require payments in advance have considerable amounts of accruals and deferred income.

Proposed dividends

Although these cannot be paid until they have been approved at the annual general meeting, they are shown as a creditor, as they have been charged to the profit and loss account. The dividends are shown net of any related ACT, which is included as part of the tax creditors.

These creditors are illustrated in the following extract from the notes to Unilever's 1996 consolidated accounts:

Extract 12.1   **TRADE AND OTHER CREDITORS (UNILEVER)**

	£ million	
	1996	1995
Due within one year:		
Trade creditors	**2820**	3155
Social security and sundry taxes	**282**	305
Accruals and deferred income	**1210**	1235
Taxation on profits	**256**	233
Dividends	**432**	483
Others	**880**	918
	5880	6329
Due after one year:		
Accruals and deferred income	**53**	47
Taxation on profits	**257**	242
Others	**101**	81
	411	370
Total creditors	**6291**	6699

SUMMARY Companies will give, in the notes to their accounts, detailed disclosures of their creditors, analysed between those falling due within a year and more than a year.

● Creditor ratios – creditor days

We have seen that we can use information from the accounts to calculate the collection period. We are also interested in the payment period – how long is the company taking to pay its suppliers? We have information about the trade creditors, in the notes to the balance sheet. The trade creditors relate to purchases. Unfortunately, purchases are only shown on a Format 2 profit and loss account (the least popular presentation in the UK), so we are unlikely to arrive at an accurate figure for the payment period.

Some analysts use cost of sales as an approximation to purchases; but this can mean different things to different companies, so others use turnover. If we are comparing companies we will need to look at creditors in relation to turnover to have a basis for comparison. The objective is to identify whether the company has a potential problem with its payments, and whether it is taking longer to pay suppliers than other companies in the sector. Even if we had perfect information, we would be unable to quantify the size of the problem exactly, as the balance sheet has already been managed to give the best view.

Whichever way is used to calculate how long the company is taking to pay its suppliers, the trend should still be the same (unless profit margins have fluctuated wildly during the period), even though the answer may be different!

To calculate how many days the company is taking to pay its suppliers we look at trade creditors in relationship to either turnover or cost of sales using one of the following formulas:

Based on sales

$$\frac{\text{Trade creditors}}{\text{Turnover}} \times 365$$

Based on cost of sales

$$\frac{\text{Trade creditors}}{\text{Cost of sales}} \times 365$$

EXAMPLE If we used the balance sheet in our example which has trade creditors of £15 000 and the profit and loss account below:

	£
Sales	100 000
Cost of sales	(60 000)
Gross profit	40 000
Administration expenses	(20 000)
Distribution costs	(10 000)
Operating profit	10 000
Interest	(6 000)
Profit before tax	4 000

we can calculate our creditor days. In our example:

$$\frac{15\ 000}{100\ 000} \times 365 = 54.75 \text{ days} \qquad \frac{15\ 000}{60\ 000} \times 365 = 91.25 \text{ days}$$

(We need to multiply by 365, as the creditors represent the amount of money owed on a given day, and the sales are the sales for the whole year.)

SUMMARY It is impossible to quantify creditor days accurately from the information given in the accounts. However, calculating creditor days should reveal trends in the payment of suppliers.

● PROVISIONS FOR LIABILITIES AND CHARGES

These are defined by the Companies Act (Sch 4, para 89) as 'any amount retained as reasonably necessary for the purpose of providing for any liability or loss which is either likely to be incurred, or certain to be incurred but uncertain as to amount or as to the date on which it will arise'. Therefore, these are the provisions that relate to future costs, rather than a write-down in the values of assets. Future rationalisation costs, pension costs and deferred taxation are commonly found under this heading. As companies use provisions to 'smooth' earnings (a full discussion of this can be found in Chapter 13), it is always worth looking at this note to see what has been charged to the profit and loss account and what has been spent.

The following extract from the notes to Railtrack's 1997 accounts illustrates the information disclosed in the note on provisions for liabilities and charges.

Extract 12.2 **PROVISIONS FOR LIABILITIES AND CHARGES (RAILTRACK)**

	At 1 April 1996 £m	Utilised in year and other reclassifications £m	Profit and loss charge in year £m	At 31 March 1997 £m
Deferred tax (Note 21)	39	(1)	–	38
Environmental liabilities	70	(2)	–	68
Performance regimes	–	20	46	66
Other	26	(9)	–	17
	135	8	46	189

The performance regimes balance at 31 March 1996 of £20m was reclassified in the year from trade debtors to provisions.

Railtrack plc inherited from British Railways Board a number of sites which are known to suffer from some degree of contamination. These sites have been inspected and assessed by professional advisors. The cost of remedial works has been estimated and a provision has been made for this in accordance with the Group's accounting policy.

SUMMARY The provisions for liabilities and charges shown on the balance sheet represent future costs that will be incurred by the company. Material provisions will be separately disclosed. The note will disclose how much has been charged to the profit and loss account, and how much has been spent in the year.

● CONTINGENT LIABILITIES

When we are looking at company accounts we are not only interested in what has happened and what will probably happen, we also need to have an indication of what may happen. The accounts reflect what has happened. Provisions are made to cover probable future expenses, and asset writedowns. Contingent liabilities are uncertain, but could have a material effect on the results of the business or its financial position. The financial statements are intended to give a true and fair view. If they do not give information about contingencies, they will clearly not do this, as without information on contingencies the financial statements could be misleading.

Contingencies can lead to a gain or a loss. Whilst the accounting treatment for gains and losses is different, the definition is the same. The accounting standard (SSAP 18, *Accounting for Contingencies*) defines a contingency as: 'a condition which exists at the balance sheet date, where the outcome will be confirmed only on the occurrence or non-occurrence of one or more uncertain future events'.

A contingency, then, could lead to a potential gain or liability which has not materialised by the date of the balance sheet, as it is dependent upon future events. There are other situations where the outcome is determined by future events (such as bad debt provisions). However, in this case, the future event would only require the revision of an accounting estimate. The accounting standard makes it clear that contingencies are different from other uncertain events that affect accounting estimates, although obviously there will be occasions when the revision could also constitute a contingency. Litigation is a classic example of a contingent liability, where the outcome is resolved by a court's decision. Guarantees and warranties would also be included in the definition of a contingent liability.

Some information on guarantees and other financial commitments is required to be disclosed by law. The Companies Act (Sch 4, para 50) requires companies to disclose the following items in their accounts:

- The amount of any third-party liabilities that are secured by charges on the company's assets.
- The amount, nature and what, if any, security has been provided in relation to any contingent liability (the accounting standards require additional disclosure).
- The total capital expenditure that has been:
  - contracted for;
  - authorised by the directors, but not contracted for.
- Pension commitments that have been:
  - provided for;
  - not provided for (additional guidance is given in the accounting standards).
- Any other commitments that are relevant to a proper understanding of the company's affairs.

Any commitments that have been given on behalf of the company's subsidiaries, or the parent and fellow subsidiaries, should be shown separately from each other, and from the other commitments.

If the contingent liability has not been provided for, the Act requires that the company disclose:

- the amount, or estimated amount of the liability;
- its legal nature;
- whether any valuable security has been offered by the company in connection with the liability, and if so, what that security is.

The accounting standard (SSAP 18) identifies the accounting treatment for contingent gains and contingent losses (Table 12.1).

Table 12.1 **SSAP 18: Accounting for contingent gains and losses**

Probability	Gain	Loss
Probable – prudence applies	Note in the financial statements, but do not anticipate the gain	Include in costs, does not have to be disclosed separately
Possible	Ignore	Does not have to be included in the accounts, but should be noted
Unlikely	Ignore	Ignore

However, the accounting treatment for contingent gains is different when the company has made an acquisition. FRS 7 (*Fair Values in Acquisition Accounting*) requires that both contingent assets and liabilities should be valued on the basis of reasonable estimates of their outcome. Therefore, contingent assets, arising from contingent gains, will be recorded if they existed in the subsidiary at the date of acquisition.

Some contingencies are regularly disclosed by companies (e.g. bank guarantees, discounted bills, performance bonds). Whereas others are only reluctantly disclosed. Most companies do not like disclosing contingent liabilities arising from court cases, as they feel that disclosure may jeopardise their position, as it may make it look as though they expect to lose the case. Companies are also unwilling to show the financial effect of a breach of the law, although the disclosure would probably result in its not being seen as a contingency, but as a liability. Few companies identify their foreign exchange exposure risks as a contingent liability, although it seems likely that disclosure will be required elsewhere in the accounts if FRED 13 (*Derivatives and Other Financial Instruments: Disclosure*) becomes a standard. Taylor Woodrow's 1996 accounts illustrate the information that may be disclosed about a contingent liability.

Extract 12.3 **CONTINGENT LIABILITIES (TAYLOR WOODROW)**

CONTINGENT LIABILITIES

The group is one of the ten contractors in Transmanche Link (TML) which built the Channel Tunnel for Eurotunnel. Eurotunnel issued in late 1995 documents to TML which purported to claim approximately £1 billion in respect of alleged failure by the joint venture arising from that part of the contract which deals with the procurement of rolling stock. TML considers that it has no liability in respect of any of the matters raised.

The group and the parent company have entered into performance bonds and agreements in the normal course of business.

The parent company has given guarantees in respect of group undertakings of £40.4m (1995 – £32.3m).

SUMMARY

The general rule is that contingent gains should not be recognised. However, FRS 7 requires that a contingent gain should be recognised as an asset if it existed, in a subsidiary, at the date of its acquisition.

Contingent losses will be charged to the profit and loss account if they are probable. Possible contingent losses are noted, as in the example above.

INTERNATIONAL DIFFERENCES

International accounting standards

Contingencies are covered by IAS 10 (*Contingencies and Events Occurring after the Balance Sheet Date*) which is broadly similar to the UK standard. However, following FRS 7 there are differences in the recognition of contingent gains. Under the international standard these can only be recognised 'when the realisation of a gain is virtually certain', when in effect it is no longer a contingency. Otherwise, probable gains would be disclosed, but not recognised.

Europe

Contingent gains are not normally recognised, although Dutch companies can account for them if they are reasonably certain. However, they are rarely included, and would usually only be disclosed in the notes. In France and Germany contingent gains would be neither recognised nor disclosed. In France any contingent losses would be provided for where they are clearly identifiable. In Germany probable contingent losses are provided for, and any others would be disclosed.

Japan

Accounting for contingencies in Japan is similar to that of IAS 14.

North America

In the USA contingent losses should be accrued when it is probable that a loss has been incurred at the balance sheet date, and a reasonable estimate of the loss can be made. If there is a possibility of a contingent loss the company should disclose:

- the nature of the contingency;
- an estimate of the possible loss, or range of the possible loss, (where no estimate can be made this should be stated).

Guarantees should be disclosed, even if the possibility of loss is remote. Contingent gains should be disclosed, but are not usually reflected in the accounts.

In Canada the definition of a contingency includes the impairment of assets. A contingent loss should be included in the accounts if it is probable that assets have been impaired, or a loss has been incurred at the balance-sheet date, and a reasonable estimate of the loss can be made. Contingent losses should be disclosed if:

- it is likely, but the size of the loss cannot be reasonably estimated;
- an accrual has been made for the loss, but it is likely that the accrual will be insufficient;
- it is not possible to determine the occurrence of the future event.

Probable contingent gains should be disclosed, but should not be included in the accounts. Companies would disclose the following information about contingencies:

- the nature of the contingency.
- an estimate of the possible loss, or a statement that no estimate can be made;

● whether the contingency is expected to be treated as a prior-period adjustment, or charged to the profit and loss account.

● CAPITAL COMMITMENTS

The note on capital commitments discloses the capital expenditure for the next year that has already been approved by the directors. It is sorted out into two categories:

(1) expenditure where the contracts have been placed;
(2) expenditure that has been approved, but contracts have not been placed at the date of the balance sheet.

This is often a useful note to refer to as it gives some indication of the company's expansion plans and future cash flows. The note in British Steel's 1997 accounts (see below) indicates that the group will be maintaining the current levels of capital expenditure into 1998.

Extract 12.4   **CAPITAL EXPENDITURE (BRITISH STEEL)**

	The Company		The Group	
	1997	1996	**1997**	1996
	£m	£m	**£m**	£m
Contracted but not provided for	**150**	73	**194**	194
Authorised but contracts not yet placed	**122**	63	**171**	152

The above figures incorporate an estimate for future inflation.

SUMMARY   The Companies Act requires that any commitments that have been made for capital expenditure be disclosed in the notes to the accounts.

JARGON   **Accrued expenses**   Outstanding invoices for items used in sales.

Contingency   Something that exists at the balance-sheet date, but the outcome is determined by the occurrence, or non-occurrence, of uncertain future events.

Deferred income   This is money that has been received by the company, or due to the company, that has yet to be earned.

Trade creditors   The money owed for the goods and services supplied during the period.

13 The profit and loss account: turnover to profit before tax

This chapter covers:

- Capital costs and revenue costs
- Turnover
- Operating costs
- Accounting adjustments
- Pension costs
- Employee share schemes
- Long-term contracts
- Operating profit
- Share of associated undertaking's profits and losses
- Share of joint venture's profits and losses
- Significant associates and joint ventures
- Exceptional and extraordinary items
- Profit on sale of fixed assets
- Profit on sale of operations
- Net interest payable
- Additional information available in the notes
- FRS 3 and the presentation of the profit and loss account
- Creating profit
- Profitability ratios

INTRODUCTION

The profit and loss account helps us to identify the return that the business is making on its sales. A profitable business sells its goods and services for more than it costs to deliver them to the customer. A loss-making one does not. The profit and loss account takes the sales the company has made in the period and deducts the costs that are associated with these sales to arrive at the profit or the loss. The costs are deducted in the following standard order, to arrive at different levels of profit:

- operating costs
- other operating income and expenses
- share of associated undertaking's and joint venture's profits and losses
- profits and losses on the sale of fixed assets and subsidiaries
- interest received and paid.

● CAPITAL COSTS AND REVENUE COSTS

Companies spend money in different places; some is spent on things the company intends to keep; some is spent on things the company intends to sell. It is important to understand the way a company classifies its costs. Costs can be either:

- **capital costs** – these relate to the purchase of, or improvement to, assets; or
- **revenue costs** – these relate to the sales that have been made in the period.

We all understand the difference between *capital costs* and *revenue costs*. Decorating our home is a revenue cost, we do not get any more money for a well-decorated house! Putting in an extra bathroom is a capital cost – you can expect to recover the money when you sell the house. Maintaining the house is a revenue cost; improving it is a capital cost.

2 + 2 = 5 The distinction is important in accounting, as only revenue costs are included in the profit and loss account. Any capital costs are charged to the balance sheet. Consequently, it is possible for companies to improve their profitability (and their apparent net worth) by capitalising costs. The opportunity for creative accounting arises because it is not always easy to work out what costs should be capitalised, even though the Companies Act defines what should comprise the cost of an asset:

- **Company purchases the asset** – if the company buys the asset, it is relatively straightforward, it is the purchase cost plus 'any expenses incidental to its acquisition';
- **company builds the asset** – this is where the problems start, as the company has to identify the cost of production. The Companies Act defines the production cost as the price of raw materials and consumables used, plus additional costs that are 'directly attributable to the production of the asset'. During the period of production companies may also include 'a reasonable proportion of the costs', 'which are only indirectly attributable to the production of the asset'. This includes 'interest on capital borrowed to finance the production of the asset'.

The problem lies in the interpretation – what is reasonable? How do you calculate capitalised interest costs when the borrowings are not necessarily specific to the construction of the asset?

UK accounting standards currently give little guidance on interpreting the Act, auditors rely on common sense and the limited guidance given by International Accounting Standards. However, it is discussed in FRED 17 (*Measurement of Tangible Fixed Assets*), issued in October 1997. This covers commissioning costs, the capitalisation of interest and subsequent expenditure. If this evolves into a standard it will provide the guidance that is currently lacking.

● TURNOVER

Turnover represents the total sales that the company has made during the period, excluding any trade discounts, VAT, or similar sales taxes. Group accounts show the external sales; inter-company sales do not show on the face of the profit and loss account, but are usually disclosed in the notes showing the segmental analysis.

Schedule 4 of the Companies Act requires the disclosure of turnover and pre-tax profits for each class of business, and the turnover for each main geographical market. However, if the directors feel that this disclosure would prejudice the interests of the company, this information need not be disclosed, but the accounts should state that it has not been disclosed. There are additional disclosures required under SSAP 25 (*Segmental Reporting*) and these are discussed in detail in Chapter 18.

There is no UK standard dealing specifically with revenue recognition, although it is affected by the principles of accruals and prudence found in SSAP 2 (*Disclosure of Accounting Policies*). Internationally it is covered by IAS 18 (*Revenue*). IAS 18 is concerned with revenues arising from:

- the sale of goods;
- the rendering of services;
- the use by others of assets that generate incomes such as royalty payments, dividends, and interest received (these would not normally be regarded as part of a company's turnover).

This only applies to the recognition of revenues arising from a company's normal trading activities, as other sources of revenue are covered by other standards.

The standard requires that revenue should only be recognised when both of the following conditions are satisfied:

(1) it is possible to measure the revenue reliably
(2) it is probable that the company will receive the revenue.

Revenue arising from the sale of goods must also satisfy the conditions below, as IAS 18 effectively prohibits revenue recognition where there are still material uncertainties that could affect the transaction:

- The company has transferred the significant risks and rewards of ownership to the buyer. This normally coincides with the transfer of legal title.
- The company does not retain control over the goods, nor has any of the continuing managerial involvement normally associated with ownership.
- The costs can be reliably measured.

IAS 18 requires that revenues arising from the provision of services should be accounted for using the percentage of completion method. So, they must additionally satisfy the following conditions before the revenue can be recognised:

- The completion stage can be reliably measured at the balance-sheet date.
- The costs can be reliably measured.

Therefore, turnover can be recognised in a number of different ways. It can be recognised when an event occurs that transfers the ownership, risks and rewards, or it can be recognised over a period of time. The precise definition of turnover will vary from one company to another.

In the Rank Group's 1996 accounts turnover is defined as 'sales of goods and services' that were 'generally recognised as goods are shipped or services are rendered. Turnover for casinos includes the gaming win before deduction of gaming duty. The sales value of work done on property developments work in progress is recognised in relation to the progress towards completion and the estimated profit of the total development contract'. Consequently, we can see how the definition of turnover differed across their businesses. Their definition of turnover in casinos had changed during 1996, previously it had included the value of gaming chips sold. The net effect of this change in accounting policy was to reduce the turnover in the previous year by £393 million.

SUMMARY

Turnover represents the total sales that the company has made during the period, excluding any trade discounts, VAT, or similar sales taxes. The only specific guidance for the recognition of turnover is found in IAS 18 (*Revenue*). This is concerned with the recognition of revenues arising from normal trading activities. It requires that revenues arising from the sales of goods should only be recognised when:

- the costs can be reliably measured;
- the revenue can be reliably measured and it is probable that it will be received;
- the risks, rewards and management involvement usually associated with ownership have passed to the buyer.

Revenues arising from the provision of services should be recognised on a percentage of completion basis when the costs and completion stage can be reliably measured at the balance-sheet date.

This means that companies bring turnover into their profit and loss accounts in a number of different ways broadly classified into those based on an event transferring the ownership, and those based on time.

● OPERATING COSTS

These are primarily the costs of materials, wages, and overheads used in sales. We have discussed, in Chapter 4, the two different ways that these can be presented in the profit and loss account. In addition to these costs, companies will include other operating income in their calculation of operating profit. Other operating income is income that does not fit into any other heading, for example royalty income.

● ACCOUNTING ADJUSTMENTS

All companies make five major accounting adjustments to ensure that the costs that are charged to the profit and loss account are those that relate to the sales that have been made in the period:

Charges are made to the profit and loss account to include:

(1) provisions for likely costs;
(2) accrued expenses;
(3) depreciation.

The following are not included in the profit and loss account:

(4) Stock – a company's policy on valuing stock can have a significant impact on the reported profits. Higher stock values can give higher profits. This is discussed in detail in Chapter 10;
(5) Prepayments.

In addition, companies involved in trading overseas must find a way to deal with exchange rates. All of these adjustments have an impact on both the profit and loss account and the balance sheet. The effect of the charges for provisions, depreciation and exchange rates are discussed below. Whilst accounting for pensions and employee share schemes are part of the operating costs, they are discussed separately, later in this chapter.

● Provisions

The Companies Act defines a provision as either any amount written off by way of providing for depreciation or diminution in the value of assets, or any amount retained, as reasonably necessary, for the purpose of providing for any liability or loss which is either likely to be incurred, or certain to be incurred but there is uncertainty about the amount or the date on which it will arise.

There are two important elements to provisions; the company does not know precisely the costs that are involved, or when those costs will be incurred. All companies must make provisions and typical provisions would include:

● bad and doubtful debts;
● obsolete stock – this may not be obsolete in the literal sense, stock must be shown on the balance sheet at the lower of cost or net realisable value. Consequently, if the net realisable value falls below the cost then a provision must be made;
● warranty claims;
● litigation;
● rationalisation costs.

The first two involve asset writedowns, whereas the last three are likely future costs. The accounting treatment for the two types of provision is different.
Provisions can be:

● specific, for example where each debtor is considered individually;
● general, for example where the same level of provision is applied to all debtors; or
● a combination of the two, for example, where perhaps large customers would be considered individually, and smaller customers on a general basis.

To illustrate the way that asset writedowns affect the accounts we will look at a doubtful debt provision.

 A company has decided to make a provision of 4 per cent to cover doubtful debts, and we will look at the impact of this decision, on the accounts, over a period of two years.

	Year 1 £	Year 2 £	Profit growth
Outstanding invoices	100 000	110 000	
Less 4% provision	(4 000)	(4 400)	
Debtors shown on the balance sheet	96 000	105 600	
Profit before provisions	110 000	115 500	5%

Let us consider two different scenarios:

(1) The company collects £98 000 from the first year's debtors.
(2) *They only collect £94 000.*

The profit after provisions would be:

First scenario	106 000	113 100	6.7%
Second scenario	*106 000*	*109 000*	*2.9%*

In the first case, the company over-provided £2000 in the first year and so only needed to charge £2400 into the second year's profit and loss account to bring the provision to £4400 (4 per cent of £110 000). In the second case, it had under-provided and thus had to increase the charge to the profit and loss account, to bring the provision to the 4 per cent of outstanding debtors that is required.

Provisions are only the managers' best guesses and are unlikely to be a totally accurate reflection of what will happen. As provisions can only reflect approximations, they are often used by companies to move profit from one year to the next, as an over-provision in one year can be written back in the next.

The writeback of provisions, and its impact on reported profits, can be illustrated by London International Group. In the group's 1993 interim results on its health and personal products business, it reported that: 'Operating results for the half year, compared with the corresponding half year have been depressed by two additional factors. Firstly, operating results last year were helped by the release of surplus provisions and the benefit of favourable exchange variances, following the UK's exit from the ERM. In total these benefits amounted to £5 million compared to this year. Secondly, the adoption of more conservative accounting policies has adversely affected results by circa £2 million.' Operating profits for the half year in this division had fallen from £16.1 million to £3.5 million.

2 + 2 = 5 Provisions clearly provide creative accounting opportunities for companies, and probably none more so than rationalisation provisions. Traditionally, companies have announced a rationalisation programme that would extend over a number of years, and take all the provision in one year. As the provision will be large, it will be shown as an exceptional item. (This is known as *big-bath accounting*.) When analysts are trying to identify an underlying trend in a business, they will usually exclude exceptional items. As the provision relates to a likely future cost, it would be included in the provisions for liabilities and charges shown on the balance sheet. The disclosures on provisions have often been insufficient to allow users of the accounts to trace through the expenditure over the rationalisation programme. So big-bath accounting pays off! But not for long.

FRED 14

This practice clearly does not follow the accounting principle of matching expenses to revenues, and in June 1997 the ASB issued FRED 14 (*Provisions and Contingencies*) to resolve the problem. The FRED is concerned with the provisions that are made to cover costs that are likely to be incurred in the future. The proposed standard states that provisions should only be recognised when the entity has a legal or constructive obligation to transfer economic benefits as a result of past events. There must be an obligation to a third party at the year end. A decision to reorganise the business does not create any obligation. Once the obligation exists, a provision should be made, unless a reasonable estimate of the amount that would be required to settle the obligation cannot be made.

In consequence rationalisation provisions would only be recognised when the company has a detailed plan for the reorganisation, and could not withdraw from the programme. The amount that could be provided would have to be a realistic and prudent estimate of the costs of the obligation at the year end. It would appear that the ASB has pulled the plug on big-bath accounting!

FRED 14 will have a major impact on provisioning if it becomes an accounting standard. It is planned that it will apply to all companies and provisions, except insurance companies making provisions resulting from insurance contracts. Where another FRS covers the provision the more specific standard should be applied if there is a conflict between the two standards. Some of the other proposals are:

Future operating losses

Companies should not make provisions for future operating losses. However they may still be made in two situations:

(1) discontinued operations – provisions for future operating losses on discontinued business can be made under FRS 3 (*Reporting Financial Performance*) if certain conditions are met;
(2) onerous contracts – these are contracts that are expected to be loss making, and where the company has to compensate the other party if it does not fulfil the terms of the contract.

The size of the provision

The amount that is recognised should take account of the risks associated with the cash flows. The estimate should be revised in future periods to reflect any material changes in either the assumptions or any future events that may affect the amount. The provision should be discounted, using a risk-free rate, where this has a material effect. The risk-free rate is thought to be the most appropriate rate to use, as the amount should already have been adjusted to reflect any risks.

Disclosure

Unless the company can argue that disclosure would be seriously prejudicial to the negotiations relating to the provisions, it must make extensive disclosures. Companies should disclose, for all material classes of provision, the following information:

● A description of the obligation and an indication of the timing of the cash payment. If there is significant uncertainty about either the amounts involved, or the timing of the payment, companies should also disclose the factors that will be relevant for determining them.
● The amount provided, and if this is an estimate, the basis of the estimate.
● If the provision has been discounted, the discount rate used should be disclosed.

The movements on the provisions during the year should disclose:

● additions to, and adjustments made to, provisions during the year;
● the amounts that have been used and any amounts that have been released unused;
● the amortisation of the discount (this will be shown on the profit and loss account as part of interest charges), if the provision has been discounted;
● exchange differences.

There are additional disclosure requirements proposed for reorganisation provisions.

● Depreciation

Depreciation is something we all familiar with. We buy something today, and it is not worth the same tomorrow. The Companies Act requires companies to make a charge for depreciation in their accounts, to reflect the shrinking in value of their assets. This is not a cash cost to the business. Depreciation is discussed in detail in Chapter 8.

The depreciation charge takes account of:

- the cost of the asset – this will not just be the purchase cost of the asset, other costs will be included;
- the asset life – in the UK this is determined by the managers, not tax tables;
- the asset's net residual value (i.e., scrap value at the end of the asset's life).

Any change in these assumptions will change both reported profits and asset values. This is compounded by the fact that there are several different methods that can be used to calculate the depreciation charge. Within the UK, companies can choose the method of depreciation. The straight-line method is usually used, although some companies use other methods. The straight-line method is the simplest of all, and allocates the costs equally over the life of the asset. The reducing-balance and the sum-of-the-digits methods are commonly used alternatives, and would give higher charges in the earlier years than the straight-line method. The earlier higher charge probably more closely reflects the reduction in the market value of the asset. Usage-based methods bring in depreciation charges that reflect the use of the asset, rather than its market value.

The different methods of depreciation will give different depreciation charges, thus a change in the accounting policy for depreciation would affect the reported profits. Material changes in the depreciation policies would be disclosed in the notes to the accounts.

● Currency adjustments

Any company trading overseas has to account for transactions in foreign currencies. It becomes more complicated when the company has subsidiaries overseas, as they have to be consolidated. Accounting for foreign currencies is discussed in detail in Chapter 20.

Exchange rates can have a direct impact on a company's reported profits. If a company sells some machinery to Germany for DM 1 million, the sterling sales would be reported as £454 545 at DM 2.2 to the pound, and £400 000 at DM 2.5 to the pound. In addition, there are two problems with accounting for exchange rates:

(1) Which rate do you use? The rate at the time of the sale may not be the rate when the company receives the cash.
(2) How do you account for any exchange differences?

In the UK these are covered by SSAP 20 (*Foreign Currency Translation*). The accounting procedures are different for individual companies and groups. For profit and loss account items individual companies use the exchange rate at the transaction date, or average rates if there have been no significant fluctuations during the period. Forward exchange rates may be used, but they do not have to be used. Exchange differences can arise from the movement in exchange rates between the date of invoicing and the date when the invoice is paid. These differences, which arise from trading transactions, are charged to the profit and loss account.

The assets and liabilities on the balance sheet are sorted out into those that are monetary (these are amounts that will be receivable or payable in cash), non-monetary items and shares in overseas companies. Monetary items are translated at the closing rate. Any resulting exchange gains and losses are taken into the profit and loss account. Shares in overseas companies are usually shown at the exchange rate when the investment was made. The only exception to this is if the investment is financed by foreign borrowings, or foreign borrowings are used to hedge the foreign investment. In this case, they may be translated at the closing rate.

This means that the reported profits of a company can be affected by exchange rates in three ways:

(1) by rising or falling exchange rates, which will directly affect the company's profits;
(2) through exchange differences arising between the time of the sales and the payment;
(3) through gains and losses arising from the retranslation of balance sheet monetary items to closing rates at the year end.

Hence, the reported profits of importers will benefit from a strengthening pound, whereas exporters' profits fall. The opposite will be true if sterling is weakening; the importers will lose, and the exporters will gain.

SUMMARY

The operating costs are the costs of materials, wages and overheads that have been used in sales made in the period. The company has to make a number of adjustments to arrive at the costs that match the sales in the period.

Companies must include charges to cover provisions, depreciation and outstanding invoices. These charges have nothing to do with cash outflows during the period. The profit and loss account excludes stock, which may have been paid for, and prepayments, which have been paid for, but the payments do not relate to the period under review. This means that the reported profit from the sales, and the cash the company has generated from its sales are rarely the same. This is compounded by the accounting treatment for exchange rates. The rate that is used in the profit and loss account may not be the rate that the company actually gets for the sale, as the company is not required to use the agreed forward rate, and the reported profitability will be affected by exchange rate adjustments.

If a profitable business is short of cash, it may be indicative of creative accounting. It is worth checking the figures on the balance sheet to see why the cash is much lower than the reported profits.

● PENSION COSTS

Whilst pensions accounting can appear very esoteric, the way a UK company accounts for pensions can have a significant impact on its apparent financial performance. For this reason, it is important to understand some of the more important principles of pension accounting if we want to be able to interpret a set of accounts.

● Different types of pension scheme

Pension schemes may be either funded (UK practice) or unfunded (often found overseas, for example in Greece). In a funded scheme the company will make a payment to the pension fund. In an unfunded scheme the company pays the pensions of its employees, therefore there is likely to be a large provision for pension payments shown in the accounts. These schemes may then be:

Defined contributions schemes

The contributions are invested and the employee's pension will be determined by the investment performance of the scheme. The accounting treatment for these schemes is simple, the contributions relating to the period will be charged to the profit and loss account.

Defined benefits schemes

In this type of scheme employees are entitled to receive a proportion of their salaries on retirement. This is totally unrelated to the investment performance of the scheme. If the scheme under-performs, the company will have to make additional contributions to honour its obligations. The company, therefore, assumes the risks involved in providing employees' pensions. Defined benefits schemes have traditionally been the type of scheme offered by large UK companies. However, there is an increasing trend for new employees to be offered defined contributions schemes, rather than defined benefit schemes.

If the company operates a defined benefits scheme, the way that it accounts for the pension costs is likely to differ fundamentally from the way that it makes contributions into the scheme.

Accounting for pension costs is covered by SSAP 24 (*Accounting for Pension Costs*). Pension costs are part of the employment costs. However, the size of the employer's contribution in any year will, in part, depend upon the performance of the fund. There may be sufficient money in the fund to meet the obligations of the scheme. In this case, the company would not have to make any contributions to the scheme, it could have a pensions 'holiday'. SSAP 24 specifies that 'the employer should recognise the expected cost of providing pensions on a systematic and rational basis over the period during which he derives benefit from the employees' services'. In other words, the cost of providing the pension is spread over the working lives of the employees. This is just a reflection of the accruals principle. So, although the company may not be paying any cash into the scheme, there may still be a charge made to the profit and loss account for pension costs.

In order to calculate the pension costs charged to the period's profit and loss account the company must:

● determine the size of the fund required to meet its obligations;
● identify whether the fund is in surplus or deficit;
● account for the surplus / deficit in calculating the pension cost for the period;
● identify the contribution rate for the scheme.

● The size of the fund

Determining the fund that is required to meet the obligations to employees is complicated, as it is based on a number of assumptions based on the following questions:

● How many of us will stay with the scheme until we retire?
● When will we retire?
● What will we be earning when we retire?
● How will the fund perform until we retire?
● Will it generate a return sufficient to cover its liabilities?

Actuaries will carry out valuations, usually every three years, to identify the size of the fund that the company needs to meet its pension liabilities. The accounts will disclose their actuarial assumptions, which are usually very conservative (they tend to over-estimate salary increases and under-estimate fund performance). They will also disclose whether the fund is in surplus or deficit. A surplus arises when the fund's value is greater than that is needed to satisfy its liabilities. Given the conservatism of the actuarial assumptions, it is easy for a pension fund to be in surplus. This was particularly true during the 1980s when returns from shares easily outpaced wage inflation. The 1990s have seen a continuation of this trend, but it is now coupled with staff reduction. Redundancies have the effect of increasing the surplus by reducing the fund's liabilities. Although, if people elect for early retirement, it can increase the fund's liabilities, as is illustrated later. However, many funds are expected to move from surplus to deficit following the abolition, from 1997, of the ACT credits paid to pension funds.

Historically, the way that companies were accounting for these surpluses (charging the actual cost, often nothing, to the profit and loss account) worried accountants as it was not consistent with the accruals principle. Costs were not being matched to revenues. It was felt that the cost of providing a pension should be matched to the time that the company was benefiting from the employees' services. In 1988, in reaction to this, SSAP 24 was issued. This requires companies to match the pension costs charged to the profit and loss account to the working lives of employees. Therefore, the profit and loss account is being charged with the cost of providing pensions over the period that the company is benefiting from the employees' services. This means that the accounting charge for pensions can be very different from the cash cost of funding pension schemes. The charges to the profit and loss account will probably not reflect the cash flows into the fund.

● Accounting for a surplus

The accounting standard states that companies should spread a surplus over the remaining service life of employees. The surplus relating to the current year could exceed the normal cost of the company's contributions. This can give rise to a 'negative cost' (effectively a credit) to the profit and loss account that will be reflected by a prepayment asset in the balance sheet. For example, the normal cost of providing the future pension (called the regular cost) could be £10 million, the surplus allocated to this period could be £12 million. The profit and loss account would not be charged with any pension cost, instead it will be credited with £2 million. A £2 million prepayment would be shown on the balance sheet to reflect this credit. The accounting treatment for pensions poses two problems for financial analysts:

(1) If the fund moves out of surplus, the company's profits will appear to collapse as the company has to charge the normal costs. In the above example the comparative profits will fall by £12 million.
(2) The current assets will be overstated, as the pension fund prepayment is not a liquid asset of the company. A small number of companies have recognised this and show the surplus separately, outside of their current assets.

Today's surplus is tomorrow's deficit. A good example of this is British Telecom (BT). In its 1990 accounts BT stated that its pension fund assets were sufficient to cover 118 per cent of the liabilities. The fund was in surplus. On 1 January 1993, it merged its two pension funds, without affecting the benefits of the members. The pension fund was valued on that date, using the same actuarial assumptions as had been used for the previous valuation. The valuation identified a deficit of £750 million, with the assets only covering 95 per cent of the liabilities. The company believed the deficit derived from a combination of three factors:

(1) the cost of providing pensions to people who had elected to take early retirement;
(2) the impact of the recession on the investment returns of the fund;
(3) the reduction in the ACT credit from 25 per cent to 20 per cent.

As the pension fund was in deficit, BT felt it prudent to charge to the profit and loss account £550 million to cover the costs of early retirement. The effect on the future annual charge is also dramatic. In its 1993 accounts, BT says that the annual charge will increase by

£90 million, from £160 million to an estimated £250 million in 1994. It also announced that during the year to 31 March 1994 it was likely to have to make a contribution to the scheme of £800 million.

The size of the surplus is a matter of judgement. There are different ways of spreading the surplus, different methods will have different impacts on reported profits over time. We cannot identify whether the fund would be in surplus if a different actuarial valuation basis were used. Perhaps the important thing for us to understand is that *any surplus apportioned to a year will reduce the charge to the profit and loss account*. This could have a significant impact on reported earnings.

It is further complicated by the fact that the accounting standard allows the company to charge a notional interest, where an asset arises from the difference between the charge to the profit and loss account and the cash cost. (This is to reflect the money that the prepayment is earning as part of the fund.) The logic may be sound, but there is no cash flowing into the company. It just represents the interest that may be earned on the surplus. Companies can use the notional interest to either further reduce the pension charge to the profit and loss account, or to reduce the interest charge. Most companies do not disclose whether they are taking interest into account or where the notional interest is being credited.

We have seen how a prepayment can be created when the normal cost is less than the proportion of the surplus relating to the year. However pension prepayment assets may not be accumulated 'negative costs', they may reflect the pension fund surplus. When the standard was issued in 1988, companies were allowed either to:

● spread the surplus as outlined above; or
● incorporate the pension fund surplus or deficit onto the balance sheet by a prior-year adjustment. A prior-year adjustment was used to create a pension prepayment reflecting the surplus (if there is a deficit an accrual was created).

We can see the combination of the two in Williams' accounts. The company disclosed in its 1996 accounts that: 'The pension fund prepayment of £117.6 million (1995 – £126.2 million), which substantially arose in respect of acquisitions, has been included in debtors. This amount represents the surplus arising on implementation of SSAP 24, adjusted for acquisitions and disposals, and subsequent credits to the profit and loss account'.

We are likely to see an increase in the level of pension prepayments shown in the accounts. FRS 7 (*Fair Values in Acquisition Accounting*) allows pension fund surpluses of acquired businesses to be treated as an asset, although it does stress that care should be taken to limit the recognition to the amount that is expected to be realised. This means that the fair value of the asset should not be solely dependent on the actuarial value – the extent to which the surplus can be realised in cash should also be considered.

● Pension accounting and financial analysis

It is always worth referring to the notes on pensions. Whilst the technicalities of pension accounting are important to accountants, it is their implications that are important for financial analysts. There are various points to check when looking at a set of company accounts:

● *Is the fund in surplus or deficit?*
● *How has this been accounted for?*

If there is a surplus, we should ask ourselves:

How much of the debtors' figure is pension fund prepayments?

In Williams' 1996 accounts the pension fund prepayment represented over 26 per cent of total debtors. In Coats Viyella's 1996 accounts they were 18.7 per cent of total debtors.

It is important to realise that these pension fund prepayments are:

- not realisable, and cannot be turned into cash;
- outside of the management's control. They are determined by an actuarial valuation.

Has notional interest been charged on the prepayment?

Note 30 of Coats Viyella's 1996 accounts discloses the following information:

Extract 13.1   **PENSION COSTS (COATS VIYELLA)**

	1996	1995
Pension costs for the year were:	£m	£m
UK		
Coats Viyella Pension Plan:		
Regular pension cost	14.8	14.2
Spreading of surplus	(4.6)	(6.7)
Interest	(9.7)	(7.7)
Net charge (credit)	0.5	(0.2)

Where is the interest shown in the accounts?

In the Coats Viyella note above the interest has been deducted from the charge for pension costs, and has therefore improved the operating profit. Some companies use the notional interest to reduce the interest charge. This will affect the interest cover ratio.

● Proposals for change

The ASB discussion paper, *Pension Costs in the Employer's Financial Statements,* reviews SSAP 24, and makes some proposals for change. It identifies a preferred actuarial approach, the accrued benefits method. This is the most common method used in the UK and is the benchmark method in the international standard (see below). It also proposes some changes in the accounting for some of the actuarial assumptions and additional disclosures.

SUMMARY

There are different types of pension scheme. In a defined contributions scheme the size of the pension is determined by the fund's performance. Whereas defined benefits schemes guarantee pensioners a certain level of pension, with the company making up any shortfall. Therefore, the company's contributions are determined by the fund's performance.

Defined benefits schemes can give rise to accounting problems. These were resolved by SSAP 24 (*Accounting for Pension Costs*). Pension accounting now follows the accruals principle, the cost of providing the pension is spread over the working lives of the employees. Consequently, although the company may not be paying any cash into the scheme, there may still be a charge made to the profit and loss account for pension costs.

If the pension fund is in surplus, this surplus should be spread over the remaining lives of employees. It is possible for the surplus to be so large that a year's share of the surplus could be greater than the normal cost of pensions. The profit and loss account would then be credited with the net amount. This can give rise to large differences in operating profit when the fund moves into deficit, and a charge has to be made.

▶

> Some companies show pension fund surpluses as part of debtors, and attribute a notional amount of interest to the prepayment. These are purely accounting adjustments and may not represent cash flows into the business.

INTERNATIONAL DIFFERENCES

International accounting standards

Pension accounting is covered by IAS 19 *Retirement Benefits*, which is similar in many respects to SSAP 24. There are some differences, and the main ones are detailed below:

- There are no provisions in the international accounting standard for accounting for material deficits, ex-gratia payments or increases.
- The following disclosures are not required under the international standard, most of which we would regard as important:
  - Outstanding or prepaid contributions in defined contribution schemes;
  - Defined benefit schemes:
    - whether the actuary is an employee or officer of the company;
    - the amounts of any deficiency based on the current funding level;
    - the percentage level of funding;
    - any commitments that have been made to make additional payments for a limited period.
- Any amendments to the plan for retired employees should reflect the present value of the amended benefits and should be recognised at the time of the amendment.
- The IAS offers benchmark (accrued benefit valuation) and allowable alternative (projected benefit method) valuation methods. There are no methods prescribed by SSAP 24.

Europe

In France most pension schemes are defined contribution schemes, and the costs are charged to the profit and loss account when they are paid. Provisions for unfunded liabilities are usually made, although it is not obligatory to provide for any commitments for defined benefit schemes. However, these must be disclosed in the notes. The French Stock Exchange and the Order of Chartered Accountants recommend that companies follow IAS 19.

In the Netherlands defined benefit schemes are normal, but they are required by law to be covered by an external pension insurance company, or by an independent pension trust fund. Companies are required to provide for the full pension obligation that arises each year in the accounts. Consequently, the pension costs charged to the profit and loss account may not be the same as the contributions paid into the fund, giving rise to a pension asset or liability.

In Germany pension obligations are not normally externally funded, but are accrued within the company. Pension accounting is one of the few areas where German accounts will understate a liability. There are significant exceptions from the need to accrue for pensions, and the accruals may well be understated because of the calculation method that is used. The actuarial assumptions are tax based, and allow for the following factors to be taken into account:

- The entry age is at 30 years, therefore, employees under 30 are not considered. This is a crude attempt to cope with employee turnover.
- The discount rate is 6 per cent.
- Standard assumptions are made on assumed mortality ages, and disability risks.

This means that the resulting provisions would be regarded as too low in the UK. This can be compounded by other factors. There has only been a legal obligation to accrue for pension obligations since 1987, and whilst pension rights granted before that date are usually covered by an accrual, this is not always the case. There is also no legal obligation to accrue for pension rights that are based on indirect undertakings, such as by the company welfare fund. This is somewhat surprising, as the courts have held that these undertakings are legally binding on the company.

Japan

In Japan provisions need not be made for unfunded pension costs. Traditionally, most Japanese companies had unfunded retirement and termination plans that allowed for amounts to be paid to employees when they left the company. Larger payments were usually made if the termination was involuntary. The amount charged to profits are the amounts allowed by tax law.

Increasingly, larger companies are establishing external funded pension plans, however, they do not usually make any provisions for unfunded prior-service costs. This means that retirement and other severance assets and liabilities tend to be understated in Japanese accounts.

North America

In the USA the principle of accounting for pensions is similar to that found in the UK, although the basis for calculation will give a different charge. However as the company, rather than the actuary, determines the assumptions, there is considerable guidance as to how both these, and the pension cost, should be calculated. There is also a requirement for more disclosure in the accounts, with things shown separately that would normally be grouped in the UK. These additional disclosure requirements are largely concerned with the calculation of the pension costs and the assumptions that have been used.

The principles of pension accounting in Canada are similar to those of the USA and UK. The main difference is that Canada specifies the method that should be used to calculate the pension cost. Pension assets are limited to the amount that the company can use, or withdraw, from the plan.

● EMPLOYEE SHARE SCHEMES

UITF 17 (*Employee Share Schemes*) is obligatory for accounting periods on or after 22 June 1997. This covers the accounting treatment of share schemes other than SAYE schemes and other schemes which are offered to all, or substantially all, employees. Thus, it is concerned with shares schemes for directors and senior employees, where shares are often given as part of a bonus payment.

The cost of the scheme should be based on the fair value of the shares when the award is made, and will represent the difference between the fair value and the consideration that has been paid, unless the shares are held in an ESOP trust accounted for in accordance with UITF 13 (*Accounting for ESOP Trusts*). Then the cost will be the difference between the book value of the shares and the consideration paid. This cost should then be recognised over the period to which the employee's performance relates. If the scheme is long term, and the award is dependent upon performance, it should be assumed that the performance criteria will be met.

SUMMARY UITF 17 stipulates that accounting for directors' and senior employees' share schemes should follow the matching and prudence principles.

These schemes are usually based on some performance criteria, with the shares forming part of the individual's bonus. In determining the cost, it should be assumed that the scheme members will achieve their performance targets. The cost of the scheme should be the difference between the fair value and any consideration paid. It should be recognised over the period to which the performance relates.

● LONG-TERM CONTRACTS

Long-term contracts span accounting years, and normal accounting rules are inappropriate. If the company waited until the contract was completed before taking the profit into the profit and loss account, the accounts would not reflect a true and fair view of its financial performance. Profits would be very erratic, with construction companies swinging from loss into profit as contracts are completed.

Consequently SSAP 9 (*Stocks and Long-Term Contracts*) allows companies to include the revenues and profits from uncompleted long-term contracts in their profit and loss account.

● Calculating turnover

Turnover is recorded as the contract progresses and profit is recorded as it arises. However, identifying the turnover is only simple if the contract is a 'cost plus' one, or one where the contract is divided into easily identifiable parts. Each part of the contract is then treated as a separate contract. A number of methods have evolved to cope with this situation, but all have their own problems.

Valuation by an independent surveyor

The surveyor certifies the percentage of the contract that has been completed. This certificate may well pre-date the end of the financial year.

Valuation by the management

The management estimates the percentage of contract completion. This would allow all turnover to be included in the profit and loss account, but it is not an independent valuation.

Cost basis

There are different formulas that can be used including:

$$\frac{\text{Costs to date}}{\text{Anticipated total costs}} \times \text{Anticipated total contract value}$$

This method would only be appropriate if the costs were incurred evenly over the period of the contract and there is a direct relationship between the degree of completion and the level of costs.

$$\frac{\text{Labour costs to date}}{\text{Anticipated total labour costs}} \quad \text{x} \quad \text{Anticipated total contract value}$$

This would only be appropriate where the labour costs were a fair reflection of the completion of the project.

The turnover should be allocated to accounting periods independently of the calculation of any attributable profit. SSAP 9 requires turnover to be recognised even when no profit is recognised.

● Calculating profit

The contract turnover is allocated to the profit and loss account independently of the calculation of any attributable profit. On long-term contracts the profit is usually calculated before the cost of sales, which is the reverse of the normal procedure. In calculating the profit, account should be taken of both the current cost levels and the costs that are likely to be incurred in the future to satisfy the terms of the contract. SSAP 9 provides no guidelines for the calculation of cost of sales, only of profit (and these are somewhat imprecise). It states that the profit should:

● only be taken if it can be 'assessed with reasonable certainty';
● be reported after deducting any future irrecoverable costs that will be incurred under the terms of the contract;
● be related to the completed work.

Profit is usually calculated on the percentage of completion basis, unless there are uncertainties about the apportionment of the profit. Profit should only be recorded when the profitable outcome of the contract is reasonably certain. Many companies believe that profitability can be assessed with some certainty when more than 30 per cent of the contract has been completed. When a contract is believed to be profitable, the profit should be allocated fairly over the different time periods. Losses are treated differently, as they are affected by the principle of prudence. Losses should be taken to the profit and loss account as soon as they are foreseen.

Once the company has decided that the profitability of the contract is reasonably certain, it must decide how much profit to attribute to this period's profit and loss account. There are many different ways to calculate this. Auditors encourage companies to use methods that are similar to those used to calculate turnover. Therefore, the company would use one of the following formulas, the one selected would reflect the way that it had calculated its turnover.

$$\frac{\text{Surveyor's valuation}}{\text{Total expected value}} \quad \text{x} \quad \text{Expected profit}$$

$$\frac{\text{Management's valuation}}{\text{Total expected value}} \quad \text{x} \quad \text{Expected profit}$$

$$\frac{\text{Costs to date}}{\text{Anticipated total costs}} \quad \text{x} \quad \text{Expected profit}$$

$$\frac{\text{Labour costs to date}}{\text{Anticipated total labour costs}} \quad \text{x} \quad \text{Expected profit}$$

● The balance sheet

The accounting for long-term contracts can have a considerable impact on the company's balance sheet, as things are not always shown where you would expect them to be.

Stock and debtors

It is more difficult to determine when ownership has passed to the customer on long-term contracts, as each contract reflects an unique combination of the legal agreement and industry practice. The amounts that are shown under 'amounts recoverable on contracts' may not meet the strict legal definition of a debtor. However, if this is realisable and reflects the substance of the transaction, the accruals principle requires it to be recognised.

The amounts recoverable on contracts represent the difference between the turnover and the accumulated payments on account. This is then shown as debtors, and not as stocks. This means that most long-term contract work in progress is reflected on the balance sheet as debtors, rather than stocks.

Creditors

It is possible that the company has received payments from its customers that are greater than the value of work shown on the profit and loss account. These are deducted from any contract work in progress, with only the balance shown as a creditor. The payments are for work done, and only the balance is deferred income – payments for work that has not been done.

EXAMPLE To illustrate accounting for long-term contracts, we will consider a company with three long-term contracts (Table 13.1).

Table 13.1 **Accounting for long-term contracts**

	Project 1	Accounting treatment	Project 2	Accounting treatment	Project 3
Turnover (the value of the work done)	765		590		850
Payments on account	(700)		(650)		(950)
Classified as amounts recoverable on contract	65	◄— to debtors on the balance sheet			
Excess payments on account		Deducted —► from long-term contract balances below	(60)	Included in creditors —►	(100)
Total project costs	710		690		750
Transferred to cost of sales	(710)		(590)		(750)
Contract balances	0		100		0
Provision for foreseeable losses		If this was —► greater than the contract balances, the difference would be shown in provisions for liabilities and charges	(20)		
Excess payments on account offset against contract balances			(60)		
Long-term contract balances			20	◄— Shown as stock	

The company would show turnover of 2205 and 135 gross profit on the long-term contracts in its profit and loss account (Table 13.2).

Table 13.2 Example of accounting for long-term contracts

Profit and loss account

	Project 1	Project 2	Project 3	Total
Turnover	765	590	850	**2205**
Contract costs	(710)	(590)	(750)	**(2050)**
Provision for contract losses		(20)		**(20)**
Gross profit	55	(20)	100	**135**

Balance sheet extracts

	Project 1	Project 2	Project 3	Total
Stock – *long-term contract balances*		20		**20**
Debtors – *amounts recoverable on contracts*	65			**65**
Creditors – *deferred income*			100	**100**

SUMMARY

The accounting for long-term contracts is different from normal accounting practice. The company does not wait until the contract has been completed before including it in the profit and loss account. The turnover is recorded as the contract progresses and profit is recorded as it arises. The turnover is incorporated into the profit and loss account on the basis of the percentage of contract completion. However, there are different ways that this can be calculated. Profit should only be recorded when the contract profitability is reasonably certain. Many companies believe that this occurs when more than 30 per cent of the contract has been completed. The basis for including the profit will follow that for including turnover. This means that most of the contract work done will go through the profit and loss account, and the residual asset will usually be shown as a debtor, rather than stock. However, some valuation methods will leave residual balances that could be shown as stock.

If the payments on account are lower than the turnover, the difference will be shown as *amounts recoverable on contracts* and included in debtors. If the amounts received are higher than the turnover, the difference will initially be deducted from any long-term contract work in progress, and the balance shown as creditors.

● OPERATING PROFIT

This is a profit figure that is shown in most companies' profit and loss accounts, but is not required to be disclosed under the Companies Act. It allows us to assess the underlying trading performance of the company. However, it may be necessary to make some adjustments before the trading profitability can be assessed. Exceptional items would normally be excluded, together with the company's share of the profits of its associates (which may be included in operating profits in accounts that were prepared before 23 June 1998).

● SHARE OF ASSOCIATED UNDERTAKING'S PROFITS AND LOSSES

An associated undertaking is another company, partnership or association where the company has a participating interest in a long-term investment. A participating interest is one where the company can influence the operational and financial decisions of its investment. A shareholding of 20 per cent or more in a company is assumed to represent a participating interest.

If an investment is classed as an associate, the company will bring its share of the associate's operating profit and subsequent profit and loss items, other than dividends, into its profit and loss account. This is called the *equity method of accounting* and is discussed in more detail in Chapter 9.

An associated undertaking is one where the company has participating interest in a long-term investment and exercises significant influence over the operating and financial policies. If an investment is classed as an associate, the company will bring its share of the associate's operating profit, and all subsequent profit and loss account items into its consolidated profit and loss account.

Income from any other equity-accounted participating interests will be separately disclosed. (If the investment is not classed as an associate or a subsidiary, only the income received from the investment will be shown in the profit and loss account.)

The investing company should include its share of the following items from associates in its profit and loss account:

● operating profit
● profits, or losses, on sale of fixed assets
● profits, or losses, on sale of termination of subsidiaries
● major restructuring and reorganisation costs
● interest
● tax.

All items shown before profit before tax should be separately disclosed on the face of the profit and loss account; whereas those shown after tax can be included in the group amounts, with the amounts relating to associates separately disclosed.

The amortisation, or write down of goodwill should be separately disclosed in the profit and loss account, as part of the investing company's share of its associate's results. The accounting treatment for associates is illustrated in the following example.

EXAMPLE Company A buys a 30 per cent stake in Company B, and the investment is classed as an associate under FRS 9 (*Associates and joint ventures*). Before including Company B's results their summarised profit and loss accounts were as follows:

	Company A £000	Company B £000
Turnover	1000	700
Operating costs	(750)	(520)
Operating profit	250	180
Interest payable	(50)	(30)
Profit before tax	200	150
Tax	(60)	(40)
Profit after tax	140	110
Dividend	(20)	–
Retained profit	120	110

Company A has to include its share of Company B's operating profits (£54 000), interest (£9000), and tax charge (£12 000) into its consolidated profit and loss account:

	Company A £000	Company B £000
Turnover		1000
Operating costs		(750)
Operating profit		250
Share of associate's operating profits		54
Interest payable:		
Group	(50)	
Associate	(9)	(59)
Profit on ordinary activities before tax		245
Tax on profit on ordinary activities*		(72)
Profit after tax		173
Dividend		(20)
Retained profit		153

* The tax change relates the following:

Parent and subsidiaries	(60)
Associate	(12)

Profit has increased, but there are no cash benefits to Company A as Company B is not paying dividends to its shareholders! This will be obvious when we look at the group cash flow statement as there will be no entry for dividends received from associates.

This associate represents an important element of the investing company's profits (nearly 22 per cent of the profit before interest). Consequently the investing company will also have to disclose the associate's turnover. The additional disclosure requirements for significant associates and joint ventures are discussed later in the chapter.

SUMMARY

Investments where a company has a participating interest, and influences the financial and operational decisions, are called associated undertakings. These are accounted for using the equity method of accounting, which brings the company's share of the associate's operating profit and subsequent entries other than dividends, into its profit and loss account. All entries shown before profit before tax will be shown separately on the face of the profit and loss account. Subsequent entries are included in the group results, but must be separately disclosed.

● SHARE OF JOINT VENTURE'S PROFITS AND LOSSES

Both associates and joint ventures are long-term investments, but the accounting treatment for their profits in the group profit and loss account will be slightly different following the implementation of FRS 9 (*Associates and Joint Ventures*) in June 1998.

A joint venture is a long-term investment in an undertaking that:

● carries on a trade or business in its own right (this is referred to as an *entity* in the accounting standard);
● is jointly controlled by the reporting company and others under a contractual arrangement.

Consequently, joint marketing agreements would not be considered a joint venture under the accounting standard, as they would not be classed as an entity, as they do not trade in their own right and are effectively an agreement to share costs. The company would account for a joint arrangement as part of the group's activities.

Joint ventures are accounted for using the *gross equity method*. (This brings the investor's share of the turnover into the profit and loss account and the total gross assets and liabilities are disclosed on the balance sheet.) The turnover arising from joint ventures should be clearly distinguished from group turnover in the segmental analysis given in the notes to the accounts.

To illustrate the accounting treatment for joint ventures we will continue our previous example, and assume that Company B is a joint venture and Company A has a 30 per cent stake in the joint venture.

EXAMPLE The consolidated profit and loss account would be as follows:

	£000	£000
Turnover: group and share of joint venture	1210	
Less: share of joint venture's turnover	(210)	
Group turnover		1000
Operating costs		(750)
Operating profit		250
Share of operating profit in joint venture		54
Interest payable:		
Group	(50)	
Joint venture	(9)	(59)
Profit on ordinary activities before tax		245

Tax on profit on ordinary activities*		(72)
Profit after tax		173
Dividend		(20)
Retained profit		153

*The tax change relates to the following:

Parent and subsidiaries	(60)	
Joint venture	(12)	

SUMMARY

A joint venture is a long-term investment in an undertaking that trades in its own right and is jointly controlled with other joint venturers under a contractual agreement. The investing company's share of its joint venture's turnover, operating profits, and subsequent entries other than dividends, will be included in its consolidated profit and loss account. The investing company's share of the turnover in its joint ventures will also be disclosed. All entries shown before profit before tax will be shown separately on the face of the profit and loss account, clearly attributable to joint ventures. Subsequent entries are included in the group results, but must be separately disclosed.

● SIGNIFICANT ASSOCIATES AND JOINT VENTURES

In some industries, associates and joint ventures could represent an important element of a company's trading activities. FRS 9 recognises this and requires additional disclosures where the investor's total share in its associates or joint ventures exceed 15 per cent of the investing group's:

- gross assets
- gross liabilities
- turnover
- the operating result (on a three-year average).

The company would be required to disclose an associate's turnover and give the additional disclosures of balance sheet items discussed in Chapter 9.

If an associate, or joint venture, exceeds 25 per cent of any of the above, the investor's share of the following profit and loss account items in the associate, or joint venture, should be disclosed:

- turnover
- profit before tax
- tax
- profit after tax.

Additional disclosures are also required for balance sheet items, and are discussed in Chapter 9.

SUMMARY

Additional disclosures have to be made where associates or joint ventures exceed certain thresholds.

● EXCEPTIONAL AND EXTRAORDINARY ITEMS

Exceptional items are events that you would expect to occur, like bad debts, but, these are so unusual or so large that they need to be disclosed separately if the accounts are to give a true and fair view.

Overseas accounts will often show, after tax, something called extraordinary items. These were commonly found in UK accounts until the implementation of FRS 3 (*Reporting Financial Performance*) in 1993. This has had a major impact on the presentation of profit and loss accounts, and is discussed in detail later in this chapter. Extraordinary items used to be described as material items that are not part of the ordinary activities of the business and were, therefore, expected to occur infrequently. Profits or losses on disposal of subsidiaries were common extraordinary items. Unfortunately, the distinction between extraordinary items and exceptional items became very blurred. Exceptional items showed before tax, and affected reported earnings per share. Whereas extraordinary items showed on the profit and loss account after tax, and did not affect earnings per share. Suddenly rationalisation and reorganisation costs were extraordinary, and profits on disposal became exceptional. Reported earnings per share grew!

FRS 3 solved the problem. First it required calculations for earnings per share to be made after extraordinary items. Second it tightened the definition of extraordinary items to the point that they have become so extraordinary that you will not find any in UK accounts!

Extraordinary items are now defined as: 'Material items possessing a high degree of abnormality which arise from events or transactions that fall outside of the ordinary activities of the reporting entity and which are not expected to recur. They do not include exceptional items nor do they include prior period items merely because they relate to a prior period.'

Most exceptional items are now included as operating costs, shown under the appropriate heading. The exceptional items are then disclosed, usually in a note to the accounts. They would only be shown on the face of the profit and loss account if this was felt necessary for a true and fair view.

The only exceptional items that are shown on the profit and loss account after operating profit, and before interest, are:

● profits or losses on the sale of fixed assets;
● profits or losses on the sale or termination of operations;
● the cost of a fundamental reorganisation that has a material effect on the nature or focus of a company's operations.

As most exceptional items are no longer shown on the profit and loss account itself, reading of the notes is essential if you want to understand the underlying trends in the profitability of the company.

SUMMARY

An exceptional item is a material event, or transaction, which needs to be disclosed if the financial statements are to give a true and fair view. Most exceptional items are only disclosed in the notes to the accounts. They would only be shown on the face of the profit and loss account if this was necessary for a true and fair view or they related to:

● profits or losses on sale of assets* or subsidiaries;*
● a fundamental reorganisation.*

Exceptional items marked * above are shown between operating profit and interest; all others are included in operating costs under the appropriate heading.

INTERNATIONAL DIFFERENCES

Internationally, there are major differences in the definition of extraordinary and exceptional items. Some countries have a very restrictive definition of extraordinary items, so they are never seen, whereas others have definitions that are so wide that most exceptional items would be classed as extraordinary.

The definition of extraordinary items is important as they are usually excluded from earnings per share calculations (although they are included in Japan), meaning that adjustments often have to be made to ensure comparability.

International accounting standards

IAS 8 (*Net Profit or Loss for the Period, Fundamental Errors, and Changes in Accounting Policies*) deals with *ordinary* and *extraordinary items*. Whilst it does not actually refer to exceptional items, it requires separate disclosure of items within ordinary activities that are 'of such size, nature or incidence that their disclosure is relevant to explain the performance of the enterprise for the period'. Therefore, exceptional items must be disclosed, usually in the notes to the accounts. The illustrative examples in Appendix 2 of the IAS show that profits or losses on disposal of subsidiaries would be classed as an exceptional item.

It defines extraordinary items as those arising from transactions that are not expected to recur frequently and arising from events or transactions, that are 'clearly distinct from the ordinary activities'. Natural disasters and expropriations of assets are examples of extraordinary items. The International Standard's definition of extraordinary items, and illustrative examples, effectively limit them to items that are outside of management's control.

Extraordinary items must be shown on the face of the profit and loss account.

Europe

In France there is a wide definition of extraordinary items, although confusingly (for us) they are called *exceptionnel* in the accounts. Extraordinary items are events outside of the normal trading activities of the business, and so would include profits on sale of assets.

The Germans have a similarly narrow definition of extraordinary items to the UK, and consequently they are rarely seen in the accounts.

In the Netherlands, exceptional items are simply abnormally large or frequent. Extraordinary items are non-recurring and fall outside the normal operations of the company.

Japan

Extraordinary items are shown before tax, and include both exceptional and extraordinary items, some of which would not even be regarded as material in the UK. It is impossible to determine the split between exceptional and extraordinary items.

North America

In the USA extraordinary items are those that are distinguished by both their infrequency and their unusual nature, given the company's operating environment. This definition is generally interpreted in a restrictive way, as infrequent is defined as 'not expected to recur in the foreseeable future'. The main exceptions to this interpretation are given below, and these would be shown as extraordinary items:

● material gains and loses arising from the extinguishing of debt;
● the tax benefits of operating loss carry forwards;
● the net adjustments that are made when a company's operations are de-regulated.

In Canada the definition of extraordinary items is very restrictive, as they must meet all of the criteria shown below to be classified as extraordinary:

- they are not expected to occur frequently over several years;
- they are not typical of the company's normal business activities;
- they do not primarily depend on decisions, or determinations, by the company's management, or owners.

Therefore, extraordinary items are effectively limited to those that are not in the management's control.

● PROFIT ON SALE OF FIXED ASSETS

Fixed assets are by definition things the business means to keep, but all businesses sell their assets when they reach the end of their useful life. The sale of assets will affect profitability if the company receives more or less than the asset value.

EXAMPLE   If the company bought a machine for £15 000 and depreciated it by £10 000, it would be worth £5000 on its books. If the machine is subsequently sold for £6000, the company will report £1000 profit on the sale of assets. If it was only sold for £3000, a loss of £2000 will be shown on the profit and loss account.

If the proposals of FRED 17 (*Measurement of Tangible Fixed Assets*) are adopted in a standard, profits on sale of assets will no longer be shown as an exceptional item. Profits and losses will be included in operating profit. (The proposals are discussed in detail in Chapter 8.)

SUMMARY   When assets are sold they have a value in the books. If the company receives more than the book value it shows as a profit, any less would show as a loss. Therefore, the profit or loss recorded on the sale of assets is determined by the value that these assets have in the accounts.

● PROFIT ON SALE OF OPERATIONS

Following a UITF ruling (UITF 3, *Treatment of Goodwill on Disposal of a Business*) in 1992, that was subsequently incorporated into FRS 2 (*Accounting for Subsidiary Undertakings*), it is more complicated to calculate the profit or loss on the sale of subsidiaries. It all stems from the way that companies currently account for *goodwill* (the premium paid to acquire a company and access its future profits).

A predator wants to buy a company. This company is only worth £50 million on the balance sheet (assets less liabilities), but last year it made £20 million in profit. When the predator buys this company it will have to pay more than the net worth of £50 million, as it will not just be buying the assets, but also buying the future profits. If the predator paid £90 million for the company, it will have paid £40 million for the 'goodwill'. This is the premium paid on acquisition. (Goodwill will be discussed in more detail in Chapter 19.)

We will assume that the acquisition is consolidated into the predator's accounts at £50 million. (This may not be true as asset values will probably be restated to reflect 'fair values' (replacement cost) when the acquisition is consolidated. This is determined by the method used to account for the acquisition.)

The predator has paid £90 million to buy this company, which has a value on his accounts of £50 million. If the predator sells it for £70 million the following year, has the predator made a profit or a loss? Common sense says that it is a loss of £20 million and this is how it must be accounted for. (Before 1992, some companies were saying they had made a profit ... they had sold assets and liabilities worth £50 million for £70 million, therefore, there was a profit of £20 million!)

SUMMARY Profits or losses on sale of subsidiaries must consider the goodwill that was paid to acquire the business, as well as the current value of the business in the company's accounts.

● NET INTEREST PAYABLE

Companies usually show a figure of net interest payable on the face of the profit and loss account. The notes would then detail the interest and similar income received, the interest paid and any interest capitalised. The notes contain important information as can be clearly seen in the extract below from Tesco's 1997 accounts.

Extract 13.2   NET INTEREST PAYABLE (TESCO)

	1997 £m	1996 £m
Interest receivable and similar income on money market investments and deposits (a)	34	63
Deduct interest payable on:		
Short-term bank loans and overdrafts repayable within five years	(32)	(49)
Finance charges payable on finance leases	(8)	(9)
9% convertible capital bonds 2005	–	(8)
4% unsecured deep discount loan stock 2006 (b)	(8)	(7)
ECSC loans 1998–9 (c)	(1)	(5)
10⅜% bonds 2002	(21)	(21)
⅛% deep discount bonds 2012 (a)		(23)
8¾% bonds 2003	(17)	(17)
Interest capitalised	29	33
	(59)	(106)
	(24)	(43)

(a) The 1/8% deep discount bonds 2012 were redeemed in June 1995. Interest payable for 1996 comprised £3m of discount amortisation and £20m loss on redemption. Gains on cancellation of the associated deposit and financing arrangement of £26m were included within interest receivable.
(b) Interest payable on the 4% unsecured deep discount loan stock 2006 includes £3m (1996 – £2m) of discount amortisation.
(c) ECSC refers to the European Coal and Steel Community.

● Investment income

There is a statutory requirement (Companies Act, Sch 4) to disclose separately the income from listed and unlisted investments. However, not all investments are made to earn investment income, some may be made in the hope of generating operating profits. These are called *trade investments*, and can represent investments in customers, suppliers or even competitors. Some companies will also disclose their income from trade investments separately.

● Interest paid

Schedule 4 of the Companies Act (para 53) requires that companies disclose the interest that has been charged for loans from outside of the group, analysed between:

- interest on bank loans and overdrafts that are repayable within five years
- any other period.

● Interest capitalised

Capitalised interest is interest charged to the balance sheet, rather than the profit and loss account. It is usually charged to tangible assets, although it can be charged to stock. It is discussed in detail in Chapter 8.

The logic for charging the interest to the balance sheet goes like this. The business could buy a building from a construction company. The construction company would look at all the costs that had been incurred in constructing the building (land, materials, labour, etc.) in determining the price that it would charge. The price would reflect the total costs that the construction company has incurred, and would include interest on any borrowings. If interest can be included when a building is purchased from a third party, surely the business should be able to capitalise interest if it constructs the building? Well, there is not a rule that says you cannot, and the Companies Act says you can!

The problem with capitalising interest is twofold:

(1) The cost of construction plus the capitalised interest could well exceed the market value of the property (we saw in Chapter 8 that the book value of assets rarely coincides with the market value).

(2) The cash cost of interest is totally unaffected by where the interest is charged. A company could be experiencing difficulties with its bankers, even if in the profit and loss account the interest is only a small proportion of the profit.

SUMMARY Net interest payable is the interest payable, less any interest receivable, and interest capitalised. Capitalised interest is interest charged to the balance sheet (usually fixed assets), and is disclosed in the notes. Capitalising interest affects reported profitability, and fixed asset values. There are currently no rules on capitalising interest and some companies do and others do not. Therefore, analysts need to adjust for capitalised interest before making comparisons.

● ADDITIONAL INFORMATION AVAILABLE IN THE NOTES

The Companies Act and the Stock Exchange rules require companies to make a number of additional disclosures in their accounts.

The Companies Act (s 390) and the Companies Act 1985 Regulations (1991) require companies to disclose the auditors' remuneration in the accounts. This should be analysed between remuneration for audit and non-audit work. This is an important note. If the audit remuneration has increased significantly, and the business has not materially changed during the period, it may be indicative that it has taken the auditors longer to determine that the accounts were true and fair. Most companies would be trying to negotiate to push auditors' fees down, and large increases should generally be treated with suspicion.

Schedule 4 of the Companies Act requires companies to disclose the following additional information in the notes to the accounts:

Hire charges for plant and machinery

There are two types of hiring and leasing agreements:

(1) short-term agreements where the company effectively rents the machinery for a defined period of time – these are called *operating leases*;
(2) longer-term leases where the machinery is leased for the life of the machine – these are called *finance leases*.

(These leasing agreements are discussed in Chapter 6.) Operating leases are charged to the profit and loss account; whereas finance leased assets are capitalised, with the commitments to leasing companies included in creditors.

As operating lease rentals are a form of off-balance-sheet borrowing, it is always useful for an analyst to monitor operating leases. The charge for the year is shown in the notes to the profit and loss account, and the commitments under operating lease agreements will be disclosed as part of the notes on contingent liabilities and capital commitments.

Amounts set aside for the redemption of shares and loans

Employees and their remuneration

This should cover both the average number of employees employed during the period; and the employment costs should be analysed between:

● wages and salaries payable during the period;
● social security costs (this should include any contributions to state-run pension schemes);
● other pension costs.

Payments to directors

This should include:

● directors' emoluments ('emoluments' is a legal term, from Sch 6 of the Companies Act, incorporating all aspects of a director's remuneration. Consequently it would include fees, any expenses that are subject to income tax, benefits in kind, and pension contributions);
● directors' pensions;
● compensation payments made to directors for loss of office;
● any amounts paid to third parties for directors' services;
● the number of directors who have waived emoluments, together with the amounts of the waived emoluments.

The Stock Exchange also requires the disclosure of the terms of any agreement where a director has agreed to waive emoluments, and following the implementation of the Greenbury Report in 1995, listed companies disclose the directors' emoluments individually for each director by name.

● FRS 3 AND THE PRESENTATION OF THE PROFIT AND LOSS ACCOUNT

Historically, companies only disclosed total revenues and costs on the face of the profit and loss account. (The notes would usually detail a divisional and geographical analysis.) There was no requirement to identify how much of the profit came from recent acquisitions or from businesses that had been closed down or sold during the period. This meant that it was often impossible to identify how much of the profit had been generated by acquisitions and disposals, and so understand the trend in underlying profitability.

Table 13.3   **FRS 3: underlying profit trends**

		Acquisitions		
	£m	£m	£m	£m
Turnover	500	300	200	1000
Cost of sales	(280)	(160)	(160)	(600)
Gross profit	220	140	40	400
Distribution costs	(70)	(40)	(30)	(140)
Administrative expenses	(35)	(15)	(20)	(70)
Other operating income	10			10
Operating profit	125	85	(10)	200
Profit on sale of fixed assets	5	2	3	10
Profit before interest	130	87	(7)	210
Net interest payable				(50)
Income from interests in associated undertakings				20
Profit on ordinary activities before taxation				180

Looking at Table 13.3, you can see how this gives us a much clearer idea of where the profits have been made this year and what the profits might be next year.

FRS 3 had mixed reviews. It has made it possible to understand the underlying trends in company profits, but in doing so has complicated the profit and loss account. It eliminated the misuse of extraordinary items, but most exceptional items are now charged to operating profits and their disclosure is in the notes, but it does give us the information to understand the underlying profitability in a way that was not possible before its introduction.

Splitting continuing and discontinued operations helps us to understand the improvement in United Biscuits' (UB) operating profit margins. In 1995, UB's discontinued operations contributed £1176.8 million to turnover, but had operating losses of £25.2 million. Whilst discontinuing these businesses reduced turnover, it improved operating profits and doubly improved the operating profit margin!

Extract 13.3   CONSOLIDATED PROFIT AND LOSS ACCOUNT (UNITED BISCUITS)

for the 52 weeks ended 28 December 1996

	Notes	1996 £m	1995 £m
Turnover			
Continuing operations		1,887.2	1,824.3
Discontinued operations		99.5	1,176.8
		1,986.7	3,001.1
Cost of sales		(1,271.5)	(1,755.2)
Gross profit		715.2	1,245.9
Distribution, selling and marketing costs		(434.6)	(983.5)
Administrative expenses		(147.9)	(166.3)
Other income		5.3	2.5
Employee profit sharing		(1.0)	–
Operational reorganisations	2	–	(27.4)
Operating profit			
Continuing operations before exceptionals		129.2	123.8
Discontinued operations		7.8	(25.2)
		137.0	98.6
Operating exceptional items		–	(27.4)
Total operating profit		137.0	71.2
Amounts written off investments	2	(3.2)	(4.3)
Loss on disposal of businesses	2 & 21	(82.9)	(102.3)
Profit/(loss) on disposal of fixed assets	2	1.4	(16.3)
Profit/(loss) before interest	2	52.3	(51.7)
Interest	3	(27.9)	(48.9)
Profit/(loss) on ordinary activities before tax			
Continuing operations before exceptionals		101.3	74.9
Discontinued operations before exceptionals		7.8	(25.2)
Total operations before exceptionals		109.1	49.7
Total exceptional items		(84.7)	(150.3)
Profit/(loss) on ordinary activities before tax		24.4	(100.6)
Taxation			
Tax charge on profit before exceptionals	5	(29.7)	(23.0)
Tax credit/(charge) on exceptionals	5	23.6	(1.2)
Taxation		(6.1)	(24.2)
Profit/(loss) on ordinary activities after tax		18.3	(124.8)
Minority interests		(1.3)	(1.4)
Profit/(loss) attributable to shareholders		17.0	(126.2)
Dividends – payable	6	(18.5)	(18.5)
Dividends – proposed	6	(34.5)	(32.8)
Reduction in reserve	19	(36.0)	(177.5)
Earnings/(loss) per share	7		
FRS 3 basis		3.2p	(23.9)p
Continuing operations before exceptionals		13.7p	10.1p
All operations before exceptionals		14.8p	4.8p

CREATING PROFIT

The various paper adjustments involved in the determination of profit allow some companies to create their own profit. Creative accounting is something that every analyst should look for, as two and two only equals five when four is not good enough! If the profit looks too good to be true, it probably is!

2 + 2 = 5 Operating profit is the key component of profit, as it is sustainable and generates 'quality' earnings. Profit before tax is the base figure for the return on capital employed calculation. Profit after tax is used for calculating earnings per share and other investment ratios. Each one can be 'managed'. In this chapter we will summarise how operating profits and profits before tax can be improved. These creative accounting opportunities are fully discussed in this, and other, chapters, but are summarised below.

Operating profit

Operating profit can be improved in one of two ways. You can either increase the sales or reduce the costs. Increasing the sales is an obvious option for the company, but is more difficult for the reader of accounts to spot. It is much easier to spot companies trying to reduce their costs.

The problems of revenue recognition

In a cash business, determining the turnover is very straightforward. It is the cash that has gone through the till. Earlier in the chapter we discussed the different ways that companies can determine turnover, any change in the definition will probably have an impact on the reported profitability, and any material change should be disclosed in the notes to the accounts.

The 1996 accounts of the Swedish company, Atlantic Container Line (ACL), stated that: 'The accounting policy for revenue and expense recognition has been changed as of 1996, from a full completion of voyages in the financial year to a pro rata of total voyage days before and after December 31. The effect of this policy change has been adjusted in the Shareholders' Equity as per January 1, 1995.' No numerical disclosures were made, therefore, we have to assume that the impact on profitability was immaterial.

In most manufacturing businesses it is the delivery of the goods, or the transfer of title, that determines turnover. That has led some companies, for example Fisons until 1994, to practice 'trade loading'. Some of next year's despatches are pulled forward into the last period of the current year. Most managers are aware of this practice – goods and invoices are often despatched or delayed at the end of the financial year. Over a period of time it probably does not matter, as this sort of manipulation cancels itself out.

Turnover becomes more difficult to ascertain when the revenue is bridging different accounting periods, for example, in long-term contracts. Companies must then determine the accounting period in which they will be recognising the revenue.

It is not unusual for companies involved in long-term contracts to have agreed stage payments, but the inclusion of turnover does not necessarily reflect the cash flow. When should the turnover be recognised on the company's profit and loss account? In the UK, turnover from long-term contracts is generally included in the profit and loss account on a percentage of completion basis. However, we have seen that there are different ways of calculating the turnover and reported profits. It almost goes without saying that different ways of calculating the percentage of contract completion will give different turnover figures.

The important thing to spot here is consistency. If the turnover has been calculated on the same basis from one year to the next, the numbers are roughly comparable. Bringing turnover forward into this year will make next year's profit figures harder to achieve. If the company has changed its definition of turnover, the comparability of the numbers will be affected.

Reducing the costs

In reality most costs cannot be changed, what can be changed is where they are charged. Every invoice has to show up somewhere in the accounts, but is it the profit and loss account or the balance sheet? Capitalising costs improves profitability. However, not all costs can be traced in this way. Some are 'paper' charges that we include to ensure that the profit and loss account reflects the costs that relate to the sales made in the period. These adjustments are paper transactions to cover things like probable bad debts. They are based on managers' judgements, and judgements can be changed. Consequently, there are two possibilities for creative accounting to reduce the costs:

(1) charging costs to the balance sheet. This would include transferring costs to stock and capitalising interest;
(2) reducing the 'paper charges' made to the profit and loss account. This would include provisions, exchange differences and depreciation.

Stock valuation

This involves:

- identifying the volume of the closing stock; and
- calculating the value of stock.

Measuring the amount of stock in the warehouse should be simple, but anyone who has been involved in stocktaking will know how difficult it is in practice! Errors in stocktaking are not usually deliberate in large companies, after all, the auditors will do a physical stock-take. (Smaller companies have been known to overstate the volume of stock. Beware of accounts where the auditors feel unhappy about the cut-off level for stock!) Some degree of error will be built into the system, and should not affect the company's performance over time. It is the valuation of stock that gives most scope for creative accounting. There are three possible options for the creative accountant:

(1) change the method of valuing stock;
(2) increase the level of overheads charged to stock;
(3) overstate the net realisable value.

Charging costs to stock and having an optimistic view of net realisable value flatters both profits and net worth. Unfortunately, the information given by companies about their stock valuation is somewhat limited, as the following note from the 1996 accounts of engineering company, IMI, shows:

Extract 13.4   **STOCK VALUATION (IMI)**

> **STOCKS**
> Stocks are valued at the lower of cost and net realisable value. In respect of work in progress and finished goods, costs include all direct costs of production and the appropriate proportion of production overheads.

Provisions

Provisions have always been used by companies to 'smooth' profits. The stock market likes to see a steady growth in profits, unfortunately life is not like that – you have bumper years and bad years. Reporting a bumper profit always gives companies problems. If the market expects a profit of £100 million and it looks like being £120 million, should the company report £120 million? The stock market behaves very much like bosses – it moves the goalposts! If the company reported a profit of £120 million, they would expect £130 million next year. For a public company, disclosing profits in one year creates an expectation for the next. For this reason, there has always been a tendency to make large provisions in good years (taking a prudent view) and smaller provisions in bad years. The only exception to this rule is when new management takes over or when the market expects a bad year, then the company will always make large provisions to depress profits. Then the following year, when the costs are probably incurred, they are not charged to the profit and loss account and the new management will have turned the business around!

Provisions are not normally detailed in UK accounts (the main exception is banks' accounts where bad-debt provisions are required to be disclosed). Any disclosure is given to ensure that the accounts show a true and fair view. However, the scope for creativity in provisioning will be limited if the proposals in FRED 14 are incorporated into an accounting standard. The FRED proposes that provisions should only be recognised when the company has an obligation to a third party at the year end to transfer economic benefits as a result of past events. Provisions would have to be based on obligations, not on guesses.

Most provisions have the effect of moving profit from one year to the next. When analysing accounts, we need to read the notes to see if any provisions have been disclosed, and to determine their impact on the financial performance of the company.

Depreciation

Depreciation was discussed in detail in Chapter 8. As a paper charge, depreciation offers considerable scope for creative accounting. There are three avenues for the decision:

(1) change the asset lives;
(2) change the method of calculating the annual depreciation charge;
(3) change the net residual value.

To spot any changes in the depreciation policy, you need to read the notes carefully and compare the accounting policies and profits declared from one year to the next. If the company declares a profit in 1996, is the same profit figure shown for comparative purposes in 1997? If not, has the fixed asset number changed on the balance sheet. If it has, there has been a change in the depreciation policy.

We cannot comment on whether a company is right or wrong in changing its depreciation policy, we are only concerned with trends in performance. We are looking for any changes in the accounting policies of the company that make the numbers less comparable. We need to exclude these changes from our analysis to establish a trend.

Exchange rates

Exchange rates are discussed in detail in Chapter 20. They offer companies two opportunities to engage in creative accounting:

(1) change the method of calculating exchange rates;
(2) the treatment of exchange differences for borrowings and deposits.

Any change in the method used to account for exchange adjustments must be disclosed in the notes to the accounts.

The general rule is that exchange gains and losses on monetary items should be taken into the profit and loss account. Whether it is prudent to take unrealised gains on foreign currency borrowings as part of profits is a matter of debate (the Companies Act says that only realised gains should be taken into the profit and loss account). This treatment is required under SSAP 20, unless the exchange gains should be excluded on the grounds of prudence, or there are doubts about the convertibility and marketability of the currency. The reported profits will reflect exchange gains and losses on monetary items, unless these have been used to finance or hedge investments.

If foreign currency borrowings have been used to hedge against, or finance, foreign equity investments, the exchange differences are written off through reserves. This is an extension of the principle of matching assets to liabilities.

The problems arise when we are looking at a multinational company with a diverse loan portfolio. This is increasingly common, as treasurers use the international capital markets and take advantage of the extensive range of funding instruments that are now widely available. How do you identify which loans have been used to finance or hedge the investments? There is considerable scope for creativity. The accounting standard tries to minimise this by insisting on consistency of accounting treatment from one year to the next, but there is still scope for improving the reported results.

The accounting policies will disclose whether the company is writing the exchange differences on hedged foreign-currency borrowings through reserves. The statement of total recognised gains and losses, and the note on reserves, should disclose the amount that has been charged to reserves during the year.

The profit before tax can be improved by:

- improving the profit on sale of fixed assets;
- reducing the interest charged to the profit and loss account.

Profit on sale of fixed assets

Since 1993, the profit on sale of fixed assets is calculated by reference to the book value of the assets. Therefore, the profit on sale of assets is determined by the book value of the assets. This is influenced by two things:

(1) the company's depreciation policy;
(2) the company's revaluation policy. If the asset is a building that the company has held for a number of years, it will probably have increased in value. This increase in value may or may not have been recognised in the accounts. If the company has not revalued its assets, it is almost certain to make a profit on disposal. It is interesting to note that following the implementation of FRS 3 a number of companies' *directors* (in conjunction with their own professional qualified staff) felt it prudent to *devalue* their properties.

The differences in depreciation policies will be disclosed in the accounts. The effects of different revaluation policies can be eliminated by using the note on historical cost profits and losses (see Chapter 15). This shows what the profit before tax would have been had the company not revalued its assets.

Companies have always capitalised costs. Any costs associated with the improvement or construction of assets have always been charged to the balance sheet, as they are capital costs that do not relate to the sales in the period. If you look at any company that has major capital projects, you will find that a significant proportion of their staff costs are capitalised.

The capitalisation of interest in property development and other areas is a more recent phenomenon. The capitalisation of interest, like any other cost, has the effect of improving the profits and the asset values on the balance sheet. One of the problems is deciding how much interest should be capitalised. It is straightforward if there is a specific loan taken out to fund the development of the asset. Problems arise when the development of the asset is funded from the general borrowings of the company. Then the amount to be capitalised can be either:

- the cost of funding the incremental borrowings required to finance the asset; or
- an average of the interest on the total borrowings of the company, applied to the cost of the asset.

Therefore, there is scope for companies to manipulate profit, and there have been occasions where the book value of properties (including the capitalised interest) has exceeded the market value.

● PROFITABILITY RATIOS

If we are looking at a company's profitability we are interested in:

- the return that the company is making on its capital – this is measured by the *return on capital employed*.

● Operating profit margin

The operating profit used in this ratio may not be the reported operating profit shown in the profit and loss account. The operating profit should reflect the profit that the company has made on trading, and would, therefore, exclude any non-trading items such as the company's share of associated undertaking's profits and losses. Thus, it would be:

$$\frac{\text{Operating profit arising from trading activities}}{\text{Turnover}}$$

This is usually expressed as a percentage.

If a company wants to improve its profitability, it must reduce costs or grow revenues. So, it can improve its operating profit margins by:

- increasing prices
- increasing the volume of products sold
- reducing the operating costs.

If a company has a higher operating margin than other companies in the sector, it will usually be a short-term difference. The other companies in the sector will recognise the profitability of the market, and will enter unless there are large barriers to entry.

● Return on capital employed

The return on capital is an important ratio. To survive in the long term, all companies must generate a return on their capital that is greater than their cost of capital. The return on the capital must also be sufficient to compensate investors for the risks involved with investing in the company.

Unfortunately, calculating the return on capital is not always as simple as it seems. The return on capital employed is:

$$\frac{\text{Profit before tax and interest}}{\text{Capital employed}}$$

This is usually expressed as a percentage. However, as is discussed in Chapter 21, there are often adjustments that need to be made to both the profit figure and the capital employed. Improving the return on capital is fully discussed in Chapter 21.

● Interest cover

The interest cover is indicative of a company's future solvency position, as it measures how many times the interest can be paid out of the available profits. It is calculated by dividing the profit before interest by the interest charge:

$$\frac{\text{Profit before interest}}{\text{Interest}}$$

This is usually expressed as a multiple.

If a company has profit before interest of £45 000 and interest of £30 000, its interest cover would be 1.5 times. It shows how many times the interest bill could be paid out of the available profits. An interest cover of 1.5 times would be regarded as low, if interest rates rose and/or profits fell, the company could experience difficulties in paying interest. Common sense tells us that if a company is having difficulties paying interest on its loans, it may not be able to repay those loans.

Whilst the principle behind the interest-cover ratio is simple to understand, its calculation may be more difficult. The different ways of calculating it and the adjustments that may have to be made are discussed in Chapter 21.

JARGON   **Associated undertaking**   A company, partnership, or association where the company has a participating interest and exercises significant influence.

Capital cost / capital expenditure   A cost relating to fixed assets. Capital costs are normally associated with the purchase of fixed assets but they could also relate to improvements to the fixed assets.

Defined benefits pension schemes   A scheme where an employee's pension is based on a proportion of the employee's salary. The pension is unrelated to the fund performance. Consequently, the company has the risks of pension provision.

Defined contributions pension schemes   A scheme where an employee's pension is determined by the performance of the fund.

Equity method of accounting   Equity accounting is consolidation on one line. The group's share of the associates' total net assets is shown on the group balance sheet. So, the individual assets and liabilities are not shown.

Exceptional item   A material event or transaction occurring in the ordinary activities of the company that needs to be separately disclosed to give a true and fair view.

Extraordinary item   Abnormal material items arising outside of the company's ordinary activities that are not expected to recur in the future. In the UK, exceptional items are specifically excluded from the definition of extraordinary items.

Joint venture   A long-term investment in an undertaking that is jointly controlled with other parties and carries out a trade or a business in its own right.

Long-term contract A contract spanning a number of accounting periods.

A participating interest The investing company can influence the operational and financial decisions of another undertaking.

Percentage of completion A way of accounting for long-term contracts, where the turnover is recorded as the contract progresses and profit is recorded as it arises.

Revenue cost/revenue expenditure A cost relating to the sales that have been made during the period.

Turnover The total sales during the period excluding trade discounts, VAT and similar sales taxes.

14 The profit and loss account: introduction to taxation

> **This chapter covers:**
>
> - **Taxable profit**
> - **The tax charge**
> - **Disclosure requirements**

● INTRODUCTION

Paying tax is one of the certainties of life. We pay taxes until we die, whereas companies pay tax when they are profitable. A UK-based company has to pay tax on any profits made in the UK, but may also pay tax overseas if it has foreign subsidiaries. There is a wide range of taxes that companies have to pay. VAT, Excise Duty and employee PAYE are not included in the separate tax charge shown on the profit and loss account, although some companies do detail VAT and Excise Duty separately (Extract 14.1).

Extract 14.1 **PROFIT AND LOSS (J. SAINSBURY)**

	Note	Continuing Operations 1996 £m	Acquisitions 1996 £m	Total 1996 £m	Total 1995 £m
Group Sales including VAT & sales taxes	16	**12,821**	**678**	**13,499**	12,065
VAT & sales taxes		771	101	872	708
Group Sales excluding VAT & sales taxes		**12,050**	**577**	**12,627**	11,357

There are three taxes that may be included in the tax charge in the profit and loss account:

(1) Corporation tax – this is the tax that is levied on a company's income and capital gains and most companies pay this tax nine months after the company's year end. Large companies pay by instalments.

(2) Deferred tax – this is a notional charge that adjusts the tax charge to reflect the tax that would have been payable if the tax allowances had been the same as the charges made in the profit and loss account. It is effectively an accrual for tax.

(3) Advance corporation tax – this is the tax that companies pay when they pay a dividend to the shareholders. It represents an advance payment of corporation tax, and is paid within 14 days of the end of the quarter in which the dividends are paid. This will be abolished from April 1999.

The tax charge in the UK is rarely calculated as simply as taking the reported profit before taxation and multiplying it by the tax rate. There are three main reasons why differences occur:

(1) some things are required to be charged to the profit and loss account that are not allowed for tax purposes; equally some income is tax free. These are referred to as *permanent differences*;
(2) some things are charged to the profit and loss account in a different period for tax purposes than accounting purposes. These are called *timing differences*;
(3) the tax charge can be affected by the past financial performance of the company. The tax rules allow past losses to be used in future years. In fact, the rules allow losses to be both carried back (for only one year following the July 1997 budget) or they can be carried forward indefinitely.

For UK tax purposes profit is sorted out into three categories:

(1) Trading profits.
(2) Investment income. This would include:
    - interest not taxed at source;
    - overseas income;
    - unfurnished lettings and certain premiums;
    - interest and other receipts taxed at source.
(3) Chargeable capital gains.

● Fiscal years and financial years

Unfortunately these are not the same. The tax year (*the fiscal year*) runs from 6 April to 5 April of the following year. (At the beginning of each fiscal year the Inland Revenue sends out a tax return to many, but not all, tax payers.) Whereas the financial year runs from 1 April to 30 March. Just to add to the confusion, the two years are described differently, the tax year ending 5 April 1997 would be described as the Income Tax year 1996–7 (we see this on our tax returns). Whereas the financial year is referred to by the year in which it starts. Consequently, in our example the financial year would be described as the financial year 1996. The corporation tax rates for the financial year are set by the chancellor in the budget. This has recently fallen in November preceding the financial year, although in 1997, following the change in government, there was a July budget that affected tax during 1997.

Company's accounting years do not always coincide with financial years (although there are a lot of companies with accounting years ending on 31 March). If the company's accounting year spans two financial years, the profits are allocated to the relevant financial year and the appropriate rate of tax is applied.

● TAXABLE PROFIT

The reported pre-tax profit shown in the accounts and the taxable profits are not the same. To calculate the taxable profits, the accounting pre-tax profits have to be adjusted to take account of:

● charges on income
● non-allowable expenditure

- capital allowances
- chargeable capital gains
- dividends received from UK companies.

● Charges on income

This covers interest and royalty payments. They will be charged to the profit and loss account on an accruals basis, but are allowed for tax purposes only when they are paid. Consequently, different amounts will be charged to the tax accounts than shown in the financial accounts.

● Non-allowable expenditure

There are several things that are required to be charged to the profit and loss account that are not allowed for tax purposes. These would include:

- **Depreciation** – this means that a company's depreciation policy makes no difference at all to its tax position (this is not true in many countries overseas).
- **Losses on the sale of assets** – any losses on the sale of assets would be added back and any profits on disposals of fixed assets would be deducted from the reported profits. Adjustments are then made to see if the company is liable for capital gains – these are discussed later in the chapter.
- **Business entertainment**.
- **Charges on income** – this would cover:
  - interest paid on UK borrowings;
  - royalties payable under a UK patent;
  - payments to charities under a deed of covenant.

  These are allowable deductions, but they are deducted from taxable profits on a paid basis, not an accruals basis (this is how they would have been charged to the profit and loss account). Therefore different figures would be included in the tax accounts than reported in the published profit and loss account.
- **General provisions**.

● Capital allowances

The Inland Revenue ignores the depreciation that a company has chosen. This is a non-allowable expense, as it can vary both from one company to another and from one year to another. Instead, the Inland Revenue gives all companies a standard tax allowance. This is called a *capital allowance*. Company tax allowances work essentially the same way as personal tax allowances, reducing the taxable profit.

For some expenditure (for example, offices) capital allowances will only be allowed in enterprise zones. The normal capital allowances, outside of designated enterprise zones, are currently:

- **Plant and machinery:** a writing down allowance of 25 per cent a year on a reducing-balance basis is available for plant and machinery. (This has been doubled for one year for small and medium sized business following the budget in July 1997, which will be able to claim a 40 per cent first-year allowance for twelve months from July 1998). However, if an asset has a life of 25 years or more, it is classed as a *long life asset* and different rules may apply. If the business spends more than £100 000 a year on these assets, after 26 November 1996 the allowance is reduced to six per cent. Ships and railway assets are excluded from long life assets until 2010.

- **Ships:** they attract an allowance referred to as *free depreciation*. This means that the company can choose how much to offset against tax.
- **Patent rights and know-how:** these have a writing down allowance of 25 per cent a year, on a reducing-balance basis.
- **Buildings:** the tax situation on buildings is complicated, and is based on Britain as a manufacturing economy. There are two qualifying hurdles: the trade of the company, and what the building is used for. The following 'trades' qualify for an allowance: agricultural services, bridges and tunnels, distribution, fishing, manufacturing, mines and oilwells, power generation and distribution, repair workshops, transport, and water companies.

  Once the trade qualifies for an allowance, the building itself then has to qualify. The building must be of a qualifying type. This means that it must be used either to pursue the company's trade, or be used for the welfare of the company's staff. Therefore, the head office of a manufacturing company would not attract a tax allowance, but the canteen would. Some buildings may be multi-purpose, for example, a factory with an office attached. These would qualify for a full allowance as long as at least 75 per cent of the building qualifies, otherwise the non-qualifying part should be excluded.

  The tax allowance for qualifying buildings is then 4 per cent a year, on a straight-line basis. Hotels with at least ten letting bedrooms, and agricultural works have the same allowance.

- **Scientific research:** this has a 100 per cent allowance.
- **Cars:** these attract an allowance that is the lower of £3000, or a writing-down allowance of 25 per cent a year on a reducing-balance basis. If the company leases cars, only a proportion of the lease rental will be allowable for tax if the car costs more than £12 000.

We can clearly see that these capital allowances will not be the same as the depreciation charges made by companies and it is this difference that gives rise to the bulk of the deferred taxation charge. Deferred taxation is discussed in detail later in the chapter.

● Sale of assets, chargeable gains and balancing charges

The tax allowances are quite complicated and may well vary from one year to another, depending on the government's fiscal policy. The company has to keep records of all its fixed assets for tax purposes, but does not necessarily have to keep individual records for each asset. Plant and machinery, excluding cars and ships, are 'pooled' and treated as a group of assets that attracts writing-down allowances.

We can see that all assets have a value in the tax accounts, either individually or within a pool. When they are sold the company may receive more or less than their value for tax purposes. If they are part of the 'pool', there is normally no problem. But if they are reported separately, such as buildings and cars, a tax charge may arise. This is illustrated in the following example:

EXAMPLE A company sells a warehouse for £15 million The warehouse had cost the company £10 million and has a written-down value of £7.6 million.

There are two aspects to the tax charge that may arise from this sale:

(1) the written-down value of the asset was lower than either the cost or the market value;
(2) the company has sold the warehouse for more than its cost.

Balancing charges

The first tax adjustment is known as a *balancing charge*. This is based on the difference between the written-down value and the lower of the cost or the sale proceeds. In this case the £10 million cost would be used, and tax would be liable on £2.4 million (10.0 – 7.6 = 2.4). This would be added to the company's taxable profits. If we had received less than the written-down value of the warehouse, our taxable profits would have been reduced by a corresponding *balancing allowance*.

Consequently, the formula for calculating balancing charges, and allowances is:

The lower of the cost or the sale proceeds minus the written down value equals the balancing charge, or allowance.

This balancing charge essentially represents an over-allowance for the warehouse. It is possible for companies to 'de-pool' assets to take advantage of balancing allowances.

Chargeable gains and losses

Companies are not liable to capital gains tax, but their chargeable gains and losses are calculated in exactly the same way. Consequently, in addition to the balancing charge the company would be liable to tax on any capital gains or subject to relief on any capital losses that it incurred on the sale of the warehouse.

Any gains arising since 31 March 1982 are taxable. In our example we sold a warehouse, and a building may be kept for many years. Basing the tax charge on the difference between the tax value and the sale proceeds (or the cost) does not seem very fair, as inflation will have affected the value of money over the period.

The tax authorities recognise this and relief is given against gains, but not losses, to allow for the fall in the value of money during the period of ownership. This allowance is called an *indexation allowance* and is based on the movement in the Retail Prices Index over the period of ownership. The indexation allowance is calculated using the following formula:

$$\text{Original cost} \quad \times \quad \frac{\text{RPI @ time of sale} - \text{RPI @ time of purchase}}{\text{RPI @ time of purchase}}$$

Continuing our example, if RPI was 108.1 at the time when the warehouse was purchased and 156.1 when it was sold the indexation allowance would be:

$$£10 \text{ million} \quad \times \quad \frac{156.1 - 108.1}{108.1} \quad = 4.44 \text{ million}$$

We appear to have made £5 million on the sale of the warehouse, but £4.4 million arose purely from the fall in the value of money. The indexation allowance is then deducted from the cash gain that we have made on the sale of the warehouse, to identify the chargeable gain:

$$£15 \text{ million} - £10 \text{ million} - £4.44 \text{ million} \quad = £0.56 \text{ million}$$

Therefore:

Sale proceeds – cost – indexation allowance = chargeable gain.

Rollover and holdover relief

Although the amount subject to tax has been reduced from £5 million to £0.56 million by the indexation allowance, it would seem a little unfair if the warehouse was sold because the company was moving to larger premises. In fact, if the asset was being replaced, it may not be subject to tax at all. If the company is buying another warehouse it will qualify for *rollover relief*. This means that the company can elect to have the chargeable gain deducted from the cost of the new warehouse.

EXAMPLE Continuing our example, if the company purchased another warehouse for £20 million, the company could elect to defer the payment of the tax on the £0.56 million by deducting it from the cost of the asset and showing it at £19.44 million. Rollover relief is subject to a number of conditions. Using rollover relief the company can effectively defer payment of the tax until the asset is sold and not replaced.

If the reinvestment is in a depreciating asset, other than cars, the capital gain may be deferred through a more limited relief called *holdover relief*. Here there is a time limit for the deferral of the tax liability. The gain will be taxable at the earlier of:

- the disposal of the asset
- when the asset is no longer used for the purposes of the trade
- ten years after the acquisition of the depreciating asset.

● Dividends received from UK companies

Dividends that have been received from other UK companies are called *franked investment income* or *franked income*. As they have been paid out of profits that have been subject to corporation tax, they are not taxed again.

SSAP 8 (*The Treatment of Taxation under the Imputation System in the Accounts of Companies*) requires that gross dividends received should be shown in the profit and loss account, with an amount equal to the tax credit being included in the tax charge.

SUMMARY Taxable profits can be very different from the reported pre-tax profits of a UK company. The taxable profits are calculated from the difference between the trading receipts and the allowable expenditure. Some expenditure, for example interest, is allowed only when it has been paid, whereas other expenditure is totally disallowed for tax purposes. Probably the largest non-allowable expense is depreciation.

The Inland Revenue disallows depreciation, but gives companies capital allowances. Most of these allowances will be the same for all companies, although small and medium-sized companies have a larger first-year allowance until July 1999. There are two exceptions to this:

(1) designated enterprise zones will offer increased allowances to encourage investment in these areas;
(2) buildings: companies have to be both operating in a qualifying trade and using the building for that trade or staff welfare to qualify for a tax allowance.

Plant and machinery, other than cars and ships, may be 'pooled', and are treated as a group for tax purposes. If a company sells an asset that is not in the pool and receives more or less than the written-down (tax) value, a balancing charge or allowance will arise. If the sale proceeds are different from the original cost adjusted for inflation, the company ▶

will have a chargeable gain or loss. Chargeable gains may be deferred if the sale proceeds arise from the sale of certain assets (e.g. buildings) and are reinvested. The reinvestment does not have to be in the same type of asset, but the period of deferral will be determined by the replacement asset type.

Dividends received from other UK companies are called franked investment income. As they have been paid out of after tax profits, they are not subject to corporation tax.

THE TAX CHARGE

The tax charge shown in the company accounts comprises four elements:

(1) UK corporation tax
(2) overseas tax (less any relief for double taxation)
(3) deferred tax
(4) unrelieved advance corporation tax.

UK corporation tax rates

Over the last ten years corporation tax rates have been falling, from 35 per cent for large companies in 1987, to 34 per cent in 1990, and 33 per cent in 1991. From April 1997, corporation tax rates have been reduced by a further 2 per cent to 31 per cent and are proposed to fall to 30 per cent from April 1999. Most companies currently pay 31 per cent, but there are lower rates for smaller companies, which currently pay 21 per cent. This will fall to 20 per cent from April 1999. The small companies rate applies to companies with taxable profits up to £300 000. There is some *marginal relief* for companies with taxable profits falling between £300 000 and £1 500 000. This marginal relief tapers out the benefit of the small companies rate.

Overseas tax and double taxation relief

The general rule in the UK is that if tax has been paid overseas, it need not be paid again in Britain. Double taxation relief works on the simple premise that a company's profits should not be taxed twice.

However, any overseas income earned by a UK-based company is subject to UK taxation. This means that any dividends that are paid by the overseas subsidiary to its UK parent may be liable to additional tax. If the overseas tax rate is lower than UK rates, additional tax will have to be paid, to bring the tax rate to the UK level. Therefore, there may be two elements to the tax charge relating to dividends that are received from overseas subsidiaries: an overseas tax charge and a UK one. First, some countries (for example, the USA) will tax any dividends, interest or royalties that are paid to UK companies. This tax is called a *witholding tax*. Second, if the overseas tax rate is lower than UK tax rates, the company will be liable to pay the difference between the UK tax rate and the lower overseas tax rate on the dividend payments. The tax that has already been paid on those dividends is subject to double taxation relief. Double taxation relief ensures that any dividends paid to the parent company will not be taxed twice, however, the total tax charge must be at least equal to the tax that would have been paid in the UK. Since the reduction in UK corporation tax rates announced in the July budget in 1997, it is unlikely that companies will pay much additional tax. The UK's tax rates are now lower than those in the USA, Japan, Canada and other large EU member states.

To illustrate the principles of double taxation relief, we will consider a simple example of a non-trading holding company with a wholly owned overseas subsidiary. A summarised profit and loss account, translated into sterling and showing only the relevant data, for the overseas subsidiary is shown below:

	£m	
Profit before taxation	20.0	
Tax @ 20%	(4.0)	
Profit after tax	16.0	
Dividends	(4.0)	This is subject to a 10% withholding tax
Retained profit	12.0	

The UK parent receives £3.6 million (£4 million less the £400 000 withholding tax).

The dividend will be grossed up in the UK tax calculation, taking into account both the withholding tax and the tax that has already been paid overseas. This equates the dividend to pre-tax income:

	£m	
Dividend received from overseas subsidiary	3.6	
Withholding tax	0.4	
	4.0	This will be 80% of the gross dividend
Gross dividend	5.0	(4.0 / 80%)

Therefore, the associated foreign tax, at 20 per cent, that has been paid is £1.0 million.

The UK tax liability can now be calculated. The gross income from the subsidiary is £5.0 million. The tax will be corporation tax less any double taxation relief. The double taxation relief will be the *lower* of the tax that has already been paid on the dividends and UK corporation tax that would be paid on the gross income:

	£m
UK corporation tax is £5.0 million x 31%	1.55
Tax already paid:	
Associated foreign tax on dividends @ 20%	1.00
Withholding tax	0.40
	1.40

Therefore, the double taxation relief will be £1 400 000 and £150 000 tax will have to be paid in the UK to bring the total tax charge to UK levels (£1.55 million).

The relevant parts of the holding company's profit and loss account will be as follows:

Profit before taxation	20.00
Taxation	(4.55)
Profit after taxation	15.45

The note on tax will disclose the components of the tax charge:

UK corporation tax	1.55
Less double taxation relief	(1.40)
	0.15
Overseas tax	4.00
Withholding tax	0.40
	4.55

• Deferred taxation

In the UK, unlike in some other European countries (such as Germany), taxable profits are not the same as the published profit before tax. Thus, it is not possible to take the pre-tax profits, and multiply them by the tax rate to arrive at the tax charge.

For this reason, UK companies prepare two sets of accounts: the published accounts that we see and the accounts prepared for the Inland Revenue. Some things are required to be charged to the published profit and loss account (e.g. entertainment costs) that are not allowed for tax purposes. Other things have different values in the tax accounts and the published accounts.

These differences between the two sets of accounts are called timing differences. They can either be permanent, where they appear in one set of accounts, but not in the other. Alternatively, they could be charged to the published accounts in a different year from that in the tax accounts. A good example of a permanent difference is entertainment costs, whereas the difference between the depreciation charge and the capital allowance is a timing difference. Over time the depreciation charge and the capital allowances will be the same, with any residual values arising from the capital allowance being reflected in the balancing allowance.

Permanent and timing differences can be simply illustrated.

EXAMPLE

In reporting its profits of £10 million in 1997, a company has included entertaining expenses of £100 000 and accrued interest payable of £250 000. The interest will not be paid until 1998, and the rate of corporation tax is 31 per cent. In calculating the taxable profits, the accounting profits will be adjusted for both the entertainment expenses and the accrued interest, as the interest will be allowable for tax purposes when it is paid. Therefore, the taxable profit will be £10.35 million (10 + 0.1+ 0.25). The corporation tax will then be £3 208 500 (10.35 x 31 per cent). There is an essential difference between the entertaining expenses and the interest charge; the entertaining expenses will never appear in the calculation of taxable profit, whereas the interest charge will be deducted from the taxable profit next year. In other words, the entertainment expense is a permanent difference, whereas the accrued interest is a timing difference. The timing difference is said to have originated when it first appears in either the profit and loss account or the tax accounts. Whereas it is said to have reversed when it has washed through, and the accumulated treatment is the same. In the case of the interest in our example, the transaction originates when the interest is accrued and reverses when the interest is actually paid.

The interest charge was included in the 1997 profit and loss account, following the accruals principle, as it related to that accounting period. Surely the related tax benefit of £77 500 (250 000 x 31 per cent) should also be included? Why should the accruals principle not apply to taxation?

Theoretically there are two possible ways of reporting the tax charge in the accounts:

(1) **actual tax** – this would charge the actual tax payable to the profit and loss account. This should normally be less than the current rate of corporation tax, as long as the capital allowances are greater than the depreciation charge and other non-allowables. In our above example this would give a total tax charge of £3 208 500.

(2) **deferred tax** – this charges the tax that *would* have been payable, had the interest been allowed for tax purposes. This would have given a tax charge of £3 286 000 (3 208 500 + 77 500). Deferred tax is simply an extension of the accruals principle. The tax is accounted for on an accruals basis, in the same way as any other cost.

Deferred taxation is required by SSAP 15 (*Accounting for Deferred Taxation*) and the calculation of deferred tax is further illustrated in the example below. Sometimes the pattern of origination and reversal is spread over a number of years. The example below illustrates this as it looks at the differences that arise from the depreciation charge and the capital allowances – the largest source of timing differences.

EXAMPLE A company buys a machine for £100,000 and plans to keep it for five years. At the end of the five years it believes that the machine will be worth nothing. To the company, depreciation is a matter of simple arithmetic – it has £100 000 to write off over five years. It chooses to depreciate the value of the machine at £20 000 a year. This depreciation charge will be charged to the profit and loss account as an operating cost, to reflect the allocation of the cost of the fixed asset to the periods benefiting from its use.

The machine qualifies for a 25 per cent capital allowance. Capital allowances are calculated differently from the way that most companies calculate depreciation. Most UK companies make an equal charge over the life of the asset, using the straight-line method of depreciation. Capital allowances for machinery are calculated on a 'reducing balance' basis. In the first year, the allowance would be 25 per cent of £100 000 (£25 000), giving a residual value of the asset of £75 000. In the second, it would be 25 per cent of £75 000 (£18 750). This capital allowance is unrelated to the use of the asset and is determined solely by the government's fiscal policy.

Consequently, the depreciation charge would differ from the capital allowance. In the early years depreciation would be lower than the tax allowance, in the later years it would be higher. This is illustrated in Table 14.1.

Table 14.1 **Capital allowance and depreciation charge contrasted**

	Capital allowance	Company's depreciation charge
Year 1	25 000	20 000
Year 2	18 750	20 000
Year 3	14 063	20 000
Year 4	10 547	20 000
Year 5	7 910	20 000
Total	76 270	100 000

The differences between the depreciation charge and the tax allowances are the *timing differences*, and are calculated in Table 14.2.

Table 14.2 **Timing differences between capital allowance and depreciation charge**

	Capital allowance	Company's depreciation charge	Timing difference
Year 1	25 000	20 000	5 000
Year 2	18 750	20 000	(1 250)
Year 3	14 063	20 000	(5 937)
Year 4	10 547	20 000	(9 453)
Year 5	7 910	20 000	(12 090)
Total	76 270	100 000	(23 730)

Deferred tax brings the tax accounts and the published accounts into line. It adjusts the tax charge to reflect the tax that would have been payable if the tax allowances had been the same as the depreciation charge. The deferred tax will be calculated on the timing difference. This is illustrated in Table 14.3, using a corporation tax rate of 31 per cent:

Table 14.3 **Deferred tax**

	Capital allowance	Company's depreciation charge	Timing difference	Deferred tax (charge) / credit in the year
Year 1	25 000	20 000	5 000	(1 550)
Year 2	18 750	20 000	(1 250)	388
Year 3	14 063	20 000	(5 937)	1 840
Year 4	10 547	20 000	(9 453)	2 930
Year 5	7 910	20 000	(12 090)	3 748

To illustrate the calculation of the tax charge in the profit and loss account (see Table 14.4), we will assume that pre-tax profits are constant over the five years at £100 000, and corporation tax rates remain at 31 per cent:

Table 14.4 **The tax charge in the profit and loss account**

	Year 1	Year 2	Year 3	Year	Year 5
Profit before tax	**100 000**	**100 000**	**100 000**	**100 000**	**100 000**
Depreciation	20 000	20 000	20 000	20 000	20 000
	120 000	120 000	120 000	120 000	120 000
Capital allowance	(25 000)	(18 750)	(14 063)	(10 547)	(7 910)
Taxable profit	95 000	101 250	105 937	109 453	112 090
Corporation tax @ 31%	(29 450)	(31 388)	(32 840)	(33 930)	(34 748)
Deferred tax	(1 550)	388	1 840	2 930	3 748
Total tax charge	**(31 000)**	**(31 000)**	**(31 000)**	**(31 000)**	**(31 000)**
Profit after tax	**69 000**	**69 000**	**69 000**	**69 000**	**69 000**

We can clearly see how accruing deferred tax has the effect of equalising the tax charged to the profit and loss account over the life of the asset.

When we charge deferred tax to the profit and loss account it has to show up somewhere on the balance sheet. It will either show as a liability or an asset. The balance sheet entries for our example will be calculated as follows in Table 14.5.

Table 14.5 Deferred tax in the balance sheet

	Year 1	Year 2	Year 3	Year	Year 5
Opening deferred tax balance		(1 550)	(1 162)	678	3 608
Deferred tax (charge) / credit in the year	(1 550)	388	1 840	2 930	3 748
Closing deferred tax (provision) / asset	(1 550)	(1 162)	678	3 608	7 356

The deferred tax asset exists at the end of the fifth year because the machine still has a resid-ual value in the tax accounts of £23 730 (31 per cent of £23 730 is £7 356.30). We can see that for the last three years our example has a deferred tax asset . However, you will rarely see these in practice, as we have been looking at one machine in isolation. A company will have assets and liabilities that cancel each other out.

Other timing differences

The profit and loss account is charged with the costs that relate to the sales, not the costs that have been paid for. So, other timing differences will arise as items will be charged to the profit and loss account in a different period than they are paid and, therefore, allowable for tax purposes. The accounting standard requires that deferred tax should be provided on the following items:

Accruals

The accruals principle means that in the published profit and loss account costs should be matched to income. This means that the profit and loss account will reflect the costs that relate to the sales or the income that relates to the period. Certain costs (for example, elec-tricity) will have been used in the period, but may not have been invoiced. Equally, some income may have been earned (such as interest), but not actually paid. The profit and loss account accrues both income and costs.

Revaluations

We talked in the chapter on fixed assets about how companies can revalue their fixed assets. The accounting standard requires that a provision for deferred taxation should be made when a tax liability may arise. This means, in practice, that companies make a provision for deferred taxation, reflecting the revalued asset, as soon as they have decided to sell the asset. That is when the liability may arise. The decision to sell will only affect the deferred tax charge if the decision to sell falls in a different accounting period from the actual sale. If the two occur in the same accounting year, the sale will be reflected in the corporation tax charge rather than the deferred tax charge.

Prepayments

Any payments in advance that are allowable for tax purposes will affect the deferred tax charge.

Accounting for deferred tax

Partial provision

Not all of the timing differences are used to calculate the deferred tax charge. Companies are constantly reinvesting, so timing differences might be permanently deferred. There seems little point in showing deferred tax assets or liabilities on the balance sheet if they are never going to give rise to a cash receipt or payment. With this scenario in mind, SSAP 15 requires a 'partial provision'. The company provides for deferred tax only when it is likely to result in a receipt or a payment. It states that deferred tax should be 'accounted for to the extent that a liability or asset will crystallise'. However, the accounting standard requires companies to disclose the full provision in the notes to the accounts.

The company should be trying to ensure that the deferred tax asset or liability is a genuine estimate of the amounts that will become receivable or payable in the future. Therefore, to calculate the deferred tax, it must make estimates of future capital expenditure.

Different methods

In our example above we made the simple assumption that tax rates would remain constant at 31 per cent. Unfortunately this does not reflect reality; we have already seen that UK tax rates have been falling. This presents us with a problem – should we use the tax rate when the differences arose or should we estimate the tax rate that will be actually be paid or recovered? Two different methods can be used to account for deferred tax adopt different answers to that question:

(1) **The deferral method** uses current tax rates. It has the advantage of reflecting the amount that the tax charge would have been had it not been for the timing difference. However, it has two main disadvantages:
   – the amounts appearing in the balance sheet will not necessarily reflect the expected receipt of the payment arising from the timing differences;
   – the amount appearing in the profit and loss account in the year when the timing difference reverses may not affect the original transaction if tax rates have changed. It will only show the effect it would have had if the tax rates had not altered.
(2) **The liability method** uses the tax rate that the company estimates will be paid or recovered when the timing differences reverse. Consequently, when there is a change in tax rates, the whole deferred taxation balance has to be recalculated. However, it has the advantage that the amount shown on the balance sheet is the best estimate on the amounts that will be paid or received for past profit and loss account transactions. The disadvantage is that the deferred tax movement shown in the profit and loss account will comprise three elements:
   – the originating timing differences;
   – the timing differences that have reversed during the year;
   – the changes in timing differences that have previously originated, but will reverse in future years.

The accounting standard requires that deferred tax should be calculated using the liability method.

INTERNATIONAL DIFFERENCES

Deferred tax does not arise in all countries, although it may be found in consolidated accounts where it can arise from balances in foreign subsidiaries, or adjustments made for the true and fair view.

International accounting standards

The international accounting standard (IAS 12, *Accounting for Taxes on Income*) requires that full provision be made for deferred tax, with a few exceptions. Either the deferral or the liability method may be used.

Europe

In France deferred tax does not usually arise in the individual company accounts, although it will be found in the consolidated accounts. It can arise in the consolidated accounts from balances in foreign subsidiaries or adjustments from the tax-based valuations that are found in the individual French companies' financial statements. They may be shown using either a full or a partial provision.

In Germany there are relatively few differences between accounting profits and taxable profits. However, a deferred tax liability should be recorded when the taxable income is lower than the accounting income. It will be seen in the consolidated accounts, where it arises from consolidation adjustments. It should be accounted for in full, using the liability method.

In the Netherlands full provision is usually made using the liability method, which is the recommended method. The balance sheet values can be shown at either nominal or present values.

Japan

In Japan deferred tax is rare, although Finance Ministry rules allow deferred tax accounting in the consolidated accounts. When it is shown, it usually relates to consolidation adjustments.

North America

The USA uses the liability method for all timing differences, irrespective of whether they will crystallise. Canadian companies also make full provision for deferred tax.

A MISTRUSTFUL THOUGHT ON DEFERRED TAX IN THE UK

Profit after tax is an important number, as it is the base for calculating earnings per share. Earnings per share is not only one of the important measures of investment performance, but is also often the basis for calculating directors' bonuses. Doubly important!

The deferred tax provision is a provision like any other, and to calculate the charge that will eventually materialise, the company has to make estimates of its future capital expenditure plans and its strategic intent. The accounting standard suggests that a projection over three to five years would be appropriate where there is a regular pattern to the timing differences; a longer period would be appropriate if there was no uniform pattern. Like all plans, the longer the timescale, the less reliable the plan (reflect on the corporate plan of your own company!) Like all other provisions charged to the profit and loss account, an overcharge in one year can be written back in subsequent years. It could be argued that the deferred tax provision is no longer needed in the light of the company's revised plans.

Deferred tax can be used for short-term 'smoothing' of reported profits. The deferred tax charge is based on a number of assumptions. We are not in a position to know whether these assumptions are realistic or not. The effect of deferred tax can only be short term, as the auditors will be in a position to see whether the proposed plans materialise.

● Advance corporation tax

Advance corporation tax will be abolished from April 1999. Currently, whenever a company pays a dividend to its shareholders, it pays advance corporation tax (ACT) to the Inland Revenue, and the shareholders receive a tax credit. These tax credits can then be used to offset UK share-holder's tax liability. As it is part of the shareholder's' tax liability, it is linked to income tax, not corporation tax. ACT is currently charged at 20 per cent of the gross dividend but will fall to 10 per cent when the starting rate for income tax falls to that level. Currently the ACT on a £40 000 net dividend would be:

(£40,000 / 80%) x 20% = £10,000

The imputation system explained

The £40 000 dividend received by the shareholder counts as a gross dividend of £50 000. On this dividend £10 000 income tax at the lower rate of 20 per cent is *imputed* to (considered to have been borne by) the shareholders. Thus, we talk about the *imputation system of corporation tax* (what a name!). Corporation tax has been around for over 30 years (it was introduced by the 1965 Finance Act), but the imputation system has only been with us since 1973. Prior to 1973, a company paid tax on its profits, and its shareholders paid tax on their dividends without receiving any relief for the tax that had already been paid by the company. Whilst the system was simple, it did lead to distributed profits being taxed twice: once as company profits, and again as dividend income. Under the imputation system share-holders are given a credit for the corporation tax that has been paid by the company.

It was intended that ACT would be:

- A partial payment of the company's tax bill – ACT must be paid to the tax authorities shortly after the dividends are paid. The balance of the corporation tax, called *mainstream corporation tax*, is payable nine months after its year end (or one month after the assessment is issued by the tax office, if this is later). From April 1999 this will change, as large companies with taxable profits over £1.5 million will have to pay corporation tax quarterly. Small and medium-sized companies are exempted from this change. (The definitions of small and medium-sized companies have been given in Chapter 3.)
- Deemed to have been borne by the shareholder as a tax credit. As it is only charged at the lower income tax rate, higher rate tax payers will be liable to pay another 20 per cent (this will rise to 30 per cent when the lower tax rate falls to 10 per cent). Surprisingly, basic-rate tax payers do not have to pay any more tax. Until 2 July 1997, these tax credits could be used by pensions funds and UK companies to reclaim the ACT from the Inland Revenue, as they were deemed to be tax-exempt investors. They will continue to be repaid to PEP (personal equity plan) holders, non-taxpayers and charities until April 1999.

Advance corporation tax is a strange tax. The government does not get any more money from companies, as long as their operations are based in the UK; it just gets the money faster. ACT is payable within 14 days of the end of the quarter in which the dividends are paid. In November 1997 the Chancellor proposed its abolition from April 1999 and this was confirmed in the 1998 budget. The Inland Revenue will get some of its money faster, as whilst advance corporation tax will be abolished large companies will have to pay their tax bills earlier.

In some situations, however, the government could get additional funds. Advance corporation tax represents an advance payment of corporation tax, and can be used to offset the corporation tax that is handed over to the Inland Revenue, but there are restrictions on the amount of ACT that can be recovered. It cannot be used to reduce corporation tax below a current minimum rate of 11 per cent, as the maximum set-off is equal to the rate of tax credit for the dividends (20 per cent). The minimum rate is calculated by deducting the ACT rate (20 per cent) from the corporation tax rate (31 per cent).

Therefore, a company may be unable to offset all the ACT if: dividends are very high, or a lot of its profit is generated outside the UK and is taxed overseas.

Company pays a high dividend

To illustrate the impact of a company paying a high dividend on its tax position, we shall consider the following example.

EXAMPLE A company has a profit before tax of £1 000 000 and proposes to pay a dividend of £950 000. There are no non-allowables or timing differences, and their summarised profit and loss account is shown below:

	£
Profit before tax	1 000 000
Corporation tax @ 31%	(310 000)
Profit after tax	690 000
Dividends	(950 000)
Retained loss	(260 000)

Calculation of gross dividend:	
Dividends paid	950 000
ACT paid (20/80 x £950 000)	237 500
Gross dividend	1 187 500

Composition of the tax charge:		
Minimum mainstream tax @ 11%	110 000	(1 000 000 x 11%)
ACT set-off	200 000	(maximum set-off @ 20%)
Tax charge	310 000	

The ACT on dividends is £237 500 and the maximum offset is £200 000, therefore the unrelieved ACT will be £37 500. If the unrelieved ACT could not be offset in the next year, it would be deemed to be *irrecoverable*, and would be included in the tax charge. This would reduce the earnings figure by £37 500 and would give the revised profit and loss account shown below:

	£	£
Profit before tax		1 000 000
Corporation tax @ 33%	(330 000)	
Irrecoverable ACT	(37 500)	(367 500)
Profit after tax		632 500
Dividends		(950 000)
Retained loss		(317 500)

The irrecoverable ACT would only be separately disclosed if the amounts were material.

Company profits are earned overseas

We have seen that if a company has overseas subsidiaries that generate profits and pay tax overseas, it does not usually have to pay UK corporation tax on those profits. However, they may be liable to pay some UK corporation tax if the overseas tax rates are lower than those in the UK, and the subsidiaries pay a dividend to the UK parent company. (This was explained in double taxation relief.) We will continue with the example we used to explain double taxation.

EXAMPLE The holding company had the following profit and loss account:

	£ m
Profit before taxation	20.00
Taxation	(4.55)
Profit after taxation	15.45

Its tax charge comprised:	
UK corporation tax	1.55
Less double taxation relief	(1.40)
	0.15
Overseas tax	4.00
Withholding tax	0.40
	4.55

Double taxation relief is offset against the company's UK corporation tax liability *before* ACT can be offset. Therefore, there is only £150 000, the tax paid in the UK, available to offset the ACT.

Hence, if the UK holding company wanted to pay a dividend of £4 million to its shareholders, it would have to pay £1 million ACT on their behalf. Only a very small amount of this could be off-set. The minimum mainstream tax at 11 per cent would be £96 774 (£150 000 x 20/31). This leaves unrelieved ACT of £903 226 (£1 000 000 – £96 774).

If the ACT was deemed to be irrecoverable their profit and loss account would be as follows:

		£
Profit before taxation		20 000 000
UK corporation tax	1 550 000	
Less double taxation relief	(1 400 000)	
	150 000	
Overseas tax	4 000 000	
Withholding tax	400 000	
Irrecoverable ACT	903 226	5 453 226
Profit after tax		14 547 774

The company's tax charge has risen by £903 226 because of irrecoverable ACT. However, had the company generated its profits in the UK its earnings would have been lower at £13.8 million, because although all the ACT would be relieved, it would be taxed at 31 per cent. The company has an effective tax rate of 27.3 per cent (5 453 226 / 20 000 000 = 27.3 per cent). Consequently, companies have the ability to offset tax payable on dividends against mainstream corporation tax. The higher the UK corporation tax, the more that can be either directly clawed back or poten-tially offset against ACT. Conversely, a company deriving most of its profits overseas will be pay-ing taxes overseas and will be limited in the amount of ACT that can be offset.

This means the origin of the profit has a major impact on the cost of the dividend. Compa-nies generating profits in the UK will be able to offset the ACT against their UK tax bills, whereas companies making profits overseas will be limited in the amount of ACT that can be relieved. It would pay ACT, but would be unable to use it to reduce its corporation tax bill. The company would then have 'irrecoverable ACT'.

Is irrecoverable ACT irrecoverable?

The straight answer is 'No'! Irrecoverable does not mean that the tax can never be recovered, only that it cannot be recovered this year. The tax accounting treatment is different from the accounting treatment of ACT, as tax accounting is not subject to the principle of prudence. Any that cannot be used this year can be carried back for six years and carried forward indefinitely. It can also be handed over to other members of the group, subject to certain restrictions.

Shadow ACT

However, the proposed changes may reduce the recoverability of ACT. The Chancellor, in his announcement in November 1997, said, 'We will phase in the change over four years and we will **substantially** preserve companies' expectations for using their existing surplus ACT.'

This will be achieved through a system of *shadow ACT*. This will be used solely to enable companies to recover surplus ACT, and does not mean that anyone will have to pay ACT, or a similar tax. It only affects those companies with surplus ACT until their ACT surpluses have been utilised. It works by maintaining the existing limit of 20 per cent on ACT set-offs. It would appear that multinationals have little prospect of recovering all their surplus ACT.

Reducing irrecoverable ACT

Companies have used three options to reduce the level of irrecoverable ACT:

(1) buy a company with UK profits
(2) issue a scrip dividend
(3) issue a foreign income dividend.

ACT and acquisitions

If a company has a problem with ACT, it can be an important factor when it is considering an acquisition. Part of the cash cost of the acquisition can be 'recovered' from the Inland Revenue as soon as the company acquires some UK profits. The GKN bid for Westland in 1994 arose primarily because of GKN's problem with irrecoverable ACT. Another example is Tomkins' acquisition of Rank Hovis McDougall. Tomkins used to make most of its profits overseas, and had built up a lot of irrecoverable ACT. When Tomkins decided to make a bid for Rank Hovis McDougall, it was able to offer more than Hanson – the rival bidder. Rank Hovis McDougall made most of its profit in the UK, and a UK acquisition would allow Tomkins to recover its erstwhile irrecoverable ACT, to thus reduce the cash cost of the acquisition.

Scrip dividends

A scrip dividend is in the form of shares rather than cash, and has the advantage of not being subject to ACT. Scrip dividends were a popular way of avoiding ACT until the introduction of foreign income dividends. To encourage investors to take the scrip dividend it is often *enhanced*, with the value of the shares being much greater than the cash alternative.

Foreign income dividends

Foreign income dividends (FIDs) were introduced in 1994 to help companies that had irrecoverable ACT as a result of their overseas profits. A foreign income dividend is paid from overseas earnings that have borne tax overseas. They are still liable to ACT, but the ACT can be reclaimed by the company, rather than the shareholder. Therefore, the FID does not carry a tax credit, and there is no liability for tax. However, the downside was that tax exempt shareholders could not reclaim the tax credit, so FIDs have tended to be enhanced to attract pension funds and similar investors.

The government announced in the July 1997 budget that FIDs will be abolished from 6 April 1999. This may also reduce the current spate of share buy-backs. Since 1996, buy-backs have been treated as though they are FIDs. A buy-back incurs ACT, which can then be offset against corporation tax. Any surplus ACT can be reclaimed as though it were a FID. Abolishing FIDs looks likely to abolish the tax efficiency of share buy-backs. This may mean a rush of buy-backs until April 1999, as companies try to maximise the tax efficiency. Buy-backs will continue to increase in popularity after 1999, as they will no longer incur ACT and equity funding remains relatively expensive in relation to debt.

Abnormal tax charges

We know that the permanent differences between the tax profits and the accounting profits mean that it is unlikely that the tax charge will ever be exactly 31 per cent. However, any analyst has to be interested in why a company's tax charge has changed. There are various reasons for abnormal tax charges, most of which have been discussed previously:

High profits overseas

Overseas profits will generally be subject to overseas tax, that may, or may not, be higher than UK tax.

Franked investment income

If there has been a change in the amount of franked income, and it is a significant proportion of the company's income, it would affect the company's tax charge, as it is not subject to further tax.

Chargeable gains

The tax charge will be affected if a company has reported sizeable profits on disposal of assets. The chargeable gain will be very different from the reported profits and may be deferred using rollover relief.

Tax losses from previous years

Tax losses can be carried forward indefinitely to offset against future profits. However, there are some exceptions:

- **offset of capital losses** – capital losses can only be offset against capital gains. They cannot be offset against trading profits;
- **restrictions on group relief** – the group-relief provisions of the Income and Corporation Taxes Act (1988) allow trading losses to be surrendered by one member of a group to another member. However, the tax losses can only be offset elsewhere within a group if the subsidiary is at least 75 per cent owned by the parent. If it is not 75 per cent owned the losses can only be carried forward within the subsidiary;
- **cross-border restrictions** – the losses of a subsidiary in one country cannot be used to offset the profits of another in a different country.

Prior-year adjustments

A company could have misjudged the tax charge for a previous year. Fortunately this has to be disclosed under FRS 3 (*Reporting Financial Performance*) which requires that material amounts should be disclosed.

SUMMARY

Tax rates have been falling in the last ten years and are currently at 21 per cent for small companies with taxable profits of up to £300 000, and 31 per cent for companies, proposed to be 30 per cent from 1999, whose taxable profits are over £1 500 000. These will fall to 20 per cent and 30 per cent respectively from April 1999. There is marginal relief available to companies with profits between £300 000 and £1 500 000 that tapers out the benefit of the small companies rate.

However, the tax charge is not just determined by UK tax rates. Other things need to be considered:

OVERSEAS TAXATION / DOUBLE TAXATION AGREEMENTS

These have been made with most countries to ensure that if tax has been paid overseas it need not be paid again in Britain. However, if dividends are remitted to the UK, the overseas tax rate, if lower, will be adjusted to the UK rate.

DEFERRED TAXATION

Some things are charged to the profit and loss account in a different period for tax purposes than for accounting purposes. These differences are called timing differences. Deferred tax charges the tax that *would* have been payable, had these timing differences been allowed for tax. Therefore, tax is accounted for on an accruals basis in the same way as any other cost.

In the UK companies only account for the deferred tax they believe will crystallise into a cash receipt or payment; this is referred to as a partial provision. In order to do this, they have to take a view on future levels of capital expenditure, and this provides opportunities for creative accounting. UK companies account for deferred tax using the liability method. This uses the tax rate that the company estimates will be paid or recovered. Consequently, the deferred taxation balance has to be recalculated when there is a change in tax rates.

ADVANCE CORPORATION TAX

Until April 1999, whenever a company pays a dividend to its shareholders, it pays advance corporation tax (ACT) to the Inland Revenue, and the shareholders receive a tax credit. These tax credits can then be used to offset UK shareholder's tax liability. Consequently, the shareholders are given a credit for the corporation tax that has been paid by the company and the dividends are not taxed twice.

Advance corporation tax represents an advance payment of corporation tax, and can be used to offset the corporation tax that is subsequently handed over to the Inland Revenue. However, there are restrictions on the amount of ACT that can be recovered. It cannot be used to reduce corporation tax below a current minimum rate of 11 per cent, as the maximum set-off is equal to the rate of tax credit for the dividends (currently 20 per cent).

Some companies are therefore unable to offset all of the ACT because:

● their dividend payments are very high;
● a lot of their profit is generated outside the UK and is taxed overseas.

The latter has led to concerns that ACT is an unfair tax, as where the profits are made determines the real cost of the dividend.

To alleviate this problem some companies issue scrip dividends. These are dividends paid in shares, rather than cash, and are not subject to ACT. In 1994, the government allowed companies, rather than shareholders, to reclaim the ACT paid on foreign income ▶

dividends (FIDs). These are dividends that are paid out of overseas earnings that have already borne overseas tax. Both scrip dividends and FIDs were usually enhanced to make them attractive to tax exempt shareholders, until 1997 when the government abolished the tax-exempt status of pension funds. FIDs are due to be abolished in April 1999.

If the company cannot recover the ACT within a year, it is usually deemed to be irrecoverable for accounting purposes, although for tax purposes it can currently be carried forward indefinitely. It should then be included in the tax charge, and separately disclosed if the amounts are material. This means that the payment of dividends affects earnings per share, as companies with irrecoverable ACT will have higher tax charges.

In response to the concerns about ACT, it is due to be abolished from April 1999, and companies left with surplus ACT should be able to recover it against future corporation tax payments under a system of shadow ACT. The abolition of ACT is likely to increase the number of share buy-backs.

● DISCLOSURE REQUIREMENTS

The Companies Act (Sch 4) requires the following disclosures in the profit and loss account:

- the tax on the profit or the loss on ordinary activities;
- the tax on any extraordinary profit or loss (these should be very rare now with the virtual disappearance of extraordinary items following FRS 3);
- other taxes.

With the exception of companies defined as small under the Act, the notes will detail the calculation of the charge for taxation. Whereas small companies will only show the total tax charge. Some of the information shown in the notes is required by the Companies Act, whereas other information is required by the accounting standards.

The Companies Act requires the notes to the profit and loss account to disclose:

- the basis for calculating the UK corporation tax charge and the amount of the charge;
- any *double taxation* relief (relief for tax already paid overseas);
- the basis for calculating the UK income tax charge and the amount of the charge;
- the amount of overseas tax charged to the profit and loss account.

Three accounting standards require additional disclosures. SSAP 8 (*Taxation under the Imputation System*) requires companies to disclose:

- any irrecoverable advance corporation tax;
- the deferred taxation charge.

FRS 9 (*Associates and Joint Ventures*) requires companies to disclose associated and joint venture's tax charge. FRS 3 (*Reporting Financial Performance*) requires disclosures of:

- any prior-period adjustments relating to under-provision or over-provision for material amounts of tax;
- any special circumstances that have affected the tax charge of the current or future periods. These should also be quantified.

These disclosures can be seen in Extracts 14.2 and 14.3 from the 1996 accounts of Cookson, the speciality materials group. Cookson's reported profit before tax in 1996 was £44.6 million and its tax charge was £35.5 million. The tax note disclosed the composition of the tax charge and reconciled it to the UK tax rate in 1996 of 33 per cent:

Extract 14.2 **TAXATION ON PROFIT ON ORDINARY ACTIVITIES (COOKSON)**

	1996 £m	1996 £m
Based on taxable profit for the year:		
UK Corporation Tax at 33.0%	**24.5**	22.7
Double taxation relief	**(3.1)**	(2.5)
	21.4	20.2
Overseas taxation	**13.7**	33.4
Deferred tax	**(5.1)**	–
Advanced Corporation Tax written off	**1.2**	–
Adjustments to prior years' provisions	**(2.0)**	1.4
Taxation attributable to profit of parent and subsidiary companies	**29.2**	55.0
Taxation attributable to Group share of associated companies' profit	**6.3**	6.0
Total taxation charge for the year	**35.5**	61.0
The Group taxation charge, as a percentage of profit before taxation, differs from the rate of UK Corporation Tax (30.0%) as follows:		
Taxation charge calculated at 33.0%	**14.7**	55.5
Exeptional items	**26.4**	10.2
Tax losses utilised	**(2.3)**	(3.1)
Tax losses not utilised	**4.8**	4.1
Excess of capital allowances	**(3.6)**	(3.2)
Other timing differences	**(1.1)**	(2.4)
Effect of overseas tax rates	**(0.3)**	2.2
Advance Corporation Tax written back	**(0.5)**	–
Other items	**(2.6)**	(2.3)
Taxation charge as reported – 1996: 79.6% (1995: 36.2%)	**35.5**	61.0

The note on provisions for liabilities and charges disclose that no amounts have been provided for deferred taxation, and show the full potential deferred tax assets:

Extract 14.3 **PROVISIONS FOR LIABILITIES AND CHARGES (COOKSON)**

Group	Disposal and Closure costs £m	Post-employment benefits other than pensions £m	Exceptional rationalisation costs £m	Other £m	Total £m
At 1 January 1996	9.2	15.5	–	16.8	41.5
Exchange adjustments	(0.7)	(1.2)	–	(1.3)	(3.2)
Expenditure during year	(5.8)	(0.9)	(2.3)	(6.0)	(15.0)
Additions	1.5	–	–	0.2	1.7
Provided during year	18.2	0.4	19.1	2.9	40.6
At 31 December 1996	**22.4**	**13.8**	**16.8**	**12.6**	**65.6**

▶

No amounts have been provided for deferred tax. The full potential liabilities and assets for deferred tax are:

	Amount provided		Full potential liabilities/(assets)	
	1996	1995	1996	1995
Group	£m	£m	£m	£m
Excess of capital allowances over depreciation	**1.8**	0.6	**36.7**	31.9
Other timing differences	**(1.7)**	(0.5)	**(35.9)**	(12.1)
Losses available for relief	**(0.1)**	(0.1)	**(26.7)**	(35.7)
Advance Corporation Tax recoverable	**–**	–	**(26.7)**	(26.3)
Total	**–**	–	**(52.6)**	(42.2)

The amounts shown above in respect of excess capital allowances are based on estimates of the future level of capital expenditure. No provision is made for any taxation liability that may arise in the event that any of the reserves of overseas Group subsidiary companies are distributed. No provision has been made for deferred taxation in respect of any future disposals of revalued properties, as the Directors do not foresee a significant crystallisation of any such liability in the foreseeable future.

JARGON

Advance corporation tax   Until April 1999 companies paying dividends have to make an advance payment of corporation tax equivalent to lower rate income tax on the dividend payment.

Balancing charge / allowance   The difference between the lower of the cost, the sale proceeds, and the written-down value of a fixed asset. It effectively represents an over-allowance or under-allowance for the asset.

Capital allowance   A tax allowance given for capital expenditure. The size of the allowance is determined by the type and location of the asset.

Chargeable gain / loss   A capital gain or loss made by a company. The original cost is indexed for inflation before calculating the gain, or loss and these have been taxable since 1982.

Corporation tax   The tax that is charged on the company's income and chargeable gains.

Deferral method   A way of accounting for deferred tax that uses existing tax rates to calculate the charge. The deferred tax balances are not adjusted when tax rates change.

Deferred taxation   An extension of the accruals principle to taxation. It is a notional adjustment that includes the tax effect of timing differences in the tax charge.

Double taxation relief   The relief given for tax that has already been paid overseas.

Holdover relief   Tax on chargeable gains on some assets, like buildings, can be deferred in the short term through holdover relief if the company reinvests in a depreciating asset, other than cars.

Irrecoverable ACT   ACT that cannot be used to offset the payment of the company's corporation tax bill in the next 12 months. It is not, in the literal sense, irrecoverable – the principle of prudence deems it to be irrecoverable. This means that it must be included in the company's tax charge and affects earnings.

Liability method   A way of accounting for deferred tax that uses current tax rates for calculating deferred tax. Consequently, deferred taxation is adjusted every time those tax rates change.

Permanent differences   Items that appear in the reported profit and loss account, but will never show in the tax accounts, or vice versa.

Rollover relief   Tax on chargeable gains on some assets, like buildings, can be deferred through rollover relief if the company reinvests in a similar asset.

Timing difference   Items that appear in the reported profit and loss account in a different period to their appearance in the tax accounts.

15 The profit and loss account: profit after tax to retained profit

• INTRODUCTION

In arriving at the profit after tax, the company has already deducted from the sales the operating costs, adjusted for any profits or losses on disposal of assets or operations, and interest and taxation. The profit after tax is not necessarily all available for the ordinary shareholders, as two more adjustments need to be made:

(1) a deduction of the profit that is not attributable to the company's shareholders – this is called *minority interests*;
(2) a deduction of the dividends that are paid to preference shareholders – these are referred to as *non-equity dividends*.

• MINORITY INTERESTS

When a company controls another company, it is required to consolidate the other company's results into the group accounts. A company can control another without owning all of the shares (this is discussed in detail in Chapter 19). If a subsidiary is not wholly owned, the shareholders that are not part of the group will receive a dividend in the same way that the parent company does. The group accounts must reflect the fact that part of the profit belongs to shareholders outside of the group.

These other shareholders in the subsidiary, that are not members of the group, are referred to as the minority interests. Their share of the subsidiary's profits or losses has to be deducted as a minority interest before arriving at the profit that is attributable to the group's shareholders.

PREFERENCE DIVIDENDS

Holders of preference shares, like all shareholders, are entitled to receive a dividend. The dividend is subject to ACT and is paid net of ACT. Preference dividends, and any arrears of cumulative preference dividends, have to be paid before the company can pay dividends to the ordinary shareholders.

EARNINGS PER SHARE

This is an important ratio and one of the key indicators used by investors to assess a company's performance, and is also a determining factor in most directors' bonuses. In simple terms earnings per share is the profit attributable to ordinary shareholders, divided by the number of shares in issue. So if the attributable profit was £2 million and there were 20 million shares in issue, the earnings per share would be 10p. If we only had one share in this company, 10p of the profit would be ours! Unfortunately, only part of this is likely to be paid as dividends, so the immediate cash benefit will probably be much smaller. However the retained earnings should have an impact on the growth in the capital value of the share.

All listed companies are required by SSAP 3 (*Earnings per Share*) to publish their earnings per share in the accounts. This is calculated on the basis of:

Profit attributable to ordinary shareholders
Number of ordinary shares in issue

The profit should be the profit after tax, minority interests and preference dividends, and extraordinary items. The number of shares in issue will be the number of shares at the year end that are entitled to receive dividend payments, unless there has been an issue for cash during the year, when the weighted average number of shares will be used.

EXAMPLE A company has 100 million ordinary shares in issue, and has issued no shares during the year. Its summarised profit and loss account for the year is as follows:

	£m
Turnover	1000
Operating costs	(900)
Operating profit	100
Net interest payable	(40)
Profit before tax	60
Tax	(16)
Profit after tax	44
Dividends:	
Preference dividend	(10)
Ordinary dividend	(30)
Retained profit	4

The profit attributable to ordinary shareholders would be £34 million (profit after tax of £44 million less £10 million preference dividend) and earnings per share would be 34p. This calculation would be referred to as using the *net basis*, or *basic earnings per share*.

Unfortunately, the calculation of earnings per share is not always this simple. It can be complicated by:

- **the company's tax position** – the payment of dividends may increase a company's tax charge (and so reduce the earnings) if it cannot recover the ACT within the next year;
- **exceptional items** – exceptional items can distort the trends revealed in analysing a company's earnings per share, some companies report a *normalised earnings* figure to eliminate the effect of exceptional items;
- **share issues** – share issues during the year will affect the calculation of earnings per share, which will be diluted unless profits have grown (share buy-backs would have the opposite effect);
- **share options** – the exercise of share options and warrants could reduce the earnings per share, which is referred to as *earnings dilution*.

Hence, a number of different profit figures can be used in the earnings calculation, which different assumptions about 'normal' profits and the distribution of dividends. We will also see that calculating the number of shares in issue is often more complicated than it sounds, as it will have to take account of shares issued during the year. The exercise of options could reduce the earnings per share if there was no increase in earnings after the exercise of the options. The options would then be seen as *dilutive*.

● Tax and earnings

ACT is the tax payable on dividends until April 1999, and was discussed in detail in Chapter 14. It is currently paid by the company, on behalf of its shareholders, within 14 days of the end of the quarter when the dividend was paid to the shareholders. As this does not reflect a tax liability of the company, it is used to reduce the corporation tax subsequently paid by the company. However, not all companies are able to offset the ACT against corporation tax.

A company could have a problem if the dividends are very high, or a high proportion of its profits are made overseas, and so not subject to UK taxation. Moreover, ACT cannot be used to reduce UK corporation tax below a current minimum rate of 11 per cent. This is calculated by deducting the ACT rate (20 per cent) from the corporation tax rate (31 per cent).

The tax treatment for ACT is different from the accounting treatment, as tax accounting is not subject to the principle of prudence. For tax purposes, any unrelieved ACT can be carried back for six years or forward indefinitely. However, for accounting purposes the carry forward would usually only be for the following year. Consequently, ACT that cannot be relieved against UK corporation tax may be deemed irrecoverable for accounting purposes, even though it may be recoverable at some future date. Any unrelieved ACT that is deemed to be irrecoverable should be included in the tax charge for the year in which the dividend is recorded on the profit and loss account. If the amount is material it should be separately disclosed in the note on taxation. This means that companies may have hidden assets in the form of unrelieved ACT balances which could be utilised if they made an acquisition generating UK tax profits.

For these reasons, earnings can be affected by dividend distribution. There are two ways to resolve the problem and ensure comparability of earnings per share figures:

(1) to assume that there are no dividends – this is referred to as calculating earnings per share based on *nil distribution*;
(2) to assume that all earnings are distributed as dividends – this is referred to as calculating earnings per share based on *full distribution*.

These are discussed and illustrated below. All examples assume that profit before tax is the same as taxable profits, and any unrelieved ACT is irrecoverable and is therefore included in the tax charge.

Nil distribution

For most companies net earnings and nil distribution earnings will be the same – they will only be different if the company has increased its tax charge because of irrecoverable ACT. The company in our example has made half of its profits overseas, and therefore pays some tax overseas.

EXAMPLE

	£000
Profit before tax	1000.0
UK tax @ 31%	(155.0)
Overseas tax @ 50%	(250.0)
Irrecoverable ACT	(12.5)
Profit after tax	582.5
Dividends	(450.0)
Retained profit	132.5

The company must pay minimum mainstream corporation tax of £55 000 (155 x 11/31), therefore the maximum offset is £100 000. The ACT on the dividends is £112 500 (450 x 0.25), so £12 500 will be unrelieved and deemed irrecoverable.

If the company has a million shares in issue, the reported earnings per share will be 58.25p (582 500 ÷ 1 000 000). If the company did not pay a dividend its tax charge would decrease, and the earnings would rise by £12 500. This gives nil distribution earnings per share of 59.5p, as the earnings would then be £595 000 (582 500 + 12 500).

Full / maximum distribution

This is the maximum gross dividends that could be paid out of the reported after tax profits. It ignores the dividend that is paid and identifies a notional earnings figure that is equal to the *gross* dividend if all of the earnings are distributed. Full-distribution earnings are those that are usually used for calculating dividend cover.

Full-distribution earnings will be the lower of:

- the nil-distribution earnings plus the attributable ACT, if the net dividend equalled the nil-distribution earnings;
- the profit before tax less the minimum mainstream corporation tax and foreign tax.

EXAMPLE

In the next example the first formula would be used to calculate full-distribution earnings, as it gives the lowest figure. If the company had a million shares in issue, the full-distribution earnings per share would be 86.25p, compared to the reported 69.0p.

	£000
Profit before tax	1000.0
UK tax @ 31%	(310.0)
Profit after tax	690.0
Dividends	(4502.0)
Retained profit	240.0
ACT paid – 25% of dividends	112.5
Maximum ACT offset – 20% of UK taxable profit	200.0
Unrelieved ACT	None
First formula:	
Nil distribution	*690.0*
Grossed nil distribution (Nil distribution x 1.25)	**862.5**
Second formula:	
Profit before tax	*1000.0*
Minimum mainstream tax (310 x 11/31)	*(110.0)*
Overseas tax	*0*
	890.0

EXAMPLE This example would base full-distribution earnings on the second formula and would have full-distribution earnings per share of 69.50p compared to reported earnings per share of 58.25p.

	£000
Profit before tax	1000.0
UK tax @ 31%	(155.0)
Overseas tax @ 50%	(250.0)
Irrecoverable ACT	(12.5)
Profit after tax	582.5
Dividends	(450.0)
Retained profit	132.5
ACT paid – 25% of dividends	112.5
Maximum ACT offset – 20% of UK taxable profit	100.0
Unrelieved ACT	12.5
First formula:	
Nil distribution	*595.0*
Grossed nil distribution (Nil distribution x 1.25)	*743.8*
Second formula:	
Profit before tax	*1000.0*
Minimum mainstream tax (155 x 11/31)	*(55.0)*
Overseas tax	*(250.0)*
	695.0

● Normalised earnings

Following the implementation of FRS 3 in June 1993, companies have been able to present a multiplicity of earnings figures in their accounts. Whilst a company must show an earnings per share calculation based on the accounting standard, they are encouraged to show adjusted figures, as long as:

- they are reconciled to the earnings figure required by the accounting standards;
- the different earnings figures are given equal prominence in the profit and loss account.

This has encouraged companies to show a number of different earnings per share figures in their profit and loss account, with most companies showing adjustments for exceptional items. However, different companies make different adjustments. Consequently, the Institute of Investment Management Research (IIMR) felt that there was a need for a standard definition of earnings that could be used for all companies to calculate standard investment ratios (e.g. price to earnings (PE) ratios). It proposed, in its *Statement of Investment Practice, Number 1*, a measure that it believes will satisfy the requirement for a standard earnings figure based on trading performance. This is not seen as a replacement for a figure based on maintainable earnings, the IIMR sees it rather as 'an unambiguous reference point'. This is referred to as *headline earnings*, and has been adopted by some companies and is used by the financial press to calculate PE ratios.

● The definition of 'IIMR headline earnings'

Headline earnings adjusts for some, but not all, exceptional items. The IIMR calculation would exclude the following items:

- the profits or losses arising from the sale or termination of an operation;
- profits and losses on the sale of fixed assets;
- the permanent diminution in the value of fixed assets;
- profits or losses arising from the reorganisation or redemption of long-term debt, when they are exceptional as defined in paragraph 5 of FRS 3;
- bid defence costs;
- goodwill amortisation;
- expropriation of assets.

The headline earnings would also make adjustments for any provisions for profits, or losses, on the sale or termination of a business to be discontinued in a subsequent year. These would be reversed, so that the expenses are charged to earnings in the year in which they occur.

Some of these adjustments have tax implications and the IIMR encourages companies to disclose sufficient information to enable the calculation of the tax effects. Some companies disclose headline earnings per share in their accounts, as we can see from the following extract from Coats Viyella's 1997 accounts.

Extract 15.1 **EARNINGS PER SHARE (COATS VIYELLA)**

Earnings per share are based on profit available for ordinary shareholders of:			55.8	109.7
and an average number of shares of:	702.1m	698.2m		
resulting in earnings per share of:	8.0p	15.7p		
Less: profit on sale of fixed assets	(1.4)p	(1.3)p	(9.5)	(9.3)
(gains) on sale or termination of operations	(0.2)p	(1.6)p	(1.6)	(11.5)
operating profit credited to provisions	–	0.1p	–	0.9
taxation relating to these items	0.3p	0.5p	2.1	3.4
minority interests relating to these items	–	–	0.1	0.1
Headline earnings per share	6.7p	13.4p	46.9	93.3

Headline earnings per share have been calculated in accordance with Statement of Investment Practice Number 1 issued by The Institute of Investment Management and Research and are provided in order to assist users of accounts to identify earnings derived from trading activities.

Exercise in full of all outstanding share options and conversion of all the £68.125m 6.25% Senior Convertible Bonds of Coats Viyella Plc would not result in any material dilution of earnings per share.

● Share issues

SSAP 3 requires companies to take account of any share issues in the earnings-per-share calculation. So, if a company has issued shares during the year, it must use a time-weighted average number of shares for calculating the earnings per share. The comparative earnings per share shown for previous years would be adjusted to reflect any bonus element in the share issue. There are different forms of share issues, and SSAP 3 gives detailed guidance on the accounting treatment – these are summarised below.

Shares issued at full market price

A weighted number of shares should be used for the earnings calculation.

Bonus issues

A bonus issue (which may also be referred to as a scrip or capitalisation issue) converts some of the reserves into shares, therefore, there is no increase in the company's cash. So, whilst the number of shares increases, there is no possibility of increasing the earnings following the issue.

In the earnings calculation, the shares are treated as though they had always been in issue and the prior year's numbers are adjusted accordingly. The original earnings per share figure is reduced by using the following formula:

$$\frac{\text{The number of shares before the bonus issue}}{\text{The number of shares after the bonus issue}}$$

EXAMPLE In 1996 a company had 800 000 shares in issue and reported earnings per share of 30p. During 1997, 200 000 shares were issued as part of a bonus issue, making for 1 000 000 shares in issue at the end of the year. The earnings in 1997 are £340 000.

The earnings per share in 1997 will be 34p (340 000 ÷ 1 000 000). The 1996 earnings will be restated to:

$$30\text{ p} \quad \times \quad \frac{800\ 000}{1\ 000\ 000} \quad = \quad 24\text{p}$$

If the company has a share spilt, where the shares are split into shares that have a smaller nominal value, the accounting treatment is identical to the bonus issue shown above.

Rights issues

If the rights issue is made at the current market price, the accounting treatment is simple – a weighted average is used to calculate the number of shares.

However, most rights issues are made at a discount to the market price, and this complicates the accounting treatment. The principle behind the accounting is that the issue is treated as though there were two separate issues:

(1) an issue at full price
(2) a bonus issue.

The comparatives have to be restated to take account of the bonus element of the rights issue. Hence, the rights issue has to be divided into the bonus element and the full-price element. The bonus element is calculated using the following formula, which measures the dilution that has been caused by the bonus element of the rights issue:

$$\frac{\text{cum-rights price}}{\text{ex-rights price}}$$

The cum-rights price is the closing mid-market price on the last day that the shares have the right to subscribe for the new issue. The ex-rights price is based on a theoretical calculation of the share price immediately after the share issue.

EXAMPLE In 1996 a company had 800 000 shares in issue and reported earnings per share of 30p. On 1 July 1997, 200 000 shares were issued in a one for four rights issue at 50p, amounting to 1 000 000 shares in issue at the end of the year. The price of the shares, on the last day of quotation cum-rights, was £1.00. The earnings for the year ending 31 December 1997 are £340 000.

CALCULATING THE EX-RIGHTS PRICE

The market value for every four shares was £4.00. When the right is exercised, each holding will subscribe 50p which increases the value of the holding to £4.50. However, there are now five shares attached to each holding consequently the theoretical ex-rights price per share will be 90p (£4.50 ÷ 5).

CALCULATING THE BONUS ELEMENT

The new issue should have caused the share price to fall, as the new shares were issued at a discount. The bonus element in the price can be calculated using the following formula:

$$\frac{\text{cum-rights price}}{\text{ex-rights price}} \quad = \quad \frac{1.00}{0.90} \quad = \quad 1.11$$

Therefore, the bonus element of the issue is equivalent to an 11 for 100 bonus issue.

IDENTIFYING THE NUMBER OF SHARES IN ISSUE

The rights issue occurred halfway through the year, and the number of shares in issue should be calculated on a time-weighted average. From 1 July, following the rights issue, there are 1 000 000 shares in issue:

$$1\ 000\ 000 \times 0.5 = 500\ 000$$

From January to the end of June there were only 800 000 shares in issue. However, the bonus element of the rights issue will have to be treated as though those shares were issued. Consequently, the number of shares in issue 1 January to 30 June should reflect the bonus element, and will be calculated as follows:

$$800\ 000 \times 1.11 \times 0.5 = 444\ 000$$

The weighted average number of shares in issue will be:

$$500\ 000 + 444\ 000 = 944\ 000$$

EARNINGS PER SHARE FOR THE CURRENT YEAR

$$\frac{£340\ 000}{944\ 000} = 36.02p$$

EARNINGS PER SHARE FOR THE PREVIOUS YEAR

These have to be adjusted for the bonus element of the rights issue, as this should be treated as though it had always existed:

$$30p \div 1.11 = 27.03p$$

Shares issued in an acquisition

Where shares are exchanged to acquire another business, the accounting treatment is dependent on the method that is used to account for the acquisition.

Acquisition accounting

This is treated as an issue at full price; consequently the shares are assumed to have been issued at the full market price, even though this may not be the case. The time-weighted average number of shares in issue is used for calculating the earnings per share. The date is determined by when the subsidiary is consolidated into the group accounts, as this is the date from which they will be contributing to earnings, rather than the actual date of issue.

EXAMPLE In 1996 a company had 800 000 shares in issue and reported earnings per share of 30p. On 1 July it acquired another company through the issue of 200 000 shares, giving 1 000 000 shares in issue at the end of the year. The earnings for the year ending 31 December 1997 are £340 000.

The weighted average number of shares in issue would be:

(800 000 x 0.5) + (1 000 000 x 0.5) = 900 000

The 1997 earnings per share would be 37.78p (340 000 ÷ 900 000) and the 1996 figure would remain unchanged at 30p.

Merger accounting

The principles of merger accounting require that the business should be treated as though they had always been combined. Therefore, earnings per share will be calculated as though the shares had always been in issue and the comparatives will be restated accordingly.

• Share options

The basic earnings per share is based on the actual earnings and the number of shares that are in issue. Although they may be adjusted, and may not reflect the numbers shown in the accounts, they are still based on the current figures. This can only give an indication of future earnings where there are no plans to issue shares in the future. However, if more shares are to be issued, there has to be a measure that will quantify the impact on earnings per share.

This measure is the fully diluted earnings per share which must be disclosed in the profit and loss account if the effect of the dilution, arising from the exercise of the options, is 5 per cent or more of the basic earnings per share. Fully diluted earnings per share recalculates the earnings per share figure as though the outstanding options had already been exercised.

Fully diluted earnings per share does not just change the number of shares, it may also use a different earnings figure. For example, if the dilution arises from convertible loans, the earnings will have to be adjusted to reflect the reduction in interest charge on the loan conversion. This is illustrated below.

EXAMPLE A company has 1 000 000 shares in issue and has £500 000 10 per cent convertible loan stock. The stockholders have the option to convert the loan stock into 200 000 ordinary shares. The earnings for the year were £340 000 and the tax rate is 31 per cent.

Basic earnings per share:

$$\frac{£340\ 000}{1\ 000\ 000} = 34\ p$$

Revised earnings on the exercise of the options:

Basic earnings	340 000
Interest saved on conversion (£500 000 x 10%)	50 000
Less tax relief (£50 000 x 31%)	(15 500)
Fully diluted earnings	374 500

Number of shares in issue after the exercise of options:

Original shares	1 000 000
Additional shares	200 000
Number of shares in issue	1 200 000

Fully diluted earnings per share:

$$\frac{374\ 500}{1\ 200\ 000} = 31.21p$$

This would need to be disclosed as there is a difference of more than 5 per cent between the basic earnings per share and the fully diluted earnings per share.

The exercise of any warrants or options will bring additional funds into the business, and this should also improve earnings. SSAP 3 states that the earnings should be adjusted on the basis that 'the proceeds have been invested in 21/2 per cent consolidated stock on the first day of the period at the closing price of the previous day'. This is illustrated below.

EXAMPLE A company has 1 000 000 shares in issue. Options have been granted to directors and employees to subscribe for 100 000 shares at £1.00 per share. The price of 21/2 per cent consolidated stock on the first day of the period is £20.50.
   Earnings for the year are £340 000 and corporation tax is at 31 per cent.
   Basic earnings per share is as before:

$$\frac{£340\ 000}{1\ 000\ 000} = 34p$$

Yield on 2½ per cent consolidated stock:

$$\frac{2.5}{20.5} \times 100 = 12.2\%$$

Revised earnings on the exercise of the options:

Basic earnings	340 000
Notional earnings (100 000 x £1.00 x 12.2%)	12 200
Less notional tax (£12 200 x 31%)	(3 782)
Fully diluted earnings	348 418

Number of shares in issue:

Original shares	1 000 000
Additional shares	100 000
Number of shares in issue	1 100 000

Fully diluted earnings per share:

$$\frac{348\ 418}{1\ 100\ 000} = 31.67p$$

This would need to be disclosed as there is a difference of more than 5 per cent between the basic earnings per share and the fully diluted earnings per share.

● FRED 16 (EARNINGS PER SHARE)

Fred 16 was published in June 1997, to achieve international harmonisation on the calculation of earnings per share. In 1993 the IASC issued a draft statement, *Earnings per Share*, and in 1994 the American Financial Accounting Standards Board announced a project to develop a standard that would be compatible with the international standard. The two standard-setting bodies published exposure drafts in 1996, and the ASB issued a discussion paper containing the text of the international exposure draft.

This resulted in FRED 16, which reflects IAS 33, *Earnings per Share*, issued in February 1997, which came into effect in January 1998. Fred 16 proposes the following changes to the calculations for basic earnings per share and fully diluted earnings per share.

● Basic earnings per share

This should be calculated using a weighted average number of shares, rather than the shares ranking for dividend.

● Fully diluted earnings per share

There are a number of changes to the calculation of fully diluted earnings per share:

(1) There will be no exemptions on the grounds of materiality, so it will be published even when the dilution is less than 5 per cent.
(2) The earnings dilution should be based on the earnings from continuing businesses. As the profit arising from continuing operations is only disclosed to the pre-interest level, FRED 16 proposes that interest and tax could be allocated in proportion to the profit arising from continuing and discontinued operations.
(3) The method used to calculate the potential-earnings effect arising on the exercise of options will change. The proceeds will no longer be deemed to have been invested in 2.5 per cent treasury stock. When the shares are to be issued below the market value, the issue is treated as consisting of:
   – a contract to issue a certain number of shares at market value;
   – a contract to issue shares for no consideration. These shares are added to the number of shares in issue to calculate the fully diluted earnings per share, as these shares are dilutive.

EXAMPLE Continuing the example used earlier for calculating the fully diluted earnings per share when the company has share options, a company has 1 000 000 shares in issue. Options have been granted to directors and employees to subscribe for 100 000 shares at £1.00 per share. The shares have been trading at an average price of £1.50. Earnings for the year are £340 000.

The proceeds from the share issue will be £100 000, so the number of shares that would have been issued at fair value are:

$$\frac{100\ 000 \times £1.00}{£1.50} = 66\ 667$$

33 333 shares will be deemed to have been issued for no consideration. These are added to the shares in issue to give a fully diluted earnings per share of 32.9p (340 000 ÷ 1 033 333). This compares to 31.67p that had been calculated under SSAP 3.

(4) The fully diluted earnings per share should be calculated in the order of dilution; with each share issue being considered in sequence from the most dilutive to the least dilutive.

EXAMPLE Our earlier examples calculated the fully diluted earnings per share assuming only one dilutive option. The company may well have convertible bonds and share options. The exercise of the share options was deemed to have increased the number of shares by 33 333 with no increase in earnings, and therefore, would be the most dilutive. The fully diluted earnings per share would be calculated as follows:

	Attributable profit	Number of shares	Earnings per share
As reported	340 000	1 000 000	34.00p
Exercise of options		33 333	
On exercise of options		1 033 333	32.90p
10% convertible loans	34 500	200 000	
On loan conversion	374 500	1 233 333	30.36p

(5) As diluted earnings per share is now seen as a measure of past performance, comparative amounts should be shown.

(6) There are additional disclosures and reconciliations required.

SUMMARY Earnings per share identifies the attributable profit for each share. It takes the profit attributable to ordinary shareholders and divides it by the weighted average number of shares in issue during the year. It is an important investment measure of the company's performance.

There are four different ways that earnings per share can be calculated:

(1) **net basis** – this is the basic measure of earnings per share, and makes no adjustments to either the earnings or the number of shares. This is the earnings calculation that is required under FRS 3 and SSAP 3;

(2) **nil distribution** – this shows what the earnings would have been if the company had not paid a dividend. This is often published by companies who are unable to recover ACT;

(3) **maximum / full distribution** – this uses a notional earnings figure, based on gross dividends, that assumes that all of the earnings are distributed as dividends. This is used as the basis for calculating the dividend cover ratio in the financial press;

(4) **fully diluted** – this includes all the outstanding share options and shows the dilution in earnings per share if these options are exercised. This is currently required to be shown when the exercise of options would dilute the earnings per share by 5 per cent, or more. There are a number of proposed changes which will affect the disclosure and calculation of fully diluted earnings per share. It is proposed that whenever the exercise of options would dilute earnings, fully diluted earnings should be shown.

The first three use slightly different profit figures, reflecting different assumptions about dividend distribution. The fully diluted basis includes outstanding share options in the number of shares.

Additionally, some companies will disclose an IIMR earnings per share in their profit and loss account. This takes the profit attributable to ordinary shareholders and makes a number of adjustments to make the profits more comparable. The two common adjustments are:

▶

(1) it deducts profits, or adds back any losses, on disposals of assets and subsidiaries;
(2) it adds back any abnormal writedowns in asset values, following a permanent reduction in their values, unless the company's intention was to sell the assets.

The different calculations are summarised in Table 15.1, which assumes that all unrelieved ACT is irrecoverable and that profit before tax is taxable profit.

Table 15.1   **Calculations for earnings per share (net basis, nil distribution, full distribution, fully diluted, IIMR)**

	All UK profits	Half UK profits, half overseas	All overseas profits
	£000	£000	£000
Operating profit	1 010	1 010.0	1 010.0
Profit on sale of fixed assets	20[1]	20.0[1]	20.0[2]
Profit on disposal of businesses	250[1]	250.0[1]	250.0[2]
Net interest payable	(280)	(280.0)	(280.0)
Profit before tax	1 000	1 000.0	1 000.0
UK tax @ 31%	(310)	(155.0)	
Overseas tax @ 50%		(250.0)	(500.0)
Irrecoverable ACT		(12.5)	(112.5)
Profit after tax	690	582.5	387.5
Dividends	(450)	(450.0)	(450.0)
Retained profit	240	132.5	(62.5)
Calculation of irrecoverable ACT:			
ACT paid – 25% of dividends	112.5	112.5	112.5
Maximum ACT offset – 20% of UK taxable profit	200	100	0
Unrelieved ACT	None	12.5	112.5
Issued shares	1 000 000	1 000 000	1 000 000
Outstanding options	50 000	50 000	50 000
Earnings increase on exercise of options	10 000	10 000	10 000
Nil distribution	690.0	595.0	500
Grossed nil distribution	**862.5**	743.8	625
Profit before tax	1 000	1 000	1 000
Minimum mainstream tax	(110)	(55)	0
Overseas tax	0	(250)	(500)
Profit after tax	890	**695**	**500**
Earnings per share – pence			
Earnings per share reported under FRS 3	69.00	58.25	38.75
Nil distribution	69.00	59.50	50.00
Full distribution	86.25	69.50	50.00
Fully diluted	66.67	56.43	37.86
IIMR	50.37	39.62	25.25

Notes:
[1] Profits are incurred in the UK, and so are subject to UK taxation.
[2] Profits are incurred overseas, and so are subject to overseas taxation.

● DIVIDENDS

The payment of dividends does not necessarily require shareholders' approval. As long as it does not break the law, interim dividends can be paid by directors without the approval of the shareholders. The final dividend, however, does require shareholders' approval at the annual general meeting, and the directors will devote a lot of time to determining how much should be paid. Only private companies like paying dividends, although they are likely to have taken money out of the business well before dividends! Private companies are generally paying dividends to themselves. Public companies are different – dividends are paid out to strangers. The more the company pays, the less it can keep in the business for the next year's development and growth.

The payment of dividends to shareholders is a discretionary cash outflow that reduces the funds that are available for reinvestment. Consequently, most companies treat dividends in much the same way as they treat salary increases – they want to pay as little as they can get away with! How much they pay in dividends is influenced by many of the same things that determine salaries:

- How much cash does the business have? If the business has a lot of cash, the shareholders would like a share of it. This could be given in the form of a share buy-back or a special dividend.
- What is the rate of inflation? Shareholders like to see their income growing in real terms too!
- How much is everyone else paying? If everyone else in the sector is increasing dividends by 10 per cent, the company will probably have to increase its dividend to that level.
- Is the company performing well? If the company is number one in its sector, that should be reflected in the share price. If the shareholders have already had a return from the increase in the value of the shares, they may be prepared to accept a lower dividend.
- Is it a high risk company? If the company is risky the shareholders are more likely to want a high dividend – there may not be a company next year!

It is a balance; the company cannot afford to disappoint its shareholders (they will vote with their feet and sell their shares), nor can it afford to create unsustainable expectations. Shareholders look for dividend growth, the dividend you pay this year creates expectations about the dividend you will pay next year.

Unfortunately, the dividend decision is not quite as simple as that for salary increases. In addition to the factors above, a company must consider both the cash that it needs for reinvestment, and the legal position.

The company will need money to maintain and expand its operations. It can use the cash it has generated from its current operations, raise shares, or borrow the money. The company needs to look at the probable returns on its investment plans to determine the best source of funds for them. In times of low interest rates, borrowing could be cheaper – but we saw in Chapter 6 that borrowings can increase a company's risk profile. If the risk increases, the shareholders will want an increased return to compensate. Share issues could be used, but there has to be a corresponding increase in earnings, otherwise the investment could be earnings dilutive. This would affect on the company's share price and cause the investors to seek their return in dividends, as there is no possibility of capital gain. It may be better for the company, and the shareholders in the long run, to reduce dividend payments and increase reinvestment.

Legal restrictions on the payment of dividends

In addition to the need for reinvestment, dividend payments may be limited by the company's Articles and by the Companies Act. Most companies have adopted the model set of company Articles found in the Act. These Articles limit the amount of dividends that can be paid as they:

- restrict the maximum dividend payment to that declared by the directors. The shareholders can only reduce or accept the dividend (this is not always true overseas, in Germany shareholders can increase the dividend to all of the available profit in a private company, and half in a public company);
- allow the directors to pay interim dividends, when they are justified by the profitability of the company;
- state that dividends should be paid out of profits.

This last condition is important, as it is now reflected in the Companies Act. Section 263 requires that dividends only be paid out of accumulated realised profits. (Prior to the implementation of the Second Directive, there were no legal provisions in the 1980 Act governing the funds that were available to pay shareholders' dividends.) There are two tests that should be applied to determine the profits that are available for distribution as dividends: the realised profits test and the net assets test

The realised profits test

This applies to all companies. Realised profits are those that have been taken in the profit and loss account, revaluation of assets would be an example of an unrealised profit. These accumulated profits are known in law as 'distributable reserves', dividends can be paid until these reach zero. The company is only able to distribute any remaining accumulated profits, therefore, the accumulation should be net of any profits that have been previously distributed or capitalised. (This process is described in Chapter 5.)

In a group, only the realised profits of the parent company are available for distribution. Subsidiaries' profits are transferred to the parent through the distribution of dividends.

Companies can, therefore, pay dividends out of losses, as long as there is enough accumulated profits to absorb the loss. This is illustrated in the following example:

EXAMPLE

	Retained profits £000
Year 1	10 000
Year 2	5 000
Year 3	7 000
Year 4	2 000
Total	24 000

In the 5th year the company makes a loss before dividend of £8000, but still wishes to pay a dividend of £10 000. This would take the retained loss for the year to £18 000, which can be absorbed by the accumulated profits. The company could pay up to £16 000 in dividends.

The net assets test

This only applies to public companies, which are subject to the capital maintenance provision of the Second Directive. Public companies have to cover net losses before making a dividend payment. So, public companies may only make a dividend distribution when the value of the net assets is greater that the total of its share capital and undistributable reserves.

Undistributable reserves are all the other reserves; namely the revaluation reserve, the share premium account, the capital redemption reserve, and any other reserve where the distribution is prohibited by the company's Articles. The payment of dividends cannot reduce the value of the capital and undistributable reserves below the net asset value.

If any company has accounts that are qualified by the auditor, the auditor must provide a statement, before a distribution may be made, of whether the qualification is material in deciding if the distribution would be a breach of the Act.

Investment companies

A company qualifying as an investment company under s 266 of the Companies Act can take advantage of alternative rules for assessing the availability of profits for distribution if:

● it is listed;
● it has not in the previous accounting period used capital profits for: dividends; paying debentures; or amounts unpaid on its issued shares;
● it has given the necessary notice to qualify as an investment company under the Act.

These investment companies have the option of modifying the realised profits to exclude accumulated capital profits from the funds available for distribution. The corresponding test for net assets requires that the value of the assets must be at least one-and-a-half times the value of the company's liabilities and provisions both before and after the dividend distribution. If the dividend distribution reduces the value of the net assets below the total of the share capital and distributable reserves, it should be disclosed in a note to the accounts (Sch 4).

● Foreign income dividends

Foreign income dividends (FIDs) were introduced by the 1994 Finance Act to enable companies with high overseas earnings to reduce the level of irrecoverable ACT. If companies earn profits overseas, they will pay tax overseas and may be unable to recover all of their ACT as their UK taxable profits may be too low.

If a company pays a dividend out of overseas income that has borne overseas tax, ACT will still be payable, but may be reclaimed by the company. However, FIDs do not carry a tax credit, so non-taxpayers are unable to claim a refund. This led to FIDs being 'enhanced' to make them more attractive to tax-exempt institutional investors like pension funds. Since the July 1997 budget, tax credits can no longer be reclaimed by pension funds and companies; they can only be reclaimed by PEP holders, non-tax payers and charities until April 1999. So the need to enhance has gone, making FIDs more attractive. Unfortunately, it looks likely that FIDs will also disappear, as in the same budget the government announced that FIDs will be abolished from April 1999.

● Scrip dividends

Scrip dividends are attractive, as they do not involve any cash outlay. A scrip dividend is where the shareholder receives extra shares instead of cash. This is often an attractive option for smaller shareholders, as it enables them to build up their stake in the company without paying dealing fees. The company also benefits from the payment of a scrip dividend as it is not subject to ACT. So everyone wins! To encourage institutional shareholders to take the scrip dividend alternative, it is often 'enhanced'. The shareholder receives more if he takes shares, rather than cash.

● Accounting for dividends

The Companies Act requires that the final dividend, together with any interim dividend that has already been paid, should be shown in the profit and loss account. The balance sheet will then show a current liability to reflect the unpaid dividend.

INTERNATIONAL DIFFERENCES

The UK practice of accruing dividends in the profit and loss accounts is not universally followed. The Dutch have a similar practice to the UK, whereas in Germany only paid or declared dividends are accounted for. The final dividend has not been approved, and so will only affect the appropriation account and the brought-forward retained earnings. Japanese accounting for dividends follows German practice. In France, whilst the legal position is the same as in Germany, many large companies will show balance sheet entries before and after dividend allocation. In the USA only the dividends paid during the year would be shown in the profit and loss account. In Canada dividends represent a capital transaction, and would therefore be shown in the statement of retained earnings, as a deduction from retained earnings.

SUMMARY

The directors determine the size of the dividend within a statutory framework. Companies can pay a dividend when they have made a loss in the period as long as they have sufficient accumulated retained profits. Public companies must comply with an additional requirement. The payment of the dividend should not, both before and after the dividend payment, reduce the value of the net assets below the total of its share capital and undistributable reserves. If the auditor has qualified the company's accounts he must state whether the qualification is material in deciding if the distribution would be a breach of the Act, before a distribution can be made.

Both the interim and the proposed final dividend will be charged to the profit and loss account in the UK. The proposed dividend will show as part of the creditors falling due within a year in the balance sheet.

● THE NOTE OF HISTORICAL COST PROFITS AND LOSSES

If a company has sold assets that have previously been revalued, the profit and loss account will be followed by a note of historical cost profits and losses. Following the implementation of FRS 3, companies are required to calculate profits and losses on the sale of fixed assets from the book value of these assets. This means that the reported profit on sale of fixed assets is determined by the value of the assets shown in the balance sheet. Therefore, these profits are influenced by the company's depreciation and revaluation policies. The note on historical cost profits and losses was introduced to improve the comparability of reported profits. It tells you what the profit would have been had there been no revaluations of assets. It eliminates the distortions in reported profit that can arise from different revaluation policies. It does not consider the effect of different depreciation policies.

The impact that revaluations can have on reported profits is clearly illustrated by the following example.

EXAMPLE Two people buy identical plots of land for £100 000, one revalues the land to £120 000 at the end of the first year. Both sell the land for £150 000 at the end of the second year. What is the profit? The cash profit for both of them is £50 000, but the reported profit will be very different. One will show £50 000 but the other, who revalued, will only show £30 000 profit. The note of historical cost profits and losses will bring both back to £50 000.

This note is useful if you were comparing the profits of two companies in the same sector, which have different policies on revaluation. In some sectors where property profits may be a significant component of reported profit and there is a variety of revaluation policies, the note becomes an integral part of the analysis.

A published note of historical cost profits and losses will show both historical cost profit before taxation and historical cost retained profits. The extract from the 1996 accounts of the distribution company, NFC, illustrates this and shows that NFC's profit before tax would have been £7.6 million higher in 1996, had it not revalued its assets.

Extract 15.2 **GROUP HISTORICAL COST PROFIT AND LOSSES (NFC)**

For the year ended 30 September 1996

	1996 £m	1995 £m
Profit on ordinary activities before taxation	**105.2**	38.5
Revaluation surpluses realised on disposals of properties	**6.7**	3.0
Difference between depreciation based on historical costs and on revalued amounts	**0.9**	1.0
Historical cost profit on ordinary activities before taxation	112.8	42.6
Historical cost retained profit / (loss)	19.8	(31.5)

● RELEVANT RATIOS

From the shareholders' perspective, this is the most important part of the profit and loss account. They want to make a return on their investment. The profit that is attributable to the ordinary shareholders is the profit after tax, less any minority interests and preference dividends. We have seen that this is the profit that is used in calculating earnings per share and also forms the basis of a number of some of the other investment ratios.

● Return on equity

The return on equity measures the return on the funds that the shareholders have invested in the business. It looks at the return on the book value, not the market value, of the investment. It is simply measured by taking the profit attributable to ordinary shareholders and dividing it by the share capital and reserves:

$$\frac{\text{Profit attributable to ordinary shareholders}}{\text{Capital and reserves}}$$

This is usually expressed as a percentage.

If the capital and reserves were £50 000 and the profit attributable to ordinary shareholders was £10 000, the return on equity would be 20 per cent. It sounds like a good return on the investment, but we would really need to know more information before we could be certain. It may also be necessary to make a number of adjustments, to ensure that our numbers are fully comparable. These adjustments are discussed in Chapter 21.

● Price/earnings ratios

The price/earnings ratio (abbreviated as the *PE* or *PER*) compares the market price to the earnings. It is sometimes referred to as the *multiple*. The *Financial Times* publishes the PE ratio for listed companies, but usually talks about the multiple in its articles.

The PE looks at the current earnings in relation to the current share price, and is calculated using the formula below:

$$\frac{\text{Today's market price for the share}}{\text{Earnings per share}}$$

The market price used for this ratio is the middle price.

The earnings per share figure used in the PE will be different from that shown in the published accounts, as the financial press use IIMR earnings per share, excluding any unrelieved ACT, in the published ratios. The earnings per share figures are updated from the interim figures, and then the preliminary figures as soon as they are published, and finally updated when the full annual results are available. The PE will change through the year; daily as prices change, but also as different earnings per share figures are fed through into the formula.

If the middle price for the share was £3.00 and the earnings per share was 10p, the company would have a PE of 30. We now know how to calculate the PE, but what does it tell us? It says that if we buy the shares at today's price, and profits remain constant, it will take us 30 years to get our money back and still hold the share. (We will get our money back from the dividend stream and the capital gain. Both are reflected in the earnings calculation. Dividends are paid out of after tax profits, and relative retained profits should affect the share price.)

Although we criticise the stock market for its short termism, there are very few of us who would be prepared to wait 30 years to get our money back! Most investors are looking for a return in five to seven years, depending on the risk profile of the investment. So if someone is prepared to pay 30 times current earnings, but expects to get their money back in five to seven years, they expect the profits to grow over the period. A high PE is usually an indication of an expectation of profit growth (although it could just be that the share is expensive). A low PE usually means that the market has an expectation that profits will fall.

The market's profit expectations affect the volatility of the share. If the market believes that earnings will rise dramatically in the next few years, and the company gives a profits warning, the share price will fall steeply. A share with a high PE is often volatile, small items of good news (supporting the market's view) will cause the price to jump, any bad news (contradicting the market's view) and the price will fall.

As the price reflects expectations of future earnings, it is often more appropriate to compare the price to the expected earnings – this is called the *prospective PE*. This uses the estimated earnings per share for the year, rather than the latest published earnings per share. The published PE uses a current share price, and an historic earnings per share. The prospective PE matches current earnings with current price. Therefore, if in our example earnings were expected to rise from the reported 10p to 30p, the prospective PE would be 10 (3.00 ÷ 0.30), compared to the historic PE of 30. We can clearly see that this is probably a more useful measure – the market has built the anticipated profit growth into the current price. The company may have had a bad year last year and is expected to recover in the current year. Our example illustrates that a high PE is not necessarily indicative of a growth stock, it may simply reflect a company that has had a temporary fall in profits.

As the prospective PE is based on an individual analyst's view of current earnings, a company's prospective PE will vary from analyst to analyst. In practice, the historic earnings are also likely to be adjusted, as most analysts do not rely on the published figures. There is a great tendency for reported earnings per share figures to be 'managed' after all, directors' bonuses and reported PEs depend on it! Consequently, if companies want to improve the earnings per share, they have two options: improve the reported earnings or have a share buy-back to reduce the number of shares.

Currently many listed companies use provisions to smooth out the earnings line, making provisions when times are good, and writing them back when times are bad. There is also considerable scope for manipulating the tax charge through the deferred tax provision. (This was discussed fully in the last chapter.) Deferred tax is charged for the liabilities that are *expected* to crystallise. This is a paper adjustment that will not affect the money handed over to the tax authorities, only the profit that is declared to the shareholders. As it is not real money adjustments can always be made. Using the reported tax charge also makes international comparisons become very difficult, as most countries require deferred tax charges to be based on a full provision rather than the partial provision required in SSAP 15 (*Accounting for Deferred Taxation*).

In consequence, most analysts will adjust the reported earnings per share to take account of:

● provisions utilised, rather than provisions charged;
● the full provision for deferred tax, rather than the provision that has been made. (Earnings calculated using the full deferred tax provision are often referred to as *fully taxed* earnings per share.)

A company's PE ratio should always be considered in the context of the expectations for the sector. The *Financial Times* publishes sector averages in the Actuaries Share Indices. It is then possible to look at the company's performance relative to the sector:

$$\frac{\text{PE ratio of the company}}{\text{PE ratio of the sector}}$$

Looking at the company's relative performance within the sector gives an indication of the market's view of its relative performance. We think that a company with a PE of 20 is believed to have a lot of potential for profit growth, but if the sector average is showing a PE of 25, our company is believed to offer less potential than most other companies in its sector.

Another way of comparing the price to the earnings is the earnings yield.

● Earnings yield

The earnings yield is the reciprocal of the PE ratio, and is calculated in the same way as the dividend yield:

$$\frac{\text{Earnings per share}}{\text{Today's market price for the share}}$$

This is usually expressed as a percentage.

● Dividends per share

Dividends per share is simply the total dividend divided by the number of shares in issue. If a company is paying £5000 dividends, and had 100 000 shares in issue, the shareholders would be receiving 5p dividend per share.

The dividends can be either net (excluding the ACT) or gross (including the ACT). Gross dividend is used in most of the published dividend ratios. Assuming ACT at 20 per cent the gross dividend per share would be 6.25p (5p ÷ 0.8).

The dividend per share shows how much the shareholder will receive in dividend, but is the company being generous or mean in its payment of dividends? To find out, we need to look at the dividend cover.

● Dividend cover

This is similar to the interest cover, and measures how many times the dividend could be paid out of the available profits.

It can be calculated in two different ways, either using the total earnings and dividends, or on a per-share basis. If a company had earnings of £10 000, paid dividends of £5000, and had 100 000 shares in issue the dividend cover would be:

ON A TOTAL PROFIT BASIS

$$\frac{\text{Profit attributable to ordinary shareholders}}{\text{Dividends}} = \frac{10\ 000}{5\ 000} = 2 \text{ times}$$

ON AN INDIVIDUAL SHARE BASIS

$$\frac{\text{Earnings per share}}{\text{Dividend per share}} = \frac{10p}{5p} = 2 \text{ times}$$

We can see that the company is paying out half of the available profit as dividends. The more the company gives to its shareholders, the less it has to put back into the business for next year's development and growth. Determining the size of the dividend is a fine balancing act for most companies. They want to pay enough to maintain a stable share price, but they need to retain funds for reinvestment. Dividend cover at two times may be verging on the imprudent, but would not be unusual in the UK, where almost half of the available profit is being paid as dividends, but like salary increases for staff, the dividend decision is largely determined by expectations, and what everyone else is paying.

For our purposes either of the definitions outlined above would be an adequate definition of dividend cover, but it is worth remembering that *where* the profit is made will have an impact on the dividend cover. This arises because of the problems associated with irrecoverable ACT, discussed earlier in the chapter. If a company has considerable overseas earnings and, therefore, overseas tax, dividend cover is calculated using full-distributed earnings divided by the gross dividend.

This is illustrated in the following example:

EXAMPLE

Profit before tax	15 516
Tax	(5 516)
Profit after tax	10 000
Ordinary dividends	(5 000)
Retained profit	5 000

279

The tax charge comprises:

UK tax charge @ 31%	1 000
Double taxation relief	(250)
Tax paid	750
Overseas tax	4 000
	4 750
Irrecoverable ACT	766
	5516

Calculation of irrecoverable ACT:

Maximum offset (750 x 20/31)	484
ACT paid (5000 x 0.25)	1 250
Irrecoverable ACT	766

We can see that part of the tax charge is irrecoverable ACT, and this affects both the earnings and the dividend cover. The dividend cover would be calculated using earnings computed on the full distribution basis. Full-distribution earnings are calculated using the lower of:

- nil distribution earnings plus associated ACT – £13 458 (10 766 ÷ 0.8);
- profit before tax less minimum mainstream corporation tax and overseas tax - £11 250 (15 516 – 266 – 4 000).

So, full-distribution earnings would be £11 250; and the dividend cover would be 1.8 (11 250 ÷ 6 250).

• Dividend yield

The dividend yield tells us what percentage we can expect to receive as dividends if we buy the share at today's price. The market price used in calculating the dividend yield is not quite the same as the cash you would receive if you sold the share. It is the average of the buy price and the sell price – the middle price. The dividend used in the ratios published in the financial press is the gross dividend (the ACT is included), not the net dividend received. The formula for the gross dividend yield is:

$$\frac{\text{Gross dividend per share}}{\text{Today's market price for the share}}$$

EXAMPLE In our example, if the middle price for the share is £2.00 and the company is paying 5p net dividend per share, the net dividend yield would be 2.5 per cent. The gross dividend yield would be 3.125 per cent (6.25/200). The share offers a poor dividend return, but may offer some scope for capital gain. This will depend on future profit growth, relative to the sector, and to see the market's view of potential we would need to look at the PE ratio.

PE ratios move in the opposite direction to the dividend yield. If the price of the share rises, the PE rises and the dividend yield falls. To illustrate this, a company with earnings of 10p a share pays a gross dividend of 7p, and has a current share price of £2.00. Therefore, the current gross dividend yield is 3.5 per cent, and the PE is 20. If the share price rises to £3.30, the PE ratio would rise to 33 (3.30 / 0.10) and the gross dividend yield would fall to 2.12 per cent (0.07 / 3.30). If the price fell to £1.50 the PE ratio would fall to 15 (1.50 / 0.10) and the gross dividend yield would rise to 4.67 per cent (0.07 / 1.50).

JARGON

Earnings per share   A measure of investment performance, showing how much of the total profit attributable to ordinary shareholders relates to each share.

Foreign income dividend (FID)   A dividend that is paid out of overseas income that has borne overseas tax. It has the advantage that the ACT can be reclaimed by the company, and so is attractive to companies with high levels of overseas earnings.

Full-distribution earnings   The maximum gross dividend that could have been paid out of the available profits.

Fully diluted earnings   This shows what the earnings would have been if all of the outstanding share options had been exercised.

IIMR/Headline earnings   An earnings figure that adjusts for most of the exceptional items shown below operating profit.

Net assets test   A legal test, for public companies, to ensure that they have covered net losses before making a dividend payment.

Nil distribution earnings   This shows what the earnings would have been had the company not paid a dividend.

Note of historical cost profits and losses   A note which would follow a UK profit and loss account if the company had sold something it had previously revalued. It shows what the profit would have been, had the assets not been revalued, so it is useful when comparing companies in some sectors.

Realised profits test   A legal test, for all companies, to ensure that dividend payments can be covered out of distributable reserves.

Scrip dividend   The dividend is paid in shares rather than cash. They are not subject to ACT.

16 The cash flow statement

This chapter covers:

- Exemptions from the accounting standard
- The construction of the cash flow statement
- Additional disclosures in the notes
- Using cash flow statements in analysis
- Ratios for calculating cash flow per share

• INTRODUCTION

The success and survival of every organisation depends on its ability to generate and acquire cash. Cash flow is a concept that we all understand. Companies survive because they have cash, and they fail when they do not. We must, therefore, be interested in a company's ability to generate cash for itself, and to acquire it from other sources. This can be clearly seen in the cash flow statement.

There is no legal requirement for companies to prepare a cash flow statement. however, the accounting standard, FRS 1, requires most companies to prepare one. The cash flow statement identifies the cash movement within the business; clearly showing where the cash has come from and what the business has spent the money on. It is purely concerned with the movement of cash. Cheques received are shown as cash *inflows* and those paid as cash *outflows*. The cash flow statement is perhaps the most important document found in the accounts, as cash is the one thing that cannot be created – the company either has cash or it does not! By looking at the movement of cash, we get a clearer idea of the company's financial stability and viability.

The cash flow statement shows a summary of the cash flows in and out of the company during the year. To help our analysis, the cash flows are shown functionally and are classified into cash flows from:

- **trading** – these cash flows are shown under the heading *operating activities;*
- **dividends from joint ventures and associates** – these are shown as a separate heading following the implementation of FRS 9 (*Associates and Joint Ventures*) in June 1998.
- **interest, dividends received and any dividends paid to 'non-equity' shares and minority interests.** These cash flows are shown under the heading of *returns on investment and servicing of finance;*
- **tax** – these cash flows are shown under the heading *of taxation;*
- **buying and selling fixed assets** – these cash flows are shown under the heading of *capi-*

tal expenditure and financial investment (if the company has not bought or sold any fixed asset investments the heading can be shortened to capital expenditure, to reflect the actual cash flow);

- **buying and selling businesses and trades** – these cash flows are shown under the heading of *acquisitions and disposals*;
- **dividends paid to ordinary shareholders** – these cash flows are shown as *equity dividends paid*;
- **short-term investments that are shown as current asset investments** – these are used to manage the position of a company's net debt or net funds, rather than for its investment potential. These cash flows are shown under the heading *management of liquid resources*;
- **shares and loans** – these cash flows are shown under the heading of *financing*.

The cash flow statement then finishes with the increase or decrease in cash. Companies also have to show a reconciliation, either in the notes or following the statement, to:

- net debt, thus linking the cash flow statement to the balance sheet;
- operating profit, linking the cash flow statement to the profit and loss account.

Before the revision of FRS 1, which became effective on 23 March 1997, companies would strike a sub-total called the *cash flow before financing*. This would have shown before management of liquid resources. (Most, although not all, cash flows now classified as part of liquid resources would have been included in cash, under the heading of *cash and cash equivalents*. The term cash equivalent is still found in accounts overseas – a cash equivalent is a highly liquid investment that usually has a maturity of three months or less when the company acquires it.) The revised standard neither requires, nor prohibits sub-totalling. It is likely that a number of companies will take a sub-total after equity dividends, as this is illustrated in the examples given in the accounting standard.

● EXEMPTIONS FROM THE ACCOUNTING STANDARD

Not all UK companies have to prepare a cash flow statement. The accounting standard exempts the following organisations:

- Private companies that are defined by the Companies Act as small companies (the definition of a small private company is given in Chapter 3).
- Subsidiary companies where:
  - more than 90 per cent of the voting rights are controlled within the group;
  - the group's consolidated accounts are publicly available (publicly available means that the accounts are disclosed in a registry, or are published in a register or gazette).
- Mutual life assurance companies owned by the policy holders.
- Pension schemes.
- Open-ended investment funds, as long as they show a statement of the changes in the net assets, and their investments are shown at their market value and are highly liquid.
- Building societies are exempted from the statement until 23 March 1999.

SUMMARY

Cash flow statements are not required by the Companies Act, however most companies are required to prepare them by FRS 1. The accounting standard requires that cash flows are classified under nine headings shown in the following order:

(1) operating activities
(2) dividends from joint ventures and associates
(3) returns on investment and servicing of finance
(4) taxation
(5) capital expenditure and financial investment
(6) acquisitions and disposals
(7) equity dividends paid
(8) management of liquid resources
(9) financing.

The cash flow statement should also show reconciliations to net debt and operating profit. Companies may show sub-totals at any point.

● THE CONSTRUCTION OF THE CASH FLOW STATEMENT

We will now look at the items shown in the cash flow statement in more detail, and prepare a simple statement. The example will show the cash flows that will be found under each heading, and the cash flow statement as it would appear in the accounts.

● Detailed cash flows

All cash flows should exclude any recoverable VAT and similar sales taxes. The standard requires that foreign currencies should be translated at the same rate used in the profit and loss account, unless the actual rate is used. The actual rate can be used for intragroup cash flows to ensure that these cancel out in the consolidated cash flow statement.

The operational cash flow

The cash flow statement starts by looking at the cash flows from operating activities. There are two different ways that this can be shown on the statement; the accounting standard refers to these as *the direct method*, and *the indirect method*. They only differ in the *way* they identify the operating cash flow. The direct method shows the cash receipts and payments, whereas the indirect method reconciles the operating profit to the operating cash flow. All companies must show the reconciliation to the operating profit in the notes to the accounts. Consequently, this is the most popular way of arriving at the operating cash flow.

The direct method

The direct method is easier for non-accountants to understand, but is less commonly found in the accounts:

CASH FLOW FROM OPERATING ACTIVITIES:

	£000
Cash received from customers	1010
Cash paid to suppliers	(530)
Cash paid to, and on behalf of, employees	(200)
Other cash paid	(100)
Net cash inflow from operating activities	*180*

The indirect method

If the company uses the direct method to calculate the operating cash flow it will still have to show the reconciliation to operating profit – this is the indirect method. It starts with the operating profit and then adds back any paper charges (primarily depreciation) that have been made in arriving at the profit to show the cash that *will* be generated from this period's trading. It is then adjusted for any changes in the working capital, to arrive at the cash actually generated from operations during the year:

CASH FLOW FROM OPERATING ACTIVITIES:

		£000
	Operating profit	70
	Depreciation	40
Less:	Increase in debtors	(50)
Plus:	Decrease in stocks	50
	Increase in creditors	70
	Net cash inflow from operating activities	*180*

In the above example, the company will only generate £110 000 (£70 000 + £40 000) from the year's sales but has managed to generate £180 000 during the year – the balance has come from the reduction in the working capital. Although debtors have increased, this has been more than offset by the reduction in stock and the increase in creditors.

Returns on investment and servicing of finance

This represents the cash flows from dividends and interest, excluding any dividends paid to ordinary shareholders. This is illustrated in the following example.

During the past year the company has had the following cash flows:

	£000
Interest received	30
Interest paid	(70)
Interest element of finance lease rentals	(10)
Dividends received	10
Dividends paid:	
to ordinary shareholders	(30)
to preference shareholders	(5)
to minority interests	(5)

The cash flow statement would show the following entries under returns on investment and servicing of finance:

	£000
Interest received	30
Interest paid	(70)
Interest element of finance lease rentals	(10)
Dividends received	10
Dividends paid to preference shareholders	(5)
Dividends paid to minority interests	(5)
Net cash outflow from returns on investment and servicing of finance	(50)

The £30 000 dividends paid to the ordinary shareholders will show on the cash flow statement under the heading of *equity dividends paid*. Had the dividends received been from an associate, or joint venture, they would have to be shown earlier in the cash flow statement under the heading *dividends received from joint ventures and associates*.

Taxation

This represents the cash payments for tax, less any cash receipts for tax rebates, etc. To illustrate this, in our example the company has paid £45 000 to the tax authorities during the period. However, it has received a cheque for £5000 in respect of a previous over-payment. Consequently, the cash flow from taxation shown on the statement would be an outflow of £40 000.

Capital expenditure and financial investment

This is a new heading. Under the old standard there was a heading called *investing activities*, which combined capital expenditure and financial investment with acquisitions and disposals.

The heading of capital expenditure and financial investment represents the investment in the company's fixed assets. However, the fixed asset investments shown here exclude investments in a business that is a joint venture, associate or subsidiary, as these would be regarded as part of acquisitions and disposals.

EXAMPLE   To illustrate this, our company has the following cash flows during the year:

	£000
Purchase of new machinery	90
Purchase of motor vehicles	40
Purchase of fixed asset investments (other than associates and joint ventures)	20
Investment in an associated undertaking	10
Proceeds from sale of machinery	20
Proceeds from sale of motor vehicles	5
Purchase of subsidiary	200

The entries on the cash flow statement shown under capital expenditure and financial investment would be:

	£000
Payments to acquire tangible fixed assets	(130)
Payments to acquire fixed asset investments	(20)
Receipts from the sale of tangible fixed assets	25
Net cash outflow from capital expenditure and financial investment	(125)

The balance would be shown under acquisitions and disposals, as shown below.

Acquisitions and disposals

These cash flows relate to the purchase or sale of any trade or business that is an associate, joint venture, or subsidiary. Using the above example, the cash flows for acquisitions and disposals would be as follows:

	£000
Investment in an associated undertaking	(10)
Purchase of subsidiary	(200)
Net cash outflow from acquisitions and disposals	(210)

Equity dividends paid

These would be the £30 000 dividends paid to ordinary shareholders. Any other dividends paid would be included in returns on investment and servicing of finance.

Management of liquid resources

Most companies do not keep their cash in a petty-cash tin. They invest it and have become increasingly sophisticated in the vehicles that are used as part of their treasury activities. Large companies do not just invest surplus cash in deposit accounts, they invest wherever they feel they will get the best return. Consequently, they invest in gilts, money markets, and even shares. These are not investments they intend to hold on a long-term basis; they are just short-term 'liquid' investments that would show as part of current assets.

These investments will be included in the management of liquid resources if the following three criteria hold true:

(1) they can be sold without harming the business;
(2) they can be easily converted into cash at the amount, or very close to the amount, that they are shown in the accounts;
(3) they are traded in an active market.

In our example we will assume that the company has sold £50 000 government gilts.

Financing

These are either receipts from or repayments to the external providers of finance. The receipts will be cash arising from share issues and additional long-term borrowings. The payments will be the purchases of shares, the redemption of bonds and loan repayments.

 To continue our example, the company had the following financing cash flows:

	£000
Proceeds from share issue	250
Increase in short-term borrowings	50
Repayment of long-term loan	(20)
Capital element of finance lease rental payments	(40)
Net cash flow from financing	140

Cash

This covers cash, any deposits that are repayable on demand, together with bank overdrafts and other loans that are repayable on demand. (Deposits are held to be repayable on demand if they are repayable without notice and penalty, or the agreed notice period is 24 hours or less.)

If the company, in our example, had opening cash balances of £30 000 and closing cash balances of £45 000, the cash flow statement would show an increase in cash of £15 000.

● The cash flow statement

The cash flow statement will follow the order shown above, although it is possible to combine the management of liquid resources with financing as long as the cash flows relating to each are shown separately. (This is allowed as some large companies manage their treasury operations in an integrated way, consequently combining the cash flows may be more reflective of the commercial reality.)

There is also some flexibility in the reporting of the cash flows. Companies may decide to report gross cash flows on the statement itself, showing the detailed cash flows in the notes.

If we assume that the company in our example chose to show the gross cash flows in the notes, it would publish the cash flow statement (as shown in Table 16.1).

Table 16.1 **Cash flow statement**

	£000
Cash flow from operating activities	180
Returns on investment and servicing of finance	(50)
Taxation	(40)
Capital expenditure and financial investment	(125)
Acquisitions and disposals	(210)
Equity dividends paid	(30)
	(275)
Management of liquid resources	50
Financing:	
Proceeds of share issue	250
Reduction in debt	(10)
	240
Increase in cash for the period	**15**

The cash flow statement would now have to include a new note, which reconciles the increase in the cash to the movement in the net debt. This is illustrated in Table 16.2.

Table 16.2 Reconciliation of net cash flow to movement in net debt

	£000
Increase in cash for the period	15
Cash used to repay debt and finance leases	10
Cash inflow from decrease in liquid resources	(50)
Change in net debt resulting from cash flows	(25)
Loans acquired with subsidiary	(25)
New finance leases	(20)
Translation difference	(13)
Movement in net debt in the period	(83)
Net debt at 1\1\199x	(150)
Net debt at 1\1\199y	(233)

The cash flow statement shows a business that is generating sufficient cash to meet its interest, tax and dividend payments. However, after making these payments the company had only £60 000 to put towards its capital expenditure and investment programme. So, it realised the government gilts, and used a share issue to fund its acquisitions.

● ADDITIONAL DISCLOSURES IN THE NOTES

We have seen that the notes will often show the detailed net cash flows. In addition the notes will show other useful information:

- further analysis of the changes in net debt;
- information about cash flows arising from acquisitions and disposals;
- exceptional and extraordinary items;
- non-cash transactions and any restrictions on the transfer of cash.

● Analysis of the changes in net debt

The notes should reconcile the opening and closing components of net debt and disclose separately any material changes that arise from:

- the company's cash flows;
- the acquisition and disposal of subsidiaries;
- non-cash changes;
- the recognition of any changes in market value or exchange rate movements.

Using our previous example, the note would be set out in Table 16.3.

Table 16.3   **Example of a note detailing changes in net debt**

	At 1 Jan 199y	Cash flow	Acquisition (excl. cash and overdrafts)	Other non-cash changes	Exchange movement	At 31 Dec 199y
	£000	£000	£000	£000	£000	£000
Cash at bank and in hand	30	10			4	44
Overdrafts	(20)	5			(2)	(17)
		15				
Debt due within a year	(60)	5	(15)	(5)	(7)	(82)
Debt due after a year	(100)		(5)	5	(8)	(108)
Finance leases	(50)	5	(5)	(20		(70)
		10				
Current asset investments	50	(50)				0
	(150)	(25)	(25)	(20)	(13)	(233)

● Acquisitions and disposals

There should be a note to the cash flow statement showing:

- ● a summary of the assets and liabilities acquired or disposed with the subsidiary, together with details of the consideration;
- ● any material effect on the company's cash flow, reported by standard heading, 'as far as is practicable'.

Exceptional and extraordinary items

These should be shown under the appropriate heading and separately disclosed and explained, either in the statement itself or by way of a note.

Non-cash transactions

Major non-cash transactions, such as debt–equity conversions, should be disclosed in the notes to the accounts.

Restrictions on remittances

Sometimes companies have operations in countries where there are severe restrictions on cash transfers, or have money lodged in a bank account that can only be used for a specific purpose. In both cases, the cash is not freely transferable within the group; the accounting standard requires disclosure when the restriction is outside the company's control. The note should specify the amounts involved and explain the circumstances of the restriction.

SUMMARY | The cash flow statement classifies cash flows into the nine headings shown in the standard. The operating cash flow may be derived on a receipts and payments basis *(the direct method)*, or by way of a reconciliation to operating profit (the *indirect method)*. The notes will also disclose:

- the detailed movements in net debt;
- the effect of acquisitions and disposals and any material cash flows arising from them;
- cash flows arising from extraordinary and exceptional items;
- material non-cash transactions;
- any restrictions on remittances that are outside the company's control.

INTERNATIONAL DIFFERENCES

The cash flow statements prepared overseas are generally less detailed than those found in the UK.

International accounting standards

The changes made to FRS 1 in 1997 have moved it further away from the international standard. IAS 7 *(Cash Flow Statements)* requires all companies to show cash flows arising from operating, investing and financing activities, leading to the change in cash and cash equivalents. There are no exemptions from the standard. Interest, dividends, and tax are usually shown under operating activities, as this is usually the appropriate heading. Gross cash flows are usually shown. IAS 7 requires that the cash flows of the subsidiary should be translated at the exchange rate on the date of the cash flow, although it permits the use of a weighted average rate when it approximates to the actual rate. The international standard does not require a reconciliation of the movement in cash flows with net debt.

The cash flow statement produced by the French automotive components group, Valeo, is a good illustration of a cash flow statement prepared under IAS 7. The net income is the profit after tax. This is shown before associated undertaking's profits, and amortisation of goodwill.

Extract 16.1 **CONSOLIDATED STATEMENT OF CASH FLOWS (VALEO)**

(millions of French francs)	1996	1995	1994
CASH FLOWS FROM OPERATING ACTIVITIES			
Net income from consolidated companies	1,047	802	804
Net dividends received from associated companies	30	25	142
Other adjustments to reconcile net income to net cash provided by operating activities:			
• depreciation and amortization	1,642	1,437	1,327
• net charges to provisions and deferred taxes	144	153	200
• (gains)/losses on disposals of fixed assets	(19)	(123)	25
• other income and deductions with no cash effect	(32)	(105)	(47)
Changes in operating working capital:			
• inventories	(55)	(165)	(266)
• accounts and notes receivable	(139)	(179)	(897)
• accounts and notes payable	202	375	1,123
• other receivables and payables	249	3	61
Net cash provided by operating activities	3,069	2,223	2,472
CASH FLOWS FROM INVESTING ACTIVITIES			
Capital expenditures:			
• property and intangibles	(2,337)	(2,067)	(1,754)
• investments and other assets	(7)	(27)	(33)
Proceeds from disposal of:			
• property and intangibles	72	23	109
• investments and other assets	9	4	15
Net cash used in investing activities	(2,263)	(2,067)	(1,663)
NET CASH PROVIDED BEFORE FINANCING ACTIVITIES	806	156	809
CASH FLOWS FROM FINANCING ACTIVITIES			
Investments in consolidated companies, net of cash acquired	(694)	(218)	(124)
Proceeds from disposals of consolidated companies, net of cash sold	95	97	
Dividends paid to parent company stockholders	(751)	(130)	(91)
Dividends paid to minority interests in consolidated subsidiaries	(9)	(8)	(6)
Proceeds from:			
• issuance of share capital	40	77	402
• issuance of long-term debt	1,013	37	24
• capital grants received	17	12	20
Principal payments on long-term debt	(808)	(11)	(54)
Net cash (used in)/provided by financing activities	(1,097)	(144)	171
Effect of exchange rate changes on cash	(2)	(10)	(6)
NET CHANGE IN CASH AND CASH EQUIVALENTS	(293)	2	974
Cash and cash equivalents at beginning of year (note 10.1)	879	877	(97)
CASH AND CASH EQUIVALENTS AT END OF YEAR (note 10.1)	586	879	877

Europe

In France a cash flow statement is recommended by the *plan comptable*, and most listed companies would prepare one complying to IAS 7. They are not required in the Netherlands and Germany, although most large companies would prepare one. The format is not uniform, but increasingly major companies are conforming to IAS 7.

Japan

Listed companies are required to prepare cash flow statements, which are similar to those required under IAS 7.

North America

Most companies in the USA have to include cash flow statements in their accounts. The only exemptions are for non-profit-making organisations such as charities, pension plans, some other employee-benefit plans, and highly liquid investment companies. The required statement is similar to IAS 7. Cash flows are classified into:

- operating activities (including interest and tax). Companies are encouraged to show the direct method, but the indirect method is allowed and is used by most companies. This reconciliation should be shown by all companies;
- investing activities;
- financing activities (including dividends).

This then leads to the change in cash and cash equivalents (which should normally have a maximum maturity of three months). Non-cash investing and financing transactions should be separately disclosed in the notes to the accounts.

In Canada a statement of changes in financial position is required for all companies, unless it would not provide any additional information as the company's operations are very simple. The cash flows are normally classified in the same way as in the USA (shown above). However, companies are required to disclose the following minimum information:

Cash flows arising from:

- operations – this should be reconciled to the profit and loss account
- discontinued items
- extraordinary items
- the sale and purchase of each major category of fixed assets
- the issue, assumption, redemption, and repayment of debt
- the issue, redemption and acquisition of share capital
- the payment of dividends.

● USING CASH FLOW STATEMENTS IN ANALYSIS

The cash flow statement shows clearly where the money has come from during the period, and how the company has spent it. This is vital information for any analyst, and would normally be the starting point in financial analysis. It answers many of the questions we need to ask:

- *Is the company living within its means?* This can be found by striking a sub-total before management of liquid resources.
- *Can the company finance its capital expenditure out of its own resources?* This can be found by

deducting the cash flows from returns on investment and servicing of finance, taxation and equity dividends paid from the cash flow from operating activities.

- *Will the company be able to repay loans from its own resources?* This can be found by:
  - striking a sub-total before management of liquid resources;
  - adding this to the cash and short-term investments shown on the balance sheet;
  - comparing this with the loan-repayment schedule.
- *Is the company generating more cash than it needs?* This may well increase the share price if the cash balances are increasing every year. This is found in the same way as identifying whether the company is living within its means, by striking a sub-total before management of liquid resources.

To illustrate this we will consider United Biscuits' (UB) cash flow statements for 1996 and 1995.

Extract 16.2 **CASH FLOW STATEMENTS (UNITED BISCUITS)**

	1996 £m	1995 £m
Net cash inflow from operating activities	193.1	196.9
Net cash outflow from returns on investments and servicing of finance	(29.5)	(45.6)
Tax paid	(18.0)	(26.3)
Net cash outflow from capital expenditure and financial investment	(90.7)	(156.5)
Net cash inflow/(outflow) from acquisitions and disposals	362.2	(15.9)
Equity dividends paid	(50.3)	(76.1)
Cash inflow/(outflow) before use of liquid resources and financing	366.8	(123.5)
Net cash inflow from management of liquid resources	(4.1)	(15.4)
Net cash outflow / (inflow) from financing	376.6	(150.8)
(Decrease)/increase in cash in the period	(5.7)	42.7
	366.8	(123.5)

● Analysis of UB's cash flows in 1996 and 1995

Disposals

The disposal of the Keebler and Ross Vegetable products businesses has a major impact on the 1996 cash flows.

Falling dividends

The cash outflow for dividends fell during 1996, although dividend per share actually rose from 9.8p per share to 10p per share and there was a small increase in the number of shares. This change in the cash flow has arisen from the fact that the 1995 cash outflow will be for the 1995 interim (3.5p) and the 1994 final dividend (9.8p).

Falling capital expenditure and financial investment

The company's inward investment has fallen by £65.8 million, and an analysis of the net cash flows shows that most of this fall has been absorbed by capital expenditure. This has fallen from £161 million in 1995 to £98.5 million in 1996.

The company's capital expenditure in 1995 was funded from external sources. The balance of operating cash flow after interest, tax and dividends was only £48.9 million (196.9 – 45.6 –

26.3 – 76.1). The figure of £15.4 million came from the realisation of short-term investments and the balance came from external sources. (This is not in itself a bad thing, but the company must ensure that the return on this investment is greater than the cost of raising the funds.) By 1996, the situation had improved with capital expenditure and financial investment covered by the funds generated during the year.

Living within its means?

UB has provided a sub-total before the management of liquid resources. This shows that in 1995 the company's cash flows during the year were not enough to cover its expenditure, although the situation improved in 1996 largely through the disposal of businesses.

Able to repay loans?

Two things make it difficult to understand the underlying cash generation potential of UB:

(1) the company is undergoing major changes;
(2) we have only two years' cash flows.

However, we do know that it used the cash surplus in 1996 to repay debt. This is clearly shown on the reconciliation of net cash flow to movement in net borrowings.

Extract 16.3   **RECONCILIATION OF CASH FLOW TO BORROWING (UNITED BISCUITS)**

	1996 £m	1995 £m
Net borrowings at beginning of year	(607.0)	(483.5)
Cash inflow/(outflow) before use of liquid resources and financing	366.8	(123.5)
Loans and finance leases disposed/(acquired) with subsidiary	19.4	(0.2)
Proceeds of issue of shares for cash	–	2.2
Foreign exchange translation difference	6.2	(2.0)
Movement in net borrowings in the period	392.4	(123.5)
Net borrowings at end of year	(214.6)	(607.0)

The loan repayment schedule below shows that loans have fallen dramatically during 1996.

Extract 16.4   **LOAN REPAYMENT SCHEDULE (UNITED BISCUITS)**

	1996 £m	1995 £m
Analysis by maturity		
Repayable as follows: After more than five years – by instalment	–	15.2
– other	1.2	85.4
Between two and five years	164.7	283.1
Between one and two years	27.3	16.6
	193.2	400.3
Under one year	117.5	320.0
Total gross borrowings	310.7	720.3

UB may have to repay £117.5 million during 1997 and £27.3 million in 1998. (It is unlikely that all will have to be repaid, as some will be facilities that are rolled over.) The notes disclose that most of this has a short maturity; £73.4 million is A$ commercial paper (covered by a revolving credit facility) and £5.8 million are bank overdrafts. In 1996, the sale of businesses (primarily Keebler and Ross Vegetable Products) generated a net cash inflow of £365.8 million. Without the cash flow from these disposals, the company had an underlying cash flow before management of liquid resources of £1 million, short-term deposits at the year end of £46.6 million and cash of £49.5 million. Unless the cash flow grows significantly, the company looks unlikely to be able to repay debt from existing resources. However, it is unlikely that the company would have to repay all the money, and even if it did UB should have no difficulty in raising additional debt.

Cash interest cover

This measures a company's ability to pay interest out of the operating cash flow and is calculated by using the following formula:

$$\frac{\text{Cash flow from operating activities}}{\text{Interest paid}}$$

United Biscuits improved its interest cover, as the interest paid was £35.1 million in 1996 and £51.9 million in 1995 giving cash interest covers of:

$$1996 \quad \frac{193.1}{35.1} \quad = \quad 5.5 \text{ times} \quad 1995 \quad \frac{196.9}{51.9} = 3.8 \text{ times}$$

The interest payments should decrease slightly in 1997, following the reduction in loans in 1996. However, this may be offset by rises in interest rates.

Operating cash flow

To illustrate how the reconciliation of operating profit to the net cash inflow from operating cash flow can be used in analysis, we will use note 20 from UB's 1996 accounts.

| **Extract 16.5** | **OPERATING CASH FLOW (UNITED BISCUITS)** | | | | | |

	Continuing	Discontinued	1996 Total	Continuing	Discontinued Total	1995
	£m	£m	£m	£m	£m	£m
Operating profit	129.2	7.8	137.0	96.4	(25.2)	71.2
Depreciation	67.7	2.9	70.6	61.6	33.1	94.7
Non-cash element of operating exceptional items	–	–	–	24.4	–	24.4
Share of retained loss of associated undertakings	0.1	0.5	0.6	0.3	1.6	1.9
(Increase)/decrease in stocks	(2.5)	(3.5)	(6.0)	(3.3)	4.8	1.5
(Increase)/decrease in debtors	(28.8)	3.8	(25.0)	6.6	(3.1)	3 5
Increase/(decrease) in creditors	35.2	3.4	38.6	49.8	(6.7)	43.1
Expenditure against rationalisation provisions	(23.5)	(0.1)	(23.6)	(23.1)	(23.1)	(46.2)
Other	0.9	–	0 9	(0.1)	2.9	2.8
Net cash inflow from operating activities	178.3	14.8	193.1	212.6	(15.7)	196.9

This shows us that:

- The operating profit improved by £65.8 million, but only £32.8 million of the improvement came from continuing operations. The balance came from discontinued operations.
- The company is undergoing a major rationalisation programme, in both continuing and discontinued operations. None of this was charged against 1996 profit (although the note on provisions actually says that £3.5 million was charged to 1996 profits), some exceptional provisions were charged to 1995 profits. This begs two questions:

(1) What is the balance on the provisions at the end of 1996? *(£29.3 million)*.
(2) What were the exceptional charges in 1995? *(Factory closures and management reorganisations of £27.4 million, and amounts written off investments of £4.3 million.)*

We can now identify the cash that will be generated from each year's trading:

Extract 16.6   **UNITED BISCUITS (CONTINUED)**

	1996 Total £m	1995 Total £m
Operating profit	137.0	71.2
Depreciation	70.6	94.7
Non-cash element of operating exceptional items	–	24.4
Share of retained loss of associated undertakings	0.6	1.9
Expenditure against rationalisation provisions	(23.6)	(46.2)
	(184.6)	146.0

The cash the business will generate from its trading has increased by £38.6m, but only £13.9 million came from continuing operations. The cash that has been generated from operating activities is higher than this figure, therefore, the working capital has been a source of funds for the business over the last two years although less so in 1996. As the turnover in the last two years has fallen from £3001.1 million to £1986.7 million, some fall in the working capital is to be expected, but to find out if the business had improved its control of working capital, we would need to calculate the working capital ratios.

● What the cash flow statement does not tell us

We can clearly see how the information in the cash flow statement can be used in analysis. We saw in Chapter 1 that the cash flow statement is a snapshot of the cash flow, and only looks at the movement of cash between the start to the end of the period. We must also remember that it cannot possibly give us all the answers as it does not tell us anything about:

- the company's borrowing facilities, or how close the company was to its maximum facility in the year (although this information may be available elsewhere in the accounts);
- why the company has spent the money. For example, the company could have more money invested in stock because it is inefficient, its launching a new product, commodity prices rose sharply at the end of the year, or because no one wants to buy its products. Again, some of this information may be available elsewhere in the accounts;

- where the cash is and where it has been spent;
- what is happening today – remember it is three months out of date when you see it!

Despite these limitations, analysing the cash flow statement will give us the information to enable us to ask better questions.

● RATIOS FOR CALCULATING CASH FLOW PER SHARE

There are several different ways of calculating the cash flow per share, and the three main ways are discussed below:

(1) the cash available for reinvestment
(2) the free cash flow
(3) the free cash flow available to the shareholders.

The cash flow before additional investment is a measure of the trading performance of the business, whereas the free cash flow is a measure of the company's ability to satisfy the providers of capital. The respective cash flows are divided by the weighted average number of shares in issue to arrive at the cash flow per share.

● Cash available for reinvestment

This method identifies the cash flow per share before any additional investment in either the working capital or the fixed assets. This shows the cash that has been generated by the business and is available for reinvestment. To calculate it you would need to take information from the cash flow statement. This cash flow measure starts with the operating profit and adds back any non-cash charges (e.g. depreciation), thus identifying the cash that the business will generate from this period's trading. Dividends, interest and tax paid are then deducted from the operating cash flow.

Free cash flow

This is a different concept. Free cash flow is defined as the cash that is available to the providers of capital, after any reinvestment in the existing business. Consequently, it starts with the operating profit plus depreciation, or similar non-cash charges. It then adjusts for changes in the working capital, cash flows from taxation, and the purchase and sale of fixed assets and companies.

Free cash flow available to shareholders

This identifies the cash that is available to the shareholders. Hence, it is the free cash flow less any loan interest and any net loan repayments.

JARGON

Cash   The definition of cash in the cash flow statement is very different from that of the balance sheet. Most companies would include money on deposit as part of cash on the balance sheet, regardless of the period of notice.

The definition used in the cash flow statement differs in two ways:

(1) it includes bank overdrafts as negative cash balances (and other loans repayable on demand or within 24 hours);

(2) cash is defined as having a maximum notice period of 24 hours, effectively restricting the definition of cash to money available, or repayable, on demand.

Cash equivalent   These are short-term, highly liquid investments that are readily convertible into cash and are subject to insignificant changes in value.

Direct method   This calculates operational cash flows on a receipts and payments basis.

Free cash flow   The cash that is available to the providers of capital, after any reinvestment in the existing business.

Indirect method   This calculates operational cash flows by reconciling the operating profit to the operational cash flow by deducting any non-cash charges to profits and adjusting for changes in the working capital.

Liquid resources   This covers current asset investments that do not qualify as cash. These should be able to be converted into cash at or close to their book value or are traded in an active market. Consequently the definition would encompass both deposits and financial instruments.

17 The statement of total recognised gains and losses

This chapter covers:

- Constructing a statement of total recognised gains and losses
- Reconciliation of movements of shareholders' funds
- Using the statement of total recognised gains and losses in financial analysis

● INTRODUCTION

This new primary statement was introduced in June 1993, as part of FRS 3. The Accounting Standards Board felt that the statement of total recognised gains and losses was necessary, as not all of the components of a company's financial performance are reflected in the profit and loss account – only the realised gains. The profit and loss account does not show all the gains and losses that are recorded in the period. Unrealised gains must be taken directly to reserves and are, therefore, not shown in the profit and loss account. This statement plugs that gap by showing the extent to which the shareholders' funds have increased from any gains that the company has included in the accounts, making them recognisable in the period. This is so, irrespective of whether they have been realised and included in the profit and loss account.

Although the statement itself is new, the information contained within it has always been found in the accounts. It was always shown in the note on the reserves, but I wonder how many of us read it? The ASB felt that most non-professional readers would be unlikely to have read this note in detail, and introduced this statement to make it possible to see at a glance the gains and losses recognised during the year. It effectively bridges the profit and loss account and the balance sheet, taking information from both statements. It is intended to be used with the profit and loss account to measure the company's financial performance during the period.

The statement of total recognised gains and losses shows us:

- the profit for the financial year;
- any revaluations of assets during the year;
- any currency translation differences on the company's net investments.

● CONSTRUCTING A STATEMENT OF TOTAL RECOGNISED GAINS AND LOSSES

The important thing to remember is that this statement is concerned with the gains and losses that have been recognised during the period. Consequently, it will not include all increases and decreases in the shareholders' funds, as some of these will relate to other items, for example, changes in the share capital, which is clearly neither a gain nor a loss. Therefore, companies are required to show a reconciliation to the movements in the shareholders' funds in addition to the statement of total recognised gains and losses.

We will derive a statement using the profit and loss account and balance sheets shown in the following pages. During the year our illustrative company has:

- had a major change in accounting policies, following the introduction of a new accounting standard. Conforming to this new standard will reduce the previously reported profits by £20 million;
- revalued properties upwards by £10 million;
- sold fixed assets, that had previously been revalued from the cost of £3 million to £4 million, for £5 million. Consequently, the company reported a profit on sale of fixed assets of £1 million;
- written £2 million off an investment, to reflect a fall in the market value following a recent valuation. The value of the investment remains above the original cost;
- issued shares with a nominal value of £5 million for £7 million;
- written off an £11 million exchange loss on overseas net investments.

These transactions are reflected in the following accounts (Tables 17.1 to 17.3).

Table 17.1 **Profit and loss account**

	This year
	£ million
Turnover	1000
Cost of sales	(650)
Gross profit	350
Administration expenses	(100)
Distribution costs	(150)
Operating profit	100
Profit on sale of fixed assets	1
Net interest payable	(11)
Profit before tax	90
Tax	(30)
Profit for the financial year	60
Dividends	(20)
Retained profits	40

Table 17.2 Balance sheets

	This year £ million	Last year £ million
FIXED ASSETS		
Tangible assets	520	500
Investments	8	10
	528	510
CURRENT ASSETS		
Stock	200	150
Debtors	300	200
Cash	36	100
	536	450
CREDITORS: AMOUNTS FALLING DUE WITHIN A YEAR		
Creditors	(350)	(300)
Net current assets	186	150
Total assets less current liabilities	714	660
CREDITORS: AMOUNTS FALLING DUE IN MORE THAN A YEAR		
Borrowings	(200)	(200)
PROVISIONS FOR LIABILITIES AND CHARGES	(70)	(60)
	444	400
CAPITAL AND RESERVES		
Share capital	55	50
Profit and loss account	280	250
Share premium account	52	50
Revaluation reserve	57	50
	444	400

Table 17.3 **Note on reserves extracted from the balance sheet notes**

	Share premium account	Revaluation reserve	Profit and loss account	Total
	£ million	£ million	£ million	£ million
At beginning of year as previously stated	50	50	270	370
Prior-year adjustment			(20)	(20)
At beginning of year as restated	50	50	250	350
Premium on issue of shares	2			2
Transfer from profit and loss account of the year			40	40
Transfer of realised profits		(1)	1	0
Decrease in value of investment		(2)		(2)
Currency translation differences on foreign currency net investments			(11)	(11)
Surplus on property revaluations		10		10
At the end of the year	52	57	280	389

The accounts and the note on the reserves contain the necessary information to construct a statement of total recognised gains and losses, reflecting the transactions previously outlined.

The statement follows a standard format. It takes the profit for the financial year and adds to it any revaluations of assets to arrive at the recognised gains and losses before currency adjustments. Currency adjustments are then deducted to show the recognised gains and losses for the year.

In our example the statement would be as shown in Table 17.4.

Table 17.4 **Statement of total recognised gains and losses**

	£ million
Profit for the financial year	60
Unrealised surplus on revaluation of properties	10
Unrealised loss on investment	(2)
	68
Currency translation differences on foreign currency net investments	(11)
Total recognised gains and losses for the year	57
Prior-year adjustment	(20)
Total gains and losses recognised since last annual report	37

The statement clearly shows the relative importance of profit, revaluations and currency adjustments to the company. It also highlights the fact that the company has adjusted its previously reported profits. Prior-year adjustments are shown for major changes in accounting policies or fundamental errors.

SUMMARY

The statement of total recognised gains and losses shows all the gains that the company has recognised during the year, regardless of whether they are realised gains shown on the profit and loss account, or unrealised gains recognised on the balance sheet. It discloses:

- the profit for the financial year;
- any fixed asset revaluations made during the year;
- the effect of currency adjustments on the company's balance sheet;
- prior-year adjustments made for changes in accounting policies or fundamental errors.

INTERNATIONAL DIFFERENCES

The statement of total recognised gains and losses is not required in other countries. However, similar information may be shown in the accounts. IAS 1 (*Presentation of Financial Statements*) requires companies to show a statement showing changes in equity, identifying the gains and losses that have been recognised during the period.

• RECONCILIATION OF MOVEMENTS IN SHAREHOLDERS' FUNDS

The profit and loss account and the statement of total recognised gains and losses are important measures of the company's financial performance during the year. However, it is important that we understand why this may not reflect the changes in the shareholders' funds, the net worth.

This is shown in the 'reconciliation of movements in shareholders' funds', which may be found either in the notes or following the statement of total recognised gains and losses. There are two ways that this can be prepared.

First reconciliation option

	£ million
Total recognised gains	57
Dividends	(20)
New share capital subscribed	7
Net addition to shareholders' funds	44
Opening shareholders funds (originally £420 million before deducting prior-year adjustment of £20 million)	400
Closing shareholders' funds	444

Second reconciliation option

The second option starts with the profit for the financial year, not the recognised gains and losses.

	£million
Profit for the financial year	60
Dividends	(20)
	40
Other recognised gains and losses relating to the year (net)	(3)
New share capital subscribed	7
Net addition to shareholders' funds	44
Opening shareholders funds (originally £420 million before deducting prior-year adjustment of £20 million)	400
Closing shareholders' funds	444

This is the format illustrated in the accounting standard, but is less 'user friendly', as it is more difficult to identify the total recognised gains. To do this we have to add the profit for the financial year of £60 million to the other recognised gains and losses of −£3 million. This gives us the £57 million gains recognised during the year.

● USING THE STATEMENT OF TOTAL RECOGNISED GAINS AND LOSSES IN FINANCIAL ANALYSIS

The statement identifies at a glance the gains that have been realised during the year.

● Profit for the financial year

You will notice that this is the profit before dividends, not the retained profits that are transferred to the reserves. The proposed dividends may or may not be approved at the annual general meeting after the publication of the accounts.

● The revaluations are not netted off

The revaluations are not netted off, with surpluses and deficits separately disclosed. We can see that the recognised gains are different to those revealed by a casual glance at the movement on the revaluation reserve (the way most non-professional readers would have spotted a revaluation). The revaluation reserve has increased by seven million, not the net eight million that has been recognised. This is because one million was transferred from the revaluation reserve to the profit and loss account on the sale of assets (as the gain is now realised).

● Currency translation differences

These are clearly shown in the body of the accounts for the first time. Whilst they have always been disclosed in the note to the reserves, the average reader of accounts would have been unaware how exposed the company's net worth was to exchange rate movements. This is illustrated in the following extract from BTR's 1996 accounts.

STATEMENT OF TOTAL RECOGNISED GAINS AND LOSSES
for the year ended 31 December 1996

£ millions	Notes	1996	1995
Profit for the financial year		431	960
Revaluations			(16)
		431	944
Exchange movements	24	(255)	20
		176	964

Exchange rates reduced the shareholders' funds by £255 million, this was more than 10 per cent of the closing shareholders' funds of £2 259 million.

● Prior-year adjustments

A prior-year adjustment is made for a major change in accounting polices or a fundamental error in the accounts. These could be critical in our analysis of the accounts. Highlighting them in the statement (again, they were always disclosed in the notes) is an important improvement for the less informed reader.

JARGON

Prior-year adjustment   A major change in accounting policies or a fundamental error.

Part 3

OTHER ACCOUNTING ISSUES

18 Other information disclosed in the notes to the accounts

This chapter covers:

- **Related party transactions**
- **Segmental analysis**
- **Post balance sheet events**

INTRODUCTION

The notes to the accounts disclose a wealth of other information that provides useful insights about a company's financial performance. We are able to understand the structure of their profits and assets by looking at the segmental information. The company's turnover, operating profit and operating assets will be analysed between different businesses and geographical locations. The company's profits and balance sheet can be affected by the way that it has accounted for pensions. The company's future performance can be influenced by things that have happened since the year end – these are called post balance sheet events. All this information can be found in the notes.

This information increases our understanding of the company's financial performance. It enables us to look at the company's performance in specific areas, identify any potential future problems and see if the company has changed between the date of the accounts and publication.

RELATED PARTY TRANSACTIONS

Relationships between related parties are a normal part of business life. However, dealings between related parties can have a material impact on a company's performance and its financial position. There could be an asset sale or trading between companies that are controlled by the same group. When these have been made at arms' length and at fair value there is no need for any concern. Unfortunately, this is not always the case. If there is any suspicion that transactions have not been fairly conducted, the shareholders have a right to know. The financial statements must contain sufficient disclosures to draw attention to the possibility that the reported financial position and profitability could have been affected by related parties and by transactions with them.

There are extensive statutory and Stock Exchange requirements (Chapter 11 and 12 in the Listing Rules) for disclosure of transactions with related parties. These cover many of the potential weak spots, such as loans made to directors, and the accounting standard (FRS 8, *Related Party Disclosures*) goes much further. It has widened the definition of related parties and requires most transactions to be disclosed if they are material to either party.

FRS 8 became effective in December 1995. It defines related parties, transactions with them and the disclosure requirements for related party transactions.

● Who is a related party?

The standard has a wide definition of related parties. A 'party' may be an individual, an entity, or a group of individuals (or entities) acting in concert. The standard identifies those who are deemed to be related parties, and those who are presumed to be related parties, unless proven otherwise.

Under the standard two or more parties are regarded as related parties in the following circumstances:

- **control** – one party has direct or indirect control over the other party;
- **common control** – the parties are subject to common control from the same source;
- **influence** – one party has the ability to influence the other party;
- **common influence** – the parties are subject to influence from the same source.

This means that other members of the group, the company's associates and joint ventures, company directors and pension funds would be related parties.

Moreover, others would be presumed to be related because of their influence within the company. The company would have to demonstrate that these had not exercised their influence 'in such a way as to inhibit the pursuit of separate interests'.

The presumed related parties are:

- **key management** – this includes the reporting company's key management, and the key management of its parent and any subsidiaries. The standard defines key managers as those who have 'authority or responsibility for directing and controlling the major activities and resources of the reporting entity'. This covers senior managers who effectively act as directors, but do not have a director's legal status;
- **controlled by a management contract** – an entity that manages, or is managed by, the company under a management contract would be presumed to be a related party;
- **control of 20 per cent or more of the company's voting rights** – any one owning, or controlling directly or indirectly, 20 per cent or more of the company's voting rights is presumed to be a related party, as such a party can clearly influence the company's operations;
- **concert party members with control or influence** – any member of a concert party who could exercise control or influence over the company is presumed to be a related party;
- **members of a related parties close family** – the standard has a wider definition than that found in the Companies Act and Stock Exchange Listing Rules (spouses and children under 18). It defines a close family as family members, or members of the same household;
- **entities controlled by related parties or their close families** – this covers partnerships, companies, trusts, or any other entities where the related party, or a member of his close family, has a controlling interest.

The standard presumes that the following parties are not related. Therefore, there is no requirement to disclose transactions that arise simply as a result of their role as:

- providers of capital
- utilities

- government departments and their sponsored bodies
- a customer, supplier, franchisor, distributor or general agent with whom the company transacts a significant volume of business.

Definition of related party transactions

Related party transactions are simply defined as the performance of a service or the transfer of assets or liabilities. The related party does not have to charge for the transaction, it can have been done for no consideration. All material transactions should be disclosed. This is a very wide ranging definition that means that all material transactions should be disclosed in the accounts, regardless of whether they were conducted on an arms' length basis or were done for no payment.

Materiality is defined as 'when their disclosure might reasonably be expected to influence decisions made by the users of general purpose financial statements'. The definition of materiality is extended if the related party is:

- a director, key manager or any other person in a position to influence, or accountable for the stewardship of the company;
- a member of that person's close family;
- an entity controlled by either of the above.

In deciding the materiality of transactions with these related parties, both the significance to the company and the significance to the related party should be considered. For this reason, transactions will be reported that are immaterial to the company, but material to the directors and their families.

Disclosure of related party transactions

FRS 8 requires that all companies disclose the name of the party that controls the reporting entity, and the name of the ultimate controlling party if this is different. This must be disclosed whether or not any transactions have taken place.

It also requires the following disclosure of material transactions with related parties:

- a description of the transaction, the amounts involved and any other information that is necessary for an understanding of the financial statements;
- details of any year-end balances that are due to or from related parties together with any provisions and amounts written off for bad debts.

Exemptions from disclosure

Whilst some parties will be defined as related parties, it is not necessary to disclose all transactions with them. The FRS does not require the disclosure of the following related party transactions:

- intra-group transactions or balances eliminated on consolidation;
- intra-group transactions in a parent's own financial statements, where these are shown with the consolidated accounts;
- ninety-per-cent subsidiaries: if 90 per cent, or more, of the voting rights are controlled within the group, disclosure is not required for transactions with other members of the group, or investees in the group, as long as the consolidated statements are publicly available;

- pension contributions paid to a pension fund;
- emoluments for services as an employee of the company;
- where the disclosure would conflict with a legal duty of confidentiality: this covers banks' legal duty of confidentiality.

The disclosures required for transactions with related parties are illustrated in the extract from the notes to Alfred McAlpine's 1996 accounts.

Extract 18.1 **RELATED PARTY TRANSACTIONS (ALFRED McALPINE)**

RELATED PARTY TRANSACTIONS

During the year, the Group entered into the following material transactions with related parties:

- Transactions amounting to £23.6m with various Civil Engineering Joint Ventures for the provision of labour at cost, plant at normal commercial rates, the recharge of costs incurred and a management fee. Balances totalling £6.4m (1995 – £2.5m) were owing to the Group by these joint Ventures at the year end, and amounts written off during the year in respect of such balances were £20 000 (1995 – £nil). In each case, a senior representative of Alfred McAlpine sits on the Board of the Joint Venture Body.

- The completion of the deferred consideration settlement with Mr E. W. Grove, who was a Director for part of the year, for the minority holding of Alfred McAlpine Homes Holdings Limited. This is referred to in note 14.

- The assignment, from Mr L. Grove, son of Mr E. W. Grove, on normal commercial terms, of a development agreement for £0.5m; and the lease of commercial premises from a company owned by Mr L. Grove at a commercial annual rent of £0.1m. Balances owing by the Group at the year end to Mr L. Grove were £0.1m and £nil, respectively.

- Two directors of the operating units within the Homes Division, acquired properties for their own occupation from the Group during the year for an aggregate consideration of £0.2m. These were acquired at discounts which are available to all McAlpine employees. There were no outstanding balances at the year end.

Except as noted above, no amounts have been written off or provided against in respect of any of the above transactions.

SUMMARY

The disclosure of related party transactions is covered by the Companies Act, the Stock Exchange Listing Rules and FRS 8 (*Related Party Disclosures*). The accounting standard goes much further than the statutory or listing requirements.

Under the accounting standard a related party is anyone who controls or influences another party, or who is subject to common control or common influence by another party.

Additionally, the following are presumed to be related, unless it can be proved otherwise:

- the key management of the company, its parent and its subsidiaries;
- any entity that manages, or is managed by, the company under a management contract;
- any one owning, or controlling directly or indirectly, 20 per cent or more of the company's voting rights;
- concert party members who could exercise control or influence;
- a related party's family members or a member of the same household. These are the related party's close family (this extends both the statutory and Stock Exchange's definitions);
- entities controlled by related parties or their close families.

▶

FRS 8 requires all companies to disclose the name of the party that controls the reporting entity, and the name of the ultimate controlling party if this is different. This must be disclosed whether or not any transactions have taken place.

All other material transactions with related parties should be disclosed unless they are:

● Transactions between group members. These are largely unnecessary as the consolidated statements treat the group as a single entity. Therefore, the following related party transactions would not have to be disclosed:
  – intra-group balances that are eliminated on consolidation;
  – transactions in the parent company accounts, where these are shown with the consolidated accounts;
  – transactions with other group members if 90 per cent or more of the voting rights are controlled within the group, and the accounts are publicly available.

● Pension contributions to a pension fund.
● Payments for services as an employee of the company.
● Disclosure would represent a breach of a legal duty of confidentiality.

There is also exemption for specific related parties whose transactions arise from their normal roles of suppliers or customers.

INTERNATIONAL DIFFERENCES

International accounting standards

IAS 24 (*Related Party Disclosures*) was originally issued in July 1984 (and reformatted in 1994), so FRS 8 is similar to the international standard. There are some differences between the UK and international standards:

● The definition of related parties does not specifically extend to close families. A related party is simply defined as 'one party has the ability to control the other party or exercise significant influence over the other party in making financial and operating decisions'.
● Only wholly owned subsidiaries are excluded from disclosure, if the parent is in the same country and provides consolidated accounts.
● IAS 24 does not require disclosure of :
  – the names of the related parties;
  – year-end balances of amounts due to or from related parties;
  – amounts written off these debts during the period.

Europe

There are statutory requirements within Europe to disclose transactions with directors. Beyond this there are few detailed disclosure requirements, although listed companies are increasingly conforming to international standards.

Japan

Japanese accounts would disclose some related party transactions, but not others.

At the end of the Second World War, Japan's huge conglomerates that effectively controlled Japanese industry, the *Zaibatsu*, were broken up into separate businesses. However, these were largely replaced with new informal *Keiretsu* enterprise groupings formed around banks. The majority of shares in a Keiretsu member would be held by other members, therefore, there is considerable cross-ownership of Japanese shares. Trading within Keiretsu members is common. Borrowings from another Keiretsu member would be shown as external debt. Related party transactions with other Keiretsu members would not normally be disclosed.

North America

The North American accounting requirements for related party disclosures is similar to the UK. The definition of a related party is similar to the definition in FRS 8. FAS 57 requires disclosures of material related party transactions other than compensation arrangements, expenses allowances, and other similar items in the normal course of business. Where there are no material transactions, common ownership or management would only be disclosed where the control could lead to significantly different operating results and statements of financial position.

Canadian companies are required to disclose when the company's operations are economically dependent on another party.

● SEGMENTAL ANALYSIS

When we are looking at large companies, the group accounts often do not give us the detailed information that we need. They are often multinational companies with diverse interests, and we want to know where the company is trading and where it is making its profits. Unless we can find out where the profits are being made and the assets are located, it is difficult to make a realistic assessment of the risks facing a company, and its long-term prospects. We must have more detailed information about the company's activities and the different markets the company trades in before we can assess a company's performance. We need to be able to understand how changes in the political and economic climate will affect the company's performance. Analysing performance and assets by different activities and markets is called *segmental reporting*.

All companies are required by the Companies Act to disclose the turnover and profit or loss before tax for each class of business and geographical market which differ substantially from one another. There is, however, an exception that is often used by smaller companies – if 'in the opinion of the directors the disclosure of any information would be seriously prejudicial', segmental information need not be disclosed.

The Stock Exchange has additional requirements and public and large private companies are required to comply with additional provisions in SSAP 25 (*Segmental Reporting*). For the purpose of segmental reporting, a large private company is defined as one that has ten times the medium-sized company criteria. Currently, a company would need to exceed two out of the following three criteria to be a large company: turnover £112 million, total assets £56 million, 2500 employees.

Companies have to report their performance by different business segments and classes of business. The accounting standard provides some guidelines for identifying these. *Business segments* are those that have different:

● returns on investment
● degrees of risk
● rates of growth
● levels of potential.

Whereas, classes of business are those where part of the company provides different products or services.

The accounting standard requires disclosure by both different classes of business and geographical segments where the turnover, or the profit and loss, or the net assets are 10 per cent or more of the total. (The rules are slightly different for associated undertakings, they would be separately disclosed where the profit and loss or net assets are 20 per cent or more of the total.)

Disclosure requirements

Companies are required to disclose turnover, profits (or losses) before tax, and operating assets by class of business and geographical segment.

Turnover

There are two ways that we can establish geographical segments. We can either look at where the company's operations are located, or where the goods and services are sold. The standard refers to these as 'origin' and 'destination'. The accounting standard requires that the disclosure of turnover should be by origin, unless the company exports a significant proportion of its goods where both origin and destination should be disclosed. The basic measure for turnover has to be one that is based on the location of the sales, as this forms the basis used for determining the profits and the operating assets.

Sales to external customers should be shown separately from inter-segment sales.

Profit

This is usually the profit before interest, tax, minority interests and extraordinary items. Interest is the one area where companies may differ. The accounting standard requires the exclusion of interest unless 'all, or part, of the entity's business is to earn and/or incur interest … or where interest income/expense is central to the business'.

Net assets

These are the operating assets and liabilities used by the business. They represent the non-interest-bearing assets less the non-interest-bearing liabilities.

Extract 18.2 from Cadbury Schweppes 1996 accounts illustrate the segmental information found in UK accounts.

Extract 18.2 **SALES, TRADING PROFIT, OPERATING ASSETS AND TRADING MARGIN ANALYSIS (CADBURY SCHWEPPES)**

for the 52 weeks ended 28 December 1996

1996	Total £m	United Kingdom £m	Europe £m	Americas £m	Pacific Rim £m	Africa & Others £m
Sales*						
Beverages	2,875	952	415	1,194	228	86
Confectionery	2,240	941	464	262	386	187
	5,115	1,893	879	1,456	614	273
Trading profit *†						
Beverages	445	113	27	271	20	14
Confectionery	267	118	28	33	67	21
	712	231	55	304	87	35
Operating Assets*						
Beverages	469	203	77	95	74	20
Confectionery	1,028	354	251	95	230	98
	1,497	557	328	190	304	118
Trading margin †	%	%	%	%	%	%
Beverages	15.5	11.9	6.5	22.7	8.8	16.3
Confectionery	11.9	12.5	6.0	12.6	17.4	11.2
	13.9	12.2	6.3	20.9	14.2	12.8

*   United Kingdom beverages includes sales, trading profit and operating assets of £921m, £124m and £214m, respectively, relating to discontinued operations

†   Excluding restructuring costs of £41m (see Note 3)

The sales analysis for 1996 and 1995 shown above is based on geographical origin and is not materially different to sales by geographical destination.

SUMMARY   Listed companies and other large companies provide segmental information in the notes to the accounts. A business, or geographical segment, is one where the turnover, or the profit and loss, or the net assets are 10 per cent, or more of the total. Geographical segments can be determined by where the operations are located (origin), or where their products and services are sold (destination). The turnover is usually shown by origin, but if the company's exports are significant the destination will also be shown.

Companies disclose the turnover, profits and net operating assets for each business segment.

INTERNATIONAL DIFFERENCES

There are differences in the reporting of segmental information, and these are detailed below for our comparative countries.

International accounting standards

Segmental accounting is covered by IAS 14 (*Reporting Financial Information by Segment*), which was revised in August 1997 and now requires more disclosures than SSAP 25. The main differences between the international standard and the UK one are:

- IAS 14 does not apply to all companies, only to those whose equity, or debt, securities are publicly traded. (This reflects international practice, as segmental reporting is usually only required for listed companies.)
- SSAP 25 requires the same quantity of information to be disclosed for industry and business segments. IAS 14 now requires companies to identify which of these is primary and which is secondary, requiring more disclosure for primary segments.

  The primary segment is the dominant 'source and nature of an enterprise's risks and returns'. Usually the management organisation will reflect the predominant source of risks and rewards, and therefore identifies the primary segment. However, if the management structure is based neither on products nor geography the directors may determine the primary segment. Consequently, if the risks and returns of the company are largely determined by differences in its products and services – business segments will be the primary segment. If both are equal, the business segment should be the primary segment.

  The primary segment has to give more disclosures than are required under SSAP 25. Additionally they would disclose:
  - assets employed (SSAP 25 requires net assets to be shown);
  - the basis of inter-segment pricing;
  - segment liabilities;
  - expenditure on tangible and intangible assets;
  - depreciation and amortisation (unless the company gives segmental cash flows);
  - other non-cash expenses;
  - the company's share of the profits, and related investment, of any equity accounted investment where the operations are largely within a segment.

Secondary segments should disclose:
  - the sales to external customers (where these are more than 10 per cent of the total) based on the location of the customers;
  - the book value of segmental assets (where these are more than 10 per cent of the total), together with any related capital expenditure.

If the primary format is based on geographical segments it is possible, where the companies export a significant proportion of their turnover, for the location of the customers to be different from the location of the assets. Additional information must then be disclosed to make these comparable.

The ASB published a discussion paper in 1996, with a view to minimising the differences between a revised IAS and the UK rules.

Europe

The Directives require that turnover should be split by sector and market, and this has been incorporated into the law of our comparative countries. Disclosure of profits and net assets would be unusual, as most companies provide only the minimum information required by law. BMW, is typical in its disclosures of net sales in its 1996 accounts, although more information is given in the operating review (Extract 18.3).

Extract 18.3	NET SALES (BMW)	

	1996 DM million	1995 DM million
Automobiles	37,966	33,547
Motorcycles	744	731
Leasing	6,054	5,044
Other sales	7,501	6,822
	52,265	**46,144**
Federal Republic of Germany	14,621	13,862
United Kingdom	8,930	8,242
Rest of Europe	12,218	10,088
North America	8,228	6,177
Asia	5,574	5,291
Other markets	2,694	2,484
	52,265	**46,144**

JAPAN

The segmental disclosures are broadly similar to those of the old international standard.

NORTH AMERICA

North American companies are required to disclose segmental information if they are listed, or are required to file financial statements with the securities commission. Operating profit is the required profit figure, therefore, interest and exceptional items showing below operating profit would not be included.

In the USA segmental reporting is not required in the interim statements. The following segmental information is required to be disclosed by industry and geographical segments:

- third-party sales and inter-segment sales. If third-party export sales are 10 per cent, or more of total third-party sales, it should be reported together with any appropriate geographical analysis;
- operating profits, excluding any results from associates;
- total assets that have been used by the segment together with a reasonable allocation of assets that are jointly used by segments;
- depreciation and capital expenditure.

If a single customer represents 10 per cent or more of the company's total sales, this should be disclosed, together with the amount of sales relating to that customer.

In Canada segments are defined in a similar way to SSAP 25. An industry or geographic segment is defined where any of the following exceed 10 per cent of the total:

- third-party sales
- operating profits

- identifiable assets.

Companies should disclose the following information for each segment:

- third-party sales and inter-segment sales
- operating profits
- total assets that have been used by the segment
- depreciation and capital expenditure
- the company should also disclose any dominant industry segment.

● POST BALANCE SHEET EVENTS

The accounts give a snapshot of the company at the balance-sheet date, but the company could have changed significantly in the three months between taking the snapshot and publishing the accounts. The accounting standard (SSAP 17, *Accounting for Post Balance Sheet Events*) recognises this and divides post balance sheet events into two types:

(1) **adjusting events:** these give extra information about conditions that the company knew about at the year end. The extra information allows the company to adjust the figures, to show a more accurate view. For example, the company could have made a bad debt provision for a customer's account. The customer has subsequently gone into liquidation, confirming the company's view. The amount would need to be written off, but would not have to be disclosed separately unless the amount was so large that separate disclosure of the bad debt was felt to be necessary for the true and fair view.

(2) **non-adjusting events:** these did not exist at the year end. Examples of non-adjusting events could be acquisitions, disposals, the resignation of directors and share issues. Material, non-adjusting, post balance sheet events would have to be separately disclosed in the notes to the accounts and an estimate of the financial impact should be provided, where it is possible.

The 1997 interim accounts for The Energy Group clearly illustrate how much can happen between the date of the balance sheet and the publication of the accounts:

Extract 18.1 **POST BALANCE SHEET EVENTS (THE ENERGY GROUP)**

SUBSEQUENT EVENTS

On 14 April 1997 Eastern Electricity plc issued £200 million 8.75% bonds due 2012.

On 24 April 1997 Eastern issued promissory notes of CZK 2,900 million (approximately £59 million) to Ceska Sporitelna a.s. in the Czech Republic redeemable no later than 29 April 2004. The notes are secured by the Group's investments in Severomoravska Energetika a.s. and Teplarny Brno a.s.

On I May 1997 the Labour Party was elected to government in the UK. It has reaffirmed its intention to impose a one-off "windfall levy" on regulated industries in the UK.

On 20 May 1997 the Group completed its acquisition of Citizens Lehman Power LLC, which has been renamed Citizens Power LLC. The acquisition involved an initial payment of £12.5 million in cash, plus a payment deferred until 31 March 2000, equivalent to the net assets as of 30 June 1997. There will be additional purchase consideration linked to profit goals up to 2002, subject to a maximum consideration for the entire transaction of $120 million.

On 10 June 1997 the company announced it was in discussions with PacifiCorp which may lead to a combination of the two companies through a recommended cash offer for The Energy Group plc.

At 12 June 1997 the Group's shareholding in Teplarny Brno a.s. had increased to 70.3 per cent at an additional cost of £4 million.

SUMMARY Many things happen to a company between the year end and the publication of the accounts. SSAP 17 (*Accounting for Post Balance Sheet Events*) identifies two types of post-balance-sheet events: those that provide additional information about the company at the balance-sheet date (adjusting events) and those that have no impact on the amounts shown in the accounts (non-adjusting events).

Adjusting events are shown in the financial statements, but are only disclosed if they are material. Non-adjusting events, such as acquisitions, do not affect the financial statements, but do affect the company's future prospects. Therefore, they are disclosed, but no adjustment is made to the accounts, as they do not relate to the state of affairs at the year end.

INTERNATIONAL DIFFERENCES

Most countries would disclose non-adjusting events, although French companies tend to only disclose them if the going concern assumption is affected.

International accounting standards

Post balance sheet events are covered by IAS 10 (*Contingencies and Events Occurring after the Balance Sheet Date*), which is similar to SSAP 17. However, it does differ to SSAP 8 (*Taxation under the Imputation System*) in the allowed accounting treatment for proposed dividends. SSAP 8 requires that dividends that have been declared and proposed should be accrued, and shown as a current liability. Whereas the international standard allows them to be either accrued, or disclosed.

Europe

Dutch practice is the same as that found in the UK. In France adjusting events should be reflected in the accounts where they can be reasonably estimated. Otherwise, they should be treated as non-adjusting events. This means that they would be disclosed if the going concern assumption is affected. Disclosure is also sometimes made when going concern is unaffected. In Germany the treatment of adjusting events is the same as in the UK; non-adjusting events are disclosed in the management report.

Japan

Japanese practice generally conforms with IAS 10.

North America

The accounting treatment for post balance sheet events in the USA is similar to that of the UK. In Canada disclosure of non-adjusting, post balance sheet events is only required if:

- they will cause significant changes to the company's assets or liabilities in the subsequent period;
- they may or will have a significant effect on the company's future operations.

JARGON

Adjusting event   Something that has happened between the year end and the publication of the accounts that gives the company additional information about conditions, such as bad debts, that the company knew about at the year end.

Geographical destination   Where a company's products are sold.

Geographical origin   Where a company's operations are located.

Non-adjusting event   Something was not known at the year end, that has occurred between the year end and the publication of the accounts. An acquisition would be an example of a non-adjusting event.

Related party   A party that controls or influences another, or who is subject to common control or common influence.

19 Group accounts, acquisitions and mergers

This chapter covers:

- Introduction to group accounts
- Accounting for acquisitions
- Accounting for mergers
- Disclosure requirements for acquisitions and mergers

● INTRODUCTION TO GROUP ACCOUNTS

In this chapter we will discuss groups and group accounts. A group is a collection of companies controlled by a parent or holding company. The group could have evolved in three ways:

(1) organically, with companies being started to cover different activities;
(2) through acquisition, with the original company buying other companies;
(3) through a merger with another company.

Acquisitions and mergers are accounted for differently. The rest of this chapter will look at the structure of group accounts, and how we account for acquisitions and mergers. As the detailed accounting procedures for accounting for acquisitions and mergers tend to be country specific, this chapter deals with UK accounting practices, unless specified otherwise.

So far we have talked about individual company's accounts, but in practice many companies belong to a group. Later in the book we will be reviewing the financial performance of Boots and the accounts we will be using are their group accounts. The Boots Group comprises the following companies:

Extract 19.1   THE BOOTS COMPANY PLC: LIST OF COMPANIES IN THE GROUP

	Percentage held by parent	Percentage held by subsidiary undertakings	Country of incorporation where operating overseas	Principal activities
Parent				
The Boots Company PLC				Manufacturing, marketing and distribution of healthcare and consumer products
Subsidiary undertakings (incorporated in Great Britain)				
A G Stanley Ltd.		100		Retailing of decorative products and interior furnishings
BCM Ltd.	100			Manufacturing pharmaceuticals and consumer products
Boots Development Properties Ltd.		100		Property development
Boots Healthcare International Ltd.	100			Marketing consumer products
Boots Opticians Ltd.		100		Registered opticians
Boots Properties PLC	100			Property holding
Boots The Chemists Ltd.	100			Retail chemists
Crookes Healthcare Ltd.	100			Marketing consumer products
Do It All Ltd.	100			DIY retailer
Halfords Ltd.	100			Retailing of auto parts, accessories, bicycles and car servicing
Optrex Ltd.	100			Marketing consumer products
Subsidiary undertakings (incorporated overseas)				Activities refer to healthcare and/or consumer products unless otherwise indicated
The Boots Company (Australia) Pty. Ltd.	100		Australia	Marketing
Boots Healthcare SA NV		100	Belgium	Marketing
Boots Healthcare SA		100	France	Marketing
BCM Cosmetique SA	100		France	Manufacturing and marketing
Laboratoires Lutsia SA		100	France	Manufacturing and marketing
Roval SA		100	France	Manufacturing
BCM Kosmetik GmbH	100		Germany	Manufacturing and marketing
Mountgrave Insurance Ltd.	100		Guernsey	Insurance company
Boots (Retail Buying) Ltd.	100		Hong Kong	Buying
Boots Healthcare Ltd.		100	Ireland	Marketing
Boots Healthcare Marco Viti Farmaceutici S.p.A.	100		Italy	Manufacturing and marketing
Boots Investments Ltd.	100		Jersey	Investment company
Boots Trading (Malaysia) Sdn. Bhd.	100		Malaysia	Marketing
Boots Healthcare BV		100	Netherlands	Marketing
The Boots Company (New Zealand) Ltd.	100		New Zealand	Marketing
The Boots Company (Philippines) Inc	100		Philippines	Marketing
The Boots Company (Far East) Pte. Ltd.	100		Singapore	Marketing
The Boots Company (South Africa) (Pty.) Ltd.	100		South Africa	Manufacturing and marketing
Boots Healthcare S.A.	100		Spain	Marketing
The Boots Company (Thailand) Ltd.	100		Thailand	Marketing
Boots Retail (Thailand) Ltd.	49	2	Thailand	Retail

All percentages relate to holdings of ordinary share capital.
All companies operate principally in the country of incorporation.

Each of these companies is a legal entity, and as such prepares accounts. A group, therefore, comprises a parent company and its subsidiaries. A parent company is one who controls another company, which is deemed to be a subsidiary. The group accounts combine the accounting statements of all the group members – this process is referred to as *consolidation*. However, the shares in all of the subsidiaries may not be owned within the group. Some shares may be owned by other shareholders. The company will have to disclose the proportion of the after tax profits, and net assets, that belong to the non-group shareholders as *minority interests*.

Historically, companies were thought to control other companies when they had more than 50 per cent of the voting rights. Unfortunately, this definition left considerable scope for creative accounting, with companies taking their debt 'off the balance sheet', hiding their profitability, or avoiding tax liabilities. Consequently, both the Companies Act and the accounting standards have been amended to broaden the definition of control.

The parent is required to prepare accounts both for itself, and the group, at the end of the financial year (Company Act 1985, s 227) unless the group is defined by the Act as small, or medium sized. The Act requires that the group accounts should consolidate both the profit and loss accounts and the balance sheets of the group. The accounting standards also require that groups have consolidated cash flow statements (FRS 1). The statement of total recognised gains and losses (FRS 3), and notes on historical cost profits and losses (FRS 3), are also consolidated statements as they are derived from information in the consolidated accounts.

• The parent

An undertaking is classified as a parent under the Companies Act (s 258) if *any* of the following conditions apply:

- It has the majority of the voting rights in the undertaking.
- It is a member of the undertaking and has the right to appoint or remove directors who hold the majority of the voting rights at meetings of the board on all, or substantially all, matters. Consequently, it effectively controls the majority of the voting rights.
- It is a member of the undertaking and, following an agreement with other shareholders or members, controls alone a majority of the voting rights in the undertaking.
- It has the right to exercise dominant influence over the undertaking. This influence can arise in a number of ways:
  - by virtue of the provisions contained in the Memorandum or Articles; or
  - by virtue of a written control contract that is permitted both by the Memorandum or Articles of the controlled undertaking, and the law under which the undertaking is established.
- It has a *participating interest* (the company holds more than 20 per cent of the shares as a long-term investment and influences the company's decision making) in the undertaking and:
  - actually exercises a *dominant influence* over the undertaking (this means that it determines the operating and financial policies of the undertaking); or
  - it and the undertaking are managed on a *unified basis* (this means that the two companies operations are integrated, and they are managed as a single unit).

• Subsidiaries

Subsidiaries may be wholly, or partly owned. A *wholly owned subsidiary* is one where all the share capital is owned by either the parent, or by another wholly owned subsidiary.

A *partially owned subsidiary* is one where some of the share capital is owned by third parties, people outside of the group.

An example of a group structure is illustrated in Figure 19.1. Companies B, C, and E are wholly owned subsidiaries, whereas companies A and D are partly owned.

Figure 19.1 **GROUP STRUCTURE: WHOLLY OWNED AND PARTLY OWNED SUBSIDIARIES**

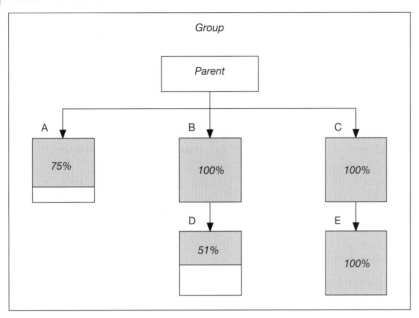

● The group

All groups have to prepare consolidated accounts, although there are detailed differences in the consolidation process that are determined by the way that the group has evolved. Different rules are used for acquisitions and mergers. The objective of the consolidation process is to combine the individual accounts of all the group members, reporting the activities of the group as though it was a single company.

This means that:

● common accounting policies should be used;
● all members of the group should ideally have the same year end;
● any inter-company transactions must be eliminated;
● minority interests in the group must be clearly stated.

The parent company is required to prepare group accounts, although there are some exceptions allowed under the Companies Act. Companies need not prepare group accounts if:

● the group is classified as small or medium sized under the Act;
● the parent is a majority, or wholly owned, subsidiary of a group incorporated within the EU, and the company complies with the requirements of s 228 of the Act;
● all of the subsidiaries are allowed or required to be excluded from consolidation under s 229 of the Act.

All of the subsidiaries should be consolidated unless:

- there are severe long-term restrictions hindering the parent's ability to exercise its rights;
- the subsidiary is held exclusively for re-sale, and has not previously been consolidated;
- the activities of the subsidiary are so different from the rest of the group that its inclusion would mean that the accounts are no longer true and fair.

The parent company is required to prepare consolidated group accounts. It must publish its balance sheet in the group accounts. However, it may claim exemption from publishing a profit and loss account, under s 230 of the Companies Act, if it discloses how much of the consolidated profit and loss has been dealt with in its own individual accounts. Most companies elect to do this.

SUMMARY

- A parent is a company which either controls the voting rights of another company, or which has dominant influence over another company.
- Unless specifically exempted by the Companies Act, the directors of the parent company must prepare consolidated accounts.
- The parent must publish its own balance sheet, but will probably seek exemption from publishing its own profit and loss account. It will, however, have to disclose the amount of the group profit that is dealt with in its own accounts.
- The parent company may also be called the holding company.

INTERNATIONAL DIFFERENCES

International accounting standards

Group accounts are covered by IAS 27 (*Consolidated Financial Statements*), which has the following main differences:

- **The definition of a parent** in IAS 27 is more restrictive than FRS 2. The definition of a subsidiary rests solely on control – the power to govern the financial and operating policies. It does not extend the definition of a parent to one who exercises dominant influence, or where unified management exists.
- **Exemption for preparation of group accounts:** only wholly owned groups (or virtually wholly owned where the parent owns at least 90 per cent of the voting power) can, with the approval of the minority shareholders, be exempt from preparing group accounts.
- **The reporting dates** of consolidated subsidiaries should be no more than three months from the parent's.
- **Unconsolidated subsidiaries:** for these there are no grounds for exclusion on the basis of dissimilarity.

Europe

Within the EU, consolidation is covered by the Seventh Directive, which requires consolidation in any of the following situations:

- there is a majority of the share voting rights;
- there is a shareholding, plus the right to appoint, or remove, a majority of the directors;
- a control contract gives dominant influence, even where there is no shareholding;
- there is a shareholding, plus the majority of the voting rights.

The Seventh Directive also allows countries to require consolidation where there is a participating interest coupled with unified management or dominant influence. It also allows parent companies to not prepare consolidated accounts if:

- it is not a listed company, and is a wholly owned subsidiary of a company in another member state;
- if there is a small minority interest of up to 10 per cent and the minority shareholders approve the exemption.

It also requires that, where tax-based values have been used for individual company's accounts, these should either be disclosed or corrected in the group accounts. In France, the numbers are 'corrected', as the group accounts are not used for tax purposes. In Germany, the 'disclosure' route is usually followed.

Small companies in our comparative European countries do not have to prepare consolidated accounts.

In France all other companies should be consolidated where:

- the company directly or indirectly has the majority of the voting rights;
- it has 40 per cent of the voting rights, and no one else has a larger percentage;
- it has a shareholding and controls the company through some form of agreement.

Since 1990, German companies have been required to prepare consolidated accounts where they either:

- effectively control one or more companies where they own more than 20 per cent of the equity;
- they are able to exercise control by having the majority voting rights, the power to appoint and dismiss directors, or a control contract.

In the Netherlands most companies would have to consolidate subsidiaries where any of the following conditions are met. The holding company:

- exercises over half of the voting rights;
- is entitled to appoint, or discharge, more than half of the directors;
- is fully liable as a partner.

Japan

Consolidation is a recent introduction to Japanese accounting, and is not required at all by the Commercial Code. The Finance Ministry requires consolidation for listed companies. Although the importance of consolidated accounts is growing with the increasing number of overseas subsidiaries, the parent company's accounts are still seen as the most important, with the consolidated accounts almost relegated to supplementary information. Listed companies are required to consolidate companies where they own the majority of the voting rights.

North America

In the USA consolidation is required for all subsidiaries where the parent, directly or indirectly, controls 50 per cent or more of the voting rights. The only allowable exception to this is where the control is temporary. This could be either because the subsidiary is going to be sold or the control does not lie with the majority shareholders (for example, bankruptcy).

In Canada all permanent subsidiaries should be consolidated. The definition of a subsidiary is similar to the UK definition, as it is not purely reliant on voting rights. A subsidiary is an 'enterprise controlled by another enterprise … that has the right and ability to obtain future economic benefits from the resources of the enterprise and is exposed to the related risks'.

● ACCOUNTING FOR ACQUISITIONS

Most business combinations are acquisitions, although some arise following a merger. Mergers will be discussed in detail later in the chapter.

A number of accounting problems arise when a company buys another company. The purchaser has to account for:

- any difference between the net asset value of the acquired business, and the cost of the acquisition – this is called *goodwill*;
- alignment of the two companies' accounting polices;
- the fair values of the acquired assets of the company;
- consolidation adjustments.

These problems will be illustrated throughout this chapter by using the following example, or variants of it.

ACQUISITION EXAMPLE

A predator wants to buy a company, which we will call the victim. The victim has net assets of £50 000, and is making £20 000 a year profit before tax. If the predator wishes to acquire the victim he will probably have to pay a lot more than £50 000. He is not just buying the net assets of the business, but also the profits, which give a good return on those assets. However, the victim's business is very seasonal, as most of the profits are made in the period September to December.

Let us consider what would happen if he decided to pay £90 000 in cash to acquire the victim's business.

The two companies' balance sheets, prior to acquisition, were as shown in Table 19.1:

Table 19.1 **Balance sheets: predator and victim prior to acquisition**

	Predator £000	Victim £000
Tangible fixed assets	100	40
Current assets:		
Stock	30	20
Debtors	70	45
Cash	100	5
	200	70
Creditors: amounts falling due within a year:		
Creditors	(110)	(30)
Net current assets	90	40
Total assets less current liabilities	190	80
Creditors: amounts falling due in more than a year:		
Loans	(30)	(30)
	160	50
Capital and reserves:		
Share capital	50	10
Profit and loss account	110	40
	160	50

• Goodwill

On acquisition the predator has spent £90 000 and gained net assets of £50 000. When the victim is consolidated into the predator's accounts, the balance sheet will not balance because of the premium the predator has paid to acquire the victim's business – this premium is called goodwill.

This can be clearly seen in the consolidated balance sheet (Table 19.2), constructed immediately following the acquisition.

Table 19.2 | **Consolidated balance sheet: predator and victim after acquisition**

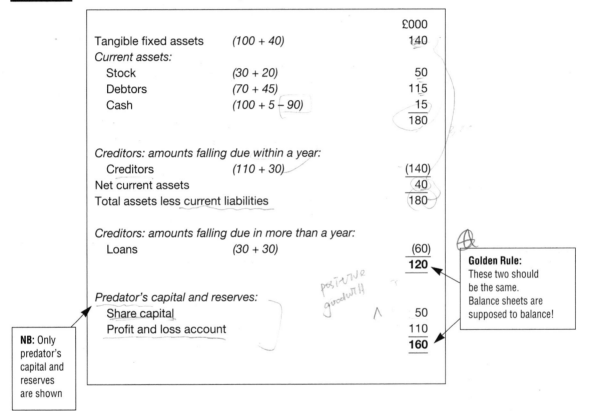

		£000
Tangible fixed assets	*(100 + 40)*	140
Current assets:		
Stock	*(30 + 20)*	50
Debtors	*(70 + 45)*	115
Cash	*(100 + 5 – 90)*	15
		180
Creditors: amounts falling due within a year:		
Creditors	*(110 + 30)*	(140)
Net current assets		40
Total assets less current liabilities		180
Creditors: amounts falling due in more than a year:		
Loans	*(30 + 30)*	(60)
		120
Predator's capital and reserves:		
Share capital		50
Profit and loss account		110
		160

positive goodwill

NB: Only predator's capital and reserves are shown

Golden Rule: These two should be the same. Balance sheets are supposed to balance!

The balance sheet does not balance! The combined business has net assets of £120 000 and capital and reserves of £160 000. The balance sheet does not balance because the predator has paid a £40 000 premium above the net asset value (goodwill) to acquire the victim. Accountants now have to find a way to resolve the problem of getting the balance sheet to balance.

There are two obvious ways to resolve the problem. We can either reduce the capital and reserves to £120 000 or we can increase the net assets to £160 000. Either approach could be used. Goodwill can be written off against the capital and reserves, or an intangible asset can be created to reflect the goodwill that has been purchased. Accounting for goodwill is probably the most hotly contested argument in UK accounting today.

These two different accounting approaches are illustrated as Option 1 (*writing goodwill off through capital and reserves*) and Option 2 (*showing goodwill as an intangible asset*).

Table 19.3 **Getting the balance sheet to balance after acquisition**

	Option 1 £000	Option 2 £000
Tangible fixed assets	140	140
Intangible fixed asset – goodwill		40
		180
Current assets:		
Stock	50	50
Debtors	115	115
Cash	15	15
	180	180
Creditors: amounts falling due within a year:		
Creditors	(140)	(140)
Net current assets	40	40
Total assets less current liabilities	180	220
Creditors: amounts falling due in more than a year:		
Loans	(60)	(60)
	120	**160**
Capital and reserves:		
Share capital	50	50
Profit and loss account	110	110
Goodwill	(40)	**160**
	120	

The first option writes goodwill off against reserves. Some companies would show goodwill as a separate, negative, reserve, as illustrated above. However currently most UK (and Dutch) companies write goodwill off through the profit and loss account, showing the cumulative goodwill written off as a note to the reserves. Their capital and reserves would then be reported as follows:

Capital and reserves:	
Share capital	50
Profit and loss account	70
	120

This means that most UK companies have written off goodwill against *past* profits. Writing goodwill off through the shareholder's funds reflects the fact that their funds have been used to acquire the victim's business. However, in exchange for this cash outflow the predator has the opportunity to benefit, in the future, from the victim's profits and cash flows. Proponents of the immediate write-off method believe that this is the best approach. They also argue that goodwill is clearly not an asset and, therefore, should not be treated as such. Nor is it a cost, as it is not used in the operations of business, nor is it depleted. They argue that this treatment is consistent with the accounting treatment of internally generated goodwill, which is not recognised as an asset. The costs are written off as they are incurred and the benefits taken into the profit and loss account when they arise.

The second option creates an intangible asset and must be followed in the UK from December 1998. By showing goodwill as an intangible asset, this treatment recognises that it is not a normal asset of the business, but is an integral part of the larger asset, the investment in the victim. The predator's management must be accountable for their management of the company's investment in the victim. Proponents of capitalising goodwill argue that the first option can be criticised on two grounds:

(1) it reduces the apparent net worth of the business following any acquisition where the cost of the acquisition is greater than the net assets of the acquired business. This may encourage companies to value their brands, and show these as an intangible asset, as a way of avoiding the goodwill write-off. As these assets are similar in nature to goodwill, the accounting treatment should be the same;

(2) it distorts many of the financial ratios – reducing the denominator increases the percentage, be it the return on capital or gearing! This makes acquisitive businesses appear to be more profitable than those who have grown organically, although the downside is that they appear to be more highly geared.

This increase in the assets opens the debate about whether the goodwill should stand for ever on the balance sheet at £40 000, or whether it should be *amortised* (depreciated) over a period. Both the international accounting standards and FRS 10, which becomes effective on 23 December 1998, suggest that goodwill should be amortised. (From December 1998 it must be amortised unless the company can prove that the value has not fallen.) This has the effect of charging goodwill against *future* profits, rather than against past profits. The amortisation periods will vary from one country to another.

Historically most UK companies wrote goodwill off against their reserve. However, FRS 10 will require them to follow the second option and show goodwill as an intangible asset. This will bring the UK into line with international accounting practice. In the past the accounting treatment, shown in Option 1, overstated the returns on the investment and made it harder to spot those companies that had overpaid for their acquisitions. The new accounting treatment will ensure that the management will be held accountable for all aspects of the acquisitions, and should identify whether the acquisition has added value for the shareholders.

Goodwill must be reviewed at the end of the first full financial year to ensure that the premium which has been paid to acquire the company will be covered by the acquisition's future cash flows. The impairment review compares the value of the acquisition with the present value of its future cash flows. It is carried out in two stages. Initially the company compares the acquired company's first year performance with the pre-acquisition forecasts for the first year. If there is evidence that the post-acquisition performance has not met the pre-acquisition expectations, a full impairment review is then undertaken. This impairment review ensures that if there has been an overpayment the loss is recognised immediately.

Goodwill arising from acquisitions made after 23 December 1998 will be capitalised on the balance sheet. However, the transitional arrangements allow goodwill that has previously been eliminated through the reserves to remain eliminated until the business is sold or terminated. This goodwill will have to be disclosed in the notes to the accounts, and be deducted from profit when the business is sold, or terminated, in the future. This means that careful reading of the notes will be required before calculating any ratios.

International Accounting Standard 22, *Business Combinations*, requires goodwill to be amortised over its useful economic life. This life should not exceed five years, unless a longer period (maximum 20 years) can be justified. The goodwill should be reviewed annually and, if the goodwill is felt to be irrecoverable, it should be written down.

Negative goodwill

We have talked about companies paying more to acquire a company than the value of the net assets, as this is the most likely scenario. However, it may be possible to buy a company for less than its net asset value. In 1996 Boots acquired the remaining shares in Do It All (Boots had previously owned 50 per cent), which had net assets of £95.6 million for £1. In this case the goodwill would be negative rather than positive. We would then have a different accounting problem. To illustrate this we will amend our earlier acquisition example.

EXAMPLE **ACQUISITION EXAMPLE (CONTINUED)**

We will now assume that the predator pays £40 000 to buy the victim. The consolidated balance sheet, before the adjustment for goodwill, will be as shown in Table 19.4:

Table 19.4 **Consolidated balance sheet (before adjustment for goodwill)**

		£000
Tangible fixed assets	(100 + 40)	140
Current assets:		
Stock	(30 + 20)	50
Debtors	(70 + 45)	115
Cash	(100 + 5 – 40)	65
		230
Creditors: amounts falling due within a year:		
Creditors	(110 + 30)	(140)
Net current assets		90
Total assets less current liabilities		230
Creditors: amounts falling due in more than a year:		
Loans	(30 + 30)	(60)
		170
Predator's capital and reserves:		
Share capital		50
Profit and loss account		110
		160

The negative goodwill has caused a similar imbalance in the balance sheet. This is currently taken directly to reserves but under FRS 10 negative goodwill should be shown separately from positive goodwill on the face of the balance sheet as an intangible asset. It is subsequently written back into the profit and loss account over the periods expected to benefit.

Acquisitions using a share exchange

So far we have considered the victim is bought for cash. However, a number of acquisitions are made by means of a share exchange, or a mixture of shares and cash. To illustrate the accounting procedure for a business acquired through a share exchange, we will amend our example.

EXAMPLE **ACQUISITION EXAMPLE (CONTINUED)**

The predator's shares are trading at £4.50. With the shareholders' permission, predator makes an offer to buy the victim by offering two shares in the predator for every share in the victim. All of the victim's shareholders accept the offer, and the predator has issued 20 000 shares with a nominal value of £20 000 and a market value of £90 000. There are two things that we now have to take into account:

(1) the goodwill arising on the acquisition – the predator has paid £90 000 for net assets of £50 000, giving goodwill of £40 000;

(2) the share premium arising from the issue of shares – the nominal value of the shares issued was £20 000, compared to a market value of £90 000. The share premium is, therefore, £70 000.

Prior to the offer, the two companies' balance sheets could be summarised as shown in Table 19.5:

Table 19.5 **Balance sheets of predator and victim prior to acquisition by share exchange**

	Predator £000	Victim £000
Tangible fixed assets	100	40
Current assets	200	70
Creditors: amounts falling due within a year	(110)	(30)
Net current assets	90	40
Total assets less current liabilities	190	80
Creditors: amounts falling due in more than a year	(30)	(30)
	160	**50**
Capital and reserves:		
Share capital *£1.00 nominal value*	50	10
Profit and loss account	110	40
	160	**50**

Immediately following the acquisition, the balance sheets of the two companies and the group would be as Table 19.6:

Table 19.6 Balance sheets of predator, victim and group after acquisition

	Predator £000	Victim £000	Predator Group £000
Note: Goodwill only arises in the group balance sheet. In the parent's the investment is shown at cost.			
Tangible fixed assets	100	40	140
Intangible asset – goodwill			40
Investment in victim	90		
Current assets	200	70	270
Creditors: amounts falling due within a year	(110)	(30)	(140)
Net current assets	90	40	130
Total assets less current liabilities	280	80	310
Creditors: amounts falling due in more than a year	(30)	(30)	(60)
	250	50	250
Capital and reserves:			
Share capital £1.00 nominal value	70	10	70
Profit and loss account	110	40	110
Share premium account	70		70
	250	50	250

Consequently, we can see that the acquisition accounting principles are applied in the same way, whether the company is acquired through a share issue or for cash. The goodwill will be calculated from the market value of the shares issues, not the nominal value. Any share issue costs can be deducted from this to arrive at the *fair value of the consideration*. (The cost of an acquisition is the cash paid plus any other consideration, like shares. The other consideration should be shown at fair value, which is usually market value.)

However, as in this case the victim was acquired through a share exchange, it is possible that the acquisition could be accounted for in a slightly different way. The Companies Act (s 131) does allow companies to create a merger reserve, rather than a share premium account. This only applies to acquisitions where shares have been issued to acquire at least 90 per cent of the equity in the acquired business. This is referred to as *merger relief*, which confusingly has nothing to do with mergers! If the merger-relief provisions apply, the company legally would be able to offset the goodwill against the merger reserve.

Unfortunately for companies, you are unlikely to see this in practice, although it is a grey area. FRS 4 requires that, in acquisitions, shares should be stated at fair value less any deductions for issue costs. This seems to mean that FRS 4 has taken away the right to use the merger-relief provisions of the Companies Act. FRS 6 and 7 mention merger relief, but the exact treatment they require is unclear.

● Alignment of accounting policies

The Companies Act and FRS 2 require the amounts shown in the group accounts to have been prepared on a consistent basis. This means that all companies within a group should have the same accounting policies, unless there are exceptional circumstances which mean that to do so would not present a true and fair view.

● Fair-value adjustments

The Companies Act (Sch 4a) states that 'the identifiable assets and liabilities of an undertaking shall be included in the consolidated balance sheet at their fair values as at the date of acquisition'. There is no guidance given in the Act about fair values, other than the requirement to value assets and liabilities in accordance with the accounting policies of the purchaser. The guidance comes from the accounting standard FRS 7 (*Fair Values in Acquisition Accounting*).

FRS 7 states that the assets and liabilities should be those that existed at the date of the acquisition, and measured at fair values reflecting the conditions at the date of the acquisition.

The fair values should be calculated as set out below:

Tangible fixed assets

The fair value should not be greater than the recoverable value, and should be based on market value, if similar assets are bought and sold on the open market, or depreciated replacement cost.

Intangible assets

These should be valued at replacement cost, which will normally be the estimated market value.

Stock

If the acquired company normally trades (both as a buyer and a seller) in a market, the stock should be valued at their current market value. All other stock should be valued at the lower of their replacement costs and their net realisable value.

Quoted investments

These should be valued at their market price. This can, however, be adjusted for unusual price movements or the size of the holding. There is no guidance given in the standard on valuing unquoted investments.

Contingencies

Both contingent assets and liabilities should be valued on the basis of a reasonable estimate of their outcome. (This goes against normal accounting practice. This would only recognise a gain when it is realised, whilst recognising all losses unless the probability of their occurrence is remote.)

Businesses held exclusively for resale

If the business is sold within one year of the acquisition the fair value, in most circumstances, should be the net sale proceeds. This must be adjusted for any assets or liabilities transferred from the business.

However, sale proceeds should not be used if:

● the value at the date of acquisition is plainly different from its value at the date of disposal;
● the acquirer has made a substantial change to the business prior to its disposal;
● the acquirer reduces the price in order to get a quick sale.

If the business remains unsold at the end of a year, it should be consolidated in the normal way.

Monetary assets and liabilities

These should be stated at their present value. This will be the anticipated receipts or payments of short-term items. However, long-term items may need to be shown at market value, or be discounted at an appropriate rate. In practice, this will be difficult to determine and may have a considerable impact on the reported values.

Pensions and other post-retirement benefits

Any funded scheme deficits, or unfunded scheme obligations should be recognised as a liability. Surpluses may be shown as assets, but only to the amount that is expected to be realised.

On 14 March 1995 J Sainsbury acquired Home Charm Group plc (which traded as Texas Homecare) from Ladbroke Group plc, shown in the notes to their 1996 accounts (Extract 19.2).

Extract 19.2 **FAIR VALUE ADJUSTMENTS (J SAINSBURY)**

	Book value	Fair Value Adjustments Alignment Revaluations to group policy		Fair value
	£m	£m	£m	£m
Tangible fixed assets	168	(23)	(16)	129
Investments	2	1	–	3
Stocks	185	(16)	(24)	145
Debtors	42	5	(10)	37
Cash at bank and in hand	9	–	–	9
Creditors (within one year)	(52)	(38)	–	(90)
Creditors (over one year)	(3)	–	(17)	(20)
Ladbroke liability	(143)	–	–	(143)
Provision for store rationalisation	(23)	(16)	–	(39)
Deferred tax	–	24	8	32
	185	(63)	(59)	63
Goodwill				103
Consideration for shares, including costs and fees				166

● Consolidation adjustments

The objective of the consolidation process is to combine the individual accounts of group members, report the activities of the group as though it was a single company. We will now look at how the various accounting documents are consolidated in the group accounts.

The balance sheet

The consolidated balance sheet of the group will show all the assets and liabilities of all the group companies. Where there are partly owned subsidiaries, the balance sheet reflects that the funds have been partly provided by the parent, and partly by the minority shareholders.

ACQUISITION EXAMPLE (CONTINUED)

EXAMPLE

A predator buys 80 per cent of the shares in a company, which we will call the victim, for £70 000. The predator buys the victim on 30 September, and its year end is 31 December. Both companies have the same accounting policies, and fair values are book values.

To consolidate the balance sheets at the end of December, we have to calculate:

- the goodwill
- the predator's share of the post-acquisition profits
- the minority interests
- any inter-company balances, and cancel these out.

The victim had the following balance sheet at the date of acquisition:

Table 19.7 **Victim's balance sheet as at 30 September (date of acquisition)**

	Victim £000
Tangible fixed assets	40
Current assets:	
Stock	20
Debtors	45
Cash	5
	70
Creditors: amounts falling due within a year:	
Creditors	(30)
Net current assets	40
Total assets less current liabilities	80
Creditors: amounts falling due in more than a year:	
Loans	(30)
	50
Capital and reserves:	
Share capital (£1)	10
Profit and loss account	40
	50

Goodwill

The predator has paid £70 000 to acquire 8 000 shares in the victim. Therefore he has acquired 80 per cent of the share capital and reserves – £40 000. The predator has paid £70 000 and purchased £40 000, the goodwill will, therefore be £30 000.

By the end of December, the two companies' balance sheets were as shown in Table 19.8:

Table 19.8 **Balance sheets of predator and victim as at 31 December**

	Predator £000	Victim £000
Tangible fixed assets	110	50
Investment in victim	70	
Current assets:		
Stock	35	25
Debtors	90	40[2]
Cash	10	10
	135	75
Creditors: amounts falling due within a year:		
Creditors	(120)[1]	(30)
Net current assets	15	45
Total assets less current liabilities	195	95
Creditors: amounts falling due in more than a year:		
Loans	(30)	(35)
	165	60
Capital and reserves:		
Share capital	50	10
Profit and loss account	115	50
	165	60

Notes:
[1] This includes £10 000 owed to the victim
[2] This includes £10 000 owed by the predator

Post-acquisition profits

At the time of the acquisition the victim had retained earnings of £40 000, by the end of December they were £50 000. Therefore, the victim's retained earnings since they were acquired by the predator were £10 000. The predator's share of the post-acquisition profits will be 80 per cent of £10 000, £8000.

Minority interests

These will simply be the proportion of the net assets not owned by the predator:

20% of £60 000 = £12 000

Inter-company balances

The consolidated balance sheet should show the true and fair state of affairs of the group as a whole. Therefore, any inter-company balances should be eliminated, as they do not involve outsiders. If these were left in the group's balance sheet, it would overstate the group's assets and liabilities. Any trading within the group should cancel out on consolidation. There are three adjustments that need to be made in this example:

(1) *Inter-company trading:* the predator's creditors and the victim's debtors should be reduced by £10 000;
(2) *Investment in subsidiaries:* the predator's £70 000 investment in the victim will not show on the consolidated balance sheet, as the consolidated balance sheet will include instead their assets and liabilities;
(3) *Subsidiaries capital and reserves:* the victim's capital and reserves are excluded. However, the goodwill will be included as this reflects the premium paid on acquisition. The group accounts will also reflect the group's share of the post-acquisition profits.

Consolidation example

The consolidated balance sheet will then be constructed as shown in Table 19.9:

Table 19.9 **Predator group balance sheet as at 31 December**

	Predator £000		Victim £000	Consolidation adjustments £000	Predator Group £000
Tangible fixed assets	110	+	50		160
Investment in victim	70			–70	
Goodwill				+30	30
Current assets:					
Stock	35	+	25		60
Debtors	90	+	40	–10	120
Cash	10	+	10		20
	135		75		200
Creditors: falling due within a year:					
Creditors	(120)	+	(30)	–10	(140)
Net current assets	15		45		60
Total assets less current liabilities	195		95		250
Creditors: falling due in more than a year:					
Loans	(30)	+	(35)		(65)
	165		60		185
Capital and reserves:					
Share capital	50				50
Profit and loss account	115			+8	123
	165				173
Minority interests					12
					185

SUMMARY

- Following an acquisition the new subsidiary's accounting polices will need to be aligned with those of the group.
- Assets and liabilities are restated to 'fair values'.
- Only third-party transactions are shown in the group accounts.
- Goodwill will be shown on the consolidated accounts to reflect the difference between the price paid and the value of the net assets acquired. Both are calculated on fair values, not book values.
- Only the post-acquisition profits of the subsidiary are included in the group accounts.
- Non-group shareholder's interest in the net assets of the group are shown as minority interests.

• The profit and loss account

So far we have just considered the balance sheet. Groups must also consolidate other accounting statements.

The group may only include the victim's profits since the date of acquisition, and must deduct the minority interests from the after tax profits. The same consolidation principles apply to the profit and loss account as applied to the balance sheet. The profit and loss account is only concerned with sales to third parties. Inter-company trading must be eliminated.

ACQUISITION EXAMPLE

EXAMPLE

The victim sold the predator £10 000 materials during the three months of ownership, these materials cost the victim £8000. The predator subsequently sold the materials for £12 000. Therefore, the overall group profit is £4000, split equally between the victim and the predator. If the inter-company transactions were not eliminated the profit and loss account would be:

	Predator £000	Victim £000	Group £000
Sales	12	10	22
Costs	(10)	(8)	(18)
Profit	2	2	4

Whilst the group profit is correct at four, neither the turnover nor the costs reflect the true nature of the group transactions. Therefore £10 000 needs to be eliminated from both the turnover and the costs.

We will also assume that the victim is proposing to pay a final dividend of £5000, 80 per cent of this will be paid to the predator.

Table 19.10 **Predator group profit and loss account for the year ending 31 December**

	Predator 1/1 – 31/12 £000		Victim 1/10 -31/12 £000	*Consolidation adjustments £000*	**Predator Group £000**
				Inter-company trading is eliminated	
Turnover	200	+	50	−10	240
Cost of sales	(120)	+	(20)	−10	(130)
Gross profit	80		30		110
Administrative expenses	(20)	+	(5)		(25)
Distribution expenses	(15)	+	(5)		(20)
OPERATING PROFIT	45		20		65
Dividends receivable from victim	4			−4	
Net interest payable	(5)	+	(1)		(6)
PROFIT BEFORE TAXATION	44		19		59
Taxation	(7)	+	(4)		(11)
PROFIT AFTER TAXATION	37		15		48
Minority interests	—		—		(3)
PROFIT FOR THE FINANCIAL YEAR	37		15	Victim's dividends are not included in group accounts	45
Dividends	(10)		(5)		(10)
RETAINED PROFIT	27		10		35

SUMMARY

- Only third-party transactions are shown in the group profit and loss account, any inter-company trading is eliminated.
- Only the post-acquisition profits of the subsidiary are included in the profit and loss account.
- Minority interests reflect non-group shareholders share of the after-tax profits.

The cash flow statement

The underlying principals of consolidation also apply to the cash flow statement. It must only reflect the cash flows of the subsidiary after the acquisition and those transactions that are external to the group. Consequently, any inter-group transactions would need to be eliminated on consolidation. This could include the following:

- intra-group loans
- dividends and interest paid to other group members
- share issues to other group members for cash
- sale and purchases of assets between group members.

Any transactions with minority interests must be separately disclosed. Cash flows to minority shareholders will usually be in the form of dividends that will be disclosed under 'returns on investment and servicing of finance'. However, companies may issue (or buy back) shares to minority interests. This will be disclosed under 'financing' on the cash flow statement.

There are two different ways that a group can prepare the consolidated cash flow statement. Either if can consolidate the individual company's cash flow statements, or it can use the consolidated profit and loss account and balance sheet to generate a cash flow statement. The latter approach is usually used, as inter-group transactions have already been eliminated and any exchange adjustments will have been made. However, they may not precisely cancel out, as different exchange rates could have been used for profit and loss and balance sheet items.

Groups with subsidiaries overseas have to translate cash flows into sterling. They must use the same rate in the cash flow statement as that used for consolidating the profit and loss account.

There are two different methods that can be used:

(1) the *net investment or closing rate method* – this uses the closing exchange rate or average exchange rates;

(2) the exchange rate at the time of the transaction, this is called the *temporal method*. Under this method, an average rate can be used if it is not materially different. The temporal method is used when the subsidiary company's operations are more dependent upon the economic environment of the investing company's currency.

SUMMARY

- Only third-party transactions are shown in the group accounts; inter-company trading should be eliminated.
- Only the post-acquisition cash flows of the subsidiary are included in the cash flow statement.
- Any transactions with minority interests will be shown under the appropriate heading.

INTERNATIONAL DIFFERENCES

International accounting standards

IAS 22 (*Business Combinations*) covers the accounting treatment of goodwill. It requires that goodwill be recognised as an asset and amortised, usually on a straight-line basis, over its estimated useful life. The period of amortisation should not exceed five years, unless a longer period (which must not exceed 20 years) can be justified. The unamortised balance of goodwill should be reviewed at each balance sheet date, and any amounts that are not expected to be recoverable should be written off. Any writedown to reflect the impairment of goodwill cannot subsequently be reversed.

The benchmark treatment for negative goodwill is to reduce the fair values of non-monetary assets proportionately until the negative goodwill is eliminated. Alternatively, it can be shown as a deferred income on the balance sheet and released to the profit and loss account on a systematic basis over five years, unless a longer period (which must not exceed 20 years) can be justified.

Europe

Dutch companies usually follow the UK practice of writing off goodwill to reserves, but the capitalisation of goodwill is allowed. In France it should normally be capitalised and written off over its useful life. There is no limit to the period of amortisation and most companies use periods of 20 to 40 years, and some companies do not amortise it all. In Germany goodwill is normally capitalised and written off over four years or the period expected to benefit. Whilst the law mentions 41 years, forty years is not an uncommon amortisation period. In both France and Germany it is possible to write goodwill off to reserves in exceptional circumstances.

Japan

In Japan, goodwill can be either written off in the current year's profit and loss account, or capitalised and amortised over five years. Common practice is to base goodwill on book values, rather than fair values, and to amortise it over five years.

North America

In the USA, goodwill should be amortised over the useful life, which should not exceed 40 years. Negative goodwill is allocated, pro rata, against all long-term assets except long-term investments in marketable securities. If these are reduced to zero, any residual goodwill is amortised to income over the period expected to benefit, which should not exceed 40 years.

Canadian practice is similar, with negative goodwill eliminated by charging it against non-monetary assets.

● ACCOUNTING FOR MERGERS

Mergers are different from acquisitions in that one party does not control another, the combination is one of equal partnership. Consequently, there are different consolidation rules covering mergers, as the principles of acquisition accounting would not adequately reflect the situation that exists in a merger.

Acquisition accounting can be seen as unfair in a merger because:

- the formerly distributable reserves become non-distributable for at least one of the parties, as only post-acquisition profits can be included under acquisition accounting rules;
- any premium paid over the net asset value, which will probably not reflect the true worth of the company anyway, has to be shown as goodwill. This will either be written off against reserves, or capitalised and amortised against future profits;
- any excess of the market value of the shares issued over their nominal value becomes part of the share premium account, a non-distributable reserve.

For these reasons, a different approach has evolved in accounting for mergers, appropriately called *merger accounting*. The Companies Act and the accounting standards have slightly different definitions of a merger, and when merger accounting can be used.

Under the Companies Act merger accounting is allowed if:

- the group has at least 90 per cent of the shares in the company and these shares have unrestricted rights to participate in distributions;
- the shares were acquired through a transaction that involved the issuing of shares by a member of the acquiring group;
- the non-equity element of the consideration did not exceed 10 per cent of the *nominal value* of the shares issued;

● the adoption of merger accounting is allowed under the generally accepted accounting principles.

The Accounting Standards Board believed that the Companies Act criteria were too lenient, as they allowed a combination to be accounted for as a merger, whereas it was in fact an acquisition. The accounting standard (FRS 6) describes a merger as 'the formation of a new reporting entity as a substantially equal partnership where no party is dominant'. Dominance is one of the cornerstones of the accounting standards criteria. The accounting standard establishes five criteria that should be used to determine whether the business combination is a merger:

(1) No one involved in the merger should be portrayed as either the acquirer or the acquired either by its management, or any other party to the combination. A share exchange which involves a premium over the market value of the shares is indicative that one business has been acquired, not merged.

(2) Everyone involved in the combination should participate in the establishment of the management structure of the merged companies, and in selecting the management personnel. This process must effectively be harmonious, as any imposition of a management structure indicates that the combination is an acquisition.

(3) The combining businesses should be of a similar size. This is important as if one company is much larger than another, it is presumed to dominate the other. The standard says that one party will be presumed to dominate if it is 50 per cent larger than the other combining parties. It is, however, possible to challenge this if it can be argued that one party's influence is disproportionate to its size, thus making all parties equal.

(4) The consideration received should be in the form of equity shares. Any non-equity element should be an immaterial proportion of the total consideration. The standard allows this total to include convertible non-equity shares and convertible loan stock, which are not normally regarded as equity. Non-equity includes cash, non-equity shares, limited voting shares, or limited distribution shares. If one of the combining companies has bought shares in another during the past two years it will affect the consideration. Any shares bought for cash, non-equity shares, or limited-rights equity shares, in the past two years will be included in the total.

(5) No shareholders in the combining businesses should retain any interest in the future performance of part of the combined business. It is felt that the merging companies should equally face the risk and rewards of the merged business. If any party retains a preferential interest in part of the business it cannot be a merger.

If the combination satisfies all these criteria, and is not prohibited to do so by law, merger accounting *must* be used.

So why all the fuss? A lot of effort has gone into ensuring that acquisitions are not treated as mergers, what are the benefits in being able to use merger accounting? It can be summed up by saying that *merged companies are treated as though they have always been combined*. This means that:

● the alignment of accounting policies is the only adjustment that has to be made to the values of the assets and liabilities. They do not have to be restated to fair values. The comparative balance sheet will also show the combined businesses;

● the trading results and cash flows, adjusted for any changes in accounting policies, are consolidated from the start of the year, not the date of the merger. The comparative numbers will be restated to show the combined business;

- merger expenses are charged to the profit and loss account in the period they are incurred;
- any difference between the nominal value of the shares issued, and the fair value of any other consideration, and the nominal value of the shares received should be taken to other reserves (normally called a merger reserve). Any existing balances on the share-premium account or capital redemption reserve of the subsidiary should also be taken to the merger reserve.

To illustrate the principles of merger accounting we will continue with our example. However, as this is a merger it will be necessary to amend our previous example and rename the predator, Friend, and the victim, Ami. After all, no one should be portrayed as the acquirer!

EXAMPLE OF A MERGER

Two companies, Friend and Ami decide to merge. It is agreed that Ami's shareholders should receive two Friend's shares for every Ami share. The Friend shares are trading at £4.50. All of Ami's shareholders accept the offer, and Friend has issued 20 000 shares with a nominal value of £20 000 with a market value of £90 000. The merger takes place on 30 September, and the group's year end is 31 December. Both companies have the same accounting policies.

On 30 September the two company's summarised balance sheets were as shown in Table 19.11:

Table 19.11 **Balance sheets of Friend and Ami as at 31 December (post-merger)**

	Friend	Ami
	£000	£000
Net assets	**160**	**50**
Capital and reserves:		
Share capital £1 *nominal value*	50	10
Profit and loss account	110	40
	160	**50**

Using merger accounting rules, the consolidated balance sheet of the Friendly Group at 30 September would be as shown in Table 19.12:

Table 19.12 **Consolidated balance sheet: Friendly Group as at 30 September**

		Friendly Group
		£000
Net assets	(160 + 50)	**210**
Capital and reserves:		
Share capital		70
Profit and loss account	(110 + 40)	150
Merger reserve*	(20 – 10)	(10)
		210

*The merger reserve just represents the difference between the nominal value of the shares issued by Friend, and the nominal value of Ami's shares.

This compares with the same balance sheet prepared under acquisition accounting rules (Table 19.13):

Table 19.13 | **Balance sheet prepared under acquisition accounting**

	Predator Group £000
Net tangible assets	210
Intangible asset – goodwill	40
Net assets	**250**
Capital and reserves:	
Share capital	70
Profit and loss account	110
Share-premium account	70
	250

The distributable reserves are much smaller under acquisition accounting, as only post-acquisition profits may be consolidated. If goodwill is capitalised, future profits will be reduced by the amortisation of goodwill.

When the group prepares its profit and loss account at the end of December, it will be able to combine both companies' full-year results under merger accounting. In our example we will assume that there has been £10 000 of inter-company trading (Table 19.14):

Table 19.14 | **Group profit and loss account under merger accounting**

	Friend 1/1 – 31/12 £000		Ami 1/1 -31/12 £000	Consolidation adjustments £000	Friendly Group £000
Turnover	200	+	150	−10	340
Cost of sales	(120)	+	(80)	−10	(190)
Gross profit	80		70		150
Administrative expenses	(20)	+	(20)		(40)
Distribution expenses	(15)	+	(15)		(30)
OPERATING PROFIT	45		35		80
Dividends receivable from Ami	(4)			−4	
Net interest payable	(5)	+	(5)		(10)
PROFIT BEFORE TAXATION	44		30		70
Taxation	(7)	+	(4)		(11)
PROFIT FOR THE FINANCIAL YEAR	37		26		59
Dividends	(10)		(4)	−4	(10)
RETAINED PROFIT	27		22		49

Whereas, under acquisition accounting the reported profit will be smaller (Table 19.15):

Table 19.15   **Group profit and loss under acquisition accounting**

	Predator 1/1 – 31/12 £000		Victim 1/10 -31/12 £000	Consolidation adjustments £000	**Predator Group £000**
Turnover	200	+	50	–10	240
Operating costs	(155)	+	(30)	–10	(175)
OPERATING PROFIT	45		20		65
Dividends receivable from victim	4			–4	
Net interest payable	(5)	+	(1)		(6)
PROFIT BEFORE TAXATION	44		19		59
Taxation	(7)	+	(4)		(11)
PROFIT FOR THE FINANCIAL YEAR	37		15		48
Dividends	(10)		(4)	–4	(10)
RETAINED PROFIT	27		11		38

The difference between the two profit figures is probably not as large as you would normally expect, as Ami/Victim's business is seasonal. Whilst the reported profit is smaller under acquisition accounting rules, the reported profit growth would be larger. To illustrate this we will assume that both companies made the same profit last year, and we will take the important profit for the financial year (the earnings).

The earnings reported under merger accounting would be the same for both years:

	This year	Last year
Profit for the financial year	£59 000	£59 000

Whereas under acquisition accounting, they will appear to have grown by 30 per cent!

	This year	Last year
Profit for the financial year	£48 000	£37 000

This is why it is important to see how much of the profit has come from acquisitions. In the UK we are lucky as the profit and loss account will disclose, down to profit before interest, the profit that has arisen from acquisitions.

SUMMARY

- Merged companies are treated as though they were always combined. This means that:
  - all of the subsidiaries' profits are included in the accounts;
  - comparatives will be restated as though the businesses were always combined;
  - there is no goodwill or share premium.
- Inter-company transactions are still eliminated.

Figure 19.2 THE MAIN DIFFERENCE BETWEEN ACQUISITION ACCOUNTING AND MERGER ACCOUNTING

	Acquisition accounting	Merger accounting
Assets and liabilities are shown at fair values	**YES**	**NO**
Pre-acquisition profits included in the accounts	**NO**	**YES**
Comparatives restated to include subsidiaries numbers	**NO**	**YES**
Share premium recognised	**YES**	**NO** *If there is a difference between the nominal values of the shares, this is shown in a merger reserve*
Goodwill	**YES** *This may be positive or negative*	**NO**

● DISCLOSURE REQUIREMENTS FOR ACQUISITIONS AND MERGERS

We have talked about the accounting procedures that must be followed in acquisitions and mergers. We will now move on to look at the additional information that must be disclosed in the accounts.

In the year that the combination has occurred, all business combinations have to disclose the following information in the accounts of the acquiring company (or the one which issued the shares in a merger):

- the names of the combining companies, if they are not the reporting company
- the date of the combination
- the method used to account for the combination.

● Acquisitions

When a company has made an acquisition, we need to know how much the company paid for the acquisition and how important it is to the existing business. In the UK, FRS 3 helps with the latter. Companies must disclose, down to profit before interest, the contribution that has come from acquisitions. However, on its own this will not be enough. We must have some idea of the underlying profitability of the acquisition. We would want to know the impact that the acquisition will have on the balance sheet and cash flow of the business. The larger the acquisition, the more important it is to have this information. The disclosure rules of FRS 6 gives us the information we need. The larger the acquisition, the more detailed the information provided. The largest acquisitions are regarded as *substantial*.

A *substantial acquisition* is one where:

- For **listed companies**, it is defined as a Super Class 1 under the listing rules. This is where either the net assets, profit before tax, or equity are 25 per cent or more of the acquirer's, or the consideration is 25 per cent or more of the acquiring company's assets.
- For **other companies**, if either the net assets or operating profits of the acquired subsidiary exceed 15 per cent of the acquirer's, or the consideration for the acquisition is greater than 15 per cent of the acquirer's net assets.
- This disclosure is necessary for a true and fair view.

Listed companies, substantial acquisitions and reverse take-overs require the permission of their shareholders. The acquiring company should give the following information in its accounts for all substantial acquisitions in the year that the subsidiary is acquired:

- A summarised profit and loss account and statement of total recognised gains and losses, from the beginning of its financial year, which must be stated, until the acquisition date.
- This summary should have the following minimum information:
  - turnover
  - operating profit
  - any exceptional items, required by FRS 3, to be shown on the face of the profit and loss account
  - profit before taxation
  - taxation and minority interests
  - extraordinary items.

They will also have to give the information required for other acquisitions. If the company has made a material acquisition, it must disclose separate information about each material acquisition. Other smaller acquisitions may be accumulated. The following information should be given:

- The composition, and fair value of the consideration: separate disclosure should be made of any *deferred/contingent consideration* (this is where additional payments are made dependent upon the subsequent performance of the subsidiary).
- A table should be given, for each class of asset and liability, showing:
  - The book values, both before the acquisition and before any fair value adjustments.
  - The fair-value adjustments analysed between:
    - accounting policy alignments;
    - revaluations;
    - other significant adjustments, together with the reasons for these adjustments.
  - The fair values at the date of the acquisition.
  - The amount of goodwill arising from the acquisition.

Any provisions made for reorganisation shown in the liabilities, and related asset write-downs, made in the 12 months before the acquisition should be disclosed separately in the table.

This table will be the same as the one illustrated earlier Extract 19.2.

- It may not be possible to ascribe accurate fair values for all acquisitions. It should be clearly stated if the values of the assets and liabilities can only be provisionally assessed at the date of the balance sheet. Any subsequent adjustment to these values should be disclosed and explained.
- The post-acquisition trading results should be disclosed in the appropriate part of the profit and loss account. This will usually be shown under acquisitions, as part of continuing operations. They could be shown under discontinued operations if they have also been

discontinued within the period. If it is not possible to determine the post-acquisition profits, the accounts should disclose the acquired subsidiary's contribution to the reported group turnover and profit.

- If the fair-value adjustments generate an exceptional profit or loss, it should be separately disclosed in the profit and loss account, which should clearly state that it relates to the acquisition.
- Any subsequent reorganisation costs arising exclusively from the acquisition should be disclosed. This includes integration costs that relate to a project initiated at the time of the acquisition, or as part of a post-acquisition review.
- The movements on acquisition provisions or accruals should be analysed between those used as intended and those released unused.
- The revised standard on cash flows (FRS 1) has changed the reporting of acquisitions in the cash flow statement. The cash flow statement should show the cash flows for the acquisition or disposal under the heading of acquisitions and disposals. Material cash flows arising from acquisitions should be reported separately under each heading, if practicable. A note to the cash flow statement should show how much of the consideration was in the form of cash.

The following information is required for material and substantial acquisitions only:

- The profit after tax and minority interests of the acquired subsidiary should be given for:
  - the period from the beginning of the subsidiary's financial year (which should be disclosed) to the date of the acquisition; and
  - the previous year.

● Mergers

The disclosure requirements for mergers are different. Whilst we still need to know how much the merger cost we also want to understand what each party is bringing to the merger. The disclosure requirements on information give us a greater understanding of this.

Any merger where one party is more than 50 per cent larger than the other must explain why the combination has been accounted for as a merger.

In addition, all mergers must disclose, in the reporting year of the merger:

- The composition and fair value of the consideration given by the issuing company and its subsidiaries.
- The current year's profit and loss account and statement of total recognised gains and losses should be analysed between:
  - the amounts relating to each party for the period before the merger;
  - the amounts relating to the merged business since the merger.
- The analysis of the profit and loss account should show, as a minimum:
  - turnover;*
  - operating profit;*
  - any exceptional items* (the items marked * should all be split between continuing operations, discontinued operations, and acquisitions);
  - profit before taxation;
  - taxation and minority interests;
  - extraordinary items.
- An analysis of the previous year's profit and loss account and statement of total recognised gains and losses.

- The aggregate book value of each party's net assets at the merger date.
- The nature and amount of any significant accounting policy alignments. If there are any other significant adjustments that have been made, after the merger, to any of the party's net assets as a result of the merger, an explanation should be given.
- A statement of the adjustments that have been made to the consolidated reserves arising from the merger.

SUMMARY

The disclosures for acquisitions and mergers help us understand the likely future profitability of the group. This can then be compared with the acquisition costs, to see if the acquisition is likely to be successful.

INTERNATIONAL DIFFERENCES

International accounting standards

Acquisitions and mergers are covered by IAS 22 (*Business Combinations*). The rules of IAS 22 are broadly similar to FRS 6, although the language used is American. The international standard talks about pooling of interests, rather than merger accounting, and purchase accounting· rather than acquisition accounting. There are slight differences in identifying the acquirer in a reverse take-over.

Europe

Merger accounting is allowed in Europe, but is rarely used. In the Netherlands it is not mentioned, although it is possible for merger accounting to be used for similar sized companies, in which case, IAS 22 would then be used. In Germany the subsidiary must be at least 90 per cent owned and the cash consideration must not exceed 10 per cent of the nominal value of the shares that are issued.

Japan

Acquisition accounting in Japan is very flexible, and it is possible to use elements from both acquisition accounting and merger accounting in the same acquisition.

North America

Merger accounting must be used in the USA if the conditions are met, whereas in Canada it should be used where an acquirer cannot be identified.

JARGON

Acquisition accounting / the purchase method   A method of accounting for an acquisition. Acquisition accounting requires that:

- assets and liabilities are restated to fair values;
- only post-acquisition profits are included in the accounts;
- goodwill is recognised as the difference between the fair value of the consideration and the fair value of the assets acquired.

Consolidated accounts   The group accounts which combine the separate accounts of all of the members of the group, showing the group as a single company. Intra-group transactions are eliminated, consequently only third-party transactions are shown in the consolidated accounts.

Contingent consideration   A payment that is dependent upon certain conditions being met.

Deferred consideration / Earn out   A payment that is held over until a future date. It is usually dependent upon certain performance criteria being met.

Goodwill   The difference between the cost of an acquisition and the value of the net assets acquired.

Fair value   This is an approximation to the market value.

Merger accounting / the pooling of interests   A method of accounting for a business combination that treats the businesses as though they have always been combined. It is rarely used, as the business combination has to be a true merger in the UK before this method can be used.

Parent / holding company   An entity that controls other entities. The control may arise from controlling the voting rights of another company, or by having dominant influence over the other company.

20 Foreign exchange

> **This chapter covers:**
>
> - SSAP 20
> - How companies cope with exchange rate movements
> - FRED 13 – the proposal's impact on currency disclosures
> - What should we look for?
> - What impact do exchange rates have on the business?

INTRODUCTION

Exchange rates affect multinational companies in two areas:

(1) How do you account for transactions that are in foreign currencies? Large companies sell globally and buy their products from the cheapest country. This means that they will have to account for a range of currencies.

(2) Multinationals have subsidiaries overseas and have to consolidate these into the group accounts.

Any company that exports or imports goods or has foreign operations in a subsidiary or associate has to find a way of incorporating different currencies into its accounts. With the increasing globalisation of capital markets, even small companies have had to find a way to minimise the impact of the erratic behaviour of exchange rates. Exchange rates can have a considerable impact on the financial performance of any company. In July 1997 when ICI reported its interim profits, it explained that £90 million of the fall in profits was solely attributable to exchange-rate movements. A third of the fall arose from the conversion of foreign profits into sterling. Two-thirds of the currency losses were due to lower margins in markets where prices were in set in Deutschmarks and other currencies that had weakened against the pound.

The ICI example clearly illustrates how currency fluctuations can have a large impact on a company's reported profit. It would be even worse in businesses whose costs are incurred in one currency and whose revenues are earned in another. This is quite common in industries such as shipping and oil, where revenues are earned in dollars, but a UK-based company could incur most of its costs in sterling.

To illustrate this problem, let us consider the profitability of the following contract. The contract earns cash revenues of US$1000 and has costs of £500. The reported sterling profit would vary widely according to the sterling dollar exchange rate:

	£1.00 = US$2.00	£1.00 = US$1.50	£1.00 = US$1.00
Sales	500	667	1000
Operating costs	(500)	(500)	(500)
Operating profit	0	167	500

The reported profit ranges from zero to £500, a 50 per cent return on sales! Unfortunately this example is too simple, there are many more problems than this. What if the cash received from the sale came in at a different rate than the exchange rate on the day of the sale? What exchange rate should we use? Should we take the sale at the rate on the day we made the sale, or the rate we actually received? This is a common problem, as most companies' sales are on credit. A multinational company like ICI has all these problems, coupled with other problems associated with consolidating the profits, assets and liabilities of their overseas subsidiaries.

There are four possible exchange rates that companies could use:

(1) the rate at the end of the financial year – *the closing, or the current, rate.*
(2) the average rate during the year – *the average rate.*
(3) the exchange rate on the date of the transaction – *the historical rate.*
(4) the rate that the company actually gets. This could be determined in advance and may be a *forward* or *contracted rate.*

In this chapter we will consider the two accounting problems that companies face in accounting for exchange rates, and how these affect the published accounts:

● *Which rate do you use?*
● *How do you account for any exchange differences that arise?*

In the UK these are covered by SSAP 20, internationally by IAS 21. The two standards are broadly similar and companies conforming to SSAP 20 would also conform to the international standard.

● SSAP 20

The objective of the accounting standard is to translate any foreign currency transactions in a way that is compatible with the effect of exchange rate changes on the company's cash flow. The financial statements should represent a true and fair view of the management's actions. The consolidated financial statements will also have to translate the subsidiaries and associates results into the parent's currency.

The accounting standard solves the two accounting problems we discussed above. It gives guidelines about accounting for foreign currencies, both the rates that should be used and the treatment of exchange differences. The rules are slightly different for individual companies and groups. We will consider the requirements for individual companies first.

● Requirements for individual companies

Any company during the financial year may enter into transactions that are in a foreign currency. These currencies have to be translated into sterling in a way that reflects the underlying cash flows of the transaction. Consequently, balance sheet items are treated differently to profit and loss account transactions.

The balance sheet

The way that we account for balance sheet exchange differences depends on the type of the asset or liability. The accounting standard classifies assets and liabilities are into three types:

(1) *monetary* – this covers both money that is held by the company (e.g. deposits and loans) and amounts that will be received and paid in money (e.g. debtors and creditors);
(2) *non-monetary* (e.g. plant and machinery);
(3) *shares in foreign companies.*

Monetary assets and liabilities

These are translated at the closing rate and any exchange differences are reported in the profit and loss account.

Non-monetary assets and liabilities

Once these have been recorded in the accounts, their value is set. Consequently, the values of the assets and liabilities do not change over time to reflect any differences in exchange rates.

Foreign equity investments

Foreign equity investments are usually shown at the exchange rate when the investment was made. The only exception to this is if the investment is financed by foreign borrowings, or foreign borrowings are used to hedge the foreign investment. In this case, they may be translated at the closing rate. Any exchange differences are then taken to the reserves on the balance sheet, where any differences arising from the borrowings may be offset against them. The borrowings used to finance the investment do not have to be in the same currency as the investment.

The profit and loss account

For profit and loss account items, individual companies should use either the rate of exchange at the date of the transaction or, if there are no significant fluctuations, average exchange rates. SSAP 20 allows, but does not require, forward rates to be used in trading transactions. (As this would be the rate that the company actually gets it would seem more compatible with the objective that the rates used should reflect the effect of rate changes on the company's cash flow.)

Exchange differences can arise from the movement in exchange rates between the date of invoicing and the date when the invoice is paid, as we discussed in our introduction. These differences, which arise from trading transactions, are charged to the profit and loss account.

EXAMPLE OF THE ACCOUNTING TREATMENT FOR EXCHANGE DIFFERENCES IN INDIVIDUAL COMPANIES

To illustrate the accounting treatment, we will consider the following example, where sterling has been strengthening against European currencies.

	Exchange rate
The company purchases:	
Machinery from a German company for DM750 000 on 1 January	£1.00 = DM 2.50
The company pays on 1 February when the exchange rate is	£1.00 = DM 2.65
Materials from France for FFr126 000 on 30 January	£1.00 = FFr 8.40
The company pays on 23 March when the exchange rate is	£1.00 = FFr 9.00
The materials are still in stock at the end of the financial year.	
The company sells:	
US$450 000 goods to an American client on 12 February	£1.00 = US$ 1.50
The company is paid on 28 March when the exchange rate is	£1.00 = US$ 1.55
SFr200 000 goods to a Swiss client on 21 March	£1.00 = SFr 2.30
The goods have not been paid for at the end of the financial year	
and the rate at the year end was	£1.00 = SFr 2.35
In addition, on 1 February the company takes out a ten-year-term loan with an American bank for US$1 000 000.	
This will not have been repaid at the year end.	
The exchange rate on 1 February was	£1.00 = US$ 1.50
and the rate at the year end was	£1.00 = US$ 1.55

If the company has a year end of 31 March, we can account for the various transactions in the following way:

Machinery purchase

The machinery will be shown on the balance sheet at £300 000 using the exchange rate on the purchase date (750 000/2.5 = 300 000).

However, the cash outflow for purchasing the machine will be £283 019 (750 000/2.65 = 283 019) and the exchange gain of £16 981 will be credited to the profit and loss account.

Materials purchase

As this is a profit and loss account item, the exchange rate used for the materials will be FFr 8.40, the rate at the time of the transaction. This means that the stock will be valued at £15 000 (126 000/8.4 = 15 000), and this will also be the cost of materials charged to the profit and loss account when it is sold. The exchange gain must now be accounted for, as the cash outflow for the materials will be £14 000 (126 000/9 = 14 000). In the current period, the profit and loss account will show an exchange gain of £1000 to balance the cash outflow with the stock value.

American sales

The sales will be recorded using US$ 1.50, the exchange rate at the date of the transaction. Therefore, the profit and loss account will show sales of £300 000 (450 000/1.5 = 300 000) whereas the cash inflow will be £290 323 (450 000/1.55 = 290 323). The exchange loss of £9677 will be charged to the profit and loss account.

Swiss sales

The sales will be £86 957 (200 000/2.30 = 86 957). However, as the debtor is a monetary asset, it must be shown using the closing exchange rate of SFr 2.35. This means that the debtor on the balance sheet will be £85 106 (200, 000/2.35 = 85 106). The exchange loss of £1851 will be taken to the profit and loss account.

American loan

The sterling cash inflow from the loan will be £666 667 (1 000 000/ 1.5 = 666 667), but the loan will be shown on the balance sheet at £645 116 (1 000 000/1.55 = 645 116). Using the closing rate means that there is another exchange loss of £21 506 to be charged to the profit and loss account.

In the unlikely event that the company had only these transactions during its financial year, the profit and loss account and balance sheet would have been as shown in Tables 20.1 and 20.2.

Table 20.1   **Profit and loss account with exchanges adjustments**

	£	£
Sales:		
American sales	300 000	
Swiss sales	86 957	386 957
Exchange adjustments:		
Machinery	16 981	
Materials	1 000	
US sales	(9 667)	
Swiss sales	(1 851)	
US loan	21 506	27 959
Profit		414 916

Table 20.2   **Balance sheet as at 31 March**

	£	£
Fixed assets – machinery		300 000
Materials stock		15 000
Cash:		
Machinery	(283 019)	
Materials	(14 000)	
US sales	290 323	
US loan	666 667	659 971
TOTAL ASSETS		1 060 077
US loan		645 161
Profit and loss account		414 916
TOTAL LIABILITIES		1 060 077

Comments on the example

So far we have only considered the mechanics of accounting for exchange-rate differences. The example shows us the impact of exchange rates on the reported profitability of a company, and there are some important conclusions we can draw.

When sterling is strengthening against other currencies, any company that is importing goods will improve its reported profits, as the exchange adjustments will be positive. Exporters lose, and they could lose in two ways. If their goods are priced in sterling, they become more expensive in local currencies, and the volume of their sales may fall. This will be compounded by the fact that the exchange adjustments will be negative, and reduce profit even further.

The opposite will be true if sterling is weakening; the importers will lose, and the exporters will gain.

● Accounting requirements for groups

We have looked at how we account for transactions in foreign currencies in the accounts of an individual company. We will now move on to look at the other area where exchange rates affect the accounts – consolidating the results, assets and liabilities of overseas subsidiaries, joint ventures and associates.

The method used to consolidate the group accounts should reflect the financial, and other operational relationships, between the parent and its foreign subsidiaries, joint ventures and associates. This means that the group financial statements should mirror the results, and the relationships, that are measured in the local currency before any consolidation. Consequently, groups would usually use the *closing rate method*, also known as *the net investment method*, for consolidating their subsidiaries and associates. This method is based on the assumption that the foreign enterprise is a largely independent business, and does not depend on the parent company for its activities. So, the subsidiary should be consolidated in a manner that reflects the fact that the parent's investment is in the net assets of the subsidiary, rather than its individual assets and liabilities. This means that most, but not all, subsidiaries are consolidated using closing rates, the exceptions are discussed later in this chapter.

The balance sheet

Balance sheet items are translated using closing rates. This may well lead to differences between the opening and closing values of assets and liabilities. These differences are taken to reserves.

The profit and loss account

The translation of profit and loss account items is based on closing or average rates. Most companies use average rates, believing that this is more representative of the actual rates during the year. Any difference between the average rate and the closing rate is taken to reserves.

The net investment method is illustrated in the example below.

CONSOLIDATION EXAMPLE USING THE NET INVESTMENT METHOD

A company acquires a German subsidiary in November 1996 for DM 30 000 000 when the exchange rate was DM2.50 to the pound. The net assets of the German company, at that time, were DM25 000 000. The parent company's year end is 30 September.

The parent company uses the net investment method for consolidating overseas subsidiaries, using average rates for the profit and loss account. The average exchange rates during the year were 2.75, and the exchange rate at its year end was 2.85.

During 1997 there was no inter-company trading and the 1997 accounts were as shown in Table 20.3 and 20.4.

Table 20.3   **Profit and loss account (using DM2.75 = £1.00)**

	Subsidiary 1/11/96–30/9/97	Subsidiary @ 2.75	Parent	Group
	DM	£	£	£
Turnover	5 156 250	1 875 000	7 750 100	9 625 100
Cost of sales	(1 638 200)	(595 709)	(3 651 720)	(4 247 429)
Gross profit	3 518 050	1 279 291	4 098 380	5 377 671
Other operating expenses	(965 600)	(351 127)	(1 401 810)	(1 752 937)
Operating profit	2 552 450	928 164	2 696 570	3 624 734
Net interest payable			(210 450)	(210 450)
Profit before tax	2 552 450	928 164	2 486 120	3 414 284
Tax	(753 200)	(273 891)	(726 100)	(999 991)
Profit after tax	1 799 250	654 273	1 760 020	2 414 293
Dividends			(820 000)	(820 000)
Retained profit	1 799 250	654 273	940 020	1 594 293

Table 20.4   **Balance sheet (using DM2.85 = £1.00)**

	Subsidiary	Subsidiary @ 2.85	Parent	Group
	DM	£	£	£
Tangible fixed assets	24 777 400	8 693 825	10 542 100	19 235 925
Investment			12 000 000	
Goodwill				2 000 000
	24 777 400	8 693 825	22 542 100	21 235 925
Current assets	2 810 350	986 088	1 725 100	2 711 188
Creditors falling due in a year	(713 400)	(250 316)	(1 040 500)	(1 290 816)
	2 096 950	735 772	684 600	1 420 372
Long-term liabilities	(75 100)	(26 351)	(134 100)	(160 451)
	26 799 250	9 403 246	23 092 600	22 495 846
Share capital	5 000 000		5 500 000	5 500 000
Profit and loss account	21 799 250		17 592 600	16 995 846
	26 799 250		23 092 600	22 495 846

Some of the numbers on the balance sheet require a little explanation; we will look at how we have calculated the goodwill and the profit and loss account reserve.

Calculation of goodwill

Consideration	12 000 000	(30 000 000/2.5 = 12 000 000)
Net assets acquired	10 000 000	(25 000 000/2.5 = 10 000 000)
	2 000 000	

Calculation of the reserve

The profit and loss account shown on the balance sheet will be reduced by the two exchange adjustments that we have to make to get the balance sheet to balance. The first adjustment arises from the difference between the exchange rate on the date of acquisition and the year-end exchange rate. Even if the net assets of the subsidiary had not changed, they would have different values purely because exchange rates have moved from 2.50 to 2.85. This adjustment will be:

Sterling value of the subsidiary:

at the time of the acquisition	10 000 000	(25 000 000/2.5 = 10 000 000)
at the balance sheet date	8 771 930	(25 000 000/2.85 = 8 771 930)
	1 228 070	

The second adjustment has to be made because we are using a different exchange rate in the profit and loss account than that used in the balance sheet. The profit and loss account uses the average rate of 2.75, whereas the balance sheet uses the closing rate of 2.85. This gives the following exchange adjustment:

Profit reported using average rates	654 273	(1 799 250/2.75 = 654 273)
Profit reported using closing exchange rates	631 316	(1 799 250/2.85 = 631 316)
	22 957	

We can now see how the reserve has been calculated:

Parent's opening reserves	16 652 580	(17 592 600 − 940 020)
Profit for the year:		
Parent's retained profits for the year	940 020	
Subsidiary's post-acquisition retained profits	654 273	
Less exchange adjustments:		
Difference between the net asset values		
reported at opening rates and closing rates	(1 228 070)	
Difference between the reported profit and		
the profit using closing exchange rates	(22 957)	
	16 995 846	

● A different way of consolidating overseas companies

Not all subsidiaries are consolidated using the net investment method. If the subsidiary/associate is not independent, and its activities are interlinked with those of the parent, another method will be used. The accounting standard offers three examples where the net investment method may be inappropriate where the subsidiary:

(1) acts as a selling agent for the parent, sending the proceeds of the sales back to the parent;
(2) is a supplier to the parent, producing parts for inclusion in the parent's products;
(3) is located overseas as a finance vehicle for the group, whether for tax, exchange control, or other similar reasons.

Here we can see that the trade of the subsidiary is really a trading extension of the parent company, and the subsidiary is not truly independent. Consequently, the subsidiary should be treated as though it were part of the parent, as this is the commercial reality. Any subsidiary which is basically an extension of the parent would be consolidated using the *temporal method*. This treats the subsidiary as though it was part of the parent, and the accounting treatment will follow that of individual companies.

● Hyperinflationary economies

Problems arise where a company has a subsidiary or an associate operating in a country experiencing hyperinflation. UITF 9 *(Accounting for Operations in Hyperinflationary Economies)* addresses this problem. It states that adjustments should be made for hyperinflation if:

- the cumulative rate of inflation is greater than 100 per cent over three years (this approximates to 26 per cent inflation each year);
- the operations in the hyperinflationary economy are material.

UITF 9 suggests that two methods could be used to account for hyperinflation, but does not preclude the use of other methods if the suggested methods are inappropriate. The suggested methods are:

- **current price levels:** the financial statements of the subsidiary should be adjusted to reflect current price levels before they are consolidated into the group accounts, with any resulting gains or losses being taken into the profit and loss account. This has been criticised on the grounds of consistency – one part of the group is being treated differently from the rest. However, it conforms to the requirement for a true and fair view;
- **functional currency:** a stable currency is used for the subsidiary company's results rather than the local currency. (This is quite common practice in parts of Latin America, where US dollars are used, rather than the local currency.) The subsidiary company's accounts could either be kept in the stable currency, or they could be translated using the temporal method.

SUMMARY   The accounting treatment for foreign currencies is different in individual companies and groups.

Individual companies

- **Profit and loss account** – they are required to use the exchange rate at the transaction date, or average rates if there have been no significant fluctuations. Forward exchange rates may be used, but do not have to be used.

- **Balance sheet** – assets and liabilities should be classified into:
  - **monetary assets and liabilities** – these are deposits, loans and other amounts that will be receivable, or payable, in cash. These are translated at the closing rate. Any resulting exchange gains and losses are taken into the profit and loss account;
  - **non-monetary assets and liabilities** – these use the rate at the date of their acquisition, so their values will not change with exchange-rate movements;
  - **shares in overseas companies** – these are shown at the rate of exchange when the investment was made, unless this investment is financed by foreign borrowings.* (This covers borrowings that have both financed, and provided a hedge against, foreign investments.) In this case they may be translated at the closing rate, and exchange differences taken to reserves rather than the profit and loss account.

● **Exchange differences** are taken to the profit and loss account, unless they relate to investments financed by foreign borrowings (marked * above), when they are taken to reserves.

Consolidating groups

● The group accounts should use the closing-rate method (also called the net-investment method), unless the subsidiary, joint venture, or associate is simply an extension of the parent's trading activities. In this case, the subsidiary should be consolidated with the parent as though it were an individual company.
● Most consolidations use the net-investment method. This uses closing rates for balance sheet items, and average (most commonly used) or closing rates for profit and loss account items. Any exchange differences that arise will be taken to reserves, usually the profit and loss account.

In hyperinflationary economies, the accounts should be adjusted to take account of the effect of price changes before consolidation into the group accounts.

INTERNATIONAL DIFFERENCES

International accounting standard

The international accounting standard (IAS 21, *The Effect of Changes in Foreign Exchange Rates*) and SSAP 20 are similar in their approach. There are, however some differences in the consolidation of group accounts. The two most important ones are:

(1) profit and loss account items should be shown at actual, or average rates. Closing rates are only allowed in hyperinflationary economies;
(2) when the company disposes of a subsidiary, the cumulative exchange differences should be recognised as income or expense.

Individual companies – accounting for transactions in foreign currencies

Europe

Within Europe it is normal for non-monetary items to be translated into the local currency once and for all. Debtors and creditors are usually shown at the year end exchange rate, but in Germany debtors are often shown at the lower of the exchange rate at the year end, or the date of the sale. Conversely, creditors would be shown at the higher of the exchange rate at the date of the sale or the year end. Long-term liabilities are usually shown at year-end rates. Exchange losses are always charged to the profit and loss account, but gains would only be taken to profit in the Netherlands and some French consolidated accounts. Exchange gains on long-term items in the Netherlands may be allocated over the period of payment.

Japan

Japanese accounting distinguishes between short-term and long-term monetary items. Short-term monetary items are translated at closing rates. However, long-term monetary items are shown at historical rates, therefore, no gains or losses arise until settlement. Monetary items that are hedged by forward exchange contracts should be shown at the contracted rate.

North America

American practice is broadly similar to that in the UK. However, the following transaction gains and losses would not be charged to the profit and loss account:

- transactions and balances designated as a hedge of a net investment in an overseas company - these would be shown as a separate component of stockholders' equity.
- a long-term inter-company foreign currency transaction – this would be shown as a separate component of stockholders' equity;
- a forward exchange contract or any other foreign currency transaction that is intended to hedge an identifiable foreign-currency commitment (for example, the purchase or sale of machinery) – these are usually deferred and included in the related transaction. However, a loss should not be deferred if it is thought that it would result in a realised loss in a subsequent accounting period. There are two methods of determining the gain or loss on forward exchange contracts. The method that should be used is dependent upon whether the contract is speculative, or used as a hedge.

In Canada exchange gains and losses on monetary items are not taken into the profit and loss account if:

- they have been included in a previous period;
- they relate to a monetary item that has an ascertainable life extending beyond the end of the next financial year.

Group accounts – consolidating overseas subsidiaries

Companies in most countries, Japan being the major exception, use the closing-rate method for consolidating overseas subsidiaries. This means that:

- balance sheets are translated at year-end rates;
- profit and loss accounts are translated at average exchange rates;
- translation differences are taken to reserves.

Europe

In France, the closing rate would be the most common method used for consolidating accounts, although the temporal method is allowed. Whereas in Germany the only legal requirement is that the translation of foreign subsidiaries and the resulting gains and losses should be fully disclosed and applied consistently. The temporal method is often used with more approximations than would be allowed in the UK. (For example, it is not unusual when translating the value of fixed assets, to use the rates for the year end in the year of acquisition rather than the rate ruling on the date of the acquisition.) In the Netherlands the accounting practice is similar to that in the UK; the closing rate method is used for independent subsidiaries, and the temporal method for integrated subsidiaries.

Japan

Japanese rules are a unique hybrid of rules from around the world. In practice, there is considerable flexibility, and different companies adopt different methods, some using the temporal method, others the net-investment method.

The Business Accounting Deliberation Council's principles, which are not necessarily followed, require profit and loss accounts to be translated using rates at the time of transaction, or average rates. However, net income (profit after tax) is translated at closing rates, necessitating an adjustment to the profit and loss account.

Generally, long-term assets and liabilities are translated at historical rates, whereas most short-term assets and liabilities are translated at closing rates. Historical rates are used for:

- non-current assets
- stocks

- capital
- non-current liabilities
- advances and deferred income.

Closing rates can be used for all immaterial amounts apart from capital and reserves. Any adjustments for these would be shown separately as currency translation adjustments. Otherwise closing rates are used for:

- cash balances
- current debtors and creditors
- stocks held at net realisable value
- balances of income and retained earnings.

Exchange gains or losses should be shown as an asset or a liability called 'foreign currency translation adjustments'.

North America

The North Americans have developed the concept of the *functional currency*. This is the main operational currency and the one in which the company generates its cash flow. This means that their standards refer to three currencies:

(1) the *functional currency* – the main operational currency and the currency of the cash flows;
(2) the *local currency* – the currency of the country in which the company operates;
(3) the *reporting* currency – the currency that the parent uses to report its results.

This has an impact on the consolidation of the overseas operations in both the USA and Canada.

In the USA, if the local currency is also the functional currency, the current-rate method is used to translate the statements into the reporting currency. This is essentially the same as the closing-rate method:

- assets and liabilities are translated at year-end exchange rates;
- revenues, expenses, gains and losses are translated at the exchange rates prevailing when these sums are recognised, although a weighted average may be used;
- exchange adjustments are shown as a separate component of equity, and are only transferred to the profit and loss account as part of the profit or loss, on disposal of the investment.

If the functional currency is different from the local currency, the accounts must be remeasured into the functional currency before consolidation using the temporal method. The same procedure should be used for companies operating in a hyperinflationary economy.

In Canada the temporal method would be used for integrated operations and operations where the functional currency is the same as the reporting currency. Otherwise the current-rate method would be used.

● HOW COMPANIES COPE WITH EXCHANGE RATE MOVEMENTS

In our opening example in this chapter, we saw how exchange rates could have a significant impact on a company's reported profits. Anyone with a large exposure to currency movements has to find a way to mitigate the effect of exchange rate movements. Exchange rates can move rapidly, and the company's investors are usually hoping for earning's stability.

Companies have found ways to protect both their earnings and their balance sheets from currency fluctuations. Companies have to protect themselves in any way they can, and this protection process is referred to as *hedging* and forms part of normal treasury activities. These activities are often referred to in the company's financial review.

There are three ways that companies can reduce the risks associated with currency movements: forward contracts, swaps, options.

● Forward contracts

We know that we can go into a bank and buy currency, we all do this for our holidays. We also know that the rates vary from day to day. A company wants to eliminate the day-to-day fluctuations. It needs to be sure that it will make a profit on a sale and that it does know the real costs of running its business. Consequently, instead of buying the currency today, the company could arrange to buy it in the future, at a predetermined rate. It could take out a *forward contract*.

In the forward markets, currencies are bought and sold for delivery in the future. You will see reference to the forward markets in the *Financial Times*. There is a table that shows the value of the pound against major currencies:

- on the day – *the spot price*
- in one month's time
- in three months' time.

Whilst these are the time periods that are published in the FT, they are not the only time periods that companies can get. A company can get almost any time period that it wants, in practice the period is very variable.

The forward price reflects the interest rate differentials between the countries concerned. To illustrate this we will consider a British company that has agreed to buy a machine in three months' time from a German company. The treasurer in the British company is concerned that the value of the Mark will rise and, therefore, the machine will cost more. Suppose that UK interest rates were 8 per cent, whereas German interest rates were 4 per cent.

The company decides to enter into a forward contract to buy the Marks today, for delivery in three months' time. This will allow it to lock in to a known exchange rate. If it had deposited the money in Britain for three months, it would have had the benefit of higher British interest rates. Consequently, the price they will pay for the Deutschmarks for delivery in three months' time, rather than today, will be higher than today's price. It must reflect the interest rate differentials, the extra 4 per cent the money could have earned in Britain. So the three-month rate will offer fewer Deutschmarks than the spot rate. This extra is described as the *premium*. If the currency the company wants to buy has higher interest rates than those in Britain, the forward price will be lower than the spot price. It will be at a discount. The premiums and discounts for the currencies in the forward market are shown in the *Financial Times*, together with the annual interest rate differential they reflect.

The advantage of a forward contract is that whatever happens to interest rates, we know the rate that we will get. The forward market buys certainty, but it does not mean that we will win. Exchange rates could move against us, but we would be locked into the contract.

● Options

If we want flexibility we go for options. An option contract gives you the right, but not the obligation, to buy the currency at an agreed rate. For example, you may have an option to buy US dollars at $1.70 in three months' time. You will only exercise the option if it is in your favour, perhaps a pound now only gets $1.60. Obviously, you will pay a premium for this flexibility.

Options are fine as long as you buy them. They will cost you money, but you will take that into account in deciding whether to exercise the option. The difficulties start when you sell options, as you may have to deliver what you have promised. In 1991, Allied Lyons (now called Allied Domecq) lost £147 million, 18.3 per cent of its trading profit, by writing options.

● Swaps

The company in our example is British. If it wanted to borrow money it would probably get a better deal if it borrowed in Britain, where it is known. But it needs US dollars to fund the expansion of its American subsidiary. It can borrow sterling at better rates than it can borrow dollars. So it takes out a sterling loan and then its merchant bank arranges a swap deal. They find an American company who wants to borrow sterling. The two companies then swap the currencies, so that each gets what it wants. A swap is simply a legal agreement to exchange cash flows over a period of time.

SUMMARY

To protect themselves against exchange rate movements companies can enter into:

● **a forward rate agreement:** which locks the company into a fixed exchange rate that is determined by interest rate differentials. Whatever happens to interest rates this is the rate that the company has to take;

● **a currency option:** the company pays a premium to have an option to buy the currency in the future at a predetermined rate. It does not have to exercise the option if it could get a better rate in the spot market;

● **a currency swap:** this tends to be used to finance overseas subsidiaries and associates. Loans are usually raised in the currency of the parent and then this loan is swapped into the preferred currency.

● FRED 13 – THE PROPOSAL'S IMPACT ON CURRENCY DISCLOSURES

FRED 13 *(Derivatives and Other Financial Instruments: Disclosures)* is concerned with the disclosure of financial information about *derivatives* and similar instruments, and it is proposed that the final standard should apply to all companies which have securities listed on a stock exchange. *A derivative* is a financial instrument that is a spin-off from a basic instrument, or market. The proposed standard defines a derivative as 'a financial instrument that derives its value from the price or rate of some underlying item'. All of the hedging instruments we talked about above would be regarded as derivatives, and would be covered by the standard.

Under the proposed standard, a listed company will be required to:

● Discuss, somewhere within its accounts, the major financial risks that it faces and how it manages its exposure to those risks. One of these risks will be a foreign currency risk. Consequently, the company will be required to discuss its policy and strategies, for managing currency risk.

● Give numerical disclosures comparing the local currencies and currencies of its operation's borrowings. The currency analysis should distinguish between matched and unmatched net assets and borrowings. (Matched assets are those that do not affect the profit and loss account. Therefore they are either assets and borrowings in the local currency, or they qualify as a hedge under SSAP 20.)

- If the unmatched net assets and borrowings are material, they should be separately analysed to show the remaining currency exposures by the principal local currencies of the operations involved.

This means that companies will be giving additional information that will enable us to better understand their exposure to exchange rate movements. An example of the sort of information companies will have to provide about their foreign currencies is given below.

This analysis excludes gross borrowings and is shown after taking into account the effect of swaps, foreign currency rate agreements and other non-optional derivative instruments (Table 20.5).

Table 20.5   **Information that companies will have to provide on foreign currencies**

Currency	Net assets by the currency of operations	Gross borrowings	Net investments
	£ million	£ million	£ million
Sterling	1150	(600)	550
Matched			
US dollar	400	(100)	300
French franc	250	(120)	130
Deutschmark	150	(30)	120
Other	50	(20)	30
Sterling plus total matched assets and liabilities	2000	(870)	1130
Unmatched assets/liabilities	110	(80)	30
Total	2110	(950)	1160

The unmatched foreign currency investments are analysed below:

Table 20.6   **Unmatched foreign currencies**

Functional currency of the group operation	Net foreign assets/liabilities					
	Sterling	US dollar	French franc	Deutschmark	Other	Total
Sterling		25				25
US dollar	20		10			30
French franc				(20)		(20)
Deutschmark	25		(30)			(5)
Other	(30)	20			10	0
	15	45	(20)	(20)	10	30

SUMMARY   If implemented in its current form, FRED 13 will give us considerable additional information about the currency exposures of UK-listed companies. This information is already available in some other countries.

WHAT SHOULD WE LOOK FOR?

There are four things we should look at when analysing company accounts:

(1) the accounting policies
(2) the impact of exchange rates on the business
(3) any further information we can find out about the company's exposure
(4) the location of the investments.

● Accounting policies

This is fairly obvious, we should always look at the accounting policies and whether they have changed. Any change in the method would have an impact on the reported profitability of the company. We saw in our earlier example that when sterling was strengthening the profit reported using average exchange rates was £654 273, whereas closing rates made it £631 316. So, if a company had decided to move from closing rates to average rates its profit would increase by £22 957 – an increase of nearly 4 per cent.

Fortunately, we should be able to spot this as:

● the accounting policy change would be disclosed in the accounting policies notes;
● the effect on profits would have to be disclosed if it was material.

This is illustrated below in the following extract from RMC Group's 1996 accounts.

Extract 20.1   **CHANGE OF ACCOUNTING POLICY (RMC GROUP)**

Due to the volatility of sterling exchange rates during the second half of 1996, the accounting policy for the translation of the results arising from the Group's operations outside the United Kingdom into sterling was changed to using average rates of exchange from using closing rates of exchange in order to reduce the effects of this volatility on the reported profits shown in the Group accounts. The consequences of this change are as follows:

(a) The Group profit and loss accounts and balance sheet movements for 1996 and 1995, and the Group profit and loss accounts for 1992 to 1994 shown in the Group Financial Review, have been translated at average rates of exchange for the relevant accounting periods.
(b) The comparative figures for 1995 shown in the Group cash flow statement have been restated to average rates of exchange.

The effect on the Group profit and loss accounts is shown below:

	1996		1995	
	As now reported	Using previous policy	As now reported	Using previous policy
Total turnover	4,559.7	4,217.0	4,548.5	4,614.2
Profit on ordinary activities before exceptional items and taxation	295.3	275.8	324.9	329.3
Earnings per share (pence)	68.5p	64.4p	76.5p	77.5p

▶

Profit on ordinary activities before taxation	**296.2**	**276.6**		
			337.1	*341.7*
Earnings per share (pence)	**68.9p**	**64.7p**	*80.3p*	*81.4p*

Group cash flow statement
The net cash outflow before financing for *1995* has become £517.2 million (previously reported £524.3 million) as a result of applying average exchange rates.

---

2 + 2 = 5

The accounting treatment for exchange differences in borrowings and deposits can present an opportunity for some creative accounting.

The general rule is that any exchange gains and losses on monetary items should be taken into the profit and loss account. Whether it is prudent to take unrealised gains on foreign currency borrowings as part of profits is a matter of debate (the Companies Act says that only realised gains should be taken into the profit and loss account). Monetary gains should be taken to the profit and loss account under SSAP 20, unless the exchange gains should be excluded on the grounds of prudence, or there are doubts about the convertibility and marketability of the currency.

The exception to this rule is where foreign currency borrowings have been used to hedge against, or finance, foreign equity investments. In this case, the exchange differences are written off through reserves. This is a development of the principle of matching assets to liabilities.

The problems arise when we are looking at a multinational company with a diverse loan portfolio. This is becoming increasingly common as treasurers use the international capital markets and take advantage of the extensive range of funding instruments that are now widely available. How do you identify which loans have been used to finance or hedge the investments? There is considerable scope for creativity. The accounting standard tries to minimise this by insisting on consistency of accounting treatment from one year to the next, but there is still scope for improving the reported results.

A company could borrow in a currency where interest rates are low (improving profit before tax), and take exchange differences to reserves arguing that the loan is a hedging or financing instrument.

EXAMPLE

To illustrate this, a company borrows US$100 million, for five years at 4 per cent when exchange rates were US$1.50 to £1.00. Interest rates in the UK were 6 per cent at the time, making the USA a cheaper place to borrow money. If we assume that the loan was converted immediately into sterling, the company would receive £66.67 million. The dollar loan could affect on the profit and loss account in two ways:

(1) the interest bill could be reduced. The cost of borrowing dollars is lower than the cost of borrowing sterling;
(2) the interest bill could even be eliminated if the company had placed the proceeds of the loan on deposit.

To illustrate this we will assume that the money had been put on deposit in the UK at 5.5 per cent. The interest would be:

		£m
Interest received	(£66.67 x 5.5%)	3.33
Interest paid	((US$100 x 4 %)/ 1.50)	2.67
Net interest received		0.66

The company has generated £660 000 in profit by investing someone else's money! If it was that simple we would all be doing it.

The problem is that a relatively low interest rate usually reflects a stronger currency, that will probably appreciate. In five years' time, when the loan has to be repaid, the dollar is likely to have strengthened against the pound. If we assume that the exchange rate, at the time of repayment, is US$1.20 to £1.00, the company has to exchange £83.88 million to repay the $100 million loan. This gives the company a capital loss of £17.21 million. This would normally be reflected in the profit and loss account during the loan period. As the dollar strengthened against the pound, the exchange loss would be taken into the profit and loss account, *unless* the company argued that the loan was being used to hedge a US investment. (It could hardly argue that it was being used to *finance* a US investment if the loan has been converted into sterling!) If this argument was accepted by the company's auditors, the profit and loss account would benefit from the interest income and they could defer the capital loss until the loan has to be repaid. Then they incur the loss, in cash terms, but it would not affect reported earnings as it would not show on the profit and loss account.

These exchange losses are revealed in the note on the reserves and the statement of total recognised gains and losses.

SUMMARY

- Any change in the accounting method will affect reported profits. However, the change and any impact on profits, if it was material, would be disclosed in the notes to the accounts.
- Reported profits will reflect exchange gains and losses on monetary items, unless these have been used to finance or hedge investments. The accounting policies will disclose whether the company is doing this.

● WHAT IMPACT DO EXCHANGE RATES HAVE ON THE BUSINESS?

● Reported profitability

The first thing we should consider is whether the business is an importer or an exporter. We saw in our previous example that if sterling is strengthening against other currencies, importers win and exporters lose. On the other hand, if sterling is weakening, the importers will lose and the exporters will gain. Most multinational businesses will disclose the key exchange rates that have been used in the preparation of the accounts. If we use this together with the segmental information, we should have some idea of the impact of exchange rate movements on the reported profitability of the company.

Extract 20.2 from Volvo's 1996 accounts illustrates the effect that exchange rates can have on reported profits.

Extract 20.2 **IMPACT OF CHANGES IN FOREIGN EXCHANGE RATES ON OPERATING INCOME (VOLVO)**

Operating income in 1996 compared with operating income in 1995 was substantially affected by changes in the foreign exchange rates.

Lower average spot rates for most currencies had a negative effect on "inflow" currencies. JPY, GBP and to some extent USD, and a positive effect on outflow currencies, BEF, NLG and DEM. As shown in the accompanying table, the total net negative effect was 450.

However, since Volvo hedges large portions of its payment flows in foreign currency through forward contracts, changes in spot rates do not affect operating income immediately. In 1996 the impact on earnings of forward and options contracts amounted to 1,100 (1995: 0) which resulted in a positive impact of 1,100 on operating income in 1996, compared with 1995.

Changes in spot rates also had an effect in connection with the translation of operating income in foreign subsidiaries and the revaluation of balance sheet items in foreign currency.

The total effect of changes in exchange rates on Group operating income for 1996, compared with 1995, was positive 800, including a gain of 1,1000 in Volvo Cars and a loss of 300 in the other operating sectors as a whole.

Total income effect due to changes in foreign exchange rates	Net flow, 1996	Income effect
Effect of changes in spot rates in each currency		
USD	2,000	(30)
JPY	75,400	(790)
GBP	450	(320)
BEF	(25,000)	560
NGL	(1,100)	440
DEM	(1,700)	240
Other		(550)
Effect of changed spot rates, net		(450)
Effect of forward contracts and options contracts[1]		1,100
Translation of foreign subsidiaries' operating income		(290)
Revaluation of balance sheet items in foreign currency		440
Total effect		800

[1] Group sales are reported at average current rates and the effect of hedging is included directly in operating costs.

Exchange rates and the financial ratios

We know that some exchange differences are taken to the profit and loss account, whereas others are taken directly to reserves. UK companies will disclose the differences that have been taken to reserves in the statement of total recognised gains and losses (and probably they will also disclose them in the note on reserves), whereas in other countries exchange differences are usually disclosed in the note on reserves. The statement of total recognised gains and losses is a useful document as it shows, in the main accounts, the exchange differences that have been written off through reserves.

There are many financial ratios that use the capital and reserves, such as return on equity, return on capital, and gearing. The analysis can be seriously distorted in a multinational business when exchange rates are moving. Consequently, for comparable purposes, it is necessary to adjust the reported numbers where a company's net worth is seriously affected by exchange rates.

The need for further information

If there are large exchange differences it is important that we get some further information, so that we can understand the impact of the exchange rates on the business. This may be found in the notes on segmental analysis, the financial or operating review, or the note on contingent liabilities. If the proposals in FRED 13 are incorporated into a financial standard, a considerable amount of information will be available in listed companies' accounts. The following extract from SmithKline Beecham's 1996 annual report illustrates the type of information that may be found in the accounts.

Extract 20.3 | **FINANCIAL REVIEW 1996 (SMITHKLINE BEECHAM)**

Table 1: Currency Impact by Quarter	Quarter one	Quarter two	Quarter three	Quarter four	Year
U.S. Dollar rate					
1996	1.53	1.53	1.55	1.65	1.56
1995	1.59	1.59	1.59	1.55	1.58
% Change	+4%	+4%	+3%	-6%	+1%
Belgian Franc rate					
1996	46.0	47.8	47.8	51.9	48.4
1995	48.4	46.0	46.3	45.7	46.6
% Change	+5%	-4%	-3%	-14%	-4%
Profit before tax (£m) (excl. exceptionals)	387	342	374	442	1,545
% Growth (actual)	7%	14%	20%	14%	14%
% Growth (comparable)	5%	15%	19%	23%	16%
% Currency impact	+2%	-1%	-1%	-9%	-2%
£m Currency impact	+£7m	-£3m	+£2m	-£35m	-£29m

\+ benefits earnings translated in Sterling
\- reduces earning translated into Sterling

Table 2: U.S. Dollar reporting – Full Year	U.S. Dollar			Sterling			
	1996 $m	1995 $m	% Change U.S$	**1996** £m	1995 £m	%Change Sterling	Underlying Comparable
Profit and Loss			Actual			Actual	
Sales	**12,363**	11,077	12%	**7,925**	7,011	13%	14%
Profit before tax (excl. exceptionals)	**2,410**	2,150	12%	**1,545**	1,361	14%	16%
Earnings per share	**59.1c**	53.6c	10%	**37.9p**	33.9p	12%	14%
U.S. dollar average rates used	**$1.56**	£1.58					
Balance Sheet							
Net borrowings	**(2,783)**	(2,883)	3%	**(1,637)**	(1,860)	12%	
Total shareholders' funds and minority interests	**4,015**	2,796	44%	**2,362**	1,804	31%	
Gearing ratio	**69%**	103%		**69%**	103%		
U.S. dollar year end rates used	**$1.70**	$1.55					

Table 3: U.S. Dollar Reporting – Fourth Quarter	U.S. Dollar			Sterling			
	1996 $m	1995 $m	% Change U.S.$	**1996** £m	1995 £m	% Change Sterling	Underlying Comparable
Profit and Loss			Actual			Actual	
Sales	**3,543**	3,004	18%	**2,147**	1,938	11%	18%
Profit before tax (excl. exceptionals)	**729**	601	21%	**442**	388	14%	23%
Earnings per share	**18.2c**	15.0c	21%	**11.0p**	9.7p	13%	22%
U.S. dollar average rates used	**$1.65**	$1.55					

● Where are the investments?

We need to look at where the company's main investments are located. Some may be in countries with weak or volatile economies. If a significant proportion of profits and net assets are derived from countries with unstable economies, the quality of the earnings and assets may be an issue.

SUMMARY

In a multinational business, exchange rates can have a significant impact on a company's reported results. Companies whose profits are affected by exchange-rate movements will give information about the impact of exchange rates. This should always be included in any financial analysis.

JARGON

Closing-rate/net-investment method A method of consolidating companies into the group accounts where:

- profit and loss accounts are translated at average or closing rates;
- the balance sheet is translated at closing rates;
- exchange differences are taken to reserves.

Forward contract A contract that locks the company into an agreed rate. It could be an exchange rate or an interest rate.

Functional currency A term used to describe the main operational currency and the currency where the company generates its cash flow.

Monetary assets and liabilities Money that is held by the company and amounts that will be received and paid in money.

Non-monetary assets Assets, like machinery, that do not represent an amount receivable in money.

Option A contract giving the right to receive an agreed rate.

Spot price Today's exchange rate.

Swap An agreement to exchange cash flows over a period of time.

Temporal method A method of accounting for exchange rates used in individual companies accounts where:

- Profit and loss account items are translated at the rate ruling on the date of the transaction, or average rates if these are a reasonable approximation to actual rates;
- Balance-sheet items are classified into:
  - monetary items, which are shown at closing rates and any exchange differences taken in the profit and loss account;
  - non-monetary items, which are permanently shown at the rate on the date of their acquisition;
  - shares in overseas companies, which are usually shown at the exchange rate at the date of acquisition. If they are financed or hedged by foreign borrowings, they may be shown at closing rate with any exchange differences taken to reserves.

Part 4

ANALYSING COMPANY ACCOUNTS

(21) Ratio analysis

This chapter covers:

- The profit and loss account
- The balance sheet
- The cash flow statement
- Solvency ratios
- Profitability
- Cash management
- The investor's ratios

● INTRODUCTION

Welcome to the world of the amateur detective! We are now moving on to the section in this book where we start to understand what the accounts do and, indeed, do not tell us about the financial performance of a company. Like any good detective, we will probably have as many questions as answers, but it should be possible to understand what is going on in the company. It is only after we have understood the wealth of information found in the accounts, that we can start to analyse and interpret it.

The most important tool in financial analysis is not found in this book. It is one you already have – your common sense! Your common sense will help you identify creative accounting, and assess the company's financial performance. It is important that you do not rely too heavily on the ratios, as most ratios only quantify what you can already see. They measure it to six decimal places, and give you a feeling of comfort as they demonstrate that you were right in the first place! Ratios are reassuring, but there is a tendency for people who are not familiar with financial analysis, to become overly obsessed with them. They often lose sight of what the ratios actually mean.

There is no need to calculate every ratio illustrated in this book, the ratios you use will be determined by your objective and the things you spotted when you read through the accounts. When analysing published accounts, you will find that ratios are not as easy to calculate as you first thought. Most people want to see nice standard formulas that they can copy into a spreadsheet, input the accounts, press the return key, and get the ratios. Sadly, it is not quite that simple. (If it was, you would not need financial analysts in the City, as computers would do the job for less money!) You need to engage your brain to identify the numbers that should be included in the ratios.

Different people will have different views about what should be included in the ratios. These views about how to calculate the ratios could even generate different opinions about the financial performance of the company. Therefore, the ratios are not always what they appear to be. Most people like ratios because they think they are an objective measure of the company's performance. Unfortunately, they are not. Reporting ratios to six decimal places is confusing precision with accuracy. We have to decide how to calculate them, and we must always remember that they are based on numbers that represent the 'best' picture that the company could present. Ratios give us a feel for what is going on in the company. In isolation they are meaningless, we always need to look at trends. Ideally we would need to look at the company's performance over a number of years, and within the context of its sector.

Despite their attendant problems, it is important that we do understand how to calculate ratios. This part of the book will show you how. First we will calculate the ratios using a simple example, then in the next chapter we will look at how to calculate them from published accounts. To illustrate this we will use Boots' 1997 accounts.

When analysing company accounts we need to consider creative accounting, solvency, profitability,and investment potential.

● Creative accounting – do we believe the numbers?

2 + 2 = 5 Published accounts are a marketing brochure, designed to market the company to banks, investors and customers. The Companies Act says that they must be true and fair, and they undoubtedly are – but they will be a version of the truth that reinforces the company's successes and minimises its failures! We always tell the truth, but the whole truth? (Just consider your CV for a moment!)

Companies have long discussions with auditors about the amount of information disclosed in their accounts. The people who advocate full disclosure, to protect investors, are never the people who run companies! You need to check for signs of creative accounting for two reasons:

(1) it is pointless working out ratios based on numbers you do not believe in the first place;
(2) creative accounting is often the first sign of business failure. Companies only need to dress up the numbers if they have something to hide!

The accounting notes are always the first place to start in any financial analysis. They will disclose the accounting policies and help to identify how the numbers in the accounts have been determined. It is always useful to look at any extra information found in company accounts, this is the information that the auditors insisted on including to ensure that the accounts give that all important true and fair view.

● Solvency – can the business pay its debts when they fall due?

This is obviously the crucial question, it is insolvent businesses that go bust, not unprofitable ones. We need to be able to identify whether the company is likely to have any problems with either its bank or its suppliers. If it does have problems, is it likely to be able to resolve them? This chapter will help you identify if the company has any current or potential solvency problems.

● Profitability – is the business profitable?

This helps you identify whether the profitability of the company has changed, what caused that change, and whether any improvement is likely to be sustainable. The profitability of the company needs to be considered in detail to find out whether:

- the company is more or less profitable than it used to be;
- the company is more or less profitable than its competitors;
- and why.

● Cash – is the business managing its cash in the most effective way?

The cash flow statement is our starting point for looking at the way that a company manages its cash. We need to identify where the company is getting its money from and what it is spending its money on. Is it tapping the right sources of funds, considering the type of expenditure? Is it living within its means? This was discussed fully in Chapter 16. What is the company's approach to managing its cash resources? Is it conservative or innovative? There will be different risks and opportunities associated with different strategies.

● Investment potential – is the company a good investment?

The company's investment potential has an obvious interest to shareholders, but is also important to other users of the accounts. It will affect the company's dividend policy and its ability to raise money through share issues. The investment potential impacts on a company's solvency.

This chapter will use the following set of accounts as a basis for both the calculation of ratios and analysis.

● THE PROFIT AND LOSS ACCOUNT

Table 21.1   Profit and loss account for calculation of ratios and analysis

	1996	1997
Turnover	1100	1000
Cost of sales	(650)	(600)
Gross profit	450	400
Administration expenses	(160)	(130)
Distribution expenses	(70)	(60)
Rationalisation provision		(10)
Operating profit	220	200
Interest received	40	20
Interest paid	(10)	(70)
Profit before tax	250	150
Tax	(60)	(50)
Profit after tax	190	100
Dividends	(100)	(60)
Retained profit	90	40
Note – Depreciation charged to operating profit	45	50

● Quick observations

The profit and loss account shows some interesting changes:

- *turnover and operating profit have fallen by 9 per cent;*
- *the company is rationalising the business;*
- *the company would appear to have increased borrowings as interest received has halved and interest paid has increased by 700 per cent;*
- *despite a fall in profit before tax of 60 per cent, the tax charge has only fallen by 17 per cent;*
- *dividends have fallen.*

● THE BALANCE SHEET

Table 21.2 **Balance sheet as at 31 December for calculations and analysis**

	1996	1997
ASSETS		
Fixed assets:		
Tangible fixed assets		
Cost / valuation	1500	1650
Depreciation to date	(700)	(750)
Book value	800	900
Investments	200	200
	1000	1100
Current assets:		
Stocks:		
Raw material	30	50
Work in progress	120	200
	150	300
Trade debtors	170	240
Cash	120	70
	440	610
TOTAL ASSETS	1440	1710
Creditors: amounts falling due in a year:		
Trade creditors	80	100
Tax	60	50
Dividends	80	60
Bank borrowings	0	0
	220	210
Creditors amounts falling due in more than a year:		
Loans	60	100
Provisions for liabilities and charges	10	20
Capital and reserves:		
Share capital (£1.00 shares)	150	200
Share premium	50	130
Revaluation		60
Goodwill	(300)	(300)
Profit and loss account	1250	1290
	1150	1380

● Quick observations

The changes in the balance sheet become more interesting when considered in the context of the observations from the profit and loss account:

- *the company is investing in new fixed assets, at the same time as it is revaluing others;*
- *the company makes to order – there are no finished goods stock;*
- *stocks, debtors and creditors have increased, even though sales have fallen. The main increase in stocks is in work in progress – this could be indicative of manufacturing problems, or a higher level of orders at the year end;*
- *the company has increased its long-term borrowings, but average borrowings must have been at a much higher level than year-end borrowings (who pays 70 interest on loans of 100?);*
- *the company had net cash in 1996 and, therefore, could have repaid the loan;*
- *the company's rationalisation programme has not started yet, as the increase in provisions is the same as the rationalisation provision charged to the profit and loss account.;*
- *there has been a share issue, at a premium, during the year. However, the company did not pay an interim dividend during 1997 (the total dividend charged to the profit and loss account is shown as unpaid on the balance sheet) and the dividend per share has fallen dramatically.*

● THE CASH FLOW STATEMENT

Table 21.3 **Cash flow statement for calculations and analysis**

	1996	1997
Operating cash flow	225	60
Returns on investment and servicing of finance:		
Interest received	40	20
Interest paid	(10)	(70)
	30	(50)
Taxation	(40)	(60)
Investing activities:		
Purchase of fixed assets	(10)	(110)
Sale of fixed assets	0	20
	(10)	(90)
Equity dividends paid	(90)	(80)
NET CASH FLOW BEFORE FINANCING	115	(220)
Financing:		
Additional loans	60	40
Proceeds of share issue	0	130
Repayment of loans		
	60	170
Changes in cash	(175)	50
	(115)	220
Calculation of operating cash flow:		
Operating profit	220	200
Depreciation	45	50
Rationalisation provision		10
	265	260

▶

(Increase) / decrease in stock	(50)	(150)
(Increase) / decrease in debtors	(20)	(70)
Increase / (decrease) in creditors	30	20
	225	60
Reconciliation to net debt		
Increase in borrowings	(60)	(40)
Change in net debt	175	(90)
Net cash / (debt) at the start of the year	(115)	60
Net cash / (debt) at the end of the year	60	(30)

● Quick observations

Some of the observations made in looking at the other documents can now be supported by evidence from the cash flow statement, plus new observations can now be made.

Supportive observations:

● *The working capital is representing a major cash flow problem for the company. In 1996 it had increased by 40, and in 1997 by 200 – even though sales had dropped. Consequently, the company's stock, debtor and creditor days must be increasing in 1997 (we cannot take a view on 1996, as we do not know 1995 sales).*
● *No cash was spent on rationalisation during 1997.*

New observations:

● *The company only just had sufficient cash from the year's trading and interest received to pay the interest.*
● *The 1996 loan was a new loan that was probably raised towards the end of the year perhaps to finance the fixed assets that were purchased in 1997.*

We are left with a few interesting questions.

● *Why is the working capital increasing? Is the company becoming less efficient or is the company changing? (Perhaps it is launching a new product and has to offer extended credit terms to get customers to take the old product.)*
● *Is the company automating or down sizing? Is the rationalisation provision tied in with the capital expenditure? Or does the capital expenditure represent normal replacements?*
● *Why have the shareholders given the company additional funds, when their current return is declining? Why do they believe the company's performance will improve?*

Looking at the financial statements themselves does not give us any answers, although other information given elsewhere in the accounts may enable us to answer these questions. We will now move on to look at the ratios, and will clearly see that all these enable us to do is to measure what we have already observed.

● SOLVENCY RATIOS

When we are looking at a company, one of our first concerns is likely to be whether the company is likely to go bust in the near future. If it is, doing any further analysis would seem largely irrelevant! Consequently, we are always interested in finding out how solvent a company is, as this gives us some idea of whether the company has a long-term future.

A business is solvent when its assets exceed its total non-shareholder liabilities (i.e. it has a positive net worth) and it can pay its debts when they fall due.

We can look at solvency on three timescales:

(1) *Will the company be able to meet its long- and medium-term obligations?*
(2) *Will the company be able to meet its short-term obligations?*
(3) *Could the company pay all its short-term liabilities immediately?*

When we are looking at solvency we are primarily using information from the balance sheet, as it is this snapshot that shows us the assets and liabilities of the business.

● Long- and medium-term solvency

There are four indicators of a company's long-term solvency: positive net worth, gearing, interest cover and the loan-repayment schedule.

Net worth

The first thing that we must check is that the company's total assets exceed its total liabilities, and by how much. This is measured by the capital and reserves, therefore the bottom line on a Format One UK balance sheet will show us this instantly. However, our example is presented in an assets and liabilities format, so we need extract it from the balance sheet. The apparent net worth of the company was 1380 in 1997 and 1150 in 1996. Unfortunately, finding the net worth is not all that simple, as the capital and reserves, and so the apparent net worth, can be influenced by a number of things:

● Net worth can be increased by revaluation of assets. In our example, assets were revalued by 60. Revaluation is an imprecise science. If the revaluation reserve is the only thing giving the company a positive net worth check the following:
  – *What assets have been revalued?*
  – *What was the basis of this revaluation?*
  – *Who carried out the revaluation?*
  – *When were the assets revalued?*

We need to consider these as it is possible that the assets were revalued to make the company look as though it had a positive net worth. (This is not uncommon in smaller companies' accounts.)
● Net worth can be reduced by the way we account for goodwill. In our example, goodwill has reduced the capital and reserves by 300. If the company has a low net worth, check its accounting policy for goodwill and whether it has had a sizeable acquisition. If the company is writing goodwill off through reserves, the net worth will be adversely affected. If the company you are analysing is a public company, it will disclose how much goodwill has been written off through reserves in the notes on the reserves.
● Net worth is reduced by the provisions that we make. In our example, the company charged ten to profit in 1997, but had spent nothing. The provisions made in 1996 were still unutilised in 1997.

If we revised the net worth to add back provisions and goodwill and deduct revaluation, the revised net worth would be 1460 in 1996; and 1640 in 1997.

Gearing

Accountants use the gearing ratios to quantify the proportion of borrowed capital. Gearing measures the proportion of borrowed money, either to the total capital employed (the traditional accountant's approach) or to the shareholders' stake in the business (the City and banking approach). Always remember that the gearing ratios you calculate are subject to the same problems discussed above. The revaluation of assets could either increase or decrease the reserves shown on the balance sheet, writing off goodwill will reduce the value of reserves. In some countries rationalisation provisions may be charged when the decision to rationalise has been made, in others when an obligation has arisen. If you were trying to make some international comparisons, or compare companies over time, you would need to:

- **exclude the revaluation reserve:** revaluation of assets is not allowed in some countries, whilst in others it is done for fiscal reasons;
- **add back goodwill:** public companies disclose, in the notes to the reserves, the amount of goodwill that has been written off through reserves. Most countries would show goodwill on the balance sheet, as an intangible asset. They would also amortise it, so however you resolve the problem, you will have a technical comparative error;
- **add back provisions:** most countries make full provision for deferred tax. In some countries other provisions are determine by tax rules, in others they can only be taken when an obligation arises (the current UK proposal). Adding back provisions for possible future costs helps to level the playing field.

To illustrate how the gearing ratios are calculated we will use the balance sheet in our example. We will use two capital-employed figures, the standard (capital and reserves plus loans) and an adjusted figure (capital and reserves less revaluation plus goodwill and loans).

Accounting gearing

The traditional way of calculating gearing measured long-term loans as a percentage of the long-term capital available to the business. This measure of gearing requires the calculation of the long-term capital employed.

- The *standard capital employed* will be 1210 *(1150 + 60)* and 1480 in 97 *(1380 + 100)*.
- The *adjusted capital employed* will be 1520 in 96 *(1150 + 300 + 10 + 60)* and 1740 in 97 *(1380 + 300 + 20 – 60 + 100)*.

This shows us what percentage of the total long-term capital has been borrowed:

Standard calculation

	1996		1997	
$\dfrac{\text{Long-term loans}}{\text{Capital employed}}$	$\dfrac{60}{1210}$	= 5.0%	$\dfrac{100}{1480}$	= 6.8%

Adjusted calculation

	$\dfrac{60}{1520}$	= 3.9%	$\dfrac{100}{1740}$	= 5.7%

Gearing calculated in this way will always be below one 100 per cent, the City of London's method of calculating gearing can generate percentages above 100 per cent.

City gearing

This looks at the relationship between long-term debt and the equity (the shareholders' stake in the business). There are a number of different ways that this can be calculated, using: long-term debt, all debt, and net debt.

As our example only has long-term loans, we will only be able to calculate two of these gearing ratios. Both will be calculated using the reported capital and reserves and adjusted capital and reserves:

Long-term debt

Standard calculation

	1996		**1997**	
$\dfrac{\text{Long-term loans}}{\text{Capital employed}}$	$\dfrac{60}{1150}$	= 5.2%	$\dfrac{100}{1380}$	= 7.2%

Adjusted calculation

	1996		**1997**	
	$\dfrac{60}{1460}$	= 4.1%	$\dfrac{100}{1640}$	= 6.1%

Net debt

This is the commonest way of calculating gearing in the City. It deducts any cash and short-term deposits from the debt. The total debt is usually the figure used. This tends to be a better measure when looking at multinational companies which may have both cash balances and bank overdrafts. These are often in different countries, with the cash balances in one country and bank overdrafts in another. There are four reasons why this may occur:

(1) It is very difficult to take cash out of some countries. Thus, companies may have an overall cash surplus, but are reluctant to use it in a country with these remittance restrictions, so they will borrow money in these countries instead of transferring the cash.
(2) Some companies take advantage of interest-rate differentials, borrowing money in countries with low interest rates and depositing in countries with high interest rates. As we saw in Chapter 13, whilst this may flatter profits in the short term, it can create problems in the long term. Countries paying higher interest rates are not doing so because they feel generous towards investors! Their economy is viewed as being a less attractive one to invest in, so they have to pay higher rates. Companies doing this always run the risk of incurring future exchange losses. If the economy does not perform well the relative value of the currency will fall.
(3) Some loans have large early-redemption penalties.
(4) It could be simply that the company has a short-term cash surplus, and needs the cash next year.

To return to the gearing calculation, net gearing would be:

Standard calculation

	1996		**1997**	
$\dfrac{\text{All debt} - \text{cash and short-term deposits}}{\text{Capital and reserves}}$	$\dfrac{-60}{1150}$	= (5.2%)	$\dfrac{30}{1380}$	= 2.2%

Adjusted calculation

	1996		**1997**	
	$\dfrac{-60}{1460}$	= (4.1%)	$\dfrac{30}{1640}$	= 1.8%

There is *negative gearing* in 1996 as the cash is greater than the borrowings.

The gearing ratios have quantified that the company has low, but increasing, borrowings that could have been repaid in 1996.

Servicing the debt – interest cover

Repaying the debt is probably not a problem that the company has to consider in the short term, as it has only just taken out the loans. Although we know from the 1997 cash flow that if the control of working capital does not improve, it would have difficulties repaying the debt. Servicing the debt may, however, be a more immediate problem. To see if the company is having any difficulties in paying the interest, we need to look at both the profit and loss account and the cash flow statement.

A quick glance at the profit and loss account shows that around a third of the profit disappeared in interest in 1997. It is obvious that the company could have problems with servicing debt, if average borrowings remain at the 1997 level. As soon as there is something that is obvious, we must have a ratio to quantify it!

This ratio is called interest cover. Interest cover divides the interest bill into the available profit to identify how many times the company could pay the interest bill. Should the interest received be included in the available profit? The company's interest received has declined over the period as the cash balances have reduced. If the trend continues, there may be no interest received next year. Consequently, it would seem prudent to ignore it. This would give an interest cover of:

	1996	**1997**
Profit based:		
$\dfrac{\text{Profit before interest}}{\text{Interest payable}}$	$\dfrac{220}{10}$ = 22 times	$\dfrac{200}{70}$ = 2.9 times

Some analysts use net interest cover, using the net interest payable shown on the profit and loss account. However this does not tell us how many times the interest could have been paid, and is rendered meaningless by capitalised interest.

Interest is paid from cash, not profit, so it is worth looking at a cash-based interest cover:

	1996	**1997**
Cash based:		
$\dfrac{\text{Operational cash flow}}{\text{Interest paid}}$	$\dfrac{225}{10}$ = 22.5 times	$\dfrac{60}{70}$ = 0.9 times

In 1997 the operational cash flow was insufficient to pay the interest, because of the additional 200 tied up in the working capital. Paying interest is becoming an increasing burden for the company. Although the company has relatively low levels of gearing at the year end, their current profits and cash flow would probably be unable to support borrowings at a higher level.

● Short-term solvency

When we are looking at short-term solvency we are trying to see if the company can meet all its short-term liabilities. To identify this, we need to look at the balance sheet and look at the relationship between the current assets and the creditors falling due within a year.

This is measured by a ratio called the current ratio:

	1996	**1997**
$\dfrac{\text{Current assets}}{\text{Creditors falling due in a year}}$	$\dfrac{440}{220}$ = 2.0	$\dfrac{610}{210}$ = 2.9

In 1997 the company has £2.90 for every pound that it owes, this is largely a result of the increased stock and debtors. Whether this is good or bad depends on a number of things based on the type of company we are looking at. For example:

- **Grocers** – when you look at grocers' accounts you will find that they have net current liabilities, as their short-term liabilities are greater than their short-term assets. They have very little stock, only give credit via credit cards, but have the usual credit terms with their suppliers. Buying grocery is a daily buying decision and so they feel fairly safe in not having their short-term liabilities covered by their short-term assets;
- **Manufacturing companies** – manufacturers need more current assets than retailers. They may be carrying the retailers' stock, give the retailers normal corporate credit terms and have the same terms with their suppliers. Consequently, we can see that a manufacturer would need more cover than a retailer. How large the current ratio needs to be depends on the type of manufacturing business. It really depends on the length of the production and sales cycle. The longer it takes them to turn their raw materials back into cash, the more they need in current assets to cover their creditors. A heavy engineering company, which may have a nine-month production cycle, may need as much as 2.5, whereas for a confectioner, a current ratio of 1.4 may be acceptable.

Hence, when we are looking at short-term solvency we need to look at it contextually:

- we need to look at the ratio over a period of time, remembering that increasing computerisation has allowed companies to reduce stock levels (a large number of companies now run on 'just in time') and so we would expect the current ratio to be falling;
- we need to look at the company's current ratio, and compare it with other companies of a similar size in the same sector.

The company in our example probably has a strong current ratio, but this is largely as a result of having increased its investment in the working capital and that may be a sign of bad management. We would need to know the industry and the length of time it takes to convert materials into cash before we could ascertain whether the current ratio was acceptable or not.

● Immediate solvency / liquidity

Immediate solvency is the same as liquidity; liquidity is the term used to describe the company's ability to pay its short-term liabilities. This is the most pessimistic view of solvency, as you are imagining that all the company's creditors falling due within a year ask for immediate payment. If we adopt this scenario, we have to identify what assets the business could turn into cash within a day. This is largely dependent on the type of company that we are analysing. Most manufacturers would be unable to sell their stock in a day (particularly as part of it would be in work in progress), but retailers could. You need to look at the company and determine its 'liquid assets' – those that could be quickly sold to generate cash. Retailers would normally be able to realise all of their current assets, most manufacturers would only be able to realise debtors (remember factoring?), short-term investments and cash. No one would be able to sell fixed assets within the timescale.

In our example, debtors and cash would be the only liquid assets. This is a pessimistic measure, but is it appropriate? That largely depends on whether we think that everyone is likely to ask for their money back immediately. To find this out, we need to see if the company is likely to be having difficulties with its suppliers. How long is it taking to pay its suppliers?

This ratio of liquid assets to short-term liabilities is called either the liquid ratio, the quick ratio or the acid test:

	1996		1997	
Liquid assets	290	= 1.32	310	= 1.48
Creditors falling due in a year	220		210	

The company's liquid ratio is improving, but this is largely a result of the increase in debtors. The company should have no difficulty paying its creditors as long as it is paid by its debtors.

SUMMARY   Solvency is measured on different timescales. Long-term solvency is measured by interest cover and the gearing ratios. Short-term solvency is measured by the current ratio. Immediate solvency is sometimes referred to as liquidity and is measured by the acid test (also called the quick ratio or the liquid ratio). As most of these ratios use figures from the balance sheet, they only represent a snapshot of the company's solvency position.

● PROFITABILITY

Imagine that you have come into a lot of money. If you suddenly won ten million pounds, what criteria would you use for your investments? You would be looking for something that gave you a good return with a minimum level of risk, after all you do not want to lose all your money and have to go back to work again! Whatever return you were offered, you would automatically compare it with the sort of returns you could get from a building society. For most of us, with very little money, this represents the risk-free rate (in as much as anything can be risk free). If we had a lot of money the risk-free rate would increase slightly, as we could now enter the money market.

Comparing risk and return is an everyday activity; we do it when we look for jobs (are you in the best paid job available?) in just the same way as when we plan our investments. Most of us are risk averse – a small increase in risk means that we want to see a substantial increase in the return. Other people are not, and embark on lifestyles (and investments) that we would find too risky to even contemplate.

In looking at a company's financial performance, we need to find a way of looking at the profitability and comparing it to the risk-free rate. That way we can decide whether investing in the company is worthwhile. This is important when you remember that investing in a company is not risk free. The level of return that we would find acceptable is determined by two factors: our personal risk profile and the risk inherent in the company. We would want to see a higher return from a car company than a grocer; we all have to eat every day, but we do not have to buy a car every year! The return on capital employed ratio (sometimes called the return on assets), discussed below, enables you to have a basis for comparing the overall profitability of companies.

● The return on capital employed

The return on capital is exactly what it says – a measure of the return being generated on the capital being used by the company. The traditional calculation defines the capital as the long-term capital tied up in the business. This is regardless of whether the capital is in the form of equity or debt. However, in recent years an increasing number of analysts have included short-term debt as part of the capital employed. Some use net debt.

The return on capital employed allows you to compare companies with different capital structures, to identify who is generating the best return overall. If you were concerned purely with the return for the shareholders' you would calculate another ratio (the return on equity) which is discussed later in this chapter.

We will discover that companies can improve their return on capital in a number of different ways, and it is important to understand the determinants of return on capital. This allows us to identify whether any improvement is a 'one-off', or whether it represents a sustainable growth in profits.

The return on capital employed is simply:

$$\frac{\text{Profit before tax and interest}}{\text{Capital employed}}$$

We look at profit before tax and interest as we want to be able to compare a company's performance in two ways:

(1) **Over time** – we need to look at profit before tax as the tax rules change from one year to the next. If we are trying to look at a company's performance over time we need to ignore the factors outside its control;

(2) **With other companies in the same sector** – not everyone operating in the same sector will be incorporated in the same country. Therefore, it is possible that they could be subject to different tax rules.

If we want to compare companies with different capital structures we have to recognise that the price that the company pays to service debt, interest, comes out of pre-tax profits. Dividends come out of after-tax profits. Using profit before interest ensures that we are comparing apples with apples!

The traditional definition of capital employed is the total assets less current liabilities (this equals the capital and reserves + minority interests + provisions + creditors falling due in more than a year). However, in recent years company treasurers have become more innovative and will switch from long-term to short-term debt if the rates are more attractive. Consequently, there has been a trend to include short-term debt in the capital employed. The return on capital employed also needs to be based on the adjusted figures discussed earlier in the chapter. Hence, adjustments should be made to the reserves, to exclude revaluation and include goodwill.

Calculating the return on capital employed

We will use the profit and loss account and the balance sheet (Tables 21.1, 21.2) given earlier in the chapter to calculate the return on capital, and all subsequent ratios.

The return on capital employed is:

Standard calculation

	1996		1997	
$\dfrac{\text{Profit before tax and interest}}{\text{Capital employed}}$	$\dfrac{220}{1220}$	= 18.0%	$\dfrac{200}{1500}$	= 13.3%

Adjusted calculation

	1996		1997	
	$\dfrac{220}{1520}$	= 14.5%	$\dfrac{200}{1740}$	= 11.5%

We can see that the return on capital has fallen over the two years, but this information on its own is not as useful as it seems. We would also need to know:

- what the company's return on capital was in preceding years;
- what the risk-free rate is (for example, building society or money market rates), and how risky the company is;
- what returns on capital other companies in the sector get.

All ratios need to be looked at in context, not in isolation.

As a concept, the return on capital is simple, it quantifies the return that the company is earning on the capital it uses. However, determining what should be included in the ratio is more problematic. The profit can be affected by a number of 'one-off' transactions, and the capital employed is influenced by the company's accounting policies.

● Improving the return on capital employed

Improving the return on capital is a combination of improving profit margins and becoming more efficient in the utilisation of capital (Figure 21.1)

Figure 21.1 IMPROVING ON THE RETURN OF CAPITAL

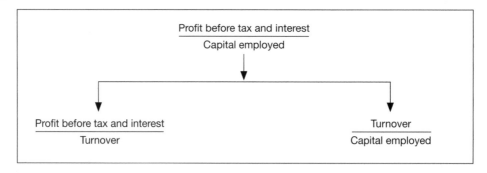

For those who can remember school arithmetic, the return on capital is a straight multiplication of the two ratios above as the turnover cancels out! Therefore, the return on capital is the multiplication of the profit margin and a ratio known as the asset turn, or the asset turnover. The asset turn tells us how many pounds worth of sales (or in this case pence) are generated for every pound of capital. It is a measure of how efficiently the company is utilising its capital. A fall in this ratio indicates the company is becoming less efficient, a rise indicates improved efficiency.

The profit margin is unchanged over the period:

	1996		**1997**	
$\dfrac{\text{Profit before tax and interest}}{\text{Turnover}}$	$\dfrac{220}{1100}$	= 20.0%	$\dfrac{200}{1000}$	= 20.0%

The fall in the return on capital arises solely from the reduction in the asset turn:

Standard calculation

	1996		**1997**	
$\dfrac{\text{Turnover}}{\text{Capital employed}}$	$\dfrac{1100}{1200}$	= 0.902	$\dfrac{1000}{1500}$	= 0.667

Adjusted calculation

	1996		**1997**	
	$\dfrac{1100}{1520}$ = 0.724		$\dfrac{1000}{1740}$ = 0.575	

Using the adjusted calculation, we can see every pound of capital generated 72.4 p sales in 1996, but in 1997 this had fallen to 57.5 p. Just to check that the arithmetic works, in 1997 the adjusted return on capital was 20 per cent x 0.575 = 0.115, or 11.5 per cent.

Therefore, if the company wanted to improve the return on capital employed it has two options:

(1) to improve its profit margins; or
(2) to use its assets more effectively to generate more sales per pound of capital invested in the business.

● Improving the profit margins

Our example is relatively simple, and does not show the complexity often found in published accounts. The profit margin we have used in the return on capital formula is the profit before tax and interest and, in published accounts, has four possible elements:

(1) operating profit
(2) share of associated companies' and joint venture's profits and losses
(3) profit on sale of assets
(4) profit on sale of subsidiaries.

The real driver of return on capital is operating profit, and there is a case that can be made for using operating profit as the profit in the return on capital employed formula. Other factors may have a 'one-off' impact on the ratio, and would need to be excluded to establish a trend. It is often necessary to prepare a number of return on capital ratios, with the main analysis showing the trend, but with supplementary data showing the ratios based on the traditional definition.

Operating profit

This is the most important component of the profit before interest and tax (PBIT) margin. It is from this profit that any sustainable improvement in the profitability element of the return on capital will be derived. Any analysis of profitability must include an operating profit margin. This is simply the operating profit expressed as a percentage of the turnover. (In our example the operating profit margin is the same as the PBIT margin.)

If a company wants to improve its profitability it must reduce costs or grow revenues. It can improve its operating profit margins by increasing prices; increasing volumes; reducing costs; changing the sales and product mix. (If a company can increase the proportion of its sales coming from higher margin activities, profits will improve.)

It may be possible to analyse some of the cost movements by looking at the company's profit and loss accounts over a number of years, but unfortunately it is not possible to make comparisons between companies in this way, as each company is likely to have slightly different definitions of cost of sales, administration expenses and distribution costs. There may be some information in the segmental information showing where the profit is made.

Share of associate's profit and losses

These may be included in the operating profit until June 1998, but will show before tax. From 23 June 1998, following the implementation of FRS 9, the group's share of associates' and joint venturer's operating profits will be disclosed immediately after the group's operating profit. It is important to recognise that whilst these profits may represent an important component of the profit before interest that may not reflect cash inflows and outflows to the company. Using them in the margin will distort the ratio, as associate's turnover is not usually included in the group turnover shown in the profit and loss account.

Profit on sale of assets

Profits and losses on sale of assets are shown after operating profit, and before tax. Consequently, they are included in the PBIT margin used in calculating the return on capital. In essence they represent an under-depreciation, or over-depreciation, of assets. For most companies, however, they would not be seen as providing an ongoing source of profits, or loss. Retailers might constitute an exception. They are always buying and selling shops to reposition themselves in the high street, and many are as much property developers as they are retailers.

Profit on sale of subsidiaries

Profits or losses on disposal of subsidiaries should be seen as one-offs. They can distort the return on capital calculation. If the company you are analysing has significant profits or losses from selling subsidiaries you would be advised to exclude them from the main analysis. You could show a second return on capital calculation, including profit or loss on sale of subsidiaries as a supplementary ratio.

Profit from discontinued operations

Following the implementation of FRS 3, companies will analyse their profit between continuing and discontinued operations. If the company has discontinued some of its operations, we would want to calculate return on capital for the continuing operations, as well as for the total business. However, the definition of discontinued operations may not be as helpful as it first appears. A discontinued operation is one that has been sold or terminated during the year, or shortly after the year end. This is defined as the earlier of:

● three months after the date of the balance sheet; or
● the approval date of the financial statements.

This means that the assets and liabilities of the discontinued operations may still be shown on the balance sheet and, therefore, included in capital employed.

Improving the asset utilisation

If a company wants to use the same amount of capital to generate more sales (or less capital to generate the same level of sales) it needs to improve its asset utilisation. So, we must look at what the company spends its capital on. A company uses the capital it raises to buy fixed assets and working capital. Consequently, improving the asset turn is a combination of doing two things: using the assets more effectively, and reducing the working-capital requirements.

Sadly, this does not have the same arithmetic simplicity of our earlier example, especially when we consider the way that these derivative ratios are usually expressed. We would normally look at how many pounds worth of sales are generated by every pound invested in fixed assets (*the fixed asset turn*). Working capital, on the other hand, is usually expressed as a percentage of sales, showing how many pence (usually, although sometimes it can be pounds) is tied up in the working capital to generate a pound's worth of sales. The ratios that influence the asset turn are set out in Figure 21.2.

Figure 21.2 | **RATIOS THAT INFLUENCE THE ASSET TURN**

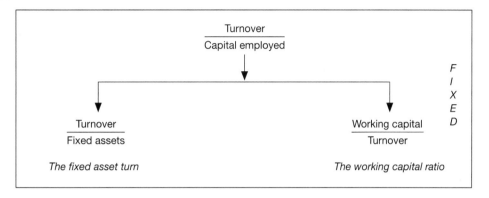

Asset turn

This would usually ignore any investments, as they do not generate sales. They generate income, either as profit from associated undertakings, or as dividend income. Associate's sales are not usually included in the turnover figure in the profit and loss account. So should investments be included in the fixed asset turn calculation? Logic says no. Should intangibles be included? If they are brand names and patents then they will generate current sales, but will goodwill or development costs? Logically we should only include those assets that make a contribution to turnover.

Revaluation would also be excluded, as it will distort the trend. In our example, the fixed asset turn would be calculated as follows:

	1996		**1997**	
$\dfrac{Turnover}{Fixed\ assets}$	$\dfrac{1100}{800}$	= 1.38	$\dfrac{1000}{840}$	= 1.19

The additional investment in fixed assets has not generated any additional sales. This would be perfectly acceptable if the investment had been made to reduce costs (many capital projects are justified by cost reduction). Unfortunately this has not happened either. However, it may be that the equipment has only recently been installed and the company has yet to receive any benefits.

Working capital ratio

The definition of working capital used in this ratio is the stock, plus the trade debtors less the trade creditors. Therefore, the working capital in our example will be:

		1996	**1997**
	stock	150	300
plus	debtors	170	240
less	trade creditors	(80)	(100)
		240	440

393

The working capital ratio is:

	1996		1997	
$\dfrac{\text{Working capital}}{\text{Turnover}}$	$\dfrac{240}{1100}$	$= 21.82$	$\dfrac{440}{1000}$	$= 44$

This can be expressed as the number of pence required to fund a pound of sales or as a percentage.

Improving the fixed asset turn

The fixed assets can be broken down into their component parts:

(1) tangible assets (land and buildings, plant and machinery, motor vehicles);
(2) intangible assets.

If you felt that it was appropriate, you could calculate ratios for these:

$$\frac{\text{Turnover}}{\text{Land and buildings}} = \text{Land and buildings turn}$$

$$\frac{\text{Turnover}}{\text{Plant and machinery}} = \text{Plant and machinery turn}$$

$$\frac{\text{Turnover}}{\text{Motor vehicles}} = \text{Motor vehicles turn}$$

$$\frac{\text{Turnover}}{\text{Intangible assets}} = \text{Intangible asset turn}$$

Clearly, it would be ridiculous to do all of these, there would be lots of facts and no information. You need to identify the type of asset that is helping to generate the sales. So, if you were analysing Tesco, it might be appropriate to do the land and buildings turn; for GKN the plant and machinery turn; for P&O the vehicles turn, and for Diageo the intangible asset turn.

Improving the working capital ratio

The working capital ratio is important as it is an indicator of management efficiency. An efficient management team would be trying to reduce stocks and debtors whilst managing creditors ethically. We have identified the cash that needs to be tied up to generate a pound's worth of sales. We can analyse the working capital in more detail to see how the company is managing the individual components of working capital, stocks debtors, and creditors.

Stocks

There are two ways of looking at stocks. Either you can see how many times a year the company turns its stock over, or you can work out how many days stock the company is carrying. You should use which ever measure you understand and are most familiar with.

Stock turn

Stocks relate to the merchandise sold in the period for a retailer and to the materials, labour and overheads used in sales for a manufacturer. These figures are not available in the published profit and loss account. If we were only analysing one company, we could use cost of sales as an approximation, but this would be inappropriate in company comparisons as it means different things to different companies. Most people use sales as the denominator. Even though it is wrong, it is consistently wrong, and allows comparisons to be made between companies! It would only be a problem if the companies being compared had very different profit margins. To illustrate the different results that are obtained using sales and cost of sales both will be prepared for the company in our example.

Sales based

	1996	1997
$\dfrac{\text{Turnover}}{\text{Stock}}$	$\dfrac{1100}{150} = 7.33$	$\dfrac{1000}{300} = 3.33$

Cost of sales based

	1996	1997
$\dfrac{\text{Cost of sales}}{\text{Stock}}$	$\dfrac{650}{150} = 4.33$	$\dfrac{600}{300} = 2.0$

Whilst the two methods give very different answers the trend from both is similar, with the ratio having more than halved between the two years.

Stock days

This is the alternative way of looking at stock and is calculated in a similar way to the way we calculate debtor and creditor days.

Sales based

	1996	1997
$\dfrac{\text{Stock}}{\text{Turnover}} \times 365$	$\dfrac{150}{1100} \times 365 = 49.8$ days	$\dfrac{300}{1000} \times 365 = 109.5$ days

Cost of sales based

	1996	1997
$\dfrac{\text{Stock}}{\text{Cost of sales}} \times 365$	$\dfrac{150}{650} \times 365 = 84.2$ days	$\dfrac{300}{600} \times 365 = 182.5$ days

(Remember that we are multiplying by 365 as we are looking at the sales for the year and the stock is the stock held on a given day.)

In both cases the stock days have more than doubled.

Using sales, rather than cost of sales, as the denominator has the effect of understating stocks. As this number is not calculated in a way that ensures its accuracy it is important that it is looked at contextually. Is the control of stocks improving, does this company have lower stocks than other companies in the sector?

Debtors

Calculating debtor days is very simple:

	1996	**1997**
$\dfrac{\text{Trade debtors}}{\text{Turnover}} \times 365$	$\dfrac{170}{1100} \times 365 = 56.4 \text{ days}$	$\dfrac{240}{1000} \times 365 = 87.6 \text{ days}$

The debtor days have increased by more than 50 per cent, and in 1997 the company is giving its customers just under 88 days of credit.

Creditors

Creditor days may be calculated using sales or cost of sales as the denominator.

Sales based

	1996	**1997**
$\dfrac{\text{Creditors}}{\text{Turnover}} \times 365$	$\dfrac{80}{1100} \times 365 = 26.5 \text{ days}$	$\dfrac{100}{1000} \times 365 = 36.5 \text{ days}$

Cost of sales based

	1996	**1997**
$\dfrac{\text{Creditors}}{\text{Cost of Sales}} \times 365$	$\dfrac{80}{650} \times 365 = 44.9 \text{ days}$	$\dfrac{100}{600} \times 365 = 60.8 \text{ days}$

In both cases the creditor days have increased by a third over the two years.

● The hierarchy of ratios

We have evolved a hierarchy of ratios, identifying the main determinants of the return on capital. This return on capital hierarchy helps us identify the profitability of the company and how effectively it is utilising its trading assets. The one area of the balance sheet that is not covered by the subsidiary ratios we have discussed in this chapter, is the return on the company's investments. Associated companies and joint ventures will be separately disclosed in the profit and loss account. Here we will see the percentage of their profit or loss that is attributable to the company. In Chapter 9 we saw that this can be very different from the cash received as dividends. However, the return from smaller investments, where the company does not have a participating interest, will be harder to quantify. These investments could be shown on the balance sheet as both fixed and current asset investments. The income will be included with the interest and dividends received. In a seasonal business where there will be peaks of cash and short-term deposits, it will be very difficult to ascertain the return on investments. We will not be able to calculate the average cash balances, so we will be unable to calculate a return on those investments.

The return on the trading assets, shown in the hierarchy of ratios (Figure 21.3), has to be a major concern for analysts. These trading assets will be generating the greater part of the profits. We can see that small changes in the subsidiary ratios will have a disproportionate effect on the return on capital. We need to identify the changes in these ratios if we want to understand the underlying performance of the company. Some changes could generate 'one-off' improvements, whereas others will give ongoing benefits. Companies have managed to improve their return on capital from the stock reduction benefits associated with the introduction of EDI (electronic data interchange). This movement to a 'just in time' stockholding policy only happens once. Subsequent improvements will have to come from other sources. We need to understand that companies improve the return on capital by improving the subsidiary ratios. They focus on improving profit margins, utilising their fixed assets more effectively and minimising their working capital.

Figure 21.3   THE HIERARCHY OF RATIOS

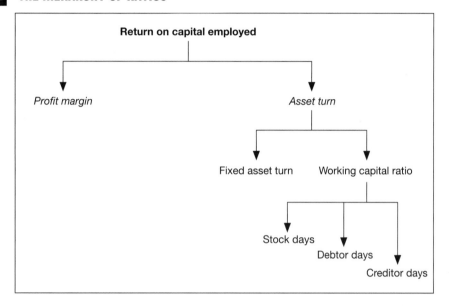

We should also understand that if the company improves its return on capital by reducing the working capital, there will be solvency implications. If the company reduces stocks and debtors whilst increasing creditors, the solvency ratios will be adversely affected. We would expect the current ratio and the acid test to fall.

SUMMARY

The prime measure of a company's performance is the return on capital employed. There are two components to the return on capital: profitability and asset utilisation. Operating profit margins are the most important element of profitability. To improve these a company must:

- increase sales volumes or prices
- reduce costs
- optimise the product mix.

Improving the asset utilisation is a combination of utilising the fixed assets more effectively and controlling the working capital. However, reducing the working capital may well have solvency implications.

● CASH MANAGEMENT

Cash management is closely interlinked with solvency. A company that manages its cash resources effectively is unlikely to have solvency problems. It should have no difficulty in paying its bills when they are due. Consequently, the way that a company manages its cash is crucial to its long-term survival. It must fund the business in the best way and optimise its cash resources. If we want to understand the company's financial performance, its opportunities and its threats, we must be able to analyse the way that it is managing cash.

To do this we need to look at:

- the operating and financial review;
- the cash flow statement;
- the working capital ratios;
- the loan profile.

The working capital ratios and the loan repayment profile have already been discussed in this chapter. The use of the cash flow statement in analysis is discussed in detail in Chapter 16, and the ratios for cash flow per share are discussed in the investor's perspective, later in the chapter. This section will focus on the operating and financial review.

● The operating and financial review

The Accounting Standards Board published a document in July 1993 called the *Operating and Financial Review*. This is a 'statement of voluntary best practice' and is intended to cover public companies and any other large company 'where there is a legitimate public interest in their financial statements'. The operating review should identify the main factors affecting the company's performance, the way that these have varied in the past, and how they are expected to change in the future. It gives a full discussion on the operating results and the company's dynamics, including the main risks and uncertainties it faces.

The financial review is of particular interest to analysts, as it should explain:

- **The capital structure of the business**:
  - maturity profile of debt;
  - types of capital instruments used;
  - currencies;
  - interest-rate structure.
- **The treasury policy**:
  - the control of treasury activities;
  - the currencies in which borrowings are made and cash and deposits are held;
  - the extent of fixed-rate borrowings;
  - the use of financial instruments for hedging;
  - the extent to which foreign currency net investments are hedged by currency borrowings and other hedging instruments.
- **The components of the tax charge**, if the overall tax charge is 'significantly different from a standard tax charge'.
- **Cash flows from operating activities**:
  - a discussion of the cash flows, and any special factors that influenced those flows;
  - segmental cash flows if these are significantly out of line with segmental profits.
- **The current liquidity**:
  - the level of borrowings at the year end;

- the seasonality of the borrowings;
- the peak level of the borrowings;
- the maturity profile of both the borrowings and the committed borrowing facilities;
- funding requirements for authorised capital expenditure;
- restrictions on the company's ability to transfer funds within the group, and any attendant restraints on the group;
- negotiations with bankers on covenants that restrict the credit facilities;
- the measures taken or proposed to remedy any breach, or probable breach, of banking covenants.
- **Whether the company is, in the opinion of the directors, a going concern**.
- **Company resources, and strengths, not reflected in the balance sheet**.

Whilst the financial review should give some useful insights into the company's financial strengths and weaknesses, the reality is a fine balance between discretion and disclosure.

SUMMARY The financial and operating review may give useful insights into the company's policies and performance. However, many companies are reluctant to disclose information that they regard as confidential and sensitive.

● THE INVESTOR'S RATIOS

Despite the determined attempts of some politicians, we still do not invest in shares because we have a fundamental belief in wider share ownership – we invest in shares because we want to get richer! No one would invest in a company if they did not believe that they were going to make a return, and preferably one that is better than they could get from a bank or a building society. There are two ways we make money from shares, a capital gain on the value of the shares, and dividends. These are reflected in many of the ratios that are prepared to express the company's performance from the investor's point of view.

Investors are interested in:

- The return on their investment. This has to be balanced with the risk and can be expressed in two different ways:
  - the overall return, the return on equity;
  - the annual return, dividends.
- The stock market's view of the future return on their investment: the PE ratio.

A number of different measures have evolved which look at the company from the shareholders' point of view. The measures can be broadly classified as traditional, or the latest fashion.

The conventional measures are concerned: assets, cash flow, dividends, earnings, sales, the current vogue is shareholder value.

Investors use a combination of these to identify if the share represents a good investment.

● Conventional valuation methods

Asset values

This ratio looks at the value of the company shown on the balance sheet and can be useful in some situations. It is often used to measure the underlying security in a share. It is generally thought that if a share is trading below its asset value, it is safer than one that is trading above the asset value. If the share is trading below the asset value and the company goes into liquidation, the investor should receive the full value of his or her shares. It is also sometimes used to identify whether the share is cheap. Brokers' reports will sometimes say that a share is cheap because it is trading below its net asset value. However, this may not be indicative of a cheap share, as trading below the asset value can occur in different situations, such as where:

- the book value of the assets is higher than their market value; or
- the company's return is lower than the cost of capital.

The main difficulty in using the asset values is deciding the right asset value to use. The figures shown in the balance sheet and the value which could be realised may be very different. In some countries revaluations are not allowed, and consequently international comparisons become very difficult. The alternative is to value the company based upon a going concern or a break-up value. However, these are subjective.

As the shareholders' funds form the basis for the net asset value per share calculation, there is, as always, the dilemma of whether to adjust for provisions, revaluation and goodwill. We have to decide which asset value to use, and we will illustrate a net asset value per share using adjusted shareholders' funds (reported shareholders' funds plus goodwill and provisions less revaluation).

The net asset value per share would be:

	1996	1997
$\dfrac{\text{Adjusted shareholders' funds}}{\text{Number of shares in issue}}$	$\dfrac{1460}{150} = 9.73$ per share	$\dfrac{1640}{200} = 8.20$ per share

The net asset value per share is sometimes compared to the share price in the *price to book,* or the *market to book, ratio.* If the company's shares were trading at £7.00 the price to book ratio would be 0.85 (700 / 820). The market values the company at 85 per cent of its asset value. If the asset values were realistic and the company went into liquidation the investor should receive some money.

• Cash flow

Cash flow measures are generally thought to be better measures than earnings, as they cannot be manipulated in the same way. There are two approaches to cash flow that are used in valuation: a cash flow per share, and discounted cash flow.

Cash flow per share

As discussed in Chapter 16, there are several ways of calculating the cash flow per share, and the three main ways are discussed below:

(1) the cash available for reinvestment
(2) the free cash flow
(3) the free cash flow available to the shareholders.

The cash flow before additional investment is a measure of the trading performance of the business, whereas the free cash flow is a measure of the company's ability to satisfy the providers of capital.

Cash available for reinvestment in the business

This method identifies the cash flow per share before any additional investment in either the working capital or the fixed assets. This shows the cash that has been generated by the business and is available for reinvestment. To calculate it you would need to take information from the cash flow statement. This cash-flow measure starts with the operating profit and adds back any non-cash charges (e.g. depreciation), thus identifying the cash that the business will generate from this period's trading. Dividends, net interest and tax paid are then deducted from the operating cash flow.

This cash flow measure for the company in our example would be as follows:

	1996	1997
Operating profit	220	200
Depreciation	45	50
Rationalisation provision		10
Net interest received / (paid)	30	(50)
Tax paid	(40)	(60)
Dividends	(90)	(80)
Cash available for reinvestment	165	70
Cash flow per share	110p	35p

The company has generated less cash in 1997 than it did in 1996. With net capital expenditure alone running at 45p per share in 1997 the company has to raise loans or have a share issue, unless it manages to reduce its working capital.

Free cash flow

This is a different concept. Free cash flow is defined as the cash that is available to the providers of capital, after any reinvestment in the existing business. Consequently, it starts with the operating profit plus depreciation, or similar non-cash charges. It then adjusts for changes in the working capital to arrive at the operating cash flow and deducts cash flows from taxation, and the purchase and sale of fixed assets.

This cash flow measure for the company in our example would be as follows:

	1996	1997
Operating cash flow	225	60
Tax paid	(40)	(60)
Purchase of fixed assets	(10)	(110)
Sale of fixed assets		20
Free cash flow	175	(90)
Free cash flow per share	£1.17	£(0.45)

This clearly shows how the company was forced into raising finance to fund its reinvestment programme in 1997.

Free cash flow available to shareholders

This identifies the cash that is available to the shareholders. Consequently, it is the free cash flow less any interest and any net loan repayments. So, in our example it would be:

	1996	1997
Free cash flow	175	(90)
Interest paid	(10)	(70)
Free cash available to shareholders	165	(160)
Cash flow per share	£1.10	£(0.80)

In 1996 the dividend payments were adequately covered by the year's cash flow, but by 1997 the company was unable to cover dividend payments from the current year's cash flow.

Discounted cash flow

This requires us to guesstimate future cash flows, and is only done by professional investors and analysts. They, and the company's management, are likely to be the only people who will have access to the detailed information required to forecast the cash flows.

Cash flows are usually calculated for two different time periods; a relatively short (generally five years) forecast period and then another time period (*the continuing period*) which represents the future cash flows to infinity. These future cash flows are then discounted using the weighted average cost of capital. The discounted value of the company is compared to the current market value to decide whether the shares are cheap or expensive.

● Dividends

Dividend-based methods of share valuation are useful when valuing small shareholdings, or shareholdings in unquoted companies. In these situations, the shareholder has little or no control over the company. When using dividend valuations, we need to know the current dividend paid and the dividend yield of similar companies. The dividend paid is simply calculated by dividing the dividend by the number of shares in issue. In our example it would be 66.67p for 1996 and 30p in 1997.

The company in our example is paying 30p dividend in 1997. Ignoring taxation, if the current dividend yield for similar companies is 5.5 per cent, an investor would want to pay no more than £5.45 for the share (30 pence divided by 5.5 per cent). If the share is trading at £5.00, the yield would imply that we have a bargain, as we are getting a 6 per cent yield. At £10 it would look expensive – or maybe not.

This analysis assumes that dividends remain constant. Whereas an investor hopes that the dividends will grow in the future. The Gordon growth model allows us to calculate share prices if we can predict the future dividend growth:

$$\frac{\text{Current dividend} \times (1 + \text{the growth rate})}{\text{Required yield} - \text{growth rate}}$$

If we expected dividends to grow by 3 per cent a year, we would be prepared to pay more to buy the share. To calculate the price we would be prepared to pay we can use the formula:

$$\frac{30 \times 1.03}{5.5\% - 3\%} = £12.36$$

With just three per cent predicted dividend growth we are prepared to pay more than twice the price! This difference arises because the dividend growth rate is very close to the required dividend yield. It would be impossible to calculate a price, using this model, if the dividend growth was anticipated to be greater than the required yield.

We are also interested in the dividend cover – how many times can the company pay the dividends out of the available profits? If we ignore any ACT implications, as in our example, we do not know where the profit are being made, the dividend cover in our example will be 1.9 times in 1996 and 1.67 times in 1997. This tells us that the company's ability to pay dividends out of profits is declining. Had the company paid the same dividend per share as 1996, the dividends would not have been covered.

Earnings

The earnings of the business are simply the profit for the financial year (i.e. after tax, minority interests and preference dividends). This is the profit that is available to the ordinary shareholders of the business, and an earnings per share figure is given in the profit and loss account. This shows the profit per ordinary share, and is calculated by taking the profit for the financial year and dividing it by the weighted average number of ordinary shares in issue. The company in our example had net earnings per share of £1.27 in 1996 and 50p in 1997.

Earnings are an important measure of a company's financial performance, and are used in two different ways as a basis for valuation: return on equity, and price earnings ratios.

Return on equity

This is effectively measuring the return on the shareholder's capital. It takes the profit for the financial year and divides it by the capital and reserves. Adjustments need to be made to the published numbers to make the numbers comparable internationally, because of the different accounting treatments of revaluations and goodwill.

In our example the return on equity will be:

Standard calculation

	1996		1997	
$\dfrac{\text{Profit after tax}}{\text{Capital and reserves}}$	$\dfrac{190}{1150}$	= 16.5%	$\dfrac{100}{1380}$	= 7.2%

Adjusted calculation

	1996		1997	
	$\dfrac{190}{1460}$	= 13%	$\dfrac{100}{1640}$	= 6.1%

Price earnings ratio

This compares the current price of the share with the earnings per share. It is also referred to as a *PE*, or *the multiple*. It tells us the number of years earnings that are reflected in the share price.

In 1997 earnings per share were 50p and if the share is trading at £7, the PE would be:

$$\frac{700p}{50p} = 14 \text{ (times)}$$

The share price is currently trading at fourteen times the company's earnings. When looking at PEs, it is important to remember that we are comparing information from two different time periods. We are comparing a *current* share price and a *historic* earnings per share figure. Analysts will also calculate *prospective* PEs that are based on next year's anticipated earnings. For example, if next year's earnings were expected to be 87.5p; the prospective PE would be 8 (700 / 87.5). Articles in the financial press will often refer to prospective PEs.

The share price represents an expectation of *future* earnings. For example, the pharmaceutical research and development company, British Biotech, is loss making and reported a loss per share of 4.5p in 1997, but at the time of writing its shares were trading at 104p and had a high for the year of 285p. The future profitability of the company depends upon getting a drug to the market, and the investors are gambling that if this happens they will make huge returns.

When looking at PEs, it is important to remember that a company's share price is affected by four things:

(1) the performance of the stock market;
(2) the performance of the sector, relative to other sectors and the state of the economy;
(3) the current performance of the company within the sector;
(4) the expected future performance of the company within the sector.

For these reasons, it is important to look at PEs relative to both the market and the sector.

A high figure is not necessarily a bargain, nor is a low figure necessarily a bad sign. A high PE is usually indicative of an *expectation* of profit growth. If a company has a high price / earnings ratio, its shares are expensive in relation to its *current* earnings. This would imply that the investing public expects the earnings to rise. If the expected increase in earnings occurs, the price earnings ratio will fall, unless investors expect the rate of increase to be sustained.

Earnings valuations tend to be used by large shareholders, who are in a position to influence both the earnings and the dividend distribution. However there are two problems associated with using earnings as a basis for valuation:

(1) comparability
(2) estimating the future earnings.

Earnings are difficult to compare across companies, as their calculation is often subjective. Private companies in the UK behave like many companies on the Continent. They are tax avoiders and so try to reduce their pre-tax profits. On the other hand, listed UK companies like to show steady earnings growth, as this leads to share price stability. Both types of company engage in creative accounting, which should be eliminated to give comparable earnings numbers.

It should also be remembered that the current fashion for share buy-backs will enhance both the earnings per share and the return on equity in the short term, but may not be in the investor's long-term best interest.

The other problem for the amateur investor is trying to guesstimate the future earnings. Without the benefit of company presentations it is difficult to predict where earnings will be in the future.

Price earnings ratios have a number of disadvantages:

- identifying the 'quality' of the earnings;
- they are very difficult to use when making cross-border comparisons. Different countries' accounting practices would generate different earnings;
- they cannot cope with cyclical earnings.

● Sales

Sales per share are used in price to sales ratios. Like all price-based ratios these need to be considered relative to the sector and are usually quoted as price to sales relative. They offer a different perspective to earnings and cash flow-based valuations. A company could be growing its market share to strengthen its position in the long term. However, this could have a detrimental effect on earnings and cash flow in the short term. They should always be considered in the light of at least one other variable – operating margins. A company may have a high price to sales relative because it has the highest operating margin in the sector. This should then work through to enhanced earnings, dividends and cash flow.

The sales per share in our example would be £7.33 in 1996, and £5.00 in 1997. If the share was trading at £7.00, the price to sales ratio in 1997 would be 1.40. This should then be compared to the price to sales ratio for the sector.

In industries where there is a need for high investment in research and development, comparison with the operating margin alone would be insufficient. There are different ways of coping with this:

● the charge for research and development could be added back to operating profit;
● the price would need to be compared to research and development expenditure;
● the price should be considered relative to other businesses in the sector.

Price to sales ratios have a number of advantages:

● sales are the same in every country, so, it is a useful measure for cross-border comparisons;
● sales are easier to predict than earnings and cash flow, as they are more stable and have fewer determining variables;
● they are a very good basis for valuing cyclical businesses.

● Shareholder value

The business cliché of the 1990s is shareholder value. Most people do not know what this means. Is it measured by profits, earnings, return on capital – or something else? Shareholders want the best total return – and this means dividends plus capital growth. However, no one seems to know what will drive long-term return and what will destroy it. Hence, the current focus on shareholder value.

The holy grail is to try to detrmine the drivers of shareholder value. It is obviously not good enough for the company just to make a profit – any profit must be sufficient to cover the cost of capital. Conventional measures of corporate performance, like earnings and cash flow per share ignore the cost of the company's capital. If the company is making enough profit to cover the cost of capital, then it must be adding value for its investors. This should be reflected in an increase in the share price. If the company is not covering the cost of capital, it will not offer a good return for its investors.

A number of different American consulting companies think that they have found the key to shareholder value. They have developed different 'packages', broadly offering the same solutions. The two main approaches are: value-based management and economic value.

Whilst the approach by the two schools is broadly similar, their jargon is so different that it is sometimes difficult to appreciate the underlying similarities. Although they have comparable approaches, it is possible that they could come up with different views of the value of the business, as their calculation bases are not identical. The adjustments made to profits are slightly different, with one company treating research and development as a fixed asset and amortising it over the period of benefit. The cost of capital used by the different consulting schools is unlikely to be the same. One school will try to calculate a cost of capital exactly, whereas another will take a more 'broad-brush' approach.

Value-based management

Value-based management (VBM) starts from the premise that a company must generate a better return than its cost of capital. If it cannot do this it is destroying value. This sounds fairly obvious, as no one would borrow at 7 per cent to earn 5 per cent!

Value-based management is based on two principles:

(1) value is only created when company's investments generate returns that are greater than the cost of its capital;

(2) the value of a company is determined by its discounted future cash flows.

VBM is a process where companies develop an understanding of how to grow value and put into place the systems and structures that will enable them to do this. It shows how to identify the most important elements of value creation in an organisation (*the value drivers*) and how to calculate the value that is being generated by the business. It has two different approaches to calculating the value of a company; the discounted cash flow *entity* method, and the *economic profit* model. The economic-profit model is similar to the economic value approach discussed below, with slightly different adjustments to the reported figures. Value-based management is a clever combination and repackaging of some old ideas – the hierarchy of profitability and discounted cash flow.

Economic value

The economic value school looks at value in a slightly different way. It compares the capital that has been invested in the business with the current market value. The difference between the two is called the *market value added* (MVA), and can be either positive or negative. If a company is worth less than the capital it was originally given, it has unsurprisingly destroyed value!

Research has shown that if a company wants to improve its market value added, and implicitly its share price, it must improve its 'economic value added' (EVA). This is an adjusted profit figure minus the cost of capital. In other words, the company must generate a return greater than its cost of capital!

Calculating economic value added

To determine EVA we must first calculate:

● an adjusted return on capital. This involves calculating:
  – an adjusted profit figure;
  – an adjusted capital employed.
● the weighted average cost of capital.

Calculating the return on capital

The return on capital used in the EVA calculation is not necessarily that shown in the published accounts. From an investor's point of view, the traditional calculation of return on capital is distorted by some of the accounting conventions. Consequently, a number of adjustments are made to both the profit and the capital employed. This gives numbers that reflect the underlying performance of the company and allows the company's performance to be compared internationally.

Calculation of adjusted profit

The adjustments that are made to the reported numbers are designed to arrive at a comparable post-tax operating profit figure. Operating profit is selected as the base for EVA as it is the 'driver' of the company's financial performance. The following adjustments are made to the published information:

- different methods of funding will give different tax charges, as interest is tax deductible. Consequently, we need to construct a tax charge that will eliminate any tax benefits arising from interest;
- taxes are only recorded when they are paid. The tax that is charged to the profit and loss account will not be the tax that is actually paid. This is because of the differences that exist in most countries between financial accounting and tax accounting;
- some companies charge costs like rationalisation expenses to the profit and loss account when incurred, whereas others charge a provision in the year that the programme is announced. Consequently, we need to deduct any provisions charged, and include any money spent (shown in the notes to the accounts as *provisions utilised*);
- under the accounting rules, some research and development expenditure can be capitalised (charged to fixed assets), whereas most is charged to the profit and loss account. Research and development has a long-term benefit to the company. So, if we are trying to work out the underlying value that has been added in a year, we would exclude it from the profit and loss account. Research and development is essentially treated as an asset, not a cost.

Calculation of an adjusted capital employed

Companies can choose to raise finance from many sources, and the long-term sources of finance are generally regarded as the capital employed by the business. However, the capital employed used for EVA reflects all the funds available to the company:

- Equity – the share capital plus any reserves.
- Interest bearing debt:
  - long-term loans;
  - short-term loans.

To make the numbers comparable, two adjustments need to be made:

(1) most countries show goodwill as an intangible asset, whereas other countries (notably the UK and the Netherlands) charge goodwill to reserves. Any goodwill that has been charged to the reserves is included in the capital employed when calculating the EVA. Goodwill would only be written off if the underlying economic value of the acquisition has fallen;

(2) provisions that have been charged to the profit and loss account, but not yet spent, will be shown as provisions for liabilities and charges on the balance sheet. These will be included in the capital employed.

Calculating the weighted average cost of capital

The weighted average cost of capital (WACC) simply reflects the cost of financing the company's funds. The cost of equity that is used in the WACC is not simply the cost of dividends – although this is the cash cost to the business of funding the equity. From the shareholders' point of view, what really matters is the opportunity cost of having money tied up in the business.

This opportunity cost comprises three elements:

(1) the return we would expect to get from a risk-free investment, like government bonds;
(2) the risk that is associated with investing in the stock market. This is reflected by the premium that investors receive when investing in the stock market;
(3) the risk of investing in a specific company. This is measured by its share volatility (called *the beta*) – it shows the movement in the individual company's shares if the market as a whole moves by 1 per cent.

A model, called *the capital asset pricing model*, calculates the cost of equity as:

The risk-free rate + (the market-risk premium x beta)

Over time, the returns on shares have been about 6 per cent higher than the return on long-term government bonds. (There is some current debate about this with many analysts believing that the current risk premium should be between 3 per cent and 4 per cent. This helps explain the high share prices during 1996 and 1997.) Bond rates have averaged 7 per cent, so an average cost of equity is around 13 per cent. Most companies also borrow, so the WACC is just the weighted average cost of the two. To calculate the WACC, the cost of each component of the capital employed by the company is weighted by its proportion of the total.

This then tells us the cost of capital to the company. Any investment the company makes must generate a return greater than the company's cost of capital if it is to increase the company's value. The WACC is usually the discount rate used in company valuation.

Example – calculating the economic value added

The economic value added is defined as:

(The return on capital – the cost of capital) x the capital employed

This is illustrated by using the figures for 1997 in our example:

(i) Adjusted profit

Operating profit	200.0
Less provisions used	0
Plus provisions charged	10.0
Plus research and development expenditure	0
Less cash taxes	(60.0)
Less adjustment for the tax impact of interest[1]	(15.5)
Adjusted after tax operating profit	134.5

[1] This is to bring the tax charge to the level it would have been if the company had not paid interest. Assuming tax at 31 per cent (50 x 0.31 = 15.5).

(ii) Adjusted capital employed

Equity	1380
Provisions	20
Goodwill	300
Short-term debt	0
Long-term debt	100
Adjusted capital employed	1800

(iii) Adjusted return on capital

$$\frac{134.5}{1800.0} = 7.47\%$$

(iv) Calculation of a weighted average cost of capital

This is actually impossible to calculate from the limited information in our example. We cannot calculate the cost of debt by dividing the interest paid by the borrowings, as we know that borrowings during the year were much higher than year-end borrowings. To calculate the cost of equity we would need to know the relevant beta factor for the company. Consequently, to illustrate the calculation the economic value added is calculated using a WACC of 7 per cent and one of 12 per cent.

(v) Calculation of economic value added

The company has adjusted capital employed in 1997 of 1800 – the economic value added would be:

WACC at 7%: 1800 x (7.47% – 7%) = *8.46*

WACC at 12%: 1800 x (7.47% – 12%) = *–81.54*

SUMMARY

There are many different measures designed to identify the potential of an investment. Shareholders can easily measure the return on equity, and know the dividends they have received in the past. What they do not know is whether:

● they will get their money back if the company is liquidated. This is measured by the asset value per share and the market to book ratio;
● the share is cheap or expensive. This can be measured by the dividend yield, the measures of cash flow per share, and the PE ratio. Sales per share may be more useful in looking at cyclical stocks. PE relatives and sales relatives help to compare the company to the market and sector. Shareholder value techniques can also be used;
● they will make a capital gain in the future.

CONCLUSION

The ratios have helped us quantify the problems facing the company in our example, but have not identified anything new. For example, we knew that debtors were increasing, by doing the ratios we have quantified the size of the problem. Debtor days have increased from 56.4 days to 87.6 days. Ratios are measurement tools that are unlikely to tell us something we cannot find out from looking at the accounts. We should always read the accounts before starting ratios, as reading the accounts will identify the important ratios and the most appropriate method for calculating them.

Beta factor   This measures the volatility of a share. It shows the percentage movement in a company's share price following a 1 percent movement in the market as a whole.

Capital asset pricing model   This is a mathematical model that is used to calculate the cost of equity. It states that the cost of equity is the risk-free rate plus a premium to reflect the specific risk associated with investing in the company. The specific risk premium is the market risk premium multiplied by the company's beta.

Economic value added (EVA)   The value that a company has created for its shareholders during the year. It is calculated by multiplying the capital employed by the difference between the return on capital and the cost of capital.

It is believed to be the main determinant of MVA (see below).

Financial review   This should give additional information on the company's financial position by discussing the company's: capital structure, treasury policy, operating cash flows, current liquidity, and additional resources that are not shown on the balance sheet.

Gordon growth model   A mathematical model used to calculate share prices based on dividend yields and dividend growth.

Market to book ratio (also called the price to book ratio)   This compares the share price with the asset value of the share.

Market value added (MVA)   The difference between the capital invested in a company and its current market value.

Negative gearing   The company's cash and deposits are greater than the total debt.

Operating review   A statement of best practice recommended by the Accounting Standards Board. It should discuss the operating results, identify the main determinants of a company's performance and the risks and uncertainties facing the business.

Shareholder return   This is the total return to the shareholders: the dividends plus capital growth in the value of the shares.

Value-based management (VBM)   An approach to management that aims to increase shareholder value. It is based on the principle that value is only created when company's investments generate returns that are greater than its cost of capital.

Weighted average cost of capital (WACC)   The cost of financing the company's existing capital.

22 A spreadsheet for analysis

● INTRODUCTION

This chapter details the construction of the spreadsheet that will have been used to analyse Boots' accounts in Chapter 23. It shows you how to construct a spreadsheet and modify it to reflect the company that you are analysing.

In Chapter 21 we analysed a company's financial performance, over two years, using the main financial statements. In practice, we would need to look at a company over a longer period. The next chapter looks at Boots over a four year period – five years would have been preferable. However, the sale of prescription pharmaceuticals business in 1995, and the associated restructuring of their over-the-counter pharmaceuticals business means that four years is currently the longest period available with comparable data.

In this chapter we will review the spreadsheet that has been used to calculate the ratios, and discuss the adjustments that have been made to the published data in the spreadsheet. The structure of the Boots group has changed over the period, with major disposals in 1995 and 1997 and acquisitions throughout the period. Profits have been made on disposals and the goodwill charged to the reserves has changed following the acquisitions and disposals. Therefore, adjustments have had to be made to ensure that the numbers are comparable.

The following spreadsheet has been used for the analysis of the Boots' accounts and is offered as an example. It cannot, in any way, be seen as a definitive spreadsheet for analysis, as adjustments have had to be made to reflect the changes in Boots over the last four years. However, it should form a good starting point for those who want to construct their own analysis spreadsheet.

● THE SPREADSHEET

Spreadsheets offer two advantages to the financial analyst:

(1) You can see a number of years' figures on the same page.
(2) Once the formulas have been entered and checked, calculating the ratios is simple and fast.

When constructing a spreadsheet, it is always necessary to balance the need for detail with the ability to see at a glance what is happening in the company. Consequently, not all of the

411

information found in a set of company accounts will be included in a spreadsheet. Unfortunately, there is not a definitive spreadsheet for you to copy and use to analyse a company's performance. You will need to have at least two basic spreadsheets to cover different formats for the accounts. If you analyse the accounts of overseas companies you will need more. Spreadsheets also have to be adjusted to reflect what you find when you read the accounts. The presentation of the data may change from one year to the next, necessitating changes and making it more difficult to see at a glance what is happening in the company.

We will consider the spreadsheet in four parts:

(1) the profit and loss account
(2) the balance sheet
(3) the cash flow statement
(4) the ratios.

Special note: all *negatives should be entered as such into the spreadsheet.*

● The profit and loss account

As the company has made acquisitions and disposals during the period it is necessary to:

● identify the operating profits arising from continuing businesses;
● input data to adjust for profits on disposal of subsidiaries, and any other material exceptional items.

Most of the data can be taken directly from the company's accounts, but some adjustments have to be made (Table 22.1).

Table 22.1   **Profit and loss acount for analysis**

1	Turnover – continuing business	
2	Turnover – total business	
3	Cost of sales	
4	GROSS PROFIT	
5	Administration expenses	
6	Selling, distribution and store costs	
7	Research and development	
8	Other operating income	
9	OPERATING PROFIT – continuing business before exceptionals	
10	OPERATING PROFIT – continuing business after exceptionals	
11	OPERATING PROFIT – before exceptional items	
12	OPERATING PROFIT – after exceptional items	
13	Share of profits of associates	
14	Profit on sale of fixed assets	
15.	Profit on sale of subsidiaries	
16	Other exceptional items	
17	PROFIT BEFORE INTEREST	
18	Interest received	
19	Interest paid	
20	Interest capitalised	
21	Change in value of bond	
22	Share of associates' interest	
23	REPORTED PROFIT BEFORE TAX	
24	ADJUSTED PROFIT BEFORE TAX	
25	Tax	
26	REPORTED PROFIT AFTER TAX	
27	ADJUSTED PROFIT AFTER TAX	
28.	Extraordinary items	
29	Minority interests	
30	Preference dividend	
31	PROFIT ATTRIBUTABLE TO ORDINARY SHAREHOLDERS	
32	ADJUSTED PROFIT ATTRIBUTABLE TO ORDINARY SHAREHOLDERS	
33	Ordinary dividend	
34	RETAINED PROFIT	
35		
36		
37	EARNINGS PER SHARE	
38	Reported	
39	Adjusted	Line 38 multiplied by (line 32 ÷ line 31)
40		
41	DIVIDENDS PER SHARE	

FRS 3 requires companies to analyse turnover, costs and operating profits between continuing and discontinued operations. This allows us to analyse profits in detail. The spreadsheet looks at turnover and operating profits from continuing operations and the total business.

Explanations

Two turnover figures are shown:

Line 1   All turnover figures should exclude VAT (some retailers show VAT inclusive and exclusive numbers). This is the turnover disclosed for continuing operations.

Line 2   This is the turnover for the total business, so it includes disposals. By looking at the difference between lines 1 and 2, we can see the turnover attributable to discontinued operations.

Operating costs have not been analysed between continuing and discontinued operations:

Line 3   This is the company's total cost of sales.

Line 4   This is the company's total gross profit.

Line 5   This is the company's total administration expenses.

Line 6   This is the company's total selling distribution and store costs.

Line 7   This is the company's total research and development expenditure. This is not always disclosed, but is a feature of Boots' accounts.

Line 8   The other operating income was generated by the prescription pharmaceuticals business that was sold in 1995.

Four figures for operating profit are shown:

Line 9   This, as the operating profit from continuing operations before exceptionals, should give an indicator of the underlying profitability of the continuing operations. The exceptional costs charged to operating profits were disclosed in the notes to the accounts.

Line 10   This shows the reported profit for continuing operations. The difference between line 9 and line 10 is exceptional items.

Line 11   This shows the operating profit for the total business, before exceptional items.

Line 12   This shows the operating profit for the total business, after exceptional items.

Line 13   Boots includes associate's profits in operating profit, but it has been shown below operating profits to ensure comparability and conformity to FRS 9.

Line 14   Profit on sale of fixed assets.

Line 15   Profit on disposal of subsidiaries.

Line 16   This line is available for other exceptional items that are required by FRS 3 to be shown below operating profits (e.g. the costs of a fundamental reorganisation).

Line 17   Profit before interest.

Line 18   This includes both interest received and similar income.

Line 19   This is the interest payable on the company's loans. Therefore, it is the interest payable less any income from interest rate swaps.

Line 20   This is the interest charged to fixed assets. It almost immaterial in the context of Boots, but is shown separately as it is important in other companies.

Line 21   This is an entry specific to Boots. A subsidiary, Boots Investments Ltd, bought back one of the parent company's bonds in 1994. The increase in the value of the bond held by the subsidiary is included in interest in the group profit and loss account.

Line 22   Operating profits for associates have only been shown since 1994, and consequently the company's share of associate's interest has only been disclosed since that date.

Line 23   This is reported profit before tax.

Line 24   The adjusted profit before tax is adjusted for:

- material exceptional items;
- profits and losses on sale of assets and subsidiaries;
- capitalised interest;
- provisions. Adds back any reorganisation provisions charged, and deducts provisions spent. There were no adjustments to Boots' accounts during the period under review.

Line 25   This is the tax charge for the year.

Line 26   This is reported profit after tax.

Line 27   The adjusted profit after tax is adjusted for the tax impact of the adjustments made on line 24, and a full provision has been made for deferred tax.

Line 28   This line is provided for any extraordinary items.

Line 29   This is the minority interests in the after-tax profits.

Line 30   This line is provided for any preference dividends.

Line 31   This is the profit attributable to the ordinary shareholders.

Line 32   This is the adjusted profit after tax less exceptional items, minority interests, which are attributable to non-exceptional profits, and preference dividends.

Line 33   This indicates the dividends paid and proposed during the year.

Line 34   This is the retained profit for the financial year.

● The balance sheet

The spreadsheet balance sheet is the reported balance sheet with some additional disclosures, found in the notes (Table 22.2).

Table 22.2 **Profit and loss acount for analysis**

42	*FIXED ASSETS*	
43	Intangible assets	
44	Tangible assets	
45	Investments	
46	Total fixed assets	(Total of lines 43 to 45)
47	*CURRENT ASSETS*	
48	Stocks	
49	Retail	
50	Manufacturing	
51	Property development	
52	Total stock	(Total of lines 48 to 51)
53.	Trade debtors	
54	Total debtors due in a year	
55	Debtors due in more than a year	
56	Investments and short-term deposits	
57	Cash at bank and in hand	
58	Total current assets	(Total of lines 54 to 57 + line 52)
59	*CREDITORS: DUE IN A YEAR*	
60	Bank loans and overdrafts	
61	Trade creditors	
62	Other creditors	
63	Total creditors due in a year	(Total of lines 60 to 62)
64	NET CURRENT ASSETS	(Line 58 + line 63)
65	TOTAL ASSETS LESS CURRENT LIABILITIES	(Line 46 + line 64)
66	*CREDITORS: DUE IN MORE THAN A YEAR*	
67	Loans	
68	Other	
69	Total creditors due in more than a year	(Line 67 + line 68)
70	*PROVISIONS FOR LIABILITIES AND CHARGES*	
71	Deferred tax	
72	Other	
73	Total provisions for liabilities and charges	(Line 71 + line 72)
74	MINORITY INTERESTS	
75		(Line 65 + line 69 + line 73 + line 74)
76		
77	*CAPITAL AND RESERVES*	
78	Share capital	
79	Share premium account	
80	Revaluation reserve	
81	Capital redemption reserve	
82	Profit and loss account	
83	Total capital and reserves	(Total of lines 78 to 82)
84		

85	Weighted average shares in issue	
86	Last revaluation date	
87	Independent	
88	Goodwill	
89		
90	LONG-TERM CAPITAL EMPLOYED	(Line 65)
91	TOTAL CAPITAL EMPLOYED	(Line 65 – line 60)
92	ADJUSTED TOTAL CAPITAL EMPLOYED	(Line 91 + line 88 – line 80)
93	ADJUSTED EQUITY	(Line 83 – line 80 + line 88 – line 73)

Explanations

Lines 49–51 Boots analyses its stocks into retailing, manufacturing and property. Using this information allows better analysis of stocks.

Line 53 This information is extracted from the note on debtors falling due within a year.

Lines 60–61 This information is extracted from the note on creditors falling due within a year.

Line 62 This information is the balance of creditors falling due within a year, i.e. those not shown in lines 60–61.

Line 67 This information is extracted from the note on creditors falling due in more than a year.

Line 68 This information is the balance of creditors falling due in more than a year.

Line 69 This information is extracted from the note on provisions for liabilities and charges.

Line 72 This is the balance of the provisions for liabilities and charges. Any increase in these should be checked to see if the company is using 'big-bath' accounting.

Line 85 This can be found in the note on earnings per share.

Line 86 and 87 It is useful to know the date of the last revaluation and whether it was independent.

Line 88 This should be the cumulative goodwill charged to the reserves. It will be disclosed in the note on reserves.

Line 90 This is the standard definition of capital employed.

Line 91 In recent years, it has become more appropriate to include short-term debt in the definition of capital employed.

Line 92 The total capital employed is adjusted to include goodwill and exclude revaluation.

Line 93 The equity is adjusted to include goodwill and provisions and exclude revaluation.

● The cash flow statement

The cash flow statement is the reported cash flow statement. Some of the lines have only shown in Boots' cash flow statement in the past, but will be found in the statements of other companies. The formulas for the totals are probably unnecessary, but form a good check to ensure that you have entered the right data. The formulas assume that cash outflows will be entered as a minus number (Table 22.3).

Two sub-totals have been included:

(1) a cash flow before management of liquid resources – this identifies if the company had surplus funds that were available for short-term investments;

(2) a cash flow before financing – this identifies any surplus or deficits that have to be matched by financing and changes in cash. (This can then be used as a further check on the entries with the total of the cash flow from financing and the movement in cash.)

Table 22.3 **The cash flow statement for analysis**

94	Net cash flow from operating activities	(Line 157)
95		
96	RETURNS ON INVESTMENT AND SERVICING OF FINANCE	
97	Interest received	
98	Interest paid	
99	Interest element on finance lease rentals	
100	Dividends received	
101	Dividends received from associated undertakings	
102	Dividends paid to minority shareholders	
103	Net cash flow from returns on investment and servicing of finance	(Total of line 97 to line 102)
104	TAXATION	
105	UK corporation tax paid	
106	Overseas tax paid	
107	Net cash flow from taxation	(Line 105 + line 106)
108	CAPITAL EXPENDITURE AND FINANCIAL INVESTMENT	
109	Purchase of fixed assets	
110	Disposal of fixed assets	
111	Purchase of own shares	
112	Net cash flow from capital expenditure and financial investment	(Total of line 109 to line 111)
113	ACQUISITIONS AND DISPOSALS	
114	Investment in and loans to associated undertakings	
115	Purchase of businesses	
116	Loan to WH Smith	
117	Investment by minority interests in subsidiary undertakings	
118	Disposal of businesses	
119	Net cash flow from acquisitions and disposals	(Total of line 114 to line 118)
120	EQUITY DIVIDENDS PAID	
121	NET CASH FLOW BEFORE MANAGEMENT OF LIQUID RESOURCES	(Line 94 + line 103 + line 112 + line 119 + line 120)
122	MANAGEMENT OF NET LIQUID RESOURCES	
123	(Increase) / decrease in short-term investments	

▶

124	Purchase of index-linked treasury stock	
125	*Net cash flow from management of liquid resources*	(Line 123 + line 124)
126	*NET CASH FLOW BEFORE FINANCING*	(Line 121 + line 125)
127		
128	*FINANCING*	
129	Issue of ordinary share capital	
130	Sale and leaseback proceeds	
131	Bond issue, net of expenses	
132	Factored rental commitments	
133	Other loans	
134	Capital element of finance lease rentals	
135	Repayment of loans	
136	Repurchase of shares	
137	Increase in other borrowings	
138	Decrease in other borrowings	
139	Investment in bond	
140	*Net cash flow from financing*	(Total of line 129 to line 139)
141		
142	*CASH*	
143		(Line 140 + line 142)
144		
145	*RECONCILIATION OF OPERATING PROFIT TO CASH FLOW FROM OPERATING ACTIVITIES*	
146	Operating profit	
147	Exceptional operating items	
148	Depreciation	
149	Loss / (profit) on sale of fixed assets	
150	Loss from associates	
151	Provisions utilised and other movements	
152	Exceptional operating cash flows	
153	Future cash generated from this year's operations	(Total of line 146 to line 152)
154	Decrease / (increase) in stocks	
155	Decrease / (increase) in debtors	
156	Increase / (decrease) in creditors	
157	*Net cash flow from operating activities*	(Total of line 153 to line 156)

● The ratios

All formulas assume that negative numbers will have been entered as such on to the spreadsheet.

Solvency ratios

Table 22.4 **Solvency ratios for analysis**

159	RATIO ANALYSIS	
160		
161	SOLVENCY	
162	Acid test	(Line 49 + line 54+ line 56 + line 57) ÷ (– line 63)
163	Current ratio	(Line 58 – line 55) ÷ (– line 63)
164	Gearing (as published):	
165	Net debt : equity	(– Line 60 – line 67 + line 56 + line 57) ÷ line 83 expressed as a %
166	Gearing (adjusted for revaluation, goodwill and provisions):	
167	Net debt : equity	(– Line 60 – line 67 + line 56 + line 57) ÷ line 93 expressed as a %
168	Profit-based interest cover (adjusted for capitalisation of interest)	Line 17 ÷ (– line 19)
169	Operating profit-based interest cover	Line 12 ÷ (– line 19)
170	Continuing operating profit-based interest cover	Line 10 ÷ (– line 19)
171	Interest cover – cash based	Line 94 ÷ (– line 98)

Explanations

Line 162   The acid test requires the identification of the company's liquid assets. For Boots, these were deemed to be the retailing stocks, the debtors due in a year, current-asset investments and cash.

Line 163   The current assets used in this ratio should exclude debtors falling due in more than a year.

Lines 165 and 167   Net debt has been chosen as the most relevant measure of Boots' gearing. Other measures could have been used.

Lines 168–171 Four measures of interest cover have been used (see below):

Line 168   This is the conventional measure of interest cover, but is distorted by the large profit on disposal of businesses in 1995.

Line 169   This uses operating profit and, therefore, eliminates the distortions arising from profit and losses on sale of assets and subsidiaries.

Line 170   This looks at the company's ability to pay interest from the continuing operations.

Line 171   This looks at the company's ability to pay interest from the operating cash flow.

Profitability

This section of the spreadsheet is concerned with the company's return on capital employed and how it is improving it (Table 22.5).

Table 22.5 **Profitability analysis**

172		
173	**PROFITABILITY**	
174	Return on capital employed:	
175	Based on published figures	(Line 23 – line 19 + line 20) ÷ line 90 expressed as a %
176	Adjusted return on capital employed	(Line 24 – line 19) ÷ (line 90 + line 88 – line 80) expressed as a %
177	Continuing adjusted ROCE	(Line 9 + line 13 + line 14 + line 15 + line 16 + line 18 + line 21 + line 22) ÷ (line 90 + line 88 – line 80) expressed as a %
178	Published return on total capital employed	(Line 23 – line 19 + line 20) ÷ line 91 expressed as a %
179	Adjusted return on total capital employed	(Line 24 – line 19) ÷ line 92 expressed as a %
180	Continuing adjusted return on total capital	(Line 9 + line 13 + line 14 + line 15 + line 16 + line 18 + line 21 + line 22) ÷ line 92 expressed as a %
181		
182	Profit margin (based on adjusted profit)	(Line 24 – line 19) ÷ line 2 expressed as a %
183	Asset turn (adjusted for goodwill and revaluation)	Line 2 ÷ line 92
184		
185	Operating margin – continuing business before exceptionals	Line 9 ÷ line 1 expressed as a %
186	Operating margin – continuing business after exceptionals	Line 10 ÷ line 1 expressed as a %
187	Operating margin – before exceptional items	Line 11 ÷ line 2 expressed as a %
188	Operating margin – after exceptional items	Line 12 ÷ line 2 expressed as a %
189		
190	Tangible fixed asset turn (adjusted for revaluation)	Line 2 ÷ (line 44 – line 80)
191	Working capital ratio	(Line 52 + line 53 + line 61) ÷ line 2 expressed as a %, or pence per £ sales

421

192	*Sales-based working capital ratios:*	
193	Stock-turn ratios:	
194	Retail stockturn	Retail sales ÷ line 49
195	Manufacturing stockturn	Manufacturing sales ÷ line 50
196	Total stockturn	Line 2 ÷ line 52
197	Stock days ratios:	
198	Retail stock days	(Line 49 ÷ Retail sales) x 365
199	Manufacturing stock days	(Line 50 ÷ Manufacturing sales) x 365
200	Stock days	(Line 52 ÷ line 2) x 365
201	Debtor days	(Line 53 ÷ line 2) x 365
202	Creditor days	(– Line 61 ÷ line 2) x 365

Return on capital employed

There are several ways that this has been calculated.

(1) the capital employed can be based on one of two figures: the long-term capital employed or the total capital employed, which includes short-term borrowings;

(2) the return on capital can be adjusted to reflect both the adjusted profit and adjusted capital employed;

(3) as Boots sold its prescription pharmaceuticals business on the last day of the financial year, a return on capital based on profit from continuing operations is the most relevant ratio for 1995.

Explanations

Lines 175 – 177   Return on long-term capital:

Line 175   This is the traditional definition of return on capital employed. It expresses profit before tax, adds back the interest paid less the interest capitalised, as a percentage of the total assets less current liabilities.

Line 176   This adjusts the return on capital for exceptional items, capitalised interest, revaluation and goodwill.

Line 177   This uses the adjusted profit from continuing operations to bring the profit in line with the adjusted capital employed.

Lines 178 – 180   Return on total capital:

Line 178   This expresses the reported profit before tax and interest paid as a percentage of the reported total capital employed.

Line 179   This adjusts both the profits and the total capital employed.

Line 180   This uses the adjusted profit from continuing operations to bring the profit in line with the adjusted total capital employed.

Line 182   This expresses the adjusted profit before tax and interest paid as a percentage of the total turnover.

Line 184   This shows how many pounds of sales were generated for each pound of total adjusted capital invested in the company. This can be multiplied by line 182 to arrive at the return on total adjusted capital employed.

Lines 186–189	*There are four operating-profit margins (see below):*
Line 186	This measures the underlying operating profit margin in the continuing business.
Line 187	This measures the reported operating profit margin in the continuing business.
Line 188	This measures the underlying operating profit margin in the business.
Line 189	This measures the reported operating profit margin in the business.
Lines 190–202	*These are concerned with the utilisation of assets (see below):*
Line 190	This measures the number of pounds' turnover generated for each pound invested in fixed assets. (This may also be calculated using gross fixed assets.)

In 1995 this was adjusted to exclude the turnover from discontinued operations, as the assets were sold by the year end.

Line 191	This measures the number of pence that have to be tied up in the working capital for every pound of turnover.
Lines 192–202	*These are concerned with the control of working capital, and they are purely indicative numbers. In 1995, these ratios were adjusted to exclude the turnover from discontinued operations, as the assets were sold by the year end:*
Line 194	This measures how many times in a year retail stocks are converted into sales. The retail sales can be found in the segmental information.
Line 195	This measures how many times in a year manufacturing stocks are converted into sales. BCM manufactures for BTC, BHI and other companies. Its total sales are shown in the segmental information.
Line 196	This measures how many times in a year total stocks are converted into sales.
Line 198	This measures how many days of retail sales are carried in stock.
Line 199	This measures how many days of manufactured sales are carried in stock.
Line 200	This measures how many days of sales are carried in stock.
Line 201	This measures the number of days' credit given. For Boots, this is fairly meaningless, with so much of its turnover in retailing, where no real credit is given.
Line 202	This measures the payment period.

● Measures of cash flow performance

This part of the spreadsheet is concerned with identifying the company's cash flows (Table 22.6).

Table 22.6   Cash ratios for analysis

203		
204	**CASH RATIOS**	
205	**Cash flow available for reinvestment:**	
206	Operating profit after provisions and exceptionals	Line 146 + line 147 + line 149 + line 150 + line 152
207	Depreciation	Line 148
208	Provisions charged	
209	Provisions utilised	
210	Net interest received / (paid)	Line 103
211	Tax paid	Line 107
212	Dividends paid	Line 120
213	*Cash flow available for reinvestment*	Total of line 206 to line 212
214	Per share	Line 213 ÷ line 85
215		
216	**Free cash flow:**	
217	Operating cash flow	Line 157
218	Tax paid	Line 107
219	Capital expenditure and financial investment	Line 112
220	Acquisitions and disposals	Line 119
221	*Free cash flow*	Total of line 217 to line 220
222	Per share	Line 221 ÷ line 85
223		
224	**Free cash flow available to shareholders:**	
225	Free cash flow	Line 221
226	Net interest received / (paid)	Line 103
227	*Free cash flow available to shareholders*	Line 225 + line 226
228	Per share	Line 227 ÷ line 85

Explanations

Line 206   This represents the reported profit adjusted for exceptional items, provisions, associates' losses and profits or losses on disposal of fixed assets.

Lines 208 and 209   This information may be found in the notes on provisions.

Line 210   This will include dividends received and dividends paid to minority and preference shareholders.

● Other measures of investment performance

Table 22.7   Cash ratios for analysis

229		
230	**OTHER INVESTMENT RATIOS**	
231	Return on equity:	
232	Published	Line 31 ÷ line 83 expressed as a %
233	Adjusted	Line 32 ÷ line 93 expressed as a %
234		
235	Reported earnings per share	Line 38
236	Reported earnings per share growth	(Line 235 ÷ previous year's earnings per share) – 1 expressed as a %
237		
238	Adjusted earnings per share	Line 39
239	Adjusted earnings per share growth	(Line 238 ÷ previous year's earnings per share) – 1 expressed as a %
240		
241	Dividend per share	Line 41
242	Dividend per share growth	(Line 241 ÷ previous year's dividend per share) – 1 expressed as a %
243		
244	Dividend cover based on full distribution	(Line 31 x 1.25) ÷ line 33
245	Dividend cover based on reported profit	Line 31 ÷ line 33
246	Dividend cover (based on adjusted profit)	Line 32 ÷ line 33
247		
248	Adjusted net asset value per share	Line 93 ÷ line 85
249		
250	Sales per share	Line 2 ÷ line 85

Explanation

Line 244   As Boots does not have a problem with irrecoverable ACT, full-distribution earnings will be the grossed up profit attributable to ordinary shareholders.

23 The Boots Company plc

This chapter covers:

- An overview of Boots
- The accounts
- Accounts analysis
- Investment potential

● INTRODUCTION

This chapter features the Boots' 1997 accounts. It uses information from Boots' last four years of published accounts, to show you how to calculate ratios from published accounts, structure a financial analysis and analyse the company's performance using ratios and common sense.

It should always be remembered that financial analysis is only one aspect of analysing a company's performance. A full analysis would need to consider other factors:

- the market for the company's products: (i.e. customers, competitors and products);
- the company's strengths and weaknesses within that market;
- the economic environment;
- the social and technological factors that could affect the company's future performance;
- the strengths and weaknesses of the company's hidden assets – people.

This book is solely concerned with using the published accounts, to enable you to analyse and understand a company's financial performance. To do this the 1997 accounts for the Boots Company plc, and relevant extracts will be reproduced here. (It is unfortunately impossible to reproduce the full accounts, as they run to 80 pages! The financial analysis will largely follow the format used in Chapter 21, but we start with an overview of the Boots group, the financial statements, solvency analysis and management of cash, profitability analysis and investment potential.

AN OVERVIEW OF BOOTS

The Boots group 1994–7

During the past five years, the group has undergone a number of changes. In 1993 the group owned four major subsidiaries that had been sold by 1997:

(1) **Sephora** (a French beauty business) – this was never a significant part of the group. In 1993 it represented 1.7 per cent of the turnover and less than half a per cent of the operating profit. It was sold in July 1993 and, therefore, was part of the group at the start of the period under review (1 April 1993 to 31 March 1997).

(2) **Boots Pharmaceuticals** – this was a prescription pharmaceuticals business that was sold to BASF in March 1995. It was a major contributor to both turnover and profits. In 1995, it comprised 9.6 per cent of group turnover and over 16 per cent of operating profits before exceptional items.

(3) **Farleys** (the infant milk and food business, part of Boots Healthcare International) was sold in 1994 to HJ Heinz Company.

(4) **Childrens World** – this was a chain of out-of-town stores that sold a wide range of children's products. The turnover peaked at £114.3 million in 1996, but the business only saw two years of profitability – 1995 when it made half a million pounds, and 1997 when it made £100 000. It was sold in May 1996 to Storehouse plc.

A number of other disposals were made during the period, and businesses have been acquired in both healthcare and contract manufacturing.

The Boots group in 1997

The activities of Boots extend beyond the famous chemist chain. Retailing currently forms the bulk of operations; in addition to Boots The Chemist, the group owns Boots Opticians, Halfords, and is involved in DIY through (1) the Homestyle chain (sold after the publication of these accounts to the private equity partnership of Alchemy Partners in August 1997), and (2) Do It All, which became wholly owned from June 1996. Whilst retailing represents the core of Boots' activities, Boots also:

- develops and markets consumer healthcare products in the UK and overseas, through Boots Healthcare International (BHI);
- develops and manufactures own brand products through Boots Contract Manufacturing (BCM);
- has a property company, Boots Properties, that is involved in retail property development and manages the group's property portfolio.

The segmental information gives a breakdown of turnover, operating profits and operating assets for these businesses. Boots The Chemist (BTC) is the largest contributor to group turnover and profits. This is clearly shown in Figures 23.1 and 23.2, which exclude Do It All because it became wholly owned during the year. (The other alternative was to treat Do It All as though it had been owned for all of the year.) The turnover excludes inter-company trading and shows that BTC represents nearly 77 per cent of the sales made to third parties.

Figure 23.1 **EXTERNAL TURNOVER**

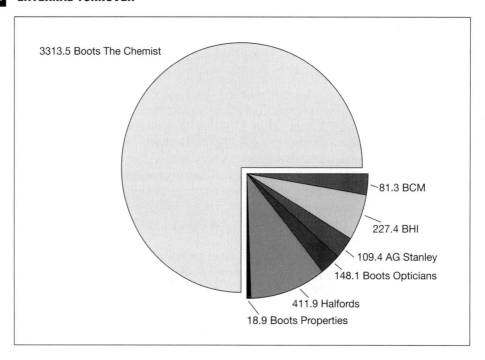

3313.5 Boots The Chemist

81.3 BCM

227.4 BHI

109.4 AG Stanley

148.1 Boots Opticians

411.9 Halfords

18.9 Boots Properties

There is a significant volume of inter-company trading that has been excluded from these figures:

Halfords:	£0.9 million
	(0.22 per cent of its total turnover, compared to 0.23 per cent in 1996);
BHI:	£16.0 million
	(6.6 per cent of its total turnover, compared to 8.1 per cent in 1996);
BCM:	£178.2 million
	(68.7 per cent of its total turnover, compared to 73.4 per cent in 1996);
Boots Properties:	£83.2 million
	(81.5 per cent of its total turnover, compared to 78.3 per cent in 1996).

Boots The Chemist is one of the major customers in other group companies, and Boots Contract Manufacturing also manufactures products for Boots Healthcare International.

The dominance of BTC also shows in the company's operating profits, which are shown before exceptional items in Figure 23.1. (BHI does not show as it made a £6.6 million operating loss in 1997).

Figure 23.2 OPERATING PROFITS (EXCLUDING EXCEPTIONALS)

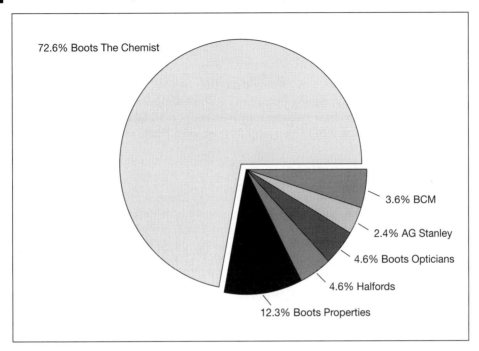

72.6% Boots The Chemist

3.6% BCM

2.4% AG Stanley

4.6% Boots Opticians

4.6% Halfords

12.3% Boots Properties

● Boots The Chemist

Throughout the period these stores have been the main contributor to profits. The operating review discloses that it has three strategic objectives:

(1) differentiaton of its business, with a focus on health and beauty to 'help its customers look good and feel good';
(2) expansion of its store portfolio in a variety of formats;
(3) the seeking out of profitable new growth initiatives.

To an outsider, the market for BTC would appear to be saturated, because of its dominance on the high street, but there is still scope for growth. During the year, the company opened 26 small stores, four large stores and five edge-of-town stores. BTC is currently testing store openings in hospitals and motorway service stations. The company is starting to expand internationally and has opened stores in Ireland. Stores have also been opened in the Netherlands and Thailand in June 1997. With its own manufacturing facilities, own brands are a driver of group profits. The company introduced over 500 new own-brand products during the year.

● Halfords

Halfords is the major retailer of bikes in the UK with over 30 per cent of the market share. It is in the process of repositioning itself from the high street to superstores. It is uniquely positioned, with no real competitor in the market place. Its retailing is a unique combination of cycles, car parts and accessories. The national market for cycles fell during 1997, although by growing market share Halfords maintained sales. The company is continuing to expand its own-brand products, which should increase profits.

In addition to the retailing business, Halfords is involved in servicing and has a sales support agreement with Daewoo. Servicing made a loss of £5 million in 1997, and plans to move to break even by growing sales.

● Boots Opticians

Boots Opticians started in 1987, and has the objective of becoming the market leader in optical retailing. The company operates in its own shops and within Boots The Chemist stores. Sales and margins have risen steadily over the period. Like all Boots retailing operations, profit growth is enhanced by concentrating on own-brand products.

● Boots Healthcare International

The company is focusing on building strong self-medication brands in analgesics, upper respiratory and skincare. It has a major presence in western Europe and Australasia, and is developing markets in eastern Europe and Asia. It has familiar brands such as Nurofen, Strepsils and E45. Heavy investment in marketing and product development has affected profits. Currently, development costs are high and the business is loss making, but BHI offers considerable future profit potential.

● Boots Contract Manufacturing

The company is trying to establish itself as a leading European supplier of private-label and contract-manufactured cosmetics, toiletries and healthcare products. Operating margins appear to have been at their highest in 1995, but this may be misleading as sales to other group companies represent 68.7 per cent of its turnover. Consequently, profits can be affected by transfer-pricing decisions. The operating margin rose in 1997 to almost 1995 levels. The business clearly used to be the manufacturing arm for the other group businesses, but external sales have grown over the past five years from £31.1 million in 1993 to £81.3 million in 1997.

● Boots Properties

Boots Properties owns and manages most of the company's store portfolio (so it is impossible to work out a return on assets for the retailing businesses, as their largest asset is excluded from their segmental information). Over 80 per cent of its turnover in 1997 came from other group companies.

● AG Stanley

AG Stanley stores specialised in co-ordinated home design, and traded during the period as Homestyle and Fads. The company has been rationalising for a number of years, by modifying store formats, closing unprofitable stores and moving out of the high street.

● Do It All

In reviewing Boots' performance, a special mention has to be made of Do It All. Boots' involvement in DIY began in 1989, when it acquired Ward White. Ward White owned Halfords, AG Stanley, Payless DIY and an American autoparts business that was subsequently sold. In August 1990, Payless was merged with WH Smith's Do It All. Each partner had 50 per cent of the merged business. Unfortunately, Boots' entry into DIY was badly timed, the fall in the housing market led to a fall in the fortunes of DIY retailers. To compound this, the merged Do It All was badly placed within this market.

The business was accounted for as an associated undertaking until June 1996 when WH Smith sold its share to Boots for £1.00. In its five-year summary Boots discloses its share of the turnover and the operating profits before exceptional items. Therefore, plotting the fortunes of Do It All is a matter of simple arithmetic.

Since the merger turnover fell, recovering slightly in 1997 (see Figure 23.3).

Figure 23.3   **DO IT ALL (TURNOVER)**

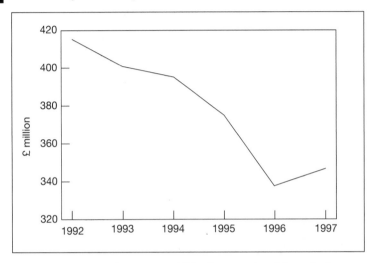

Profitability has been more difficult to attain, although there was an improvement in 1997 (see Figure 23.4).

Figure 23.4   **DO IT ALL (OPERATING PROFIT BEFORE EXCEPTIONALS)**

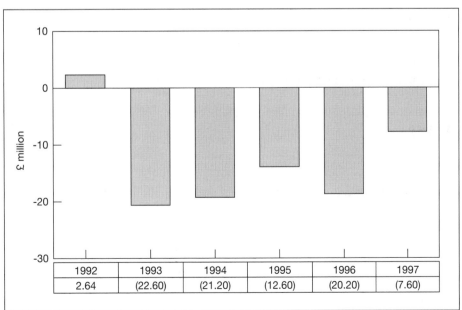

1992	1993	1994	1995	1996	1997
2.64	(22.60)	(21.20)	(12.60)	(20.20)	(7.60)

During this period both companies were investing money in the business. The difficulties in the business led WH Smith to pull out in June 1996. The structure of the deal is interesting. Prior to completion of the deal, WH Smith invested an additional net £50 million in Do It All. (It injected £63.5 million new share capital and Do It All repaid a £13.5 million loan.) This injection left £14.5 million cash on the balance sheet at acquisition. The Boots group also loaned WH Smith £40 million, repayable in four equal instalments.

On acquisition, Do It All had net assets of £95.6 million This was reduced by £5.6 million to align accounting policies, and other adjustments reduced the company's value by £79.1 million. (These other adjustments were primarily writing down fixed assets to their recoverable amounts and the onerous contracts provisions discussed later in this chapter.) This left net assets of £10.9 million. As Boots only paid a pound for the company, it was accounted for as negative goodwill.

Since acquisition, Do It All has made an after-tax loss of £17.4 million, and this has affected the cash flow statement with cash outflows of £40.1 million comprising:

- a cash outflow from operations of £35.8 million;
- interest paid of £1.0 million;
- tax received of £6.2 million;
- capital expenditure of £8.5 million;
- finance lease capital repayments of £1.0 million.

However, the news is not all bad. Some stores have been closed, or earmarked for closure, and ongoing stores are being reformatted around major DIY projects. In the 1997 operating review, the company reported a number of successes:

- like-for-like sales (sales from existing stores) were up by 6.6 per cent;
- sales in the stores that have been reformatted were 10 per cent higher than in other stores;
- the company expects the 'ongoing stores to be cash positive' during 1997/8.

● THE ACCOUNTS

● The accounting policies

The only changes in the group's accounting policies in the last five years have been caused by the introduction of accounting standards. The company does not depreciate shop properties as 'in the opinion of directors' they 'are maintained to such a standard by a programme of repair and refurbishment that the residual value of these properties ... are sufficiently high to make any depreciation charge unnecessary'. Some retailers depreciate shop properties and others, such as Boots and Marks & Spencer, do not. This could affect comparisons, and it may be necessary to make adjustments to the accounts if Boots' accounts are being compared to other retailers with different accounting policies.

The other interesting item in the accounts is that properties were last revalued in 1993. The directors revalued most of the group's properties 'in conjunction with their own professionally qualified staff'.

The profit and loss account

Extract 23.1 THE BOOTS COMPANY PLC, GROUP PROFIT AND LOSS ACCOUNT (year end 31 MARCH 1997)

	Notes	Before exceptional items 1997 £m	Exceptional items (note 3) 1997 £m	Total 1997 £m	Before exceptional items 1996 £m	Exceptional items (note 3) 1996 £m	Total 1996 £m
Turnover							
Continuing operations – excluding acquisitions		4,291.8	–	4,291.8	4,010.4	–	4,010.4
– acquisitions		273.3	–	273.3	–	–	–
Turnover from continuing operations		4,565.1	–	4,565.1	4,010.4	–	4,010.4
Discontinued operation		12.9	–	12.9	114.3	–	114.3
Total turnover	1	4,578.0	–	4,578.0	4,124.7	–	4,124.7
Operating profit							
Continuing operations – excluding acquisitions		496.4	8.6	505.0	444.0	12.8	456.8
– acquisitions		(4.7)	–	(4.7)	–	–	–
Operating profit from continuing operations		491.7	8.6	500.3	444.0	12.8	456.8
Discontinued operation		0.1	–	0.1	(1.4)	–	(1.4)
Total operating profit	1,2	491.8	8.6	500.4	442.6	12.8	455.4
Profit/(loss) on disposal of fixed assets	3						
Continuing operations		–	11.3	11.3	–	1.2	1.2
Profit on disposal of businesses	4						
Continuing operations		–	–	–	–	0.2	0.2
Discontinued operation		–	15.0	15.0	–	–	–
Profit on ordinary activities							
before interest		491.8	34.9	526.7	442.6	14.2	456.8
Net interest	5	44.4	–	44.4	50.9	–	50.9
Profit on ordinary activities							
before taxation		536.2	34.9	571.1	493.5	14.2	507.7
Tax on profit on ordinary activities	6	(175.0)	(3.3)	(178.3)	(163.4)	(3.7)	(167.1)
Profit on ordinary activities							
after taxation		361.2	31.6	392.8	330.1	10.5	340.6
Equity minority interests		0.5	–	0.5	–	–	–
Profit for the financial year							
attributable to shareholders	7	361.7	31.6	393.3	330.1	10.5	340.6
Dividends	8			(586.1)			(176.4)
(Loss)/profit retained				(192.8)			164.2
Earnings per share	9	39.5p	3.4p	42.9p	34.7p	1.1p	35 8p

Initial observations on the profit and loss account

- *There was real growth in the turnover on their existing business during 1997 (turnover rose by over 7 per cent).*
- *Existing continuing business operating profit before exceptionals grew by nearly 12 per cent, so margins have increased.* $\left(496.4 - 444 \big/ {}_{444}\right) \times 100 \ \%$
- *The company's exceptional items improved profit in both years.*
- *The company has made acquisitions and disposals during the period. The profit and loss account shows a profit on disposal, therefore, the companies were sold above book value.*
- *The acquisitions are not profitable, and the disposals were only marginally profitable.*
- *The company is a net interest receiver, therefore, has considerable cash balances and may have negative gearing. The cash balances may have gone down, or borrowing up, as the interest received has fallen in a time of relatively stable interest rates.*
- *The company does not own all of the subsidiaries.*
- *There is a huge increase in dividends in 1997.*

These comments generate the following questions, which are set out below.

What were the exceptional items?

There were three exceptional items affecting the accounts in 1997:

(1) following a high court decision that VAT is not payable on the dispensing of spectacles, £12.7 million (1996 – £12.8 million) was recovered from HM Customs and Excise;

(2) restructuring provisions – these are shown net of £3.6 million received by BHI to bring forward the transfer of products to BASF. The net charge is £2.3 million;

(3) in BCM a provision of £1.8 million has been made to withdraw from soap manufacturing.

What were the acquisitions and disposals made during 1997?

The main acquisitions were Do It All (for £1.00) and Laboratoires Lutsia (a French skincare specialist for £117.8 million). Other acquisitions made during 1997 were an Italian skincare specialist (Farmila Dermical, for £4.1 million) and the Roval personal-care/toiletry operations in France and Spain, for £15.2 million.

The main disposal was Childrens World, sold for £62.5 million.

The cash flow for the year included a final payment, from BASF, of £73.0 million for the sale of Boots Pharmaceuticals in 1995.

Why did the dividend increase?

The company paid three dividends during 1997: an interim dividend of 6.2p (an increase of 8.8 per cent over 1996), a special second interim of 44.2p per share, and a final dividend of 14.3p per share (an increase of 11.7 per cent over 1996). The special dividend was decided following the tax changes on share buy-backs, and allowed institutional investors to reclaim the tax credit, as the dividend was paid before the July 1997 budget. It was payable to all shareholders on the register on 4 June 1997, so has not been paid at the date of the 1997 accounts.

Why did the profit margin increase?

The segmental information disclosed that the operating losses of Do It All as an associate were included in the operating profit shown in the profit and loss account. As the business is an associate, the relevant turnover is not included. When the losses are deducted, operating profit for 1996 is £465.5 million after exceptionals, and £501.1 million in 1997. This gives operating profit margins of 11.3 per cent in 1996 and 10.9 per cent in 1997 – so operating profit margins fell slightly in 1997.

The segmental information discloses the operating profit and turnover, however, we know that sizeable acquisitions were made during the year. The notes on segmental information disclose that BHI's £18.7 million turnover and £1.5 million profit during 1997 came from acquisitions. Numbers have been adjusted accordingly, to reflect the profits on existing business. The segmental information revealed that operating margins have improved in all of the existing continuing businesses. (These margins have been calculated by using the operating profit before exceptionals and dividing it by the total turnover.)

Table 23.1 **Comparison of 1996–7 operating margins**

OPERATING MARGINS	1996	1997	Margin improvement?
BTC	12.38%	12.87%	✓
Halfords	5.66%	6.49%	✓
Boots Opticians	8.24%	9.32%	✓
AG Stanley (Homestyle)	(11.63%)	(10.79%)	✗
BHI	(3.97%)	(3.60%)	✗
BCM	6.98%	8.17%	✓
Boots Properties	66.28%	70.62%	✓

Do It All's margins also improved. Unallocated group costs and international retail development costs rose during 1997 and a slight change in the profit mix led to the fall in the group's operating profit margins.

● The balance sheet

Extract 23.2 | **THE BOOTS COMPANY PLC BALANCE SHEET, AS AT 31 MARCH 1997**

	Notes	**Group 1997 £m**	Group 1996 £m	**Parent 1997 £m**	Parent 1996 £m
Fixed assets					
Intangible assets	10	**33.8**	26.6	**3.2**	2.6
Tangible assets	11	**1,769.7**	1 624.4	**584.8**	205.2
Investments	12	**0.5**	46.4	**944.3**	962.2
		1,804.0	1697.4	**1,532.3**	1,170.0
Current assets					
Stocks	13	**667.3**	522.1	**186.1**	168.4
Debtors falling due within one year	14	**347.2**	358.9	**545.7**	735.3
Debtors falling due after more than one year –	14	**133.2**	2.2	**293.9**	186.0
Investments and deposits	15	**603.0**	893.9	**584.0**	868.6
Cash at bank and in hand		**30.9**	15.3	**119.0**	0.1
		1,781.6	1,792.4	**1,728.7**	1,958.4
Creditors: Amounts falling due within one year	16	**(1,597.2)**	(1,092.1)	**(1,075.8)**	(1.264.1)
Net current assets		**184.4**	700.3	**652.9**	694.3
Total assets less current liabilities		**1,988.4**	2,397.7	**2,185.2**	1,864.3
Creditors: Amounts falling due after more than one year	17	**(274.9)**	(150.5)	**(1,162.5)**	(562.5)
Provisions for liabilities and charges	19	**(92.0)**	(45.7)	**(12.8)**	(15.8)
Net assets		**1,621.5**	2.201.5	**1 009.9**	1 286.0
Capital and reserves					
Called up share capital	20,21	**226.5**	238.4	**226.5**	238.4
Share premium account	20	**233.7**	226.9	**233.7**	226.9
Revaluation reserve	20	**351.9**	321.4	**–**	
Capital redemption reserve	20	**36.8**	24.0	**36.8**	24.0
Profit and loss account	20	**772.7**	1,390.8	**512.9**	796.7
Equity shareholders' funds		**1,621.6**	2201.5	**1,009.9**	1,286.0
Equity minority interests		**(0.1)**	–	**–**	–
		1,621.5	2,201.5	**1,009.9**	1,286.0

(handwritten: 3585.6 above the 1,781.6 figure)

Initial observations on the balance sheet

- *The company has intangible assets.*
- *Stocks have increased by 28 per cent, whereas total turnover has only increased by 11 per cent. Total debtors falling due within a year has fallen, but this may not be reflected in the trade-debtor position (in fact trade debtors have increased from £181.1 million in 1996 to £208.8 million in 1997). Control of working capital may be worth a look.*
- *Debtors falling due after one year have increased by £131 million – what are they?*

- *The cash and short-term investments have fallen by over £275 million, and this is before the payment of the special and final dividends.*
- *The creditors falling due in a year have increased by half a million pounds, probably reflecting the increased dividends.*
- *The company's solvency has declined during 1997 with net current assets now standing at £184.4 million.*
- *Provisions for liabilities and charges have increased by over £46 million.*
- *The company has had a share buy-back during the year. This probably explains the fall in cash flow.*

These observations generate the following questions, which are set out below.

What are the intangible assets?

The intangible assets are patents, trade marks or other product rights that the company has acquired. They are amortised over their useful life, with a maximum life of 20 years. Any similar assets developed in the business are charged to the profit and loss account and are not capitalised.

What are the debtors falling due in more than a year?

The increase in the other debtors in 1997 is advance corporation tax of £100.1 million (this is the tax relating to the special dividend) and other debtors, undisclosed, have increased by £30.9 million.

Why have the creditors falling due in more than a year increased?

The note on creditors for the group confirms the suspicion that the main reason for the increase in creditors is the dividend payment, which has increased both the dividends and ACT.

Extract 23.1　CREDITORS: AMOUNTS FALLING DUE WITHIN ONE YEAR

	Group 1997	Group 1996
	£m	£m
Borrowings (note 18)	167.9 √	274.8
Trade creditors	331.1	269.6
Bills of exchange	4.5	0.3
Due to subsidiary undertakings	–	–
Corporation tax	135.8	128.2
Advance corporation tax	156.0	42.7
Taxation and social security (including VAT and other sales taxes)	32.8	60.9
Other creditors	127.5	103.7
Accruals and deferred income	111.6	89.9
Dividends (note 8)	530.0	122.0
	1597.2	1092.1

What provisions has the company made during 1997? Have they affected the profit and loss account?

During 1997 the Boots group had three provisions: a provision for deferred tax, an acquisition provision (created in 1997) and a disposal provision.

Extract 23.4   PROVISIONS

Group	Deferred taxation £m	Acquisition provisions £m	Disposal provisions £m	Total £m
At 1st April 1996	26.1	–	19.6	45.7
Profit and loss account	4.2	0.7	3.7	8.6
Purchase of businesses (see note 4)	(14.5)	97.6	–	83.1
Utilised	–	(40.8)	(4.4)	(45.2)
Currency adjustments	–	(0.2)	–	(0.2)
At 31st March 1997	**15.8**	**57.3**	**18.9**	**92.0**

Disposal provisions created during the year relate to the sale of Childrens World.

The majority of the disposal provisions at 31st March 1997 relate to the sale of Boots Pharmaceuticals in March 1995 and include amounts in respect of possible environmental liabilities arising from former involvement in an agro-chemical joint venture in the US.

Most of the acquisition provision was not charged to the profit and loss account, and mainly relates to the acquisition of Do It All (which accounted for £82.6 million). Note 4 tells us that the provisions were 'to provide for onerous contracts mainly in connection with property leases and adjusting for estimated tax benefits'. These provisions have been charged to Do It All's balance sheet on acquisition and have reduced the negative goodwill.

How much did the share buy-back cost?

The company paid £300 million to buy back shares. The company bought back £511.3 million in 1994/5, bringing the total amount spent on share buy-backs in the last three years to £811 million. The company says it wants to 'achieve a more efficient capital structure, in line with the policy of delivering shareholder value. It is sensible for companies to finance a proportion of their capital requirements with borrowings, and this is especially so when the business consistently produces strong cash flows'.

● The cash flow statement

Extract 23.5   GROUP CASH FLOW STATEMENT (YEAR ENDED 31 MARCH 1997)

Reconciliation of operating profit to operating cash flows

	Notes	1997 £m	1996 £m
Operating profit		**500.4**	455.4
Exceptional operating items	3	**(8.6)**	(12.8)
Operating profit before exceptional items		**491.8**	442.6
Operating loss of associated undertaking		**0.7**	10.1
Depreciation and amortisation		**111.8**	104.8
Loss on disposal of tangible fixed assets, excluding properties		**4.9**	5.5

		(73.5)	(30.5)
Increase in stocks, including property development stock		**(73.5)**	(30.5)
Increase in debtors		**(6.9)**	(19.3)
Increase in creditors		**9.6**	11.0
Other non-cash movements		**1.5**	(0.5)
Net cash inflow before expenditure relating to exceptional items		**539.9**	523.7
Exceptional operating cash flows	22	**(24.8)**	12.8
Cash inflow from operating activities		**515.1**	536.5

The cash inflow from operating activities includes £2.2m (1996 £Nil) relating to discontinued operation.

Group cash flow statement

	Notes	1997 £m	1996 £m
Cash inflow from operating activities		**515.1**	536.5
Returns on investment and servicing of finance	22	**39.1**	16.2
Taxation		**(174.4)**	(152.7)
Capital expenditure and financial investment	22	**(169.6)**	(197.3)
Acquisitions and disposals	4	**(40.4)**	(48.4)
Equity dividends paid		**(169.8)**	(154.4)
Cash outflow before use of liquid resources and financing		**–**	(0.1)
Management of liquid resources	22	**288.5**	122.8
Financing	22	**(258.1)**	(125.4)
Increase/(decrease) in cash		**30.4**	(2.7)

Cash is defined as cash in hand and deposits repayable on demand, less overdrafts repayable on demand.

Reconciliation of net cash flow to movement in net funds

	Notes	1997 £m	1996 £m
Increase/(decrease) in cash		**30.4**	(2.7)
Cash inflow from decrease in liquid resources	23	**(288.5)**	(122.8)
Cash (inflow)/outflow from change in borrowings and lease financing	23	**(34.1)**	134.5
Movement in net funds resulting from cash flows		**(292.2)**	9.0
Investments and borrowings of businesses acquired		**(9.9)**	(1.1)
Finance lease additions		**(8.7)**	(6.7)
Increase in value of investment in 10.125% bond 2017		**13.6**	12.5
Currency and other non-cash adjustments		**0.5**	(4.7)
Movement in net funds during the year		**(296.7)**	9.0
Opening net funds		**526.2**	517.2
Closing net funds	23	**229.5**	526.2

Net funds comprise cash, liquid resources, finance leases and all other borrowings.

Initial observations on the cash flow statement

● *The group is cash generative.*
● *Exceptional cash flows (£24.8 million) in 1997.*
● *The financing cash outflows must have arisen largely from the share buy-back.*

This leads to the following question:

What were the exceptional cash flows?

These are primarily contract termination costs arising from the acquisition of Do It All and are disclosed in the detailed analysis of cash flows shown below.

Extract 23.6   **DETAILED ANALYSIS OF GROSS CASH FLOWS**

	1997 £m	1996 £m
Exceptional operating cash flows:		
VAT recovered from H M Customs & Excise	12.7	12.8
Expenditure on terminating onerous contracts at Do It All	(35.1)	–
Restructuring and integration costs paid	(0.7)	–
Cash flows relating to prior year disposals	(1.7)	–
	(24.8)	12.8
Returns on investment and servicing of finance:		
Interest received	74.4	55.8
Interest paid	(35.3)	(39.6)
	39.1	16.2
Capital expenditure and financial investment:		
Purchase of fixed assets	(222.8)	(225.1)
Disposal of fixed assets	53.9	27.8
Purchase of own shares	(0.7)	–
	(169.6)	(197.3)
Management of liquid resources:		
Sale/(purchase) of index linked treasury stock	199.7	(199.7)
Decrease in other current asset investments and deposits	88.8	322.5
	288.5	122.8
Financing:		
Capital element of finance lease rental agreements	(2.9)	(1.0)
Factored rental commitments	148.2	–
Redemption of US$175m 9% bond 1997	(107.2)	–
Decrease in other borrowings	(4.0)	(133.5)
Cash inflow/(outflow) from change in borrowings and lease financing	34.1	(134.5)
Issue of ordinary share capital	7.8	9
Repurchase of shares (see note 21)	(300.0)	–
	(258.1)	(125.4)

SUMMARY Boots is a profitable, cash-generative company committed to enhancing shareholder value. Boots The Chemist is the major contributor to both profits and turnover. Not all of the other business are profitable. BHI, AG Stanley, and Do It All are loss making.

BHI was created, as a separate business, in 1993. It is currently investing in product development and marketing to create new business opportunities in eastern Europe and Asia. These heavy promotional costs mean that the business is loss making in the short term, but as these costs are converted into sales, profits will inevitably follow. It is also expanding its product range through acquisitions, and in 1997 acquired Laboratoires Lutsia and Farmila Dermical. There should be scope for considerable profits once the company is fully established in the markets and the acquisitions are fully integrated.

Of the two DIY businesses, AG Stanley, has been sold, and Do It All became a subsidiary during 1997. The jury is still out on Do It All, but there have been some improvements made during 1997.

Boots has a lot of cash, and generates more each year. The group is committed to improving shareholder value and has had a buy-back and paid a special dividend in 1997.

● ACCOUNTS ANALYSIS

This analysis looks at the financial performance of Boots over the last four years, as this is the longest period where the group has had the same structure, and the same accounting policies and presentation.

● Solvency

By any measure, Boots is solvent. It has a positive net worth, net current assets and has an operational cash flow averaging over £1.4 million a day. However, the conventional solvency ratios show solvency declining in 1997.

The acid test

$$\left(\frac{Current\ Asset - Stock}{C/L} \right)$$

	1994	1995	1996	1997
Acid test	1.27	1.64	1.57	0.95

The acid test shows that liquid assets (defined as retail stocks, plus debtors due within a year, current asset investments and cash) did not cover current liabilities for the first time in 1997. Short-term solvency improved in 1995, but this was undoubtedly linked to the timing of the cash payment for the sale of Boots Pharmaceuticals. The cash payment was received from BASF at the year end, 31 March. Since then, solvency declined slightly in 1996 as liquid assets fell (primarily investments) and current liabilities rose. In 1997, the acid test dropped below one as the share buy-back cost £300 million and the special dividend increased current liabilities by £521.3 million. (There was a £408 million increase in dividends and £113.3 million increase in the associated ACT.) However, this is hardly a cause for concern, as no one is going to ask Boots to repay *all* of its current liabilities immediately. We are more likely to argue that the company had too much money in liquid assets in earlier years.

$$\frac{\text{Current Assets}}{\text{Current Liabilities}} \quad \rightarrow 97 \rightarrow \quad \frac{1781.6 - 133.2}{1597.2} = 1.03$$

The current ratio

The fall in solvency is also reflected in the current ratio (debtors falling due in more than a year have been excluded from this ratio, as they are not current).

	1994	1995	1996	1997
Current ratio	1.37	1.70	1.64	1.03

Gearing

With large cash balances and current asset investments, the net debt to equity is the most appropriate measure of gearing. The company has negative gearing throughout the period. The total debt has been a mixture of long- and short-term debt, with the balance changing through the period:

	1994	1995	1996	1997
Bank loans and overdrafts	166.5	288.8	274.8	167.9
Loans	267.9	224.2	108.2	236.5
Total debt	434.4	513.0	383.0	404.4

In 1997, debt rose slightly and current asset investments and equity fell, reducing the group's net cash position. Boots is in the process of changing its capital structure, increasing the balance of debt to equity 'to help achieve a more efficient capital structure'. The company has had negative gearing throughout the period.

	1994	1995	1996	1997
Net debt : equity	−4.29%	−25.77%	−23.90%	−14.15%
Adjusted net debt : equity	−2.61%	−19.58%	−18.58%	−9.61%

Interest cover

The interest cover ratios show that the company could have much higher levels of debt, and this is supported by high and relatively stable returns on capital.

	1994	1995	1996	1997
Interest cover – profit based	10.7	22.1	14.1	22.9
Interest cover – cash based	16.6	15.6	13.5	14.6

SUMMARY

The Boots group is very solvent, using all solvency measures. Solvency declined slightly during 1997, as the group had a share buy-back and paid a special dividend. Solvency is expected to continue to decline as the company changes its capital structure, switching from equity to debt.

● Profitability

During the four-year period the company has had a number of exceptional items charged to profits. The following exceptional items were charged or credited to operating profit:

1994	(£35.0 million)	to write off the heart drug, Manoplax;
	(£36.6 million)	Do It All restructuring costs;
	(£2.2 million)	privity of contract costs.
1995	£2.8 million	VAT recoverable on dispensing.

1996	£12.8 million	VAT recoverable on dispensing.
1997	£12.7 million	VAT recoverable on dispensing;
	(£2.3 million)	BHI restructuring and integration costs, net of payments from BASF for product transfers;
	(£1.8 million)	BCM for withdrawal from soap manufacture.

The profit on sale of subsidiaries during the period was:

1994	£9.3 million	profit on disposal of Sephora.
1995	£273.1 million	profit on disposal of Boots Pharmaceuticals;
	£47.0 million	profit on sale of Farleys.
1996	£0.2 million	The company sold the remaining part of its print business and BHI sold its Kenyan subsidiary; the profit is not attributed.
1997	£15 million	profit on disposal of Childrens World.

This has meant that an adjusted profit figure is the most relevant measure of the group's performance. Most profitability ratios fell in 1996, as the group lost the profit contribution from discontinued operations (over 16 per cent of operating profit in 1995).

Adjusted profit before tax and interest and operating profit increased in 1997.

	1994	**1995**	**1996**	**1997**
Adjusted PBIT	523.6	562.6	522.7	554.1
Operating profit	537.2	525.9	452.7	492.5

Long-term capital employed, adjusted for provisions, revaluation and goodwill fell slightly in 1995, following a share buy-back and the write-back of goodwill following the disposals. The total capital employed increased slightly to reflect the increase in short-term debt. Both the capital employed figures rose in 1996, and fell significantly following the share buy-back in 1997.

	1994	**1995**	**1996**	**1997**
Adjusted long-term capital	2967.3	2906.7	2983.1	2663.4
Adjusted total capital	3133.8	3195.5	3257.9	2831.3

The unadjusted return on total capital shows the need to make adjustments, as the 1995 figure has been heavily distorted by the exceptional profit on disposals.

	1994	**1995**	**1996**	**1997**
Return on total capital employed	21.39%	34.00%	20.09%	27.32%

When the numbers are adjusted they show a slightly different trend.

	1994	**1995**	**1996**	**1997**
Adjusted return on total capital employed	16.71%	17.61%	16.04%	19.57%

The pharmaceuticals business was sold on the last day of the financial year in 1995, so on the balance sheet its operating assets, plus a profit, were exchanged for cash. This will distort the 1995 ratio, but there is no sensible way to account for it. By 1997 return on capital had almost reached 20 per cent and was well above the 1995 figure. The return on capital, based on profits arising from continuing business, was 16.38 per cent in 1995 – therefore, profitability fell in 1996.

As the group is rationalising its capital structure, and the mix of debt has changed over the period, the subsequent analysis will be based on the total capital employed. However, the adjusted return on long-term capital shows a similar trend.

	1994	1995	1996	1997
Adjusted return on long-term capital	17.65%	19.36%	17.52%	20.80%

Profit margin and asset turn

The return on capital improved significantly in 1997 – the important question is why? To answer this, we need to look at the two components of the return on capital; the profit margin, and the asset turn:

	1994	1995	1996	1997
Adjusted profit margin	12.57%	13.06%	12.67%	12.10%
Asset turn based on total capital	1.33	1.35	1.27	1.62

The improvement in the return on capital in 1997 has arisen from improving the utilisation of assets, as the profit margin fell, as the improvement in profits was less than the increase in turnover.

The asset turn improved in 1997 as the total turnover rose by nearly 11 per cent, and the total capital employed fell by 13 per cent. Profit margins fell, this was a combination of two factors; falling interest received, and lower operating margins.

The operating profits are the most important component of the profit before interest and tax. On the face of it operating margins appear to have fallen in 1997:

	1994	1995	1996	1997
Operating margin – after exceptional items	11.12%	12.27%	11.29%	10.95%

However, the operating margin from continuing, existing business before exceptionals shows a slightly different picture. The 1996 margin was the same as 1995 – 11.1 per cent, and it increased in 1997 to 11.7 per cent. Consequently, the problems lay in exceptional items, acquisitions (which have yet to be fully integrated into the group), and the disposals. When the additional business development costs start to generate increased profits, and the acquisitions are integrated, the return on capital should show a marked improvement. If the profit margin could have been maintained at 1996 levels, the return on capital would have been 20.52 per cent. A half a per cent improvement in the profit margin adds 0.8 per cent to the return on capital, assuming that asset turn is constant.

The asset turn improved in 1997, but this was not totally as a result of an improvement in operational efficiency. Whilst tangible asset utilisation improved, the group increased its investment in working capital.

The tangible asset turn

The tangible asset turn fell steadily until 1997, when it rose. (The 1995 numbers were based on continuing business turnover, as only continuing business tangible assets were shown on the balance sheet.) As the trend has only been reversed in the last year, we do not know whether this improvement is likely to continue.

	1994	1995	1996	1997
Tangible fixed asset turn (adjusted for revaluation)	3.56	3.28	3.17	3.23
Tangible asset turn based on cost	2.30	2.18	2.10	2.14

The working capital ratio

Whilst tangible assets generated more sales, the control of working capital slipped in 1996 and 1997. (The 1995 calculation was based on continuing business turnover.)

	1994	1995	1996	1997
Working capital ratio	0.11	0.10	0.11	0.12

In 1997, Boots needed 12p in working capital to fund £1.00 sales.

Stock days

The main contributor to the working capital increase is stock days, which rose during the period.

	1994	1995	1996	1997
Stock days	45.7	45.9	46.2	53.2

Property stocks rose significantly during 1997, from £5.6 million to £38 million (a stock days calculation is inappropriate for a property company). Retailing stock days fell in 1997.

Manufacturing stocks

The problem lies in manufacturing stocks, which rose by over 28 per cent during 1997. BCM gross sales rose by 8 per cent. This is reflected in the figures for manufacturing stock days.

	1994	1995	1996	1997
Manufacturing stock days	53.4	94.0	101.7	120.5

This could have arisen from:

- a change in corporate policy, with BCM carrying the stock for other parts of the group;
- a change in the nature of the business. The company is expanding internationally into different markets, and BCM is broadening the nature of its client base.

These trading assets represent only part of the total capital employed. The improvement that we have seen in the tangible asset turn has been partially offset by the increase in the working capital. Therefore, part of the improvement seen in asset utilisation must have come from non-trading activities. The company has non-trading assets in the form of patents and investments.

Non-trading returns

If the improvement cannot be totally explained by the trading activities, it must have arisen from the investing activities. The returns from the company's investments over the period were as follows:

	1994	1995	1996	1997
Share of profits of associates	(49.3)	(5.7)	(10.1)	(0.7)
Interest received	29.5	32.7	71.1	49.2
Change in value of bond	7.8	11.4	12.5	13.6
Return from investments	(12.0)	38.4	73.5	62.1

The share of associate's losses is primarily Do It All, although there was a small associated undertaking sold with the pharmaceuticals business. It is debatable whether the change in the value of the bond should be included, but as it affects the profit before tax and, therefore, the return on capital, its inclusion seemed appropriate.

The value of the investments are set out below.

	1994	1995	1996	1997
Fixed asset investments	57.1	30.6	46.4	0.5
Investments and short-term deposits	491.9	1015.6	893.9	603
Total investments	549.0	1046.2	940.3	603.5
Return on investments	–2.2%	3.7%	7.8%	10.3%

It clearly does not make sense for a business with a return on capital of 20 per cent to have large cash balances that only earn 8 per cent. This is the argument for share buy-backs. Reducing the cash balances to operational requirements improves the return on capital.

SUMMARY

Most profitability measures appear to have peaked in 1995. However, when we consider the underlying profit margins and the adjusted return on capital, 1997 becomes the best year. The return on capital improved in 1997 following an improvement in tangible asset utilisation and a more efficient capital structure. The underlying improvement in the operating profit margin bodes well for the future. Once the development costs pay off and the acquisitions are fully integrated, profitability should improve markedly. Whilst large short-term deposits helped solvency in previous years, they did nothing to improve profitability as the returns were significantly lower than those achieved within the business.

● INVESTMENT POTENTIAL

Boots is committed to improving shareholder value. From an investor's perspective, the share buy-back and the special dividend have clearly added value. In its five-year summary, Boots discloses information on its share price:

	1994	1995	1996	1997
Share price:				
Highest	605p	582p	627p	701p
Lowest	417p	458p	500p	555p

On the face of it this looks impressive, but the stock market has risen significantly over the last four years, and any share price movements need to be looked at in the context of movements in the retail sector. Boots has slightly underperformed its sector over the last five years, but has outperformed it significantly over the last year. The decision to return cash to the shareholders has had a marked effect on the company's investment performance.

● The investment ratios

Return on equity

	1994	1995	1996	1997
Published return on equity	17.92%	32.85%	15.47%	24.25%
Adjusted	12.82%	14.11%	11.15%	14.69%

The underlying return on equity, as shown in the adjusted calculation improved in 1997 following an improvement in the underlying profits and the share buy-back.

Earnings and dividends

Adjusted earnings per share in 1997 were slightly above the 1995 level, and dividends per share have risen throughout the period.

Figure 23.5   **DIVIDENDS AND EARNINGS GROWTH**

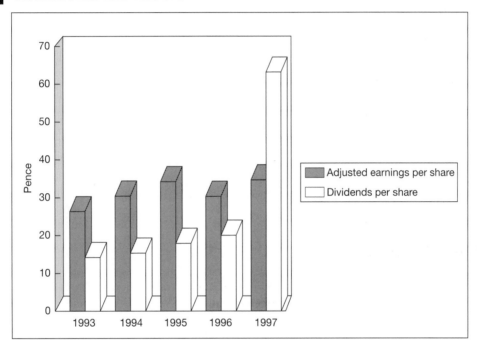

Without the special dividend, the 1997 dividend would have been 20.5p per share, representing a 10.8 per cent increase over the previous years. Dividend growth has averaged just over 11 per cent during the period.

Dividend cover

Whichever way dividend cover is calculated:

- the dividend payments are around half of the available profits;
- dividend cover has fallen in the last two years (although without the payment of the second interim dividend cover would have risen in 1997);
- the special second interim dividend was not covered by the profits in 1997.

	1994	1995	1996	1997
Dividend cover based on full distribution	2.31	4.95	2.41	0.84
Dividend cover based on reported profit	1.85	3.96	1.93	0.67
Dividend cover (based on adjusted profit)	2.17	2.24	1.79	0.60

Gross dividend yield

Dividend yield has hovered around 3 per cent during the period.

	1994	1995	1996	1997
Dividend yield (%)	2.9	3.3	3.1	3.0

Price/earnings ratios

The PE ratios are specific to a certain date, and we have seen that there is a considerable difference between the high and low share prices during the year. The PE ratios below are based on year-end share prices.

	1994	1995	1996	1997
PE ratio	17.0	14.4	16.8	16.8

At the time of writing, the shares were trading at 824p and had a PE of 20.5. The PE for the sector was 17.9, so Boots was expected to outperform the sector. Earnings for 1998 are expected to be around 43.5p, giving a prospective PE of 18.9.

Sales per share

Sales per share have been increasing over the period, with large increases following buybacks.

	1994	1995	1996	1997
Sales per share	4.01	4.30	4.33	4.99

Net assets per share

The net asset value per share fell in 1997, as the reduction in the net assets was greater than the reduction in the number of shares.

	1994	1995	1996	1997
Adjusted net asset value per share	2.54	2.63	2.98	2.61

The shares are trading well in excess of the net asset value indicating that it is the profit potential, rather than the asset values, that is driving the share price.

Cash flow available for reinvestment

The group is cash generative and is living within its means. It has managed to generate more cash available for reinvestment in the business than it has spent in the existing business, leaving a balance for acquisitions and financing.

	1994	1995	1996	1997
Cash flow before reinvestment – £m	393.6	385.9	271.2	274.9
Per share	0.38	0.38	0.29	0.30
Net capital expenditure per share	0.18	0.23	0.21	0.18

Free cash flow

Free cash flow peaked in 1995 with the large cash flows arising from disposals. It has never reached the 1994 levels as operating cash flows have fallen, whilst tax payments have risen.

Free cash flow fell in 1997 as the fall in the operating cash flow plus the increase in tax paid was greater than the reduction in net capital expenditure and acquisitions.

	1994	1995	1996	1997
Free cash flow	332.1	1156.0	138.1	131.4
Per share	0.32	1.15	0.15	0.14

Free cash flow available to shareholders

As Boots has been a net interest receiver for the last three years the free cash flow available to shareholders has been higher than the free cash flow.

	1994	1995	1996	1997
Free cash flow available to shareholders	284.5	1163.4	154.3	170.5
Per share (£)	0.27	1.16	0.16	0.19

The free cash flow per share available to shareholders has been less than the dividend per share for the last two years, indicating that dividends have been paid out of previous cash balances. The dividend would not have been covered from the 1997 cash flow, even if the second interim dividend had not been paid.

Dividends per share	15.0	17.0	18.5	64.7

SUMMARY

Boots is a cash-generative business that has been rewarding shareholders through buy-backs and dividend growth. Over the last four years it has returned £1.2 billion to investors through special dividends and buy-backs. The return on equity will grow as some of the newer businesses move into profits, and this should enable underlying dividend growth to be maintained at over 10 per cent.

The shares are probably fully priced, and currently my investment view would be to hold the shares if you already have them, but not necessarily buy.

CONCLUSION

The analysis has shown that Boots is a strong company, both in terms of profit and cash flow. It is clearly focused on shareholder value and has given its shareholders exceptional returns in the last year, but the business still has its problems, and it will be interesting to see how it resolves the situation in Do It All.

Boots was chosen, partly because it is such a strong UK household name, but mainly because in order to illustrate the principles of financial analysis it is necessary to look at a large, complex company that has undergone a number of changes in recent years. Change is the 'norm' these days, and you need to be able to pick your way through these changes to arrive at the underlying trends, and to view them in context.

Only then will you have a real understanding of a company's performance and the ability to make accurate decisions about it.

It is appropriate at this point to thank the management of Boots for their kind permission to use their accounts as the example in this book.

Part 5

APPENDICES

Appendix 1
Introduction to discounted cash flow

- Present value and compound interest
- Comparing projects that have different degrees of risk
- The present value formulas
- The internal rate of return
- Assumptions in discounted cash flow appraisals

● INTRODUCTION

We know that cash received today is always worth more than cash received in a year's time because:

- it can be invested, and the interest it will earn will make it worth more in a year's time;
- inflation reduces the real value of money over time;
- the cash today is certain, next year it may be less certain;
- we may not be around to spend it next year.

The objective of discounted cash flow is to relate the future cash flows back to their value to us today – the resulting cash is called *the present value*.

● PRESENT VALUE AND COMPOUND INTEREST

Present value works on the same principle as compound interest:

- Compound interest takes a present value and tells you what it will be worth in the future. It answers the question, 'How much will I receive at the end of the first year if I invest £100 at 5 per cent interest?'

    £100 x 1.05 = £105

- Discounted cash flow takes a future value and tells you what original sum you would have needed to have invested to receive that amount of money in the future. It answers the question, 'How much do I need to invest to receive £105 at the end of the first year if interest rates are 5 per cent?'

    £105 / 1.05 = £100

We can see that the two formulas used to calculate compound interest and discounted cash flow are related because we are looking at the same question from a different point of view.

To illustrate this consider the following example.

The compound interest approach

Q. *What will I receive at the end of five years if I invest £100 at 5 per cent compound interest?*

A. I need to use the compound interest formula:

Initial investment x $(1 + \text{rate of interest})^{\text{number of years invested}}$

=   Initial investment x $(1.05)^5$

=   *£100 x (1.2763) = £127.63*

The present value approach

Q. *How much do I need to invest to receive £127.63 in five years' time if interest rates are at 5 per cent?*

A. I need to use the present value formula:

$$\frac{\textit{Cash received at the end of five years}}{(1 + \textit{rate of interest})^{\textit{number of years invested}}}$$

= $$\frac{\text{Cash received at the end of five years}}{(1.05)^5}$$

= $$\frac{\textit{£127.63}}{(1.05)^5} = \textit{£100}$$

Either approach could be used for investment decisions, but discounted cash flow is the most commonly used method in investment appraisal. Discounted cash flow has won the battle with compound interest simply because most people find it easier to understand a current value rather than a future value. You may even be forced to consider present value in your personal life!

This is illustrated by imagining that you have just won £100 000 on the lottery and have approached a financial adviser. He gives you two options:

(1) Investing the money, for two years, at 10 per cent; or
(2) Lending the money to a company which would repay £125 000 in two years' time.

We have to find some way of comparing the two investment opportunities. Because present value works in the same way as compound interest ,we can use either technique to compare the two investment options.

Compound interest

If I invest the money at 10 per cent compound interest for two years, it will be worth £121 000 in two years' time. (This has been worked out by using the compound interest formula £100 000 x 1.1^2. The alternative investment opportunity seems better as it gives me an extra £4000 in two years' time.

Present value

If I lend the money to the company, I will receive £125 000 in two years' time. To receive this amount from the bank, I would have had to invest £125 000 divided by $1.1^2 = £103\ 306$. I seem to be £3306 better off with the loan.

You will notice that the two approaches give us different answers … or do they? Money received in two years' time is not worth the same as money received today – even in an inflation-free world. To receive £125 000 in two years' time, I would normally have to invest £103 306. If I had had the additional £3306, I could have invested it at 10 per cent compound interest. At the end of two years my investment would have been worth £3306 x 1.1^2 = £4000 (it is actually £4000.26, if you work it out on your calculator – there is a small error from rounding). So the numbers are comparable after all – they just reflect the different ways of looking at the same problem.

● COMPARING PROJECTS THAT HAVE DIFFERENT DEGREES OF RISK

The difficulty is that neither method has really helped you to solve your investment dilemma. You are still not sure which is the best investment. Unfortunately, we need to know 'what bank?' and 'what company?' before we can make the decision. Imagine the bank is the Bank of England and the company is McKenzie's Suspenders Ltd. How would you feel then? I suspect that the company loan is looking a little less attractive! McKenzie's Suspenders sounds considerably more risky than the Bank of England. We seem to be comparing a certain return from the bank with an uncertain return from the company.

There are two ways of solving this dilemma:

(1) You ask yourself how much you would want today in exchange for £125 000 in two years' time. This is called the *certainty equivalent*. Perhaps you may be prepared to exchange £80 000 today for the £125 000 you will receive in two years' time from McKenzie's Suspenders;
(2) Ask yourself what return you would expect from an investment with a similar risk to McKenzie's suspenders, let us say 25 per cent. If we discount the £125 000 by 1.25^2, we find that the loan has a present value of £80 000.

Certainty equivalents are easy to calculate if you are the investor, as you know what you would be looking for. That is why, in this case, the numbers worked out to be the same. But usually we are not the investor and then our certainty equivalent could be different from theirs. Thus, in practice, it is easier to use the second approach, as it is possible to 'guessti-mate' the return an investor would require for a similar risk investment.

Our previous example illustrated the fact that an investor will want to balance return and risk – the greater the risk the greater the required investment return. If we want to compare the two investment opportunities, we need to consider the project risk. McKenzie's Suspenders will have to generate a much bigger return than the Bank of England if it is to compete for funds.

● THE PRESENT VALUE FORMULAS

Let us now consider another investment opportunity. We will assume that we have decided that investments with this degree of risk should be generating a 12 per cent return. We initially need to invest £50 000 in the project and would get the following return over five years:

Cash received in:

	£
Year 1	20 000
Year 2	30 000
Year 3	30 000
Year 4	20 000
Year 5	10 000
	110 000

We know that the real value of the cash flow will not be £110 000 – so the total is pretty meaningless. Let us work out the present value. First of all we need to work out the 'present-value factors' – these tell us how much we need to invest to receive a pound in one year, two years, etc. with interest rates at 12 per cent.

We just use the present value formula:

Year 1 $\quad \dfrac{1}{(1.12)} \quad = \quad 0.893$

Year 2 $\quad \dfrac{1}{(1.12)^2} \quad = \quad 0.797$

Year 3 $\quad \dfrac{1}{(1.12)^3} \quad = \quad 0.712$

Year 4 $\quad \dfrac{1}{(1.12)^4} \quad = \quad 0.636$

Year 5 $\quad \dfrac{1}{(1.12)^5} \quad = \quad 0.567$

(We do not normally have to work these out – these present value factors may be found in present value tables, which are also programmed into most computer spreadsheet packages.)

Another way of calculating these would be to express them as follows:

Year 1	$(1.12)^{-1}$	=	0.893
Year 2	$(1.12)^{-2}$	=	0.797
Year 3	$(1.12)^{-3}$	=	0.712
Year 4	$(1.12)^{-4}$	=	0.636
Year 5	$(1.12)^{-5}$	=	0.567

Consequently, we can find the present value by using one of two formulas:

$$\frac{Cash\ received}{(1 + rate\ of\ interest)^{\ number\ of\ years\ invested}}$$

or

$$Cash\ received\ \times\ (1 + rate\ of\ interest)^{\ -\ number\ of\ years\ invested}$$

We can now apply the present value factors we have calculated to our cash flows:

	Cash flow £	Present value factors for 10%	Present value of the cash flows
Year 1	20 000	0.893	17 860
Year 2	30 000	0.797	23 910
Year 3	30 000	0.712	21 360
Year 4	20 000	0.636	12 720
Year 5	10 000	0.567	5 670
		Total present value	81 520
		Cost of the investment	(50 000)
		Net present value	31 520

To get these cash flows at 12 per cent interest, we would need to invest £81 520, but we are only investing £50 000, so the investment looks a good bet. The difference between the cost and the present value is called the *net present value*. Conventionally the data in the above table would be expressed slightly differently. We would take today as Year 0, and the data would be shown as follows:

	Cash flow £	Present value factors for 10%	Present value of the cash flows
Year 0	(50 000)	1	(50 000)
Year 1	20 000	0.893	17 860
Year 2	30 000	0.797	23 910
Year 3	30 000	0.712	21 360
Year 4	20 000	0.636	12 720
Year 5	10 000	0.567	5 670
		Net present value	31 520

Looking at the net present value tells us that the investment gives us a better return than the 12 per cent we would expect to get on an investment of similar risk. But what return is it giving us? Is it giving as good a return as an investment earning 25 per cent?

	Cash flow £	Present value factors for 25%	Present value of the cash flows
Year 0	(50 000)	1	(50 000)
Year 1	20 000	0.800	16 000
Year 2	30 000	0.640	19 200
Year 3	30 000	0.512	15 360
Year 4	20 000	0.410	8 200
Year 5	10 000	0.328	3 280
		Net present value	12 040

We are still doing better than an investment earning 25 per cent. We may want to work out what return we are actually getting; this is measured by the internal rate of return.

● THE INTERNAL RATE OF RETURN

This investment is actually earning us almost 37 per cent:

	Cash flow £	Present value factors for 37%	Present value of the cash flows
Year 0	(50 000)	1	(50 000)
Year 1	20 000	0.730	14 599
Year 2	30 000	0.533	15 984
Year 3	30 000	0.389	11 667
Year 4	20 000	0.284	5 677
Year 5	10 000	0.207	2 072
		Net present value	(1)

The present value of the cash flows is almost the same as the cost, and we have only £1 negative net present value. The 37 per cent return (or, to be accurate 36.99 per cent) we are getting is called the *internal rate of return, IRR,* or the *yield.* We find it, by trial and error, when the present value is the same as the cost.

The internal rate of return is the rate of return generated on the funds that repays the original investment, over a given time period. This is illustrated in the Table A.1.

Table A.1 **The internal rate of return**

	Amount invested at the start of the year	Cash flow	37% interest on the amount invested at the start of the year	Cash left to reduce the amount invested	Amount invested at the end of the year
Year 1	50 000	20 000	18 500	1 500	48 500
Year 2	48 500	30 000	17 945	12 055	36 445
Year 3	36 445	30 000	13 485	16 515	19 930
Year 4	19 930	20 000	7 374	12 626	7 304
Year 5	7 304	10 000	2 702	7 298	6

According to our Table A.1, we still have £6 invested in the project, however, this is just a rounding error.

The internal rate of return seems a nice, useful tool as it seems to give us the compound interest return of the project. However, there are technical problems when dealing with projects that have non-conventional cash flows. Usually when we invest in a project, we have an initial cash outflow (the investment) and a number of subsequent inflows (the return). The internal rate of return does not work when the cash outflow occurs in the middle of the investment. It is possible to have multiple IRRs or no IRR at all, whereas net present value gives us a clear idea of the investment regardless of the pattern of the cash flows.

● ASSUMPTIONS IN DISCOUNTED CASH FLOW APPRAISALS

There are three main assumptions in discounted cash flow analysis:

(1) **We know the appropriate discount rate to use:** in practice most companies use the weighted average cost of capital as the discount rate, because all investments must exceed the cost of funding.

(2) **Uncertainty and inflation do not exist:** uncertainty is the main problem, as inflation can be accounted for in the calculations. It is usually difficult to predict the precise cash flows and their timing, so it is necessary to do sensitivity analysis on major projects, identifying a range of cash flows and the point at which the project becomes unviable.

(3) **There is a perfect capital market, where unlimited funds can be both borrowed and invested at any time.**

Appendix 2
International accounting formats

- Profit and loss account – France
- Balance sheet – France
- Profit and loss account – Germany
- Balance sheet – Germany
- Profit and loss account – The Netherlands
- Balance sheet – The Netherlands
- Profit and loss account – Japan
- Balance sheet – Japan
- Profit and loss account – North America
- Balance sheet – North America

● PROFIT AND LOSS ACCOUNT – FRANCE

(Two-sided version)

EXPENSES	INCOME
Operating expenses:	*Operating income:*
Purchases of goods for resale	Sales of goods bought for resale
Variation in stocks produced	Sales of goods and services
Purchases of raw materials	Net turnover (including exports)
and consumables	Variation in stock of finished goods and work
Variation in stocks	in progress
Other purchases and external charges	Work performed for own purposes and
Taxes and similar payments	capitalised
Wages and salaries	Operating subsidies
Social security costs	Provisions written back
Valuation adjustments:	Other operating income
On fixed assets: depreciation	
On fixed assets: other amounts written	
off	
On current assets: amounts written	
off	
Relating to provisions for liabilities	
and charges	
Other operating expenses	
TOTAL operating expenses	TOTAL operating income
Share of loss on joint ventures	*Share of profit on joint ventures*
Financial expenses	*Financial income*
Value adjustments	From participating interests
Interest and similar expenses	From other investments and loans forming
Losses on foreign exchange	part of the fixed assets
Net loss on transfers of short-term	Other interest receivable and similar income
securities	Provisions written back
	Gains on foreign exchange
	Net gain from transfers of short-term
	securities
TOTAL financial expenses	TOTAL financial income
Exceptional expenses	*Exceptional income*
Operating	Operating
Non-operating	Non-operating
Depreciation and other amounts written off	Provisions written back
TOTAL exceptional expenses	TOTAL exceptional income
Profit share of employees	
Tax on profit	
TOTAL expenses	TOTAL income
Balance – Profit	Balance – Loss
SUM TOTAL	SUM TOTAL

● BALANCE SHEET – FRANCE

ASSETS

Issued share capital not called

Fixed assets:
Intangible fixed assets:
  Formation costs
  Research and development costs
  Concessions, patents, licences,
  trade marks and similar rights
  and assets
  Goodwill
  Other intangible fixed assets
  Payments on account
Tangible fixed assets:
  Land
  Buildings
  Plant, machinery, tools
  Other tangible fixed assets
  Tangible fixed assets in the
  course of construction
  Payments on account

Investments:
  Shares in group and related
  companies
  Amount owed by group and
  related companies
  Other fixed-asset investments
  Other loans
  Other investments

Current assets:
Stocks and work in progress:
  Raw materials and consumables
  Work in progress (goods and services)
  Goods for resale
Payments on account and deposits
Debtors:
  Trade debtors
  Other debtors
  Called up share capital not paid
Investments:
  Own shares
  Other investments
Cash at bank and in hand

Prepayments and accrued income
  Prepayments
  Accrued income

Debenture redemption premiums

Translation differences

CAPITAL AND LIABILITIES

Capital and reserves:
Share capital (of which paid up ...)
  Share premiums
  Revaluation reserves
Reserves:
  Legal reserve
  Reserves required by articles or contract
  Reserves required by regulations
  Other (optional) reserves
Carry forward from the profit and loss account:
  (credit or debit balances)
  Profit / loss for the accounting period
Sub-total: Net worth
  Investment subsidies
  Provisions required by regulations

Provisions for liabilities and charges:
  Provisions for liabilities
  Provisions for charges

Creditors:
  Convertible debenture loans
  Other debenture loans
  Loans and sundry creditors
  Payments received on account
  Trade creditors
  Debts relating to fixed assets
  Taxation and social security
  Other creditors
  Accruals and deferred income

Translation differences

● PROFIT AND LOSS ACCOUNT – GERMANY

Sales
Cost of sales
Gross profit on sales
Selling expenses
General administration expenses
Other operating income
Other operating expenses
Income from participations, of which from affiliated enterprises:
Income from other investments and long-term loans, of which from affiliated enterprises:
Other interest and similar income, of which from affiliated enterprises:
Amortisation of financial assets and investments classified as current assets
Interest and similar expenses, of which to affiliated enterprises:

Results from ordinary activities
Extraordinary income
Extraordinary expense

Extraordinary results
Taxes on income
Other taxes

Net income / loss for the year

● BALANCE SHEET – GERMANY

FIXED ASSETS

Intangible assets:
   Concessions, industrial and similar
   rights and assets
   and licences in such rights and
   assets
   Goodwill
   Payments on account

Tangible assets:
   Land, land rights and buildings,
   including buildings on third-party
   land
   Technical equipment and machines
   Other equipment, factory and
   office equipment
   Payments on account and assets
   under construction

Financial assets:
   Shares in affiliated enterprises
   Loans to affiliated enterprises
   Participations
   Loans to enterprises in which
   participations are held
   Long-term investments
   Other loans

CURRENT ASSETS

Inventories:
Raw materials and supplies
Work in process
   Finished goods and merchandise
   Payment on account

Receivables and other assets:
   Trade receivables
   Receivables from affiliated enterprises
   Receivables from enterprises in which
   participations are held
   Other assets
Securities:
   Shares in affiliated enterprises
   Own shares
   Other securities
   Cheques, cash in hand, central bank and
   postal giro balances, bank balances

PREPAYMENTS

EQUITY

Subscribed capital
Capital reserves
Revenue reserves:
   Legal reserve
   Reserve for own shares
   Statutory reserves
   Other revenue reserves

Retained profits/accumulated losses brought forward

Net income / loss for the year

ACCRUALS

Accruals for pensions and similar obligations
Tax accruals
Other accruals

LIABILITIES

Loans, of which convertible:
Liabilities to banks
Payments on account of orders
Trade payables
Liabilities on bills accepted and drawn
Payable to affiliated enterprises
Payable to enterprises in which participations are
held
Other liabilities:
   of which taxes:
   of which relating to social security and
   similar obligations

DEFERRED INCOME

● PROFIT AND LOSS ACCOUNT – THE NETHERLANDS

Net turnover

    Cost of sales

Gross margin on turnover

    Distribution expenses
    General administrative expenses

Total expenses

Net margin on turnover

    Other operating income

Operating profit or loss

    Profit or loss on fixed-asset investments
    Other interest receivable and similar income
    Changes in value of financial fixed assets and investments
    Interest payable and similar expenses

Balance of financial income and expense

Profit or loss on ordinary activities before taxation

    Tax on profit or loss on ordinary activities

Profit or loss on ordinary activities after taxation

    Extraordinary income
    Extraordinary expense
    Tax on extraordinary profit or loss after taxation

Profit or loss after taxation

● BALANCE SHEET – THE NETHERLANDS

Fixed assets

Intangible fixed assets
Share issue and formation expenses
Research and development
Concessions: licences and intellectual
property rights
Goodwill
Payments on account

Tangible fixed assets
Land and buildings
Plant and machinery
Fixtures, fittings, tools and equipment
In the course of construction and
payments on account
Not employed in the production process

Financial fixed assets
Group companies
Amounts owed by group companies
Other participating interests
Amounts owed by related companies
Other investments
Other loans

Current assets

Stocks
Raw materials and consumables
Work in progress
Finished goods and goods for resale
Payments on account

Debtors
Trade debtors
Amounts owed by group companies
Amounts owed by related companies
Other debtors
Called up share capital not paid
Prepayments and accrued income

Investments
Shares, or depository receipts therefor,
in group companies
Other investments

Cash at bank and in hand (liquid assets)

Capital and reserves
Share capital
Share premium account
Revaluation reserve
Statutory reserves and reserves required
by the Articles of Association
Statutory reserves
Reserves required by the
Articles of Association
Other reserves
Retained profits

Provisions for liabilities and charges

Pensions
Taxation
Other

Long-term liabilities

Creditors due after more than one year
Convertible debentures and other loans
Other debentures and private loans
Amounts owed to credit institutions
Advance payments received on orders
Trade creditors and trade credits
Bills of exchange and cheques payable
Amounts owed to group companies
Amounts owed to related companies
Taxation and social security
Pensions
Other creditors
Accrual and deferred income

Current liabilities

Creditors due within one year
Convertible debentures and other loans
Other debentures and private loans
Amounts owed to credit institutions
Advance payments received on orders
Trade creditors and trade credits
Bills of exchange and cheques payable
Amounts owed to group companies
Amounts owed to related companies
Taxation and social security
Pensions
Other creditors
Accruals and deferred income

● PROFIT AND LOSS ACCOUNT – JAPAN

TURNOVER
Turnover in affiliates
Turnover to other customers

COST OF SALES
Opening stock
Purchases
Sub-total
Closing stock

　GROSS PROFIT

DISTRIBUTION COSTS AND ADMINISTRATIVE EXPENSES
Packing and freight
Commission
Warehouse
Advertising
Directors' remuneration
Payroll
Bonuses
Welfare benefits
Travelling
Postage, telephone and telex
Utilities
Insurance and maintenance
Taxes and dues
Provision for accrued enterprise tax
Depreciation
Provision for allowance for doubtful accounts
Research and development
Others

OPERATING PROFIT

NON-OPERATING INCOME
Interest income and dividends
Interest income from affiliates
Interest income on securities
Dividend income
Dividend income from affiliates
Gain on sale of marketable securities
Others

NON-OPERATING EXPENSES
Interest and discounts
Interest on bonds payable
Amortisation of deferred charges
Valuation loss on marketable securities
Exchange loss
Others

▶

ORDINARY INCOME

EXTRAORDINARY GAINS
Gain from sale of fixed assets
Recovery of bad debts written off
Gain on sale of shares in subsidiary
Gain from sale of investment securities

EXTRAORDINARY LOSSES
Adjustment of depreciation provided in previous years
Fire loss
Loss on sale of fixed assets

Income before income taxes
Corporate income and inhabitants tax
NET PROFIT
Unappropriated retained earnings brought forward
Reversal of reserve for self-insurance
Interim dividends
Legal earned reserve appropriated in respect of interim dividend
Unappropriated retained earnings as at the end of the year

● BALANCE SHEET – JAPAN

ASSETS	LIABILITIES
CURRENT ASSETS:	**CURRENT LIABILITIES:**
Cash in hand and at bank	Trade notes payable
Trade notes receivable	Trade accounts payable
Allowance for bad debts	Trade notes and accounts payable to affiliates
Trade accounts receivable	Short-term borrowings
Allowance for bad debts	Current portion of long-term borrowings
Trade notes and accounts receivable from affiliates	Other accounts payable
Allowance for bad debts	Accrued corporation and inhabitants tax
Marketable securities	Accrued enterprise tax
Treasury stock	Accrued expenses
Merchandises	Deposits received
Finished goods	Deferred income
Semi-finished goods	Allowances:
Work in progress	Allowance for bonus payments
Raw materials and consumables	Allowance for damages
Supplies	Allowance for repairs
Advance payments	Allowance for warranty
Pre-paid expenses	Other current liabilities
Other accounts receivable	Total current liabilities
Other accounts receivable from affiliates	
Short-term loans	**LONG-TERM LIABILITIES:**
Allowance for bad debts	Bonds payable
Short-term loans to affiliates	Bonds with warrants
Allowance for bad debts	Convertible bonds
Other current assets	Long-term borrowings
Total current assets	Long-term borrowings from shareholders, officers and employees
	Long-term borrowings from affiliates
FIXED ASSETS:	Allowances:
Tangible fixed assets:	Allowance for severance payments
Buildings	Allowance for special repair
Accumulated depreciation	Other
Structures	Total long-term liabilities
Accumulated depreciation	Total liabilities
Machinery and equipment	
Accumulated depreciation	
Vehicles	
Accumulated depreciation	
Tools fixtures and fittings	**CAPITAL**
Accumulated depreciation	
Land	**SHARE CAPITAL**
Construction in progress	**CAPITAL RESERVE**
Total tangible fixed assets	**LEGAL EARNED RESERVE**
Intangible assets:	**OTHER SURPLUSES**
Mining rights	
Land rights	Other capital surpluses
Trade mark rights	Reserves for government grants
Patents	Reserves for gain on insurance claims
Telephone rights	Voluntary reserves
Goodwill	Reserve for overseas investment losses ▶

Total intangible fixed assets
Investment and other assets:
Long-term cash at bank
Investment in securities
Investment in subsidiaries
Investment in affiliates
Investment in partnerships
Long-term loans
   Allowance for bad debts
Long-term loans to shareholders,
      officers and employees
   Allowance for bad debts
Long-term loans to affiliates
   Allowance for bad debts
Doubtful receivables
Long-term prepaid expenses
Other
      Total investment and other assets
      Total fixed assets

DEFERRED CHARGES
Organisation expenses
Pre-operating costs
Experimental research costs
Development costs
Stock issuing costs
Bond discounts
Interest during constructions
      Total deferred charges
      Total assets

Reserve for dividend equalisation
Reserve for business extension
Reserve for additional equipment
Reserve for sinking fund
General reserve
Unappropriated
   Total capital
   Total liabilities and capital

● PROFIT AND LOSS ACCOUNT – NORTH AMERICA

CONSOLIDATED STATEMENT OF INCOME / STATEMENT OF EARNINGS

REVENUES
Sale of goods
Sale of services
Other income

Total revenues

COSTS AND EXPENSES:
Cost of goods sold
Cost of services sold
Interest and other financial charges
Other costs and expenses
Minority interest in net earnings of consolidated affiliates

Total costs and expenses

EARNINGS FROM CONTINUING OPERATIONS BEFORE INCOME TAXES
Provision for income taxes

EARNINGS FROM CONTINUING OPERATIONS
Earnings from discontinued operations net of taxes

NET EARNINGS

NET EARNINGS PER SHARE (in dollars)
Continuing operations
Discontinued operations

Net earnings per share

DIVIDENDS DECLARED PER SHARE (in dollars)

● BALANCE SHEET – NORTH AMERICA

BALANCE SHEET / STATEMENT OF FINANCIAL POSITION

ASSETS

Cash and equivalents
Marketable securities
Securities purchased under agreements to resell
Current receivables
Inventories
Other receivables
Property plant and equipment
Intangible assets
All other assets
Net assets of discontinued operations

TOTAL ASSETS

LIABILITIES

Short-term borrowings
Accounts payable
Securities sold under options to repurchase
Dividends payable
All other current costs and expenses accrued
Long-term borrowings
All other liabilities
Deferred income taxes

Total liabilities

Minority interests in equity of consolidated affiliates

Common stock
Other capital
Retained earnings

Total share-owners' equity

TOTAL LIABILITIES AND EQUITY

Index